The New Book
of California Tomorrow

The New

of

Reflections and

William Kaufmann, Inc.
Los Altos, California

Book
California Tomorrow

Projections from the Golden State

JOHN HART, Editor

All selections in this book first appeared in publications of California Tomorrow and are reprinted by permission of California Tomorrow and of the authors.

Book and cover design by Wolfgang Lederer.

Cover illustration based on a drawing by Earl Thollander.

Drawings: Ken Alexander, 371; John Beyer, 225, 229, 231; Gerald Bowden, 323; Masami Daijogo, 147; Dan Hubig, 275, 295; Steven M. Johnson, 31. 68, 74, 75, 94, 101, 111, 118, 151, 188, 281, 303, 307, 397, 399; John Kriken, 235; Wolfgang Lederer, 183, 393; Alfred Marty, 165; Osborn/Woods, 103, 115, 145; Robert Miles Parker, 354, 362; Gabriele von Rabenau, 25, 313, 331; Don Ryan, 161; Earl Thollander, 139, 171, 179, 189, 192, 255, 261, 321, 379, 385, 403.

p. 87: from *Hutchings California Magazine,* courtesy of the California State Library

p. 272: adapted courtesy of Santa Clara County Planning Department

p. 409: California Tomorrow logo designed by Wolfgang Lederer

Library of Congress Cataloging in Publication Data

The New book of California tomorrow.
  Bibliography: p.
  Includes index.
    1. Pollution—California.   2. Environmental protection—
California.   3. Environmental policy—California.   I. Hart, John, 1948–
TD181.C2N48   1984   363.7'3'09794   84-17106
ISBN 0–86576–077–2

Printed in the United States of America

To Julie

Contents

I California Going, Going . . .

II *Cry California:*
The Gadfly Years

III The California Tomorrow Plan

IV *Cry California:*
Notes on a Mild Revolution

V California 2000

Acknowledgements

Credit for the existence of this collection is due first of all to the authors, an impressive group. (For more about them, please see Appendix I: *The Contributors*.)

I worked closely with Alfred Heller in the preparation of this manuscript; my warm appreciation for his enthusiasm, persistence and vast fund of information.

Other California Tomorrow veterans provided insight into the workings and progress of that organization: particularly Walt Anderson, Harold A. Berliner, Gil Bailey, Cheryl Brandt, Marilyn Bronson, Jean Fortna, Richard A. Grant, Anne Jenkins, Weyman I. Lundquist, Proctor Mellquist, Richard Reinhardt, Richard Wilson, and Samuel E. Wood. Lewis Butler and Bruce Kelley were similarly helpful with regard to the revival of California Tomorrow in 1984.

For help in providing updates on specific issues I turned to many people, including James Deacon, Dr. Charles Goldman, Huey Johnson, Louise Kane of Friends of the Farm and Garden, David Livermore of The Nature Conservancy, Yale Maxon, John Miller, Mark Palmer of the Sierra Club, Richard Spotts of Defenders of Wildlife, Cindy Williams, and planning officials in several cities and offices of state government.

I could hardly have written the introduction to this book if I had not had before me one invaluable resource: the assembly of oral histories titled *Statewide and Regional Land-Use Planning in California, 1950–1980 Project,* published in 1983 by the Regional Oral History Office, The Bancroft Library, University of California, Berkeley. This three-volume set contains lively and thorough interviews with Samuel Wood, Alfred Heller, and ten other significant figures in the California planning and government world. The set fills in, as no other combination of sources could, the background against which California Tomorrow functioned. Thanks to Malca Chall and Willa Baum of the Oral History Office, and to Heller, Wood, and William R. MacDougall for permission to use quotations from their own interviews.

Thanks also to Juliette Hickey, Bruce Johnson of the California Historical Society, Linda Knox, and Marlene Wine of the President's Office, Stanford University.

The New Book
of California Tomorrow

Editor's Introduction:
A Narrative of California
Tomorrow

• It is almost hard to call to mind, after all these years of alarm and debate about the degradation of the California land, the clamor that followed the publication in 1962 of a little book called *California Going, Going. . . .*

That pamphlet (it has been compared to *Common Sense*) was the first real outcry about what was happening to the landscape, water, air and civilization of a state that was absorbing a huge population growth and making little attempt to absorb it gracefully. The issues it raised have been so familiar to us ever since that we forget where they were first articulated. But it is here, if we trace it back, that we find one of the opening guns in the statewide freeway revolt. It is here that we find the first serious complaint about the quality of the vast new suburban rings then forming around the old center cities. It is here that we find the first alarm about the loss of agricultural land to diffuse development, and the first systematic critique of the California Water Plan.

And it was in these pages that a general reader could first encounter the idea that, to meet the problems of headlong growth, government might have to take new shapes and act in fundamentally new ways. This idea—till then the province of academics and a tiny handful of frustrated legislators—became, for the first time, a matter of public debate.

California Going, Going . . . was the platform and first product of an organization that, for two decades, would serve as a sort of think-tank and agenda-setter for the planning and conservation movements in California: California Tomorrow.

The record of this small, determined, and rather patrician outfit makes uncommonly interesting reading, from (at least) two standpoints. First, we have California Tomorrow as an actor itself on the scene, a strong if intermittent influence on the thinking of California planners, conservationists, and government officials. Second, we have California Tomorrow as an unmatched mirror of the scene it sought to influence. To read these documents and articles is to get the flavor of a quarter-century of hope and struggle: the failures and successes, the

1

swinging of the political pendulum this way and that, the changing public attitudes and the more erratically changing attitudes of those who govern.

Through California Tomorrow's eyes we pass in review the governors: the elder Brown, the first chief executive to recognize that there was such a thing as a conservation issue in the public mind; Ronald Reagan, who in his California years spoke as an uncritical booster of growth yet did little to oppose the unprecedented controls on development that were taking shape at that time; the younger Governor Brown, who strode into office promising a virtual transformation of policy— whose accomplishments, in fact, would seem magnificent if he had not promised so much more than he could deliver; and eventually George Deukmejian, whose ideas on planning and the environment seemed to be those of 1960—or somewhat before.

It is the story of a legislature in which the majority, regardless of party, has seldom really cared to grapple with environmental problems.

It is the story of a public that started early to care about clean air, clean water, livable cities, open land—that seems to care more deeply year by year, whatever other issues have the spotlight of the day. But a public, too, that came to distrust deeply the government and everything it does at every level—even in service of these goals.

It is the story of a conservation movement, national and local, that widened out from its early focus on parks and wilderness and billboards to claim as its subject the whole of the environment we live in: a movement that exploded in size and vigor late in the 1960s and that, in the sometimes difficult years since, has established its place as one of the major, permanent powers in American society.

It's the story of another movement, never quite identical with the environmental cause, that dedicated itself to better planning and more responsive government—that seemed, in the early 1970s, on the verge of achieving much of its program—and has been balked ever since.

It is the story of the end of a resource abundance we carelessly thought would last forever: the arrival, very sudden, of an era of chronic shortages—"crises" of energy, of water, of housing, of revenue.

It is the story of people adjusting to these shortages in ways that may, in the end, prove more important to the health of the future environment than any plan so far made.

Almost a quarter-century after the founding of California Tomorrow, we seem in some ways to have come full circle. Everything is changed, yet the situation is quite recognizable. If our solutions are more sophisticated, the problems we seek to solve are revealed as still vaster than we thought and more complex. If our tools are better than they were, they are hardly better matched to the tasks to be done. The need cried out in *California Going, Going . . .*—the need to get a fresh start, a new grip on the future of California—is still before us.

From the beginning to the end, California Tomorrow—you might call it the first of the "futures" groups—was out there scouting the way. It was, quite deliberately, "ahead of its time." But the times may catch up to many of its ideas. As attitudes shift and policies change in the next few decades, I think Californians will recognize more than once, in the landscape of that future-become-present, some of the old California Tomorrow cairns and blazes.

Origins

California Tomorrow was the invention and tool of two remarkable, self-assertedly difficult men.

The first was Alfred Heller, then of Nevada City, a man with at least three hats. He was, first, the manager of a middle-sized inherited fortune. Second, he was an able but frustrated writer. And third, he was a conservationist of deep feeling—a habit of mind that he dates to a summer in 1947 when he went on a Sierra Club trip to the Kings Canyon region of the High Sierra, led by David Brower. "Those evening campfires," says Heller, "were great educators."

Heller's three interests converged late in the 1950s, when Nevada City—though not on the main drag from anywhere to anywhere—found itself in the path of a singularly questionable freeway project. At this point Heller acquired a failing local newspaper, the *Nevada County Nugget,* and threw it into the fight against the road. (The result, a number of years later, was a none-too-satisfactory compromise: a somewhat smaller freeway, but still through the middle of town. In those days it was a real achievement even to slow the freeway builders down.)

What Heller got out of it, though—along with what came to be known as a first-rate paper—was another dose of education. He saw more and more clearly that his local freeway problem was part of a much larger one: a statewide crisis of disorganized and sprawling growth. And he got a good look at what the state government was not doing to help. "That fight took me into all realms of state government, up to and including a meeting with [Governor] Pat Brown," Heller recalls. "He was very sympathetic, but I think he didn't want to be annoyed by it all."

Disappointed by the reaction of administration Democrats, Heller turned next to the liberals and tried to interest the California Democratic Council in taking a stand on environmental issues. He got no echo there. The time had simply not arrived.

Along the way, Heller became a member of the Nevada County Planning Commission and began pushing for the creation of a county general plan (something not many counties had, or saw the need for, in those days). Looking for staff, he sought the advice of a friend on the planning and housing faculty at the University of California, Berkeley, Catherine Bauer Wurster. She sent him to a fellow he had already been hearing about off and on: a Sacramento planner named Samuel E. Wood.

Wood's background could hardly have been more different. He was, in a word, a bureaucrat—though never a conventional one. For years he worked for the federal Bureau of Reclamation, the big dam-building agency, mostly on the vast Central Valley Project. As time went on he grew appalled at the waste and abuse of water supplies developed with public money. One of his concerns was the family farm. Under the law, subsidized project water was to be sold only to small farms—but in fact most of that water was flowing to big corporate operations.

In 1953, with the beginning of the Eisenhower administration, Wood lost his job. "I was a Democrat, and believed in the [pro-small farm] 160-acre limitation. Eisenhower and his people did not. So they kicked us out."

Landing on his feet, Wood hired on as staff to a committee of the California legislature: the powerful Committee on Conservation, Planning and Public Works, chaired by maverick Republican Francis G. Lindsay. Wood was in fact the first—and for some time the only—professional staff member to a legislative committee, more influential, probably, than some of the legislators themselves. During those years he turned out a library of studies, reports and legislative proposals. ("Still there," he supposes, "if the janitor hasn't thrown them away.") Just about every piece of significant planning law enacted during that period bears Wood's and Lindsay's stamp.

In the course of this work, Wood arrived at the conviction that government in California simply did not have the tools to deal with the tremendous problems brought about by population growth. To avoid real disaster, he concluded, two dramatic reforms were necessary. First, the state must establish an authoritative *state development plan* setting the broad outlines of land use and the location and size of such great city-shaping facilities as freeways and aqueducts. Second, the legislature must act to establish a new kind of home rule: *regional government*. Each metropolitan area must be given a multicounty government, limited but real, able to deal with the problems that afflict whole regions and can't be solved by any city or county acting alone.

Wood and Lindsay proposed a number of bills tending in these directions. Few passed. One that did was the law setting up the multicounty San Francisco Bay Area Air Pollution Control District. (Ironically, this helped set a legislative fashion of establishing powerful *single purpose* agencies on a regional scale—not at all what Wood was ultimately shooting for.)

And a second important proposal made it into law: the 1959 bill that established the State Office of Planning and ordered it to prepare a wide-ranging state plan. Though this was not to be the binding state plan Wood wanted, he hoped that, once it was prepared, the legislature would see the need to back it up with authority.

Wood the planner (and conservationist), Heller the well-connected conservationist (and planner): in that combination was the spark of California Tomorrow.

Following Catherine Wurster's suggestion, Heller invited Wood to Nevada City to talk to the planning commission. Wood spent more time talking with Heller; they stayed up half the night. But the spark did not catch—not just yet.

In 1958 the Democrats swept into the legislature. Among the casualties was Wood's boss Francis Lindsay. In 1959 the committee had a new chairman, less concerned with planning, and a lessened area of responsibility. Wood's job was no longer so interesting. He was ready for something more.

Heller, meanwhile, had reached that point of frustration and alarm at which he was ready to invest both time and money to arouse the public about what was happening to the California landscape. Catherine Wurster once more urged him to join forces with Sam Wood. This time it took. Together the two men resolved to do what nobody, back then, was doing: to raise an outcry about the assault on the California environment, and to push the idea of better planning and better government machinery as the means—the indispensable means—of turning things around.

This formula was unique. Though planners certainly were committed to planning as a way to help conserve the environment, conservationists, by and large, were not. They believed in specifics: saving the

5

redwoods, stopping the dams in the Grand Canyon, fighting off this or that misplaced freeway. The gap between these approaches has never been closed entirely; in the western states, it was California Tomorrow that first built the unsteady bridge between.

What Wood and Heller proceeded to set up was not so much an organization as a partnership, with the minimum of institutional trappings: no memberships, a tiny board of directors. Heller provided the basic budget of $35,000 a year. He took the title of president; Wood was executive director. Also in the core group were William Matson Roth of the steamship family; Catherine Wurster; and Harold Berliner, a Nevada City attorney, printer of the *Nugget,* and an old friend of Ruth and Alfred Heller. Then there was the advisory board, which reads like a page of a California Who's Who. Francis Lindsay, Wood's old boss, was on it; so was Wallace Stegner; so was Caspar Weinberger, then a member of the state assembly. The advisory board was permanent. "You get off," Wood was to remark, "by dying."

What to call the new organization was a problem. Wood initially wanted to call it the Foundation for Environmental Quality in California. Heller proposed calling it the Resource Policy Institute. It was Proctor Mellquist, editor of *Sunset,* who averted these disasters by suggesting the name we know.

By 1960 the framework was in place. In a tiny office in the Forum Building in Sacramento, Wood and Heller turned to their first project: a book or pamphlet with the ominous title: *California Going, Going. . . .*

California Going, Going . . .

It was to be a book of heresy.

Those were the days, after all, when growth was good. The State Water Project had just been approved by the voters. The Freeway Revolt had only begun. Governor Pat Brown had just celebrated the moment when California's population surpassed that of New York State. The elder Governor Brown, as his son the junior Governor Brown was to recall, was fascinated by that growth: by the fact, for instance, that in theory a new school had to be built every 24 hours. Ironic misgivings were not in style. Except for a few wistful reactionaries easily dismissed, who was looking at the cost?

This Heller and Wood set out to do.

Going, Going was a collaboration. Wood did the meticulous, voluminous research, Heller most of the final writing. They set what was to be the California Tomorrow tone: a combination of eloquent distress (supplied mostly by Heller) and a planner's technical solutions (offered chiefly by Wood).

The authors went for the emotions. "Angry but not screaming," Wood remembers. "We had a rule against screaming. We'd state it as far as you could without weeping or screaming . . . It worked, as a statement of the feelings of the people. Somehow we captured that."

Taking its theme from the old Gold Rush song: *And when I get my pocket full in that bright land of gold . . .,* the pamphlet asked: "How polluted can a bright land become, and still be bright? . . . The answer to that question is being written right now, across the surface of this chaotically growing state."

It detailed the expected dimensions of that growth (the curves were rising a lot more steeply then) and the tremendous effort that would be required to provide roads, water, and other basics to the people pouring in. "But there is one *must* that qualifies all the rest: in accommodating our growing population, we must somehow maintain the beauty and fertility of the land, its good water and its surrounding mantle of breathable air, upon which all Californians depend for their prosperity and their good comfortable lives."

Going, Going listed many ills, took after many targets. Chief among them, though, was suburban sprawl, which it compared to wildfire. To capture the feeling of the commercial strips and featureless subdivisions of the post-war urban fringe, Wood and Heller came up with a new word, a term that has made it into the dictionaries: *slurb.* These *slurbs* they defined, in a burst of alliteration, as "our sloppy, slovenly, slipshod semi-cities." ("I had other words that I could put in there too," Wood recalls with a grin, "but Alf wouldn't go for it.")

This indictment of the cluttered or monotonous suburb is familiar to us now. It has become a conventional wisdom. We have heard it a thousand times, heard the rebuttals, heard the rebuttals to the rebuttals. But in 1962 it was virtually new. In California, at least, this is where somebody first said: This won't do.

Who was responsible for the mess? In *California Going, Going . . .,* Wood and Heller focused on what state government might do, and was not doing, to manage growth more gracefully. They took the state to task for single-purpose planning—for turning its freeway planners, highway planners, recreation planners loose on the California landscape without providing any guiding vision of the total result to be sought. As a solution, they recommended steps much like those Wood had been

7

advocating with the legislature. They demanded preparation of a state development plan to ask and answer basic questions about growth; they also called—though not quite so loudly—for the setting up of new regional authorities to guide the growth and protect the quality of wide urban regions.

The response was startling. Editor Scott Newhall of the *San Francisco Chronicle* treated the book as front-page news. Other major newspapers (mostly in Northern California) followed the *Chronicle's* lead. Several papers printed the entire text. The booklet went back to press, then back to press again (20,000 copies eventually saw print). And Governor Brown called up his staff, so the story goes, and said: "What is this thing? Who the hell are these people who are saying we're planning so badly?" As one result, the State Office of Planning, the anemic funding for which was criticized in *Going, Going,* got a raise.

In the 1958 election for governor, conservation had not been mentioned at all. In his 1962 race with Richard Nixon, Pat Brown made a point of it. The public mood was changing—and California Tomorrow had quite a bit to do with helping that change along.

It was not coincidental, either, that a formal conservation lobby was established in Sacramento a year after the appearance of *California Going, Going . . .,* or that this lobby called itself the *Planning* and Conservation League.

Phantom Cities, Federal Threats

In 1963 appeared the second in the series of early California Tomorrow manifestos, *The Phantom Cities of California.* In *Phantom Cities,* billed as a look "through the other end of the telescope," the performance of local government was up for scrutiny. It was here that Wood and Heller really presented their case for regional governments to deal with the many problems that cities, counties, and the multitudes of single-purpose local districts were simply too small, too parochial, too shortsighted or (not seldom) too venal to confront. (This was in the days before campaign contributions were reported, much less controlled in any way. "Financial deals," as Heller puts it, "were a regular part of local statesmanship.")

Only the regional metropolis, the book contends, is the *real* city; anything smaller is actually only a neighborhood. Without the guidance of a regional government, the neighborhood governments are "phantoms," not equipped to deal with the real, regional, world. (To my mind,

Phantom Cities is one of the best pieces of work California Tomorrow ever produced.)

The third of California Tomorrow's early books did not appear until 1967. Ronald Reagan was governor then; in Washington, Lyndon Johnson was pouring federal money into local problems faster than in any period since the Great Depression. With accidental good timing, the third book focused on the federal role. Entitled *The Federal Threats to the California Landscape,* it diagnosed the central government's failure to manage well its vast holdings of park, forest, and desert lands (nearly half the state); to properly plan its development of California water; to promote any other transportation method than the lavishly subsidized private automobile.

But the primary complaint, this time, was directed at the management of the burgeoning "Great Society" programs of the day. The millions the federal government was investing in planning, urban renewal, affordable housing, open space and the like could not be well spent—so the authors charged—by local government as it stood. The federal agencies must insist that effective regional governments be set up to receive their grants and spend them in accordance with comprehensive regional plans. If this requirement were set, the authors reasoned, regional governments would form almost overnight.

Wood's coauthor of *Federal Threats* was not Alfred Heller but Daryl Lembke, a reporter on the *Los Angeles Times*. California Tomorrow was changing. What had been a partnership was becoming a broader organization; a magazine had been launched; and there simply wasn't time for the effective but cumbersome working arrangements Wood and Heller had had.

There was, originally, to have been a fourth in this series of books. Never given a title, it would have directed at private enterprise the same kind of scrutiny given the three levels of government in *Going, Going, Phantom Cities* and *Federal Threats*. "That would have been the juiciest one of all," Wood says with some regret. But the focus had shifted from special reports to the organization's new regular publication, the journal *Cry California*.

Cry California

Why now a magazine? To speed up reaction time. Heller: "The issues were evolving all the time. We had a lot to say. And with those special reports, we were only saying it every two years."

9

The first issue of *Cry California*—this name too had been provided by *Sunset*'s Proctor Mellquist—appeared in the winter of 1965–66. Editor was William Bronson, an author known especially for his history of the 1906 earthquake, *The Earth Shook, The Sky Burned*. Among the contents of Volume I, Number 1, were a piece on the gradual invasion of a Los Angeles park by roads and buildings ("A Grisly Case of Terracide"); a call by Heller for quick federal action to halt the degradation of Lake Tahoe; a piece of black humor called "Some Psychological Aspects of Driving through Sacramento"; and Bill Bronson's own small classic, "The Nervous Sign."

The tone of the magazine was set: a mixture of outrage, humor, and sober analysis. Bronson insisted on factual accuracy, but the magazine made no pretense of sitting on the fence: it knew where it stood.

With the addition of Bill Bronson, the original two strong personalities in California Tomorrow became three. Life on the troika could be interesting. The subjects to be covered in the journal were picked in advance, writers then being contacted to take them on. Wood recalls: "We would say, 'Bronson, this is an area!' And he'd say, 'No, I don't think it's an area.' Then we'd go into a room and lock the door and fight . . . We came out when we had decided on it, one way or another."

However they did it, they did it. *Cry California* established itself with speed as a distinct and leading voice in the environmental press. Its stories were routinely picked up by the dailies. It achieved, in the sense that really matters, scoops; it was often the first to take a thorough look at an issue that was on its way to notoriety. It was *Cry California* that brought to statewide attention the accelerating loss of agricultural land in the state; the galloping destruction of Lake Tahoe; the possibilities of geothermal power. It took a strong and early stand against the wholesale use of chlorinated hydrocarbon pesticides. It was even the first statewide publication to focus on that obscure, endangered, and scientifically priceless creature, the desert pupfish.

And *Cry California* was *used*. "If there was a hot one going," Heller says, "Bill Bronson would generate a really good article on the subject. You'd hear all the time about people holding *Cry California* up in meetings. It had a certain authority." Key articles were issued as reprints by the thousand.

During this period California Tomorrow was becoming a somewhat larger and more formal body. When the magazine began to appear, the organization was opened to membership. By the early 1970s, about 5,000 people belonged. The staff had grown to five people. And

California Tomorrow had moved: from its cramped, old-fashioned, welcoming quarters in Sacramento to a very similar set of rooms in San Francisco, in the solid old Monadnock Building at Third and Market. (The Monadnock can almost claim to have survived the earthquake—it was under construction when the 1906 disaster hit.)

"This pile of mush . . ."

During the late 1960s, *Cry California,* for all its effectiveness, seemed occasionally to lose sight of the original formulas of California Tomorrow: state planning and regional government. At the end of the decade, the focus swung back in a hurry.

Back in 1959, the legislature had ordered the governor to produce a State Development Plan. According to that law (largely written by Sam Wood) the plan was to include, among other things, "recommendations for the most desirable general pattern of land use and circulation within the state and . . . recommendations concerning the need for, and the proposed general location of, major private and public works and facilities." In 1962, Heller and Wood had surveyed the small progress made to date and urged, in *California, Going, Going . . .,* that the state get off the dime.

Late in 1968—ten years and $4 million later—the Reagan administration published the result. It was called the "State Development Plan Program Phase II Report." It was massive, full of information, and very difficult to read. It contained not one of the specific elements the legislature had required.

In a *Cry California* editorial, Alfred Heller exploded. "Over and over again, this document, which should itself be the major State Development Plan authorized by the legislature, merely calls for bits and pieces of planning, to be undertaken sometime in the future. . . . What was to have been the State Development Plan actually looks you in the eye and says, 'There exists an urgent need for comprehensive state land-use planning to be undertaken as early as possible.' "

Worse, said Heller, as he ticked off the document's failures point by point, "this pile of mush is clearly intended as a barricade against the future. There is no State Development Plan; there will be none, for the report says that from now on, the State Office of Planning is to concern itself with 'updating of information; improvement of interprogram relationships; improvement of intergovernmental relationships.' "

"And the State Office of Planning just sank slowly in the West."

11

He placed the blame about equally on the Reagan administration, with its antiplanning bias, and the Pat Brown administration that had preceded it. (His attack drew a rebuttal, almost equally sharp, from Caspar Weinberger, who was then Governor Reagan's finance director—and also a member of California Tomorrow's advisory board.)

Heller was later to remark that he felt a certain responsibility himself, because his organization had not done much since 1962 to track just what the state planners were up to. "I suspect it was almost as much outrage at myself for having let the thing get away as at them for putting together such garbage. . . . We didn't even follow the process, and I think it was a real failing."

The California Tomorrow Plan

What came to disturb Heller more than the failings of the state report itself was the general reaction to that failure among professional planners. It seemed to become a conventional wisdom that planning on a statewide scale in a state as complex as California was simply not possible: that the state effort had failed because it was doomed to fail. Says Heller: "That was when we decided, 'Well, then maybe we'll show them how it can be done.' "

This was the germ of that extraordinary challenge, parable and artifact, *The California Tomorrow Plan*.

The California Tomorrow Plan, as its authors hurried to point out, was never meant to be a substitute for the plan the state should do. A small private organization simply didn't have the right, let alone the money, to rush in where the legislature and the governor evidently feared to tread. But a private group could sketch the necessary contents of such a plan, and explore the processes necessary to put the real thing together. The whole operation would be a prototype, an experiment or, as Heller called it, a "metaphor."

The California Tomorrow crew was not, by any means, unanimous about the idea. In an interesting reversal of roles, Wood, the planner, had his doubts. The undertaking simply looked too huge to be practical. "In fact," he recalls, "I thought it was a lousy idea. I still think that if we'd put our effort into trying to work with the state, [we might have gotten them to do] something like this."

But Heller doubted that the state would ever move unless confronted with a tangible example, an independent demonstration that large-scale planning could be done. He was determined to go ahead. When an all-but-promised grant from the San Francisco Foundation did not materialize, he solicited funds from the members, and the response amazed him: "We got over $20,000 in the mail. It was the best thing that ever happened to us."

A plan task force was assembled, again a collection of leading names. Harvey Perloff, dean of Architecture and Urban Planning at the University of California, Los Angeles, was chairman. Willie Brown, already a powerful assemblyman, was a member. So was architect Nathaniel Owings; his San Francisco firm, Skidmore, Owings and Merrill, provided the staff, led by architect Marc Goldstein.

Where to begin such an undertaking? Goldstein got started by applying what was then a very new and rather dazzling concept: systems analysis. The idea was to put together a list of the problems besetting the state and try to figure out what the "underlying causes" of all these disorders were. Heller says: "It allowed us to group problems, causes and solutions in a logical way, and relate them to government policy. I thought it was magic. It was absolutely magic."

Sam Wood, on the other hand, confesses to having thought it was "crap."

"Since then," Heller goes on, "you see nothing but that matrix kind of thing in the planning process. But I think we were just about the first to use it."

And what were the "underlying causes" of California's troubles, according to this analysis? They were four:

1. *Lack of individual political strength.* Because of the cumbersome and often undemocratic structure of government, people cannot, or feel they cannot, make it respond to their needs.

2. *Lack of individual economic strength.* Many Californians are poor, or don't have equal access to jobs, education, services and such "amenities" as parks and recreation.

3. *Damaging distribution of population.* There are too many of us, and we are living in the wrong places.

4. *Damaging patterns of resource consumption.* We consume resources wastefully.

During the debates that surrounded *The California Tomorrow Plan* when it appeared, there was quite a bit of skepticism as to whether these are *the* four underlying causes of California's troubles, or whether, indeed, "underlying causes" exist at all. Clearly, though, the framework helped the planners put the project together, and provided a dose of excitement. They really felt they were on to something.

13

A second device was pioneered by *The California Tomorrow Plan* team, and that was the presentation of alternative futures. Planners, of course, are always looking at alternatives and trying to guess results, but here the idea was used as the dramatic basis of the whole presentation, a sort of morality play. The starting point is the idea of a "California Zero": the present, the state we have now, warts and all. Next we are invited to look at a California One: the sort of place California will become as problems continue to mount if we keep on trying to deal with them in a piecemeal, halfhearted way. Finally, there is California Two—a considerably better future that could be brought about by the coordinated attack proposed in the final *California Tomorrow Plan*.

But there was a still more fundamental innovation in the way this plan was built, and that was simply that the planners resolved, from the beginning, to exclude no important need or problem from consideration. Though the focus was indeed on "environmental quality," the meaning of that phrase was made very broad. This was not to be a plan about land use only, or a plan about housing, or a plan about water or smog or jobs. It was to be a plan about *everything* that then seemed important— "comprehensive," in the argot of the trade. Nothing that mattered to public policy could be excluded. No legitimate interest could be left unserved.

In this, California Tomorrow went beyond its own original pro-gram—and far, far beyond anything the planners in state government had ever considered doing. By giving equal weight to problems that were not, in the standard sense, environmental at all, the organization really established itself as a new kind of advocate. It made itself completely invulnerable to the old taunt: "What do you care about, trees or people?" It now commanded a position all its own.

It also laid itself open to the criticism that it wanted "supergovern-ment": that the institutions it sought to establish would tend to intervene unduly in every aspect of people's lives. Though safeguards were built in to counter such a tendency, many critics found the tone of the final plan "authoritarian"—and still do.

Just what, then, did *The California Tomorrow Plan* propose?

The State Plan

As a first step, the legislature would set up a State Planning Council and instruct it to develop the basic policies on which all further steps would depend. This council would consist of the governor himself and ten of his appointees, confirmed by the legislature. (In making the council a creature of the governor, the authors were acknowledging a reality: that state planning prospers or flounders according to whether the chief executive favors it.)

This council would prepare, and update yearly, a California State Plan. In that plan would be goals, policies, specific programs and, most important of all, a proposed budget. State *plan* and state *budget* would, under this proposal, be one and the same thing. The proposed plan would then be turned into law just as a budget is today. The governor would amend it to his liking and send it to the legislature, which would make its own changes and adopt it.

Fundamental to the state plan would be a system of four state zones: *agricultural, conservation, urban* and *regional reserve*. (The first three of these were modeled on the state zones applied since 1961 in Hawaii under that state's precedent-setting general plan.) The agricultural zone would protect good farmland; the conservation zone would apply to forest, desert, and much of the coastline. Land use in both these territories would be controlled directly by the state. The urban zone would initially contain only the built-up areas of today. Any outward growth of cities would be accommodated by the regional reserve: large areas in each region whose use would be decided more locally.

The state plan would include as well a *state infrastructure plan* showing transportation corridors of all kinds, power plants and transmission lines, waterworks, and other basic facilities.

Then there would be the *California standards*. These would amount to a bill of rights for a livable environment. Citizens would be guaranteed access to reasonably clean air and water; safety from contamination by pesticides and other toxic substances; accessible open space in stated amounts; freedom from excessive noise; decent, affordable housing; and public facilities and services meeting specified standards of quality.

Finally, there would be a *population policy*. Suggested was a goal of halting the state's population growth by the year 2000 at a level of about 30 million. (It is not surprising that this section brought a lot of controversy. A proposal to limit income-tax deductions to two children per family raised many hackles but remained in the final plan; a proposal to charge immigrants $1000 per head as a contribution to the cost of the added services they require was dropped.)

15

Regional Governments

The territory of the state would be divided into regions, ten or so; each would have its own government: "regional home rule." Power would lie in regional legislatures, directly elected. These general-purpose regional governments would absorb the many single-purpose regional agencies that had been set up over the years.

Like the state, each region would be required to produce a plan of its own for land use and much more. As the *Plan* puts it: "[The regional governments] are intended to solve the major problems of the region, including those related to employment, housing, education and health, transportation, recreation, and conservation."

The regional government, in *The California Tomorrow Plan,* is the powerhouse, the place where most of the work gets done. It takes over jobs and powers both from the state government above it and from the local governments below it. Within broad limits set by the state, it is the region that decides what is built where, how dollars for aid to housing are spent, and the like.

Regional governments would collect all property taxes and redivide them among the local jurisdictions by formula. Cities would no longer have to compete to attract taxpaying commerce and industry. Federal and state aid would also flow to the region; part would be passed on to the localities according to the regional plan.

Local Government

The California Tomorrow Plan insists—a shade unconvincingly— that city and county governments would actually be strengthened under this system. They would lose their responsibility for the broad outlines of land use, but would remain responsible for the local services they now provide, and for the details of development. Cities and counties would gain in stature, moreover, by taking on many jobs and powers that now belong to hundreds of local single-purpose agencies and districts.

Community councils. In some urban areas today, a single city councilman or supervisor may represent a million citizens. It is hard to argue in such cases that traditional home rule is "close to the people." Noting this, the plan calls for the creation of yet one more layer of general-purpose government: a set of community councils to address problems at a neighborhood level. What powers these neighborhood bodies would have is left open.

Comeback

In order to mimic the way a real state plan might be put together—as well as to collect good ideas and criticisms—the California Tomorrow planning team put its show on the road. The first product, issued in summer 1971, was a tabloid "Sketch Plan." It was presented at a two-day conference in San Francisco in August. More than 600 people took part. Reaction was mixed, lively, largely favorable. Then the plan was taken around the state in a series of seminars with smaller groups. Heller recalls:

"I remember when Harvey Perloff put it on at UCLA. He had a lot of minority people in. They started off by being extremely hostile to it: 'This thing looks like somebody's telling me what to do!' Then we would say 'Okay, let's try it out. What is it that you care about?' So whatever the issue was, we would test it against the structure of the proposed plan to see if people felt they were getting a fair shake. . . . The general pattern of these meetings was that people would start hostile . . . and at the end of the day they would be playing the thing like a keyboard and finding potential in it."

A year after the sketch plan, the final version appeared as a number of *Cry California* and, simultaneously, as the first book of a new California publishing house, William Kaufmann, Inc. As a book, the plan was a rather solid commercial success, with over 20,000 copies distributed. It is still in use as a textbook today.

To the Edge

Once again, the reception was striking. The Reagan administration, though cool to the idea of state planning, felt compelled to take somewhat favorable notice. Democrats Willie Brown and Nicholas Petris and Republican Paul Priolo spoke of bills to implement parts of the proposal. "It may be the most important document ever published in California," wrote Roger Olmsted in the *Sierra Club Bulletin,* calling it "a doctrine of hope for conservationists." The excitement extended to other states; in several, "Tomorrow" groups were formed on the California Tomorrow model.

With this momentum going, Heller and company were faced with a difficult decision: Where could they go from here? A political columnist on the *Los Angeles Times* told Heller at one of the working meetings: "Well, there's only one thing to do now. You'll have to have a political convention and decide to go for *The California Tomorrow Plan,* and really get a political movement going." "We were right up on the edge there," Heller recalls.

But the founders decided not to take that step: to pursue the proposal, rather, in the "idea realm." And pursue it they did, in a long series of seminars, public meetings and occasional publications. The most substantial of these was the report *Democracy in the Space Age,* a case study of what a regional government might look like in a particular region: the San Francisco Bay Area. And for several years after the publication of the *Plan,* virtually every article in *Cry California* was fitted with a plug for the state plan and regional government—even when, as sometimes happened, the idea had to be dragged in by the heels.

How much, in the end, did this prodigious effort accomplish? Obviously it was not enacted into law. (Neither Willie Brown's nor Paul Priolo's bills moved.) Yet the *Plan* had, through the rest of the 1970s, a considerable influence. The concepts it originated or dramatized went into the atmosphere, so to speak, and could be encountered in proposal after proposal by other groups and agencies. Nor was all this just talk. The 1970s were in fact a time of remarkable reforms in planning and government, and *The California Tomorrow Plan* was a powerful yeast in the ferment. Most significant, perhaps, it was at the root of Governor Jerry Brown's 1978 "Urban Strategy" for compact growth.

The Later Years

During this period, California Tomorrow's cast of characters was shifting. In 1968 Sam Wood had retired as executive director (but worked for some years after as consultant to the organization). In 1972 Bill Bronson left *Cry California* to take over the editorship at the *Sierra Club Bulletin.* (He died four years later.) Finally, in 1974, Alfred Heller withdrew both as president and as financial angel.

Both Wood's and Bronson's tasks were eventually taken on by John W. Abbott, a journalist and public relations expert who had worked intermittently with the group for years. Abbott brought to the job his own wide connections and a genial diplomacy that had not, till then, been a feature of the California Tomorrow style. It was during Abbott's time that *Cry California* stuck most faithfully to the comprehensive planning theme.

When Heller retired, the board of directors was expanded; the presidency passed to founding member William Matson Roth. At this point, the California Tomorrow leadership had undergone a complete turnover.

Meanwhile, the world of state and local planning—the world Wood and Heller had confronted, analyzed, scolded, prodded, lectured to and frequently despaired of—had been going through some changes of its own.

The Planning Boom

The *California Tomorrow Plan* project had begun in a moment of near despair. The mountain of state planning had labored and brought forth a ridiculous mass of paper. It appeared that nothing was happening in the field—that nothing was likely to.

But quite suddenly—even as California Tomorrow was refining its model plan—a very great deal began to be done, though not in the elegant "comprehensive" style that the citizen-planners favored. Consider this partial list:

— In 1969, the Bay Conservation and Development Commission was made permanent. The filling of San Francisco Bay—possibly the most egregious single environmental insult of the 1960s—came to a probably permanent end.

— In 1972, after years of frustration with the legislature, the voters passed Proposition 20 and established a system of coastal commissions to control development along the thousand-mile California shore.

— Meanwhile, state laws specifying the content of local plans became much more strict. For the first time a local plan became a somewhat *binding* document, not a mere piety to be set aside at the first whiff of a tax dollar.

— In 1973, the "energy crisis," gas lines, hysteria and all, was upon us. In Washington, President Nixon proposed a farcical "Operation Independence," but California did rather better. The legislature established an Energy Resources Commission with real authority in some areas and a mandate to conserve.

— Meanwhile, federal and state legislators, shaken by the Watergate debacle, had begun to write new laws requiring candidates for office to disclose where their financial support was coming from. This scarcely made politicians less beholden to special interests, but it did make the debts a matter of public record—and thus made it more embarrassing for an elected official to do the will of his known creditors.

19

— And in 1974, Californians elected a governor who talked, or seemed to talk, California Tomorrow's language: Edmund G. Brown, Jr.

With all this going on, California Tomorrow's position on the scene inevitably changed. Where once had been a tiny, deeply committed group proposing what was truly a radical reform against a background of no reform at all, there was now a larger, calmer organization that was kept busy watching and assessing a succession of more-or-less promising reforms. For the rest of the decade, California Tomorrow served mainly as a sort of intelligence service, tracking what various governments were doing.

In 1976, Jack Abbott died; and in 1977 the presidency passed to director Weyman Lundquist, a lawyer and long-time activist working especially on the Lake Tahoe problem. Abbott's quietly capable assistant Richard Grant became both executive secretary and editor of the magazine. For the next five years, Lundquist and Grant were the engine of California Tomorrow.

At this point, largely at Wey Lundquist's urging, *Cry California* changed its format. One issue a year became a book-length anthology of reports on different aspects of the scene: an annual review. The three remaining issues were often devoted to single subjects: water planning, say, would fill an entire issue, energy planning the next, farm issues a third. The general review issues were edited, superbly, by freelancer Walt Anderson.

With Heller, Wood, Bronson, and Abbott all out of the picture, there was now no one at California Tomorrow who was deeply committed to the particular set of reforms that the first crew had proposed. *The California Tomorrow Plan* was quietly dropped as part of the organization's program. What remained was an intelligent but less-specific commitment to the idea of planning in general, and to the principle that better government machinery does make for better real results.

Meanwhile, the rest of the environmental press—the environmental movement in general—had caught up with California Tomorrow. The link between planning and conservation had become a commonplace, largely because Wood, Heller, Bronson, and Abbott had worked so hard to make it so.

Cry California, however, remained an unmistakable voice. There was, to the end, a kind of coverage available in its pages for which there was no substitute. Under Dick Grant it set itself, and often mastered, a very difficult double task: to explore technical matters of planning and

20

government without obscuring the real drama and importance of the issues the machinery is laboring to solve.

California 2000

As the tenth anniversary of *The California Tomorrow Plan* approached, the organization's board began to wonder what to do for an encore. The first thought was to do an update, a "California Tomorrow Plan, 1982." Eventually, however, it was decided to dub the new undertaking "California 2000."

California 2000 was designed as a more elaborate—and expensive—undertaking than its predecessor. Lundquist and Grant went after, and got, generous funding. A vast amount of initial research was done by Charles Warren, head of the President's Council on Environmental Quality under Jimmy Carter and an author of the widely discussed *Global 2000* report. Again, as with *The California Tomorrow Plan,* the public's advice was sought. Major "2000 Conferences" were held in six cities up and down the state. This time, though, the public was not reacting to a fixed proposal but, at least in theory, helping to shape one.

In the end, all this data, input and instruction funneled onto the desk of a single beleaguered writer, frequent *Cry California* contributor Richard Reinhardt. His task was not easy. What was missing this time around was the clear guidance and single-minded vision that had gone into *The California Tomorrow Plan.* The organization was less focused than before, less set on any particular formula, and Reinhardt's eloquent text reflects this faithfully.

The final report, entitled *California 2000: The Next Frontier*, is in large part an exploration of the very desirability of planning—something that the earlier California Tomorrow never thought was required. The text acknowledges, as the earlier work did not, the real failures of planning, the real difficulties of predicting what a present action will mean for the future—all before making the strong case that better means of shaping the future we want must nonetheless be found.

As it gets down to details, the *California 2000* report seems less a new program than an elegant restatement of themes set in the pages of *Cry California* for a decade or more: that air pollution must be combatted; that water supplies can be and ought to be better managed and conserved; that energy use must be more frugal; that land-use policies have to improve; that the health-care system is fundamentally awry. A new theme, largely Reinhardt's own, is the idea that people's habits and ways of thinking need to change before government structures are likely to. "The underlying problem for the future . . . is not in our institutions—our monetary system, our governments, our schools, our churches, our families—but in our attitudes toward the earth and our place in its sphere. And, to change our attitudes, we will have to arrive at a new perception of California and of the life it could offer."

In its discussions of energy and air pollution, for instance, *The Next Frontier* does more than talk about the need for better transportation systems than the gasoline-burning automobile—it goes on to question whether we may not, in fact, be traveling too much, and suggests that, for the sake of health and conservation both, our addiction to rapid and constant motion has to be outgrown.

An End . . .

Had anyone expected California Tomorrow to suspend its work in 1983, the 1982 publication of *California 2000: The Next Frontier* might have served as a natural conclusion. Instead, however, the group was gearing up for a third decade, with another almost complete change of personnel. Weyman Lundquist, after five years as president, was ready for a change; director Ron Olson of Los Angeles replaced him. Richard Grant, too, was moving on. New executive director was Isabel Wade; Stephanie Mills, formerly of *CoEvolution Quarterly,* was the last editor of a magazine now to be known not as *Cry California* but simply as *California Tomorrow*.

New staff, new style: In the months after the transition California Tomorrow's work took on yet another distinctive flavor. The renamed magazine under Mills seemed on its way to becoming a more political, more opinionated, more controversial journal, with more attention paid than ever before to social issues other than the traditionally environmental ones—and less than ever before to the planning idea itself. The last three issues analyzed the November 1982 elections; reviewed, in more traditional style, some problems of agricultural land; and, finally, probed the dramatic state revenue shortage that had at length resulted from the passage of Proposition 13 (combined with a deep recession).

But the new direction could not be well explored before it became clear that California Tomorrow itself was foundering. Years of gradual membership loss had weakened it; a membership drive based on *California 2000* had not been a success; foundation backing was proving harder and harder to get. Perhaps more fundamentally, there was a feeling that the initial impetus of this extraordinary organization had been spent—that if a new start was to be made, it would have to be entirely new, made by other people, in some other way.

. . . and a Beginning

In spring 1983 California Tomorrow went into mothballs: it continued to have a legal existence, but conducted only one activity—the preparation of this book.

But a new beginning occurred more swiftly, and closer to home, than anyone expected. The driving force this time was Lewis Butler, a veteran San Francisco conservationist who had moved on to leadership in the field of health policy. (Butler had been an early president of the Planning and Conservation League and later a high official at the Department of Health, Education and Welfare, where he helped smooth the way for creation of the Environmental Protection Agency.) For assistance in this newest undertaking, he turned to journalist Bruce Kelley.

Somewhat like Alfred Heller and Sam Wood before them, Butler and Kelley were looking for a way to get the attention of a rapidly changing society that seemed in no mood to consider where change might take it. What troubled them was the lack, not just of planning, but even of awareness, dialogue, debate. And if some of their priorities were different—urban sprawl concerned the new founders less, and the problems posed by the changing ethnic and family structure of the California populace more—the fundamental approach was the same: to force attention to long-term issues; and to "reiterate, over and over, a fact many Californians seem not to understand: that the primary instrument we . . . have for meeting our obligations to the future is state government."

This new program, clearly, had much in common with the previous ideas of California Tomorrow. The obvious thought arose. After a series of meetings, it was agreed that the caretaker board members of California Tomorrow would elect members of the new group as fellow directors; these people would then take responsibility for the future work of the organization.

The plans for the renewed California Tomorrow are still taking shape at this writing. It appears that there will be no magazine, but instead a series of reports on particular issues, each based on thorough research and well publicized when it appears. A major hope is to involve

23

a younger group in public affairs through a fellowship program. Young men and women will study long-term problems and possible solutions and, after this preparation, will be assigned to particular political campaigns. It will be their job to serve as fulltime gadflies—to make sure that voters and reporters ask the hard questions about the future of California, and that candidates at least attempt to answer them.

But that is the beginning of another story.

The fading-out of the original California Tomorrow, almost coinciding with the inauguration of the first governor in decades to seem thoroughly uninterested in the ideas it espoused, is a convenient punctuation mark in the history of planning and conservation in California. After more than a decade of enthusiastic attempts at reform (with mixed and partly favorable results), we are, for the time being, bogged down. Many frustrated activists in the field are laying aside any hope of progress at the state or regional level and looking to what they can do on the smallest scale, community by community. It is a good way to work and one perhaps neglected in the past. But if certain things can be accomplished locally, without approaching a skeptical governor or a preoccupied legislature, many more cannot.

We are, indeed, in the slack of the wave—but a new wave may be building. As I write, there are indications that the next rise of interest in planning and government reform may be on its way—witness the revival of California Tomorrow itself. Certainly the circumstances that led to the creation of California Tomorrow in the first place have not disappeared. The pressures have changed somewhat, but they are pressing still: rising and shifting populations, falling revenues, new and old environmental threats, spiraling resource demands, the cost and comedy of government structures that simply can't do the job.

Statements about the need for reform are coming from surprising sources. One such is William R. MacDougall, the former general manager of the County Supervisors Association of California. His job for years was to defend the doctrine of local "home rule" against such heresies as the regional government proposals of *The California Tomorrow Plan*. But in 1981 MacDougall remarked: "I'm not totally sure now. If there are continuing failures to perform . . . in desperation, persons are going to be turning to this type of [regional government] approach." And again: "Something is going to give, something is going to break

24

down. . . . I just can't conceive of everything just staying frozen in status quo."

When the next pulse of reform takes place—as it must—the ideas and proposals hammered out over the decades at California Tomorrow will be still vital, on the agenda still. To whatever degree their source is recognized, they are an indispensable part of any debate about the shaping of the future. It is quite possible—I would even call it likely—that their greatest influence is yet to come.

On Reading This Book

In this anthology the editor will speak up a lot: introducing articles, reacting to articles, interrupting articles to summarize omitted material. My words are distinguished from the authors' as follows: Whenever I take the floor as editor, the column width narrows. When the authors are talking, the column widens again. In addition, please note two other signals. When I introduce a selection or add a postscript, a bullet • precedes my words. When I interrupt an article in progress, a smaller type-size and the narrower column are used.

Most of the items anthologized in this book have been shortened a great deal (with the gracious permission of the authors); some are mere excerpts of the original texts. This cutting—necessary to avoid repetition, to delete material that has lost current interest, and to keep the book at manageable length—was done with all possible care. To avoid an unpleasantly choppy text, I elected not to indicate deletions with ellipses or other devices. Please bear in mind that some of the major points made by writers in the original pieces may have been eliminated. To locate California Tomorrow publications in the original form, see the sources given in Appendix II: *A Short Bibliography of California Tomorrow.*

Many outstanding articles from *Cry California* do not appear in this collection at all—not because of any lack of value but simply because the subjects they address are not the ones I chose as the framework of this book. For example, California Tomorrow was by no means silent about forestry, wilderness, and the management of public lands; but because what it said about these issues was also being said by others, this concern is hardly reflected here. Any reader of the original magazine will notice other subject areas that are not represented. Again, there is no substitute for the original.

—JH

I *California Going, Going . . .*

1 *Three Broadsides*

• The three short books that California Tomorrow brought out in the 1960s treat the same theme: the destruction of the California environment in an era of unmanaged growth. And they identify the same general culprit: government that fails, at every level, to take up its basic task of guiding that growth. The original report, *California Going, Going . . .* surveys the gloomy territory and focuses on the need for a state development plan. The second, *The Phantom Cities of California*, gives closer scrutiny to the inadequacies of local and regional planning and administration. The third, *The Federal Threats to the California Landscape,* finds that the federal government is contributing its share to the confusion and missing its chance to insist on better administration of the money it grants to state and local governments.

Much has changed in the fifteen years and more since this early three-part survey was concluded. Some of the most flagrant abuses have been stemmed, and mechanisms have been developed to deal with some of the problems Sam Wood and Alfred Heller pointed out. But the case California Tomorrow made during the 1960s remains disconcertingly cogent today.

SAMUEL E. WOOD and ALFRED HELLER 1961

From *California Going, Going . . .*

"I love you, California . . ."

"Where bowers of flowers bloom in the spring.
Each morning, at dawning, birdies sing and everything . . ."

"And when I get my pocket full in that bright land of gold,
I'll have a rich and happy time: live merry till I'm old."

Over the years the tunes change, the rhythms vary, but the message remains: at the western shore of the American continent there lies a temperate land of unlimited beauty and unlimited bounty, which may be shared by all who choose to follow the sunset.

The message remains today; we still sing in praise of the golden state, notwithstanding the smog, the water pollution, the crowded roads, the dirty blighted cities, the disappearing open space.

Perhaps we sing out of nostalgia—for the old uncrowded ways of life. Most likely, and hopefully, we sing out of belief—California is a unique bright land, and somehow or other we must keep her so.

There is, however, a limit to our credulity: how polluted can a bright land become, and still be bright? The answer to that question is being written right now, across the surface of this chaotically growing state.

Californians are beginning to recognize that the great asset of their state, the very goose that has laid and will lay the golden eggs of their pleasures and profits, is their golden land. This land, our bright land— the charm of its open spaces, the vitality of its soils—is the true economic base of our state, its attraction as a place to live.

Within the past decade, at all levels of government, there have been efforts to control the development and the uses of California land, in order to conserve it and protect it from unnecessary encroachments of new towns, new people, new roads, new sewage—to protect it, that is, from *us*. Plans have been laid, laws and policies made.

In certain ways, California is America's most progressive state. Each county in California is now required under law to have a planning commission and to develop for itself a "master" plan for the use of its lands. Each city planning commission must do the same. Dozens of

California cities and counties are carrying on active planning programs and adopting policies that say: this area is especially suitable for homes and gardens, this for industry, this for park land, this for schools, this for agriculture, and so on.

The various departments of state government are hard at work planning for land uses. The Division of Highways, for example, in fighting out where freeways must go, is trying to plan to meet the highway needs of millions of people decades from now. For its part, the federal government is giving generous financial aid to California communities willing to plan for the future of their lands.

At all levels, good people are at work and working hard. Their wish is everyone's wish—to keep the land bright, make it brighter.

Unfortunately, although the dough looks good, the cake is not rising, and the reason is simple: nobody wrote out a recipe. A number of good cooks (and some amateur ones) have measured out a cup of this or a tablespoon of that, but the ingredients do not blend, they do not work together, they are inadequate. There is in California a serious, progressively disastrous lack of coordinated land planning and development.

In spite of all efforts to the contrary, California's unique bright land is increasingly defiled by badly located freeways and housing subdivisions and industries that needlessly destroy beautiful scenery and entomb agricultural land; by reservoirs and aqueducts that unwittingly encourage the growth of mislocated communities; by waste products; by cars and jeeps and cycles that preempt our very living and breathing space. Already, the state's nose is bloody. How long before its whole magnificent body is beaten to deformity? How long before the bright lands are dead lands?

Wildfire: The Land-consuming Slurbs

With every daily increase of 1,500 people in California, 375 acres of open farmland come under the blade of the bulldozer, to be used for subdivisions, roads, industry, public and private facilities. This amounts to 140,000 acres annually. At this rate, we can expect three million acres of bright open land to disappear by 1980, under the searing progress of growth.

A wildfire moves by wind and by whim, burns ferociously in one spot, jumps clean over another, resumes its devastation in scattered tracts far out from the original center of the holocaust. And it moves fast. So it is with our urban areas. Wildfire-like, they consume a bit here, a

33

piece there. (Whereas you can stop a fire and re-seed the burned area, it is harder to stop this urban growth, and there seems to be no way to restore built-over or paved-over land to its former open state.)

The character and quality of such urban sprawl is readily recognized: neon-bright strip cities along main traveled roads; housing tracts in profusion; clogged roads and billboard alleys; a chaotic mixture of supermarkets, used-car lots, and pizza parlors; the asphalt plain of parking spaces; instead of parks, gray-looking fields forlornly waiting to be subdivided. These are the qualities of most of our new urban areas— of our *slurbs*—our sloppy, sleazy, slovenly, slipshod semi-cities.

The term *slurb* should, we feel, be readily understood by nine out of ten of our readers, since nine out of ten Californians may soon live in the slurbs, if they are not so located already.

A typical example of the scattered, checkerboard character of California's slurban expansion may be seen in what happened in Santa Clara County—along El Camino Real, and throughout the rich orchard lands—despite the county's planning program, which has become recognized as one of best in the state.

If all the land put into urban use in Santa Clara County between 1947 and 1956 had been placed in one parcel, that parcel would have consisted of about 26 square miles. But development in Santa Clara County was so disorderly that there existed in 1956 not a single square mile in a 200-square-mile area that had not been invaded by one subdivision or more. The result was that all 200 square miles were in effect held hostage for eventual development.

This situation is more or less duplicated up and down the state. The effect is that much of our land is being driven out of farm production and present or eventual recreational use, and the costs of services in slurban areas have risen beyond the ability of people to pay for them.

Only one-sixth of the state's land is suited for intensive agriculture. Of these sixteen million acres only about five million have top-rated soils, but it is these very lands in the fertile San Joaquin Valley, the Los Angeles Basin and the Santa Clara Valley that are receiving the major impact of slurban growth.

The wildfire, checkerboard pattern of slurban growth causes small, unself-sufficient subdivisions to be scattered through our finest agricultural land. Because of the small size of these subdivisions and their distance from more heavily serviced areas, the people there are unable to support the educational, public health, and safety services they require. As a result, taxes are increased on neighboring farm lands to pay for these services, services the farmer doesn't need or desire. Speculative pressures and increased taxes force the premature subdivision of farm lands that should not be subdivided for decades.

Seldom, however, are the total costs of government in these isolated areas met by increased taxes on surrounding open lands. In the long run it is the general taxpayer of the city or county who contributes in a major way to the support of disorderly slurbanization.

Not only is the loss of this land a great economic loss to the state, the nation, the world, and the locality, but it constitutes an additional social loss to the locality, for it means the disappearance of open spaces for future park and recreation areas necessary to a truly decent life for the city dweller.

In fact, virtually all city designers and planners today insist that there must be extensive open spaces within our massively populated city areas, to be used primarily for agriculture and recreation, but also for alleviation of air and water pollution, for flood damage reduction, and for preservation of the bright open lands that mean so much to Californians. (In spite of this insistence, the slurbs are even encroaching upon the San Francisco Bay and its tidelands.)

The loss of our lands to the slurbs may also be considered as an affront to the intrinsic worth of the lands themselves, quite apart from many human considerations. There are those who say that land is to be respected for itself, just as people are to be respected for themselves.

In any case, our land can be respected as a resource as well as a commodity, to the end that we can have good new homes, in better and more healthy communities, while saving at least half of the beautiful and productive acres now marked out to become slurbs.

There is no question that California is growing and will grow. The question is, shall we have slurbs, or shall we plan to have attractive communities that can grow in an orderly way while showing the utmost respect for the beauty and fertility of our landscape? If present trends continue, we shall have slurbs.

The Local Planning Failure

California's basic planning legislation calls for the establishment of planning commissions, the development of local master plans, zoning, subdivision control, capital improvement programming, and urban renewal and redevelopment.

The Conservation and Planning Law requires every county and permits every city to create a planning commission. Each planning commission must prepare and adopt a comprehensive, long-term, general plan for the physical (land-use) development of the city, county or region, and of any land outside the boundaries that in the commission's opinion should be considered.

The local planning commission's job is to advise the city council or board of supervisors. Final responsibility for carrying on a local planning program is directly in the hands of the locally elected legislators, council members or supervisors. The planning commission is responsible for giving advice about the physical development of the community and for preparing a general plan.

Ideally, city and county planning have separate if complementary interests:

City planning ranges throughout the city from the older downtown area to the developing fringe (slurbs?) that the city will eventually inherit from the county through annexation. The city has much to gain from orderly, not scattered, development on its fringes. If it can control this development, it can avoid the usual slurban costs and chaos.

County planning, on the other hand, is actually responsible for development on the fringe because the fringe is still in the county. While concerned with the effects of planning and development within the cities, the county assumes a broader and more comprehensive responsibility for the full and balanced development of its entire area. In cooperation with its neighboring counties it is concerned with maintaining and developing its lands and planning public facilities. County planners work with state public works departments in deciding where water facilities, freeways, and beaches and parks should be located to be of most benefit to the county as a whole.

Planning budgets for cities during the 1960 fiscal year totaled more than seven million dollars, while counties spent over four million dollars. In general, the major cities and counties have mature planning programs under way, in many cases supported by federal matching funds.

Judging by all this local activity, you would think California's communities could proceed to take a sanguine view of the future of their bright lands. Such is hardly the case.

It isn't the case, in the first place, because the major planning effort in people and money is being expended in cities that have already used up most of their land suitable for well-planned development. These cities, in built-up metropolitan areas, extend clear to the back fence of neighboring cities. (Often you cannot tell where one ends and the next begins.) The surrounded city and its neighbors are spending money trying to correct errors made when there was plenty of land. By investing large sums of public money these cities hope to close the barn door after the horse is gone—after ugly slurban fringes, for example, are an accomplished fact—supported by city tax money. The money required to straighten out, widen, and improve one narrow street so it can carry present traffic may exceed the planning budgets of some of the largest and best staffed cities in California!

The amount of public and private money being spent regrouping and reorganizing industrial and commercial land uses to bring order out of chaos is counted in the millions, but very little money is being spent in small towns that will be big cities tomorrow, or in the cow counties that will hold the metropolitan areas of tomorrow.

In these growing areas, poorly financed planning is often carried on by the laymen of a planning commission without technical help. These volunteer commissioners spend night after night trying to settle subdivision controversies, granting variances to existing zoning regulations, and zoning areas without any general plan guidance. Untrained but public-spirited people are often donating their time in futile and unguided efforts to preserve and to maintain what they believe is good about their communities.

So busy are they with the day-to-day problems of the small community's growth that they have neither the energy nor the ability to look to the future and to prevent the mistakes the larger cities of California are now spending large sums of money to correct.

We cannot be too happy about our local planning effort, in the second place, because planning still does not have the public understanding and support necessary to make it successful. Some professional planners annoy the public and confuse the issues by using technical jargon to explain simple ideas, or propose solutions that are unattainable for political or economic reasons, or prepare meaningless studies. (Some, of course, do better.)

Our local planning is weak, in the third place, because our problems are bigger than our planning jurisdictions.

The Regional Planning Failure

With California's growing population spreading out across the land, most local governments are confined within areas too small to allow those governments to meet the problems facing them and their lands.

For example, public health problems know no artificial boundaries. Stream and lake pollution affects health and recreation in metropolitan areas 300 miles away. Air pollution covers the entire atmospheric basin and has no respect for political boundaries. Recreation and water conservation concern areas much larger than the typical local jurisdiction.

Many a citizen finds his political loyalty divided when he lives in an unincorporated area and has no voice in the city that serves him and influences his life. Economically and socially he is a member of the city community. Politically he is often a citizen of several special districts and of a county ill-prepared to furnish citylike services.

Because local planning is inadequate for dealing with area-wide problems, the state legislature has authorized the creation of advisory regional planning commissions. But there is, in fact, no planning authority in California extending over a full region or metropolitan area. The only commissions that have been established have been in small areas for only parts of total regions. Even here disagreements between cities and counties or among counties themselves have hamstrung both the financing and the programs.

Carrying out any areawide plan in the absence of areawide *government* is almost impossible. Think of the difficulty involved in convincing the 76 municipalities and nine counties of the San Francisco Bay Area that a plan dedicated to the overall benefit of the area should be adopted by each. A metropolitan planning commission developing a general transportation plan for the Bay area would be dealing with the state-created single-purpose Rapid Transit District, the State Division of Highways, the San Francisco Port Authority, and a toll bridge authority, in addition to 85 public works agencies in local jurisdictions.

> The idea that regional government is necessary for good results in dealing with urban problems is by no means new, the report points out: rather, it is a commonplace among planners.

Metropolitan "problems" and "solutions" have been studied almost ·to death in this country. They have been researched, conferenced and reported ad infinitum. The resulting tonnage of words reaches up to the roof; the costs of the research reach down into every pocket.

It hardly seems necessary to study the problem another ten years as recommended by the chairman of the Assembly Committee on Municipal and County Government when it killed legislation that would have permitted the formation of metropolitan governments in 1959.

Then there was the Governor's Commission on Metropolitan

Problems. In 1961, after two years of hearings and careful study and the expenditure of another $30,000 in state money and hundreds of contributed man-days of time and effort, the distinguished twenty-member commission came back with a call for regional planning legislation. The commission also called for improving laws concerning incorporation and annexation, and for creating a State Metropolitan Commission to assist local areas and the state in the solution of metropolitan problems. The commission's reports add 215 outsized pages to the mass of California literature in the field.

But these scholarly reports and their realistic proposals failed to impress the same Assembly Committee on Municipal and County Government, and again it has relegated the proposals to "interim" study.

Why is such legislation so important? In the absence of areawide planning, backed up by effective areawide government, here is what happens in a given area:

— Private enterprise prepares its own projections, its own plan for physical growth and the use of the land—it must to survive.

— Each and every government and district plans its single-interest program for the use of the land.

— State and federal agencies without areawide land-use plans to guide them, without coordinated state or federal policy to guide them, put in their freeways, great conservation works, waterways and ports, air transportation systems as, individually and separately, they see fit.

— No agency reconciles these programs, these various demands on the land, or even records them.

— In the absence of areawide government, special single-purpose, politically irresponsible districts spring up like toadstools, to supply demands for water, or power, or ports, or bridges, or flood control—the list is endless. These districts often have taxing powers that allow them to grow with virtually no political checks; in effect the citizen is experiencing taxation without representation.

The result, as we have noted, is the slurbs—wasteful of money, wasteful of lives, wasteful of the bright land that makes life possible.

State Planning: A Call for Action

California needs to bring more water to new homes and industries and new irrigated pastures: The Department of Water Resources creates and the legislature adopts the California Water Plan.

39

California wants better highways: The Division of Highways proposes and the legislature adopts the California Freeway System.

California needs more recreation areas, campgrounds, campsites: The Outdoor Recreation Plan Committee produces the California Outdoor Recreation Plan.

California needs to preserve for posterity historic buildings and sites: A plan shall be made by the Division of Beaches and Parks.

Thus, our state government not only gives expression to the demands being made upon our land, but takes action to meet those demands. There is, in truth, more and more planning being done by the separate departments of our state government, as the state recognizes its rising responsibilities for meeting the needs of a growing population.

Increasingly, however, state officials from the Governor down have come to question the adequacy of this "single agency" planning. Single-purpose planning can turn out to be extremely costly to the taxpayer in the long run. It can create new problems and conflicts and aggravate old ones. It can squander, not conserve, the bright lands of California. By it we tamper with the lands in piecemeal and uncoordinated fashion. By it we lose the opportunity to plan and develop California's lands according to a comprehensive vision of how they may most happily serve and inspire the people who live on them.

It is, most notably, planning unguided by basic answers to basic questions: How do we want to live our lives in this state, now and in the years to come? How can we manage our lands so as to help us achieve our goals?

Here are a few examples of how uncoordinated, single-interest, single-agency planning has worked in California.

There follow case histories of abuse: freeways dismembering parks and business districts, water supplies developed without regard to what they mean for growth, chaos in planning for recreation.

No state coordinating policy, no general land development plan: this is the controlling situation in California that makes planning difficult up and down the line.

Yet the need for clearly defined state planning policy has been widely recognized, ever since Governor Hiram Johnson set up the Commission of Immigration and Housing in 1913. And in 1959, the legislature passed a full-fledged planning law establishing the State Office of Planning in the Department of Finance. This office exists today. It has four primary responsibilities:

40

1. To prepare, maintain, and periodically revise a comprehensive State Development Plan.

2. To coordinate public works programs of federal, state, and local agencies.

3. To help local and regional governments carry out planning programs, and to supervise federal planning aid programs in California.

4. To give advice and help to the Governor and the legislature on planning and land development matters.

As authorized, the Development Plan must include:

Recommendations for the most desirable general pattern of land use and circulation within the state and for the most desirable use and development of land resources of the state; recommendations concerning the need for, and the proposed general location of, major public and private works and facilities.

According to the law, the plan must be "comprehensive"—that is, it must be concerned with all the demands we are making upon our lands, for highways, for recreation, for industry, for farmland, for homes. And presumably it will have to reconcile these demands with answers to those basic questions: How do we want to live our lives in this state, now and in the years to come? How can we manage our lands so as to help us achieve our goals?

The plan must also be "general"—that is, it must be concerned with our general goals for the development of our land. It would, perhaps, have a map indicating how we could best use our lands in certain broad areas—for agriculture, for forests, for urban expansion, for recreation—but it would not go into engineering or design details, or specific locations. Those matters would have to be left to the separate state agencies, local planners, and private enterprise, operating under the broad guidance of the plan.

A development plan for an area such as California must be general because the demands upon its land are constantly changing. The plan's objectives, target dates and policies regarding land use must constantly be modified to meet new conditions and circumstances. The existing legislation requires not only periodic review and revision of the plan but a biennial report to each general session of the legislature on the status of the plan.

According to the law, the plan must further be "long range"—that is, it must be concerned with how we use our land several decades in the future. It is only through prudent forecasting that the plan would be able to give us the guidance we need today in using our lands so that they will remain bright and productive tomorrow.

Thus, a state development plan could serve these special purposes, and would do so if adopted by the legislature:

— It could furnish background information to our state government as it adopts policies for land use and development.

— It could, standing as official public policy, guide public and private land development agencies.

— It could give the Governor and the legislature a means of evaluating the never-ending flood of proposals they receive to construct new public works.

— It could help state, federal, and local governments decide when to budget, when and where to build, and when and where not to build public facilities to serve the people of California.

— It could help the state administration, responsible as it is for coordinating public works programs in California, to bring method out of the present chaos of planning by state agencies.

— It could—it will—require us to make some basic policy decisions about how we choose to live on our lands, how we choose to use them. For example, before a plan is completed, it will have to take into account the answers of hundreds of state and local officials, businessmen, citizens, to questions such as the following: Do we really want the area between Marysville and Bakersfield to become one big slurb, as present growth trends indicate it will? What kind of development should be permitted? Is slurban sprawl necessary? Does it contribute to the long-term health of the state? How big should a given city be, anyway? Is there any way to determine the optimum size for a city? Was it good policy for Los Angeles to trade orange groves for homes? Should we make the same trade for vineyards in Napa County? Should there be a limit to the number of people living right on top of our best agricultural land? Couldn't people live on the rim of the valley out of the smog, in more delightful foothill country? Couldn't we bring some freeways and reservoirs to these valley rim areas, to encourage their growth? Should we encourage more "tree farms" in our mountain counties? What kind of air transport terminals will we need, and where should they be located? Is rapid transit the answer to congested freeways in the cities? The preparation of a state development plan would encourage us to answer basic policy questions like these—questions the people of California and their representatives have failed to answer.

But, though the mandate is there, the legislature has not provided the money needed to build such a plan. The State Office of Planning is undernourished. It receives less financial support than that received by individual planning departments in many of our California cities and counties. Because the state office has limited funds, the State of California has been barred from taking advantage of federal grants-in-aid available for the development of state plans.

With growth problems that dwarf those in every other state, California spends less per capita on statewide physical and economic planning than every state and possession of the Union, with the exception of Indiana.

The lack of adequate supporting funds for the State Office of Planning is almost incomprehensible in light of the fact that California will spend some $55 billion on public works programs in the next twenty years. Can anyone imagine a private corporation spending that sum without the guidance of a comprehensive plan to make every dollar count? Yet by failing to appropriate an additional sum of about $125,000 annually to the State Office of Planning, California is acting in just such a spectacularly unbusinesslike way.

A full-scale state planning program, backing up strong local and regional programs, would conform to the traditionally progressive nature of California government. California has, after all, pioneered in planning, in housing, in water development, in education and social welfare. By and large, Californians seem to believe in state government, and they find in their state government fewer weaknesses and debilitating conflicts than are found in most other states. Millions of Californians identify with the state more than with the metropolitan agglomerations in which they live and work.

Now Californians are confronted by an old challenge that has reached emergency proportions: the challenge of growth. As we have noted, they are acting, individually and in their communities and through their single-interest state agencies, to meet the challenge. But this is not enough. The new challenge must surely be met by further, decisive action in Sacramento and in all parts of the state.

For we continue to have 1,500 new neighbors a day, a half-million a year; monstrous misplaced freeways; salty groundwater supplies; park land scuffed and trampled like a pitcher's mound; a gray stink in the air. And like the great California grizzly, the slurb paws its way across that land of gold.

• In *The Phantom Cities of California,* Heller and Wood take a
much more detailed look at the struggle to deal with development problems at the local level ("The Local Battle for Beauty")
and show how each admirable "small effort" is overwhelmed by
a "large failure." Their conclusion: local government in California, as presently constituted, simply cannot do what has to be
done. It cannot lessen the public's dependence on the private
automobile for transportation, with the attendant costs to land,
air, water, and pocketbook. It cannot create suburbs that are
good to live in; preserve the land that produces food for Californians and the world; or prevent depressing, universal clutter. It
cannot preserve the beauty and vitality of old urban centers or
establish vital new ones. It cannot stem the pollution of air and
water. It has great difficulty even in getting a billboard taken
down.

The second section of the study, from which the title is taken,
explores the reasons why. Its theme: the "phantom city." Most
Californians live in urban places, but the local governments that
run these urban places are all, in one degree or another, unreal:
fragmented, ineffective, in some cases all but invisible. They
are phantoms because none of them corresponds to, or can
intelligently shape the future of, the *real* city, the home town
that truly dominates our lives: the regional metropolis itself.

SAMUEL E. WOOD and ALFRED HELLER 1963

From *The Phantom Cities of California*

Why have our governments failed so miserably to protect that great
basic heritage common to all and treasured by most, the beauty and
productivity of the land?

It seems clear enough that the scattered, disorganized, uncontrolled
growth in our city areas is attributable in large part to scattered and
disorganized responsibility for that growth. We have few effective
institutions of government to guide the growth of our city areas.

Instead we must depend for such guidance on an anarchic mess of
special-interest governments incapable individually or together of creating or conserving a wholesome California environment.

44

These various institutions operate within areas that have some of the characteristics of the traditional city. They are thickly settled, urban in nature. But they are not cities in the traditional sense of being more or less self-contained settlements controlling their own destinies. They are phantom cities. They are not what they seem to be.

Their common predicament is that the institutions that define and control and service them function irresponsibly, as if they need not see beyond their own jurisdictions and limited interests.

By way of portraying the irresponsibility of these various institutions of local government with regard to the regional landscape, we propose to discover each in its native habitat—the phantom city. There seem to be six kinds of phantom cities in California, and almost 90 percent of the people of the state now live in one kind or another.

First phantom: the unincorporated city. Today most of the five million urban acres in California are located outside of established cities, in the surrounding unincorporated area. Right now, about 75 percent of the new development in the state is taking place in the unincorporated lands bordering our established cities. About 50 percent of all Californians live in these areas.

The tremendous growth of urban areas bordering legally established cities is essentially a post-World War II phenomenon. After the war, California's population was nine million. Today it is close to 18 million, and still growing by more than a half-million a year. The people had to go somewhere, and there is one place most of them decided *not* to go, in getting established: to the old downtown areas, the old apartments and row houses, the old Elm Streets.

In their cars, they went out of town, lured by the lower land costs and easy home financing and the "country atmosphere" of the fringe.

This is the home of the galloping slurbs, of the lengthy neon alley, of the helter-skelter subdivisions and "regional" shopping centers, of crowded and narrow local roads. It is a new urban area, lacking a center, a fixed boundary, a city government, a discernible urban purpose, any clear relation to adjoining cities or farmlands.

The disorganized form of this new urban area, which might be called the unincorporated city, is an inevitable result of its hydra-headed government. Typically, it is serviced and governed locally by the county in which it is located and several "special districts."

The special district is probably the least understood, least cared about, the most used of any class of government in California. There are more than 2,000 nonschool special districts in the metropolitan areas of the state alone, whereas we have but 58 counties and 380 cities.

Political subdivisions of the state, special districts are created either directly by act of the legislature or by vote of the property owners within the proposed district boundaries, according to state law. All districts have property taxing powers. To furnish service to the area requiring it, the special district crosses city and county lines while in most instances remaining independent of those governments.

The districts are brought into being by people pursuing special interests. A group in the neighborhood wants street lighting, and induces a majority of the residents to approve the creation of a street lighting district. Another group wants road improvement and forms a road improvement district. A fire district is formed, a park district, a garbage removal district, a water district, a sanitary district, and so on.

There is nothing wrong, of course, with the desire of people to have these services. But what is the effect on the community of the formation of these special districts, each usually created to serve a single need?

For one thing, special districts pile up in the unincorporated cities like an uneven stack of pancakes. Many a citizen of these areas finds himself located in eight or ten special districts. He pays taxes to each— as well as to his county. And his tax rate is usually one of the highest in the state.

The governing boards of the various districts have little interest in the overall scheme of development within the neighborhood. Why should they? It is not their responsibility. Nevertheless, the special districts are shaping the neighborhood—and entire regions. For example, when a water main is laid by a utility district, the spread of housing developments is determined and assured—in an area that might best be reserved for a park.

The most powerful special district in California is the Metropolitan Water District, which controls the distribution of Colorado River water serving the counties of Los Angeles, San Diego, Ventura and Orange, the western part of Riverside County, and a considerable portion of San Bernardino County. Because of this control, the District has had the strength to affect the development of practically all of the area south of the Tehachapis, containing approximately one-half of the people of California and one-half of the state's tax resources.

Smaller districts are equally influential within their spheres of operation. The Richvale Irrigation District proposes to develop diversion dams and powerhouses along the Middle Fork of the Feather River.

The result would destroy the trout fishery and the great recreational appeal of the area. The power generated would be sold to pay for the project and to reduce the cost of water to the Sacramento Valley farms of Richvale and associated irrigation districts. But Plumas County would lose not only some beautiful scenery, but also a good income that could be provided by a planned recreational development of the Middle Fork. Obviously, the special interest of the irrigation district hardly comprehends the many other valid interests in the area.

Although special districts are governed by elected boards, the voters do not truly control them, because voters have neither the time nor the knowledge to equip themselves to do so effectively. The specialized purpose of each district cannot possibly interest a broad segment of the electorate. And when a voter lives under eight or ten special districts, he does not have the time to take an interest in each. Ask a Californian who represents him in his fire district, his water district, his sewer district, and it is likely he will have no idea. In fact, he might never have heard of the district itself.

In Sacramento County, about 10 percent of the voters will turn out for district elections, as against 65 percent for general city elections. Often there are no elections at all. In 1962, of the 62 fire commissioners in the 22 autonomous fire districts in Sacramento County, only one was an elected official. The other 61 had been appointed.

It might be reasonable to expect the county government to guide and control the development of the land, including district land, within the county boundaries. But district actions affecting land use are often beyond county authority.

Perhaps the greatest obstacle in the way of effective county control of the fast-growing, fringe-area unincorporated city is an apparent lack of county interest in that most vital area. It is an area, after all, that borders the established city. It may be annexed to the city some day. Or it may incorporate and itself become a city. Why should the county worry about the fate of this area, when it will likely become divorced from county control?

State legislation passed in 1963 may cause the county to take a greater interest in the unincorporated city. The legislation requires a local board of review made up of city and county representatives to pass on all annexation proposals and on all proposals for the creation of new cities or districts. This requirement should induce the county to work more closely with cities in setting and sticking to standards for land development in the unincorporated city.

Nevertheless, there is one thing that legislation cannot automatically produce—understanding, a general and widespread understanding among county and special-district officials that in the fate of the unincorporated city lies the fate of California as a land of beauty and fertility. Do the independent officials of this phantom city have the stature, the strength, the guts, the wherewithal, the imagination, the cooperative spirit to control the excessively wasteful spread of the slurbs? Are they even interested? The physical evidence shows they do not and are not.

Second phantom: the special-interest city. A curious incorporated phenomenon, the special-interest city is not a city at all in any traditional sense. Like the special district, it serves to solve a particular local problem.

What kinds of special-interest cities are there?

We have cities dedicated almost entirely to industry—Emeryville, Vernon, Union City, Irwindale, Industry, and Commerce. Vernon, where over 70,000 people work but only 236 people live, has an assessed valuation of about one-half million dollars per capita—hence it has a wonderfully low tax rate with which to attract new industry, in order to raise the assessed value and lower the tax rate even more. What could be nicer for the property owner (in one tiny corner of Los Angeles County)?

Industry, which is 18 miles long and from two miles to 200 feet wide, supports itself completely through sales tax receipts—and has forced every adjoining school district onto state aid. Industry's public library consists of sixteen books, nearly all of which are owned by the city administrator. Land prices are high, but you only have to pay for land once, whereas taxes must be paid every year.

We have cities set aside almost exclusively for beautiful homes on large lots in pleasant country surroundings—Woodside, Los Altos Hills, Rolling Hills. These sparsely populated cities have little or no commerce and no manufacturing and their municipal problems are minimal. Again, land prices are high. The residents of these cities are intent upon preserving the character and beauty of the land against insensitive development, given the unreliability of county zoning practices or the zoning practices of cities that might annex the territory.

We have cities for many cows and few people—Dairyland, Dairy Valley, Cypress.

We have "strip commercial" cities organized along main traveled roads mainly for the purpose of picking up sales tax receipts. Here there are many retail stores, but few permanent residents. One such proposed city, El Sobrante, will be about 500 feet wide and two miles long.

It has even been proposed that cities be formed mainly for the purpose of persuading the state that it should or should not build freeways in particular locations. Leaders in the community of Fair Oaks near Sacramento almost succeeded in creating a city to block the construction of what they believed would be a mislocated freeway. Conversely, local interests seeking a freeway through the South Tahoe area proposed to form a city to help them achieve their goal.

Besides having cities for cows, industries, developers, freeways, retail stores, and country-lovers, we also have cities for ordinary wage earners and those with low incomes: San Pablo, or Seaside, for example. This specialization has become necessary because other municipalities like Palo Alto make room only for selected industries and high-value homes, and must rely on neighboring communities to provide the "bedrooms" for industrial and low-income workers.

Perforce, the government of the special-interest city has a primary reason for existing: to serve that special narrow interest. Thus it contributes additionally to the hopeless scattering of governmental responsibility for such regional concerns as the massive and widespread loss of hilltops, flood plains and farmlands.

Third phantom: the contract city. Under state law, all incorporated communities regardless of size are classed as "cities." In order to be eligible for incorporation, an area need only be in one county and have 500 inhabitants. Large or small, California cities have great local autonomy, guaranteed by state law.

The generosity of the law may have represented wise policy a century ago, when our cities were farther apart than they are now, more isolated, more truly independent. Today, however, the law simply abets the creation of certain kinds of phantom cities.

We have described the special-interest phantom. Closely related to it is another phantom, also a child of our permissive state law—the contract city.

The contract city is formally incorporated, then contracts to buy municipal services from Los Angeles County (or some other county) out of a catalogue.

From 1954 to the present there have been 28 incorporations of new cities in Los Angeles County. All except the City of Downey, created in 1956, are contract cities, buying service packages from the county for a stipulated price at a predetermined level.

Seldom does a contract city buy all of the services it wants from the county. Usually the city desires to do its own planning in order to control the quality and direction of its growth. But the county provides for the sale of this service too. The contracts are renewed yearly and services provided vary as the desires of the community change.

The contract city's great appeal is that it manages to operate and provide a variety of services without having to collect high property taxes. It does so by various means: by agreement with the county, it picks up a sizable share of sales taxes; it also receives motor vehicle in-lieu taxes, gasoline taxes, liquor license fees, fines and forfeitures.

The financial load on the contract city would often be much heavier, however, if special districts within the city did not continue to provide a variety of services. The districts finance themselves, of course, by imposing property taxes. Thus the resident of a contract city may be getting a "bargain rate" city government, partly because he is paying taxes to a variety of uncoordinated, costly special-purpose districts!

The contract city might well be regarded as but another special-interest institution within the city area—cloaked in robes of respectability to be sure, but scrambling like all the other special-interest governments for more than its share of the tax dollar, contributing in its way to the scattering of responsibility for the land and landscape of the region.

Fourth phantom: the seasonal city. It is becoming normal for residents of metropolitan areas to occupy second homes or camping areas in the mountains and on the seacoast during summer or winter seasons. The result is that recreation communities become bustling "cities" during the recreation season.

Today it is not uncommon for populations to increase 300 or 400 percent in the three summer months in these areas. Yet within 20 years, the seasonal pressure will be much greater as the demand for recreation increases some 400 percent. For example, Southern California's natural resource counties of Imperial, Riverside and San Bernardino will receive a demand impact of about 95.2 million visitor days—six times the present use. Over one-half of these visitors will be nonresidents.

The outsiders pour in. The area is somewhat isolated. The building season may be short. Skilled labor is often both scarce and prohibitively expensive. Materials are limited. A killing must be made, and quickly. And the seasonal city grows in makeshift confusion. It is dusty, smelly, dirty, ugly. Ramshackle stands and blockhouses and motels invade the pine forest, and dogs howl at neon signs instead of the moon. Roads are inadequate. Sewage disposal is a perennial problem.

This is the city built for "recreation": another slurb. The summer resident complains that something must be done. His summer home or campground or beach is being "ruined." But there is little he can do. He cannot go to the mayor or city council for a redress of grievances because the seasonal city, being unincorporated, has no such officials. Instead, at vacation's end he goes home, only to return the following year to find matters worse than ever.

Nor would it do him much good to go to officials of the county or special districts responsible for the recreation area, since he is not a permanent resident and thus has no vote. Not that the thought would be likely to enter his mind, for the summer resident of the seasonal city goes there to enjoy himself, not to fight political battles.

The development of the community is really left in the hands of the small year-round population. Normally commercially oriented, that population successfully pressures the county government to approve the

installation of various unsightly facilities in the area, including freeways, and to reject proposals that would control the use of land or the
design of buildings.

Permanent Lake Tahoe residents largely engaged in the "recreation"
trade, for example, have favored a low-level highway through Bliss
State Park, and across Emerald Bay, while opposition has come from
impractical, nature-loving summertime residents—citizens of major
metropolitan areas, including California's Governor and her State Park
Commissioners.

Unless he is a homeowner paying property taxes, the visitor to the
seasonal city contributes little except sales taxes to support the county
government that builds and repairs the seasonal-city roads, provides fire
and police protection, sanitary and hospital services, and cleans up the
beaches and public toilets and the roadside litter of snaptop beer cans. It
is not surprising that the mountain county—typically a poor county
anyway—is often both unwilling and unable to provide the municipal
services, including land-use planning, needed for the area.

The question of who is the true proprietor of the California seasonal
city has never even been discussed by all of the parties concerned about
its fate. If it were not for the millions of residents of metropolitan areas,
there would be no seasonal city, yet these millions do not pay for the
services it requires. They and their metropolitan regions have a
tremendous stake in the future of the recreation area—it is really an
extension of their own community—but the visitors have no voice in the
government that determines that future.

Fifth phantom: the legitimate city. Its name is Pasadena or Palo
Alto or Sacramento, San Diego, Los Angeles, San Francisco. Traditionally it encompasses a central business district, some industry, and
surrounding residential and recreational areas. It has a city hall, police
and fire departments, a jail, and an array of agencies and facilities
through which a broad range of the people's needs are served. Incorporation of this traditional city and annexation to it of adjacent developing areas were the normal and logical result of community growth.

This is the city that assumed a good deal of civic responsibility at an
early stage. It is what most of us think of when we think of "city." Until
World War II it had a set of boundaries beyond which could be found
"the country."

Today the legitimate city, long accustomed to tackling its own
problems, is in the position of being unable to solve many of the major

problems it faces. In this sense, it is no less a phantom than the seasonal city or the special-interest city or the contract city or the unincorporated city. It is faced by a variety of problems extending beyond its boundaries and beyond the reach and often the understanding of its government.

At its perimeter, for example, it is typically hemmed in by and bled by other phantom cities. New shopping centers and subdivisions spring up in the amoeba-like unincorporated fringe area, draining away retail customers and middle-income residents from the old downtown center of the legitimate city.

The legitimate city complains that it is being forced to subsidize neighboring unincorporated or contract cities, through property taxes collected within the city by the county and redistributed in one form or another to the adjoining phantom.

The city suffers from smog and traffic congestion generated by other phantoms and dumped within its boundaries. Yet by more or less blindly widening local roads, constructing local parking lots, approving state plans for freeways passing through, the city itself invites more cars to putter around in the vicinity and manufacture more smog and ultimately full-scale, big-league traffic congestion.

Often the city does not act as if it understands that the changes and developments taking place in the entire surrounding urban region affect its vitals. Instead of seeking somehow to extend its voice and its authority into the full range of regional affairs, it seems content to engage in petty local thievery of land, people, and industry—inviting a like response from neighboring communities, and engendering a general regional deterioration.

For example, few cities in California pursue orderly, positive annexation programs, involving the full developing area on the city fringes. More likely, a city will carry on piece-meal annexation, acquiring the most valuable fringe areas, and leaving to the county the remaining fringe areas with low tax bases, thus making them unsuitable for incorporation and undesirable for annexation. In making a momentary gain, the city at the same time consigns much of the land surrounding it to sloppy, ugly development.

Maps of California city boundaries show a confusion of bumps and hollows, resulting from unsound annexation programs. These strange configurations complicate planning problems, and hinder cities from providing services efficiently. The cities in Santa Clara County have perhaps the most irregular boundaries in the state. The boundaries of Covina, West Covina and San Bernardino are similarly irregular.

Boundaries in Sacramento County look good on a map, but create difficult problems in the field.

Almost every city, of course, competes fiercely with its neighbors for new industry. But the result is not inevitably of benefit, even to itself. For example, the destruction of the San Francisco Bay tidelands by individual cities seeking to raise their tax bases may in the long run depress the vitality of these communities as well as the beauty and recreational appeal of the entire area, and counterbalance the anticipated economic gains.

The government of today's legitimate city ekes out its living by foraging where it can for the tax dollar, destroying the attractiveness of its surroundings, and denying through ignorance or inertia its responsibility for the region to which it belongs.

Sixth phantom: the regional city. If our problems are regional and not local, and our governments are local and not regional, how can we face up to those problems?

Perhaps as a start we could recognize and appreciate the evidence before us, that we now have in physical form what amounts to several regionwide cities in California.

The U.S. Census Bureau gathers statistics on the basis of ten California "Standard Metropolitan Statistical Areas," while the Governor's Commission on Metropolitan Area Problems lists nine metropolitan areas in the state. They are the San Francisco Bay Area, and the city areas surrounding and including Bakersfield, Fresno, Los Angeles, Modesto, Sacramento, San Diego, Santa Barbara, and Stockton.

The average citizen of these areas does not have to read a statistical compilation to find out that he lives in a regional city. The fact is apparent the moment he takes a ride on the freeway through nine or ten communities that are really one continuous settlement, or climbs a hill at dusk and looks out over trees, smokestacks, houses, shopping centers, all connected by processions of headlights. The physical fact of the regional city is hard to deny.

Equally hard to deny are the tremendous economic and political forces that seem to demand that substance and life be breathed into the regional form.

The separate governments of the various phantom cities that make up the regional city cannot meet the problems of the region—the loss of open space and spread of the slurbs, the deterioration of downtown centers, the crowding of roads, the pollution of air, water and landscape.

Their jurisdictions and interests do not extend far enough. Nor can it be expected that all of the small governments within the region will voluntarily work together to solve their common problems.Local plans cannot be placed end-to-end to produce a regional composite, a rational and comprehensive view of the area's destiny, because of basic differences in the purposes of the studies and in the data they contain.

Consider the San Francisco Bay Area. For many years all nine counties and almost all the cities have had zoning ordinances, subdivision ordinances and building codes. Yet even a casual look at Bay Area development is enough to convince anyone that there are huge discrepancies between planning and enforcement, between the sum of regional needs and the sum of local achievements. After 15 years of community planning and expenditure of a great deal of public money, it is doubtful whether the cities and counties of the Bay Area are significantly closer to solving their basic development problems today than they would be if they had started on their programs last week.

The regional land development problems remain, they get worse, in the Bay Area and in the other regional cities of California, and there exists no combination of local governments with the authority to solve them.

We need to devise a formula for the establishment of a political jurisdiction for the regional city, through which the public can look squarely at regional problems: a government that will assume responsibilities that are not now being assumed by any of the cities and counties, and that will carry out projects of areawide importance according to a general plan prepared by its own planning department.

A number of agencies have been formed during the past few years to assume some political responsibility for our huge city regions.

Regional planning agencies have been formed to produce comprehensive development plans for the Lake Tahoe Basin and for the Fresno area. The Association of Bay Area Governments (ABAG), a voluntary association of cities and counties, intends to create a general land-use plan for the region. A similar group is being formed in the Los Angeles area. The San Diego metropolitan area has developed a unified sewage-disposal system; there are several regional air- and water-pollution control districts in the state.

A full-scale transportation study for the Bay Area has been authorized by the legislature. In the meantime, the Bay Area Rapid Transit District, now consisting of San Francisco, Alameda, and Contra Costa counties, is very much in business. But how can you make a sensible

55

area transportation plan if there is no area land-development plan? As much as any single factor, the location of transportation facilities influences the growth of our city areas. A transportation plan should logically meet the overall land development goals of the people of the area—not determine those goals.

A rapid transit district, a bridge and highway district, a pollution control district, a unified sewage district, a regional utility district—although regional in scope, do these agencies constitute anything more than another stack of single-purpose districts piled atop the already burdened citizen of the regional city? It cannot possibly be expected that these single-purpose agencies, any more than the governments of the phantom cities, all have the same vision of how the region's lands should be conserved and developed.

On the contrary, it is clear that the recent proliferation of regional districts and agencies represents a further scattering of responsibility for regional growth and constitutes a further argument in favor of a broad and unified political jurisdiction for the regional city. Similarly, current efforts to make regional land-use plans will have little effect if there is no political authority to back up the plans. And if there is inefficiency and scattered responsibility today, what will the situation be in 20 years if present trends continue?

The political realities that suggest the need for some form of regional city government are strongly bolstered by economic arguments.

As things stand, each phantom city within the region is engaged in a perpetually vicious scramble with its neighbors for the element that gives it life—the tax dollar.

The cities within an area all shamelessly wander the boulevards, wearing greasepaint and their longest eyelashes, in an attempt to attract new industry and new tax sources. What happens to the land—to the tidelands, orchards, fields, forests—is unimportant, so long as the dollars roll in to the separate city governments.

Local tax assessment policies also encourage the spread of the slurbs. Under present practices the property tax is based on what the assessor judges to be the value of a given parcel of land, assuming that the parcel were developed according to its "highest and best use." This value is based on the highest price for which similarly situated land has sold. Thus when a subdivider buys a field in the middle of nowhere, the assessed value of neighboring land goes up. When taxes go too high, neighboring farmers sell their fields too—and the slurbs jump across hill and plain. The ultimate cost to the community—economic and spiritual—of this kind of development is ignored. The important thing is that this year's tax returns must increase!

Regional governments could establish tax assessment and equalization policies of lasting benefit to the land and the people involved.

The regional city exists in physical form but has no government. It is thus a phantom, just as the various communities that constitute it are phantoms.

It is clear that these county, city, and special district governments are incapable by themselves of producing or maintaining a sane and amenable urban life for their citizens. The regional city might be able to help them, if it were given the breath of political life.

• In *The Federal Threats to the California Landscape,* Samuel Wood and Daryl Lembke survey a number of problem areas. They discuss the role of the federal government as landlord of 44 million of California's 102 million acres, and the thorny conflicts concerning the proper uses of this land. They single out Washington as the great supporter of our auto-dominated transportation system, and brief the promising but still very inadequate federal efforts at pollution control. They reveal that the federal folk have at least as much trouble as the state in getting their act together: often "the federal right arm doesn't know (or like) what the federal left arm is doing."

The most striking thesis of the report, however, concerns the relationship between federal funding agencies and the regional metropolis. Since the state "refuses to breathe life into the regional city," Wood and Lembke suggest, it is up to the federal government to do so.

SAMUEL E. WOOD and DARYL LEMBKE   1967

From *The Federal Threats to the California Landscape*

Our outrage would be unbounded if we went out to our garden some morning and found that while we slept, a night marauder had plowed up the lawn, uprooted the flowers, cut down fruit trees, and generally created a shambles of what was a thing of beauty and productivity. We would call the police, and if the culprit could be found, we would demand that he pay for the damage.

Under the assault of expanding population, a similar kind of destruction is going on in California. This is the same kind of brutality toward the environment, magnified to the millionth power, and it is taking place before our very eyes. Yet this attack isn't as easy to recognize or to stop as vandalism in the garden.

Unfortunately, when it comes to large-scale despoliation, there isn't always a police agency to call. Sometimes the agency we assume to be providing protection is in fact the culprit. Often blame is hard to place in a state as big and complex as California.

Two earlier California Tomorrow reports attempted to assess the damage and suggest remedial action. Both studies found California inflicted with a serious case of shortsightedness.

Now *The Federal Threats to the California Landscape* examines primarily the effect of federal programs on the way California grows, and recommends ways in which these programs could be improved.

Consider these facts: The federal government owns almost half of the state's 102 million acres. Defense and space industries account for 37 percent of all manufacturing employment in the state. The federal government is the state's biggest single employer. It pours about $13 billion into California annually (equal to one-fifth of the state's personal and corporate income). Virtually all construction in California is financed, underwritten or otherwise affected by the federal government.

Without doubt these programs exercise a most profound influence upon the growth of our state; we must be sure that they help the state maintain and enhance its beauty and productivity.

Federal financial aid to states and cities is increasing rapidly, primarily because of the serious problems confronting urban centers across the nation. This aid rose from $1 billion in 1946 to $15 billion in 1966. The magnitude of the problems and the money it will take to meet them should not make us falter: the nation can well afford whatever it takes to meet the challenge of population growth.

It is not just a question, however, of money. It is also a question of method, organization, coordination, and vision. There have been some efforts by Congress to coordinate policies and programs. But with few exceptions, agencies have great difficulty meshing their projects with those in other, related fields.

The usual process by which a project is conceived, planned, financed and carried out produces single-purpose monstrosities like San Francisco's high-rise Embarcadero freeway and the concrete sluiceway that was once the Los Angeles River. Under this process each agency moves according to its own legislative authorization, developed in most cases by its own supporting congressional committee and backed by special interests that stand to benefit financially from the program.

A large number of programs bypass state government and deal directly with special districts, local governments, and single-purpose agencies, thereby discouraging state initiative. For example, federal aid to local rapid-transit districts bypasses the State of California. Federal agencies also deal directly with local jurisdictions in water development and flood control, public housing, and urban renewal.

Even where a federal agency deals directly with state government, it deals with a counterpart special-purpose agency, which in turn deals with a similar local agency. Thus our federal highway men speak to state highway men who speak to city and county highway men, and highways that needlessly defile the landscape get built.

Often the programs of one agency cancel out those of another, and at times programs within the same department are at variance. In a typical example, $250,000 of federal open-space money was granted to Sacramento County to help create a parkway along the American River. The Bureau of Reclamation now proposes to destroy this parkway by diverting the river water to the San Joaquin Valley and Southern California.

We are not suggesting that the federal government retreat from the field. On the contrary, it should use these programs and its full powers to goad California into creating administrative machinery that could most effectively coordinate federal and state expenditures within its borders.

In 1963 the state legislature established the framework for a system

59

of regional planning districts that would cover the entire state. The districts can be activated by joint action of the boards of supervisors representing the counties involved, but to date, none has been activated. Instead, a rather strange animal has been conceived in response to federal and state pressure for regional planning. Voluntary associations of local governments have been formed. They are made up of elected officials from the cities and counties that choose to join.

The Association of Bay Area Governments (ABAG), formed in 1961, was the pioneer organization in this new approach. San Francisco was reluctant to join but eventually did so. Eight of the Bay Area's nine counties and 85 of its 91 cities are now members.

Originally formed as a "forum for discussion" of regional problems, the association accepted responsibility in 1962 for regional planning. This function has been bolstered by federal grants from HUD.

ABAG has also been given authority to review local government applications for federal grants in the urban field, thus fulfilling requirements that such projects conform to a regional policy.

Following ABAG's lead, the Southern California Association of Governments (SCAG) began operations in the fall of 1965. It is made up of six counties and 86 of their 141 cities. Formation of similar voluntary regional associations for the San Joaquin Valley and the North Coast area is in the talking stage.

Like ABAG in the north, SCAG has been sanctioned by HUD to review local applications for federal grants and will prepare a federally financed regional plan.

Even then, with the completion of the plans, ABAG and SCAG will have only advisory power to see that the plans are observed by the many jurisdictions within the associations.

An ABAG committee late in 1966 recommended that the legislature be asked, in effect, to convert the association into a regional government. Initially, the new agency would have authority for regional planning, refuse disposal, open space and parks, and airports. Decisions receiving a two-thirds vote of cities and a similar majority from counties would be binding. The proposal was surprisingly well received by city and county officials, although some labeled it a supergovernment plan that would wipe out home rule.

Actually ABAG hardly proposes a super anything . . . only a too-limited, unwieldy government with such meager tax resources that even these enumerated functions could not be handled properly. Nevertheless, ABAG has taken a step in the right direction.

The facts are that California's regional cities have almost 90 percent of the state's population, contain over four-fifths of all taxable wealth and business activity, and provide at least 90 percent of the return from federal personal income taxes. They also demand and receive the greatest proportion of the federal domestic budget expended in California. In each regional city is found most of the wealth and most of the poverty in the state, but poverty is in one jurisdiction and wealth in another, industrial land in one jurisdiction and land that should be kept open in another. Disadvantaged minorities are confined to the central city ghettos while higher income families and industrial properties are located mainly in the suburbs.

The home-rule myth that the public interest is served no matter how irresponsibly local jurisdictions act in relation to their neighbors dies slowly. Federal and state officials have been slaves to it too long.

To meet the unsolved regional problems of California in a coordinated way, the federal government should stop pussyfooting and insist that the state create general-purpose governments for its regional cities. Strong regional governments can most effectively coordinate state and federal programs in order to protect the regional environment and the interests of the people who live in our regional cities. We can no longer afford to rely for such protection upon local governments, or upon the many single-purpose agencies that have popped up to meet our pressing regional problems.

We suggest further that the federal government require its own agencies to establish interagency coordinating offices or "little cabinets" in each of the regional cities.

Under such an arrangement, all federal programs affecting the regions could be developed by the Bureau of the Budget in cooperation with the federal and state coordinating offices and the regional governments, and programs and budgets for each activity (such as open-space preservation) could be developed showing the contributions of federal, state, and regional governments to joint projects.

II *Cry California:*
The Gadfly Years

CHAPTER

2   *The Nervous Sign*

• In 1966, when Lady Bird Johnson put together a high-level conference on what we now would call environmental issues, she labeled it "The White House Conference on Natural Beauty." The First Lady was right in step. In those days, "beauty" was almost *the* environmental issue. Though California Tomorrow, from the start, marked out a wider focus—though it helped to nudge the rest of the movement along the path from "beauty" to "conservation" and from "conservation" to "environment"— it shared that starting point, that belief in the central value of esthetic things. The three early books, and *Cry California* in the Bronson years, reflect this bias plainly.

Maybe this Sixties attitude seems dated now. A broadening was certainly required. But as we have widened our attention, we may lose sight of something valid, too. The way things around us look and sound and smell and feel does, after all, matter to people. It matters a great deal.

Not infrequently, too, the obvious esthetic loss is a sign or index of greater, or at least additional, damage under way. The pesticides that start by killing songbirds are found, a few years later, to be endangering people. The same aggressive irresponsibility that leaves the beer can by the road—a tiny insult—may be allowing toxic industrial wastes to seep into a public groundwater supply. The big elevated roadway that looks so bad in the middle of town may also be draining commercial life away to the suburbs.

Without pushing the point too far, it seems safe to say that ugliness is a sign that somebody does not, or cannot, care. And not caring is, in this dangerous, promising, surprising world, a luxury we cannot well afford.

Ugliness, monotony, visual and auditory noise: maybe they don't kill us, but the fact that we let them happen all around us is, indeed, a nervous sign.

WILLIAM BRONSON   1965

The Nervous Sign

Anyone with 20/400 vision or better who has driven along a few of California's thousands and thousands of miles of cheap commercial strip development is familiar with what I choose to call the Nervous Sign. It is everywhere. Its forms are few, but its numbers are many. And each one beckons with a syncopated visual shriek that cannot be ignored. The Nervous Sign is a vulgar tic on the face of California's small-business life, and like other excesses in the jungle world of outdoor advertising, it is ultimately self-defeating.

The Nervous Sign carries no message. It is designed for one purpose, to attract the eye of the motorist to *another* sign. In the words of one proud manufacturer:

"The unique lighting action of the Superior Animator attracts the conscious and unconscious eye. Its unusual action compels people to look at your sign from three to five times as they approach. From a great distance it appears to be moving at one speed—as you approach, the speed appears to change—the closer you come the more rapid its change. The action borders on hypnosis.

"The Animator with its Unique Design, Fast Action, Bright Color and Intense Brilliance compels people to look at your sign and place of business whether they want to or not.

"Its design delivers a message—'read this sign!' 'this is the place!' 'stop here!' 'buy here!'

"Survey tests have proven that there is nothing more penetrating to the human memory than the design of the Animator. It stays with everyone and is never forgotten."

They do not mention that the Nervous Sign is, at least to the moderately sensitive onlooker, about as comfortable as a wart under the eyelid.

The Nervous Sign people, unlike the balance of the industry, sell through straight-commission salesmen working on a door-to-door basis. Mass production allows a big margin for the cost of sales. The Nervous Sign makers are also alone in the industry in that they do not install their own product.

The sales technique is simple. In the trade it's called a "one shot flop." Typically, the salesman walks into the prospect's place of business "cold" and, with the suggestion that he can show a way to increased profits, proceeds to give a spirited pitch. The dramatic and often clinching moment comes when he plugs in his demonstrator and lights up the room with multicolor pyrotechnics.

The first Nervous Signs sold for about $200 and the salesman took the $40 down payment as his commission. Legend in Sacramento has it that a young fellow arrived there with the first model a couple of years ago and sold 80 in three days, netting himself $3,200.

Once the factory gets the order, the sign is sent off C.O.D. and the buyer then looks for someone to install it. In many cases the buyer is surprised to find that the cost of installation is considerably more than he somehow got in his mind it would be.

Although the sign's mechanisms are guaranteed (one manufacturer gives two years) the light bulbs are not, and for good reason. Bulb life is affected not only by normal voltage fluctuation, but also by the amount of vibration the filaments are subjected to, and the average Nervous Sign is exposed to much—gusty winds, passing trucks, and slammed doors all hasten filament failure. It is rare to find a fully functioning Nervous Sign.

As the novelty wears off and the bulbs begin to go, the owners either don't have replacements on hand, or they don't have the time and money to bother with it, or they just don't care. And the sign becomes shabby and offensive for its shabbiness, just as it offended with its vulgar intrusiveness when new.

A fully functioning Nervous Sign works with the compelling brilliance of an arc welder, but when it fades it has no more appeal than a broken toy or a cigarette butt.

Perhaps we deserve the Nervous Sign. Certainly the man who makes it and the man who buys it are not the root of the problem. The Nervous Sign is a symptom, not a disease in itself. It is the natural outgrowth of the slurbanization of California. Strip development, stupidly allowed to spread like wild morning glory from our urban centers, is utterly dependent on the motoring shopper—be it in San Bernardino or San Jose.

To compete for the passing eye, signs along the strips were made bigger, more exaggerated, more vulgar; flags and spinning plastic discs were draped from poles and rooftops; where one sign had once been sufficient, three or six had to be added.

Then into this visual chaos came the Nervous Sign, so brilliant and irritating that wherever it was placed it stuck out like a sore thumb.

But this was only the beginning of another cycle, a cycle that has not yet reached its conclusion.

For while one Nervous Sign per mile may work to good effect for its owner, that effect is completely lost when the neighbors begin putting them up. And that is where we are today. We have chaos on top of chaos. The outdoor display struggle is a real-life version of the old radio game, "Can You Top This?" The process demands the heaping of one excess upon another merely to stand still in the race for attention.

I don't know what the next outdoor advertising excess will be. I only know that it will come in the absence of controls.

The term "sign control" throws many businessmen into a fit, and this is unfortunate, for the fact is that sign control does not mean economic loss, as the shopkeepers of Menlo Park, Carmel, La Jolla, Santa Barbara and Palm Springs, among other towns, will testify. These towns and a few counties, including Marin, Monterey and Santa Barbara, have already written laws that should stand as inspiration and guide to the eyesore cities and counties most of us are forced to live in.

Effective sign control means more than stamping out the gnatlike Nervous Sign and other grotesqueries of the on-premise advertising world. It means the creation of restrictions on sign size, height, motion, brilliance, etc., all aimed at restoring order to the process of business identification, and eliminating the burdensome, ineffective, strident ugliness we have blindly led ourselves into.

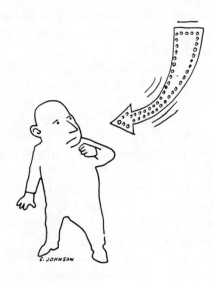

STAN CLOUD and RAY MARCH   1967

The Great Billboard Sellout

It is known as the Highway Beautification Act. In it are provisions to screen roadside junkyards from view, to aid in the building of roadside rests, to purchase strategic scenic easements, and to eliminate nearly 900,000 billboards along the nation's interstate and primary highway systems. It was signed October 22, 1965, by the President of the United States, with the qualified approval of conservationists. As for Mr. Johnson himself, he admitted it was not the law it should have been.

Nevertheless, the act was received enthusiastically by a great many people—including the President's wife, who lent her own considerable prestige to the campaign for its passage. It was a time for celebration. Beauty had at least become national policy. A renaissance of sorts was at hand. Or was it?

As the act became law, the word went forth that a meaningful blow had been struck for the elimination of billboards—those towering, ubiquitous and distracting fixtures the courts have called "nuisances." Such claims now seem discouragingly premature. It is clear that, today, the billboard companies are in a better position than ever to confound efforts by public agencies to unclutter the landscape *because* of the Highway Beautification Act.

Despite the considerable merits of the act, and they are many, inclusion of a clause that requires payment of compensation to billboard owners when they are forced by law to remove them has set the antibillboard campaign back a long way. Added as a last-minute amendment under heavy pressure from the powerful billboard lobby, this requirement constitutes a major flaw in legislation. It was a severe blow to many local governments that have been working independently for a long time to clean up the visual blight under their jurisdiction.

Thus, the billboard control section (Title I) of the Highway Beautification Act, regardless of its lofty intent, did not mark a victory in the war against billboards; instead, it was merely the first shot of a crucial battle that is only just beginning in Washington, in Sacramento and in such areas as Monterey County where an independent, local effort to force the removal of illegal signs has bogged down.

Cloud describes the Monterey County case, concluding: "The billboard companies are aware that they can turn delays into money, and they are not anxious to bow out gracefully."

Title I requires the removal of advertising signs from within 660 feet of interstate and primary highway systems, excluding those in districts that are "zoned commercial or industrial." But the provisions of the act are not operative until the states adopt them. If a state fails to do so before January 1, it stands to lose 10 percent of its federal highway funds. In the case of California, which is still considering the matter, that could mean a loss of $35 million a year.

The big catch is that the act requires the payment of "just compensation" for the removal of signs: if they were in existence when the act was signed October 22, 1965; or are on any highway made a part of the interstate or primary highway systems after the act was signed and before January 1, 1968; or are erected after January 1, 1968. Seventy-five percent of the cost of compensation would be borne by the federal government, with the states paying the remainder—a burden that many legislatures might consider too heavy. (It has been estimated that California's share of compensation could total as much as $75 million.)

County and city officials are concerned that the act may set a precedent requiring the payment of compensation for the removal of nonconforming billboards *not* located on interstate or primary highways. It would be difficult to justify a refusal to pay compensation for the removal of billboards from one type of road when payment is made for removal from another type. If the provisions of the Highway Beautification Act are adopted by the California legislature, the billboard companies would be able to claim—with considerable logic—they were entitled to compensation whenever and wherever their signs were zoned out of existence.

As things stand now, the lawmakers in Sacramento must adopt the federal act, compensation clause and all, or lose a sizable chunk of federal highway money. This has created a cruel dilemma, because if they *do* adopt the act, they may find they have helped to wreck local antibillboard programs.

The basic question is whether billboards should be treated as a *bona fide* use of the land—just another business—or whether, as the courts have held, they should be classed as a "franchise on the public investment [whose] sole value consists of being viewed from public ways." That question will be debated now in Congress and the state legislatures.

The Highway Beautification Act could have helped stem the tide of billboard blight, but Congress emasculated it to satisfy the outdoor advertising lobby. The result was a chain reaction affecting areas such as Monterey County that are working independently to eliminate the visual clutter of our thoroughfares.

Now local government and the people can only look to Congress, realizing that, unless something is done to rectify the situation, those nuisances known as billboards will continue to proliferate, and most efforts to control or eliminate them will be futile.

> • *Update:* California did, of course, accept the provisions of the Federal Highway Beautification Act. And billboards did come down at a pretty good clip—so long as the federal money flowed. But within a few years the federal government retrenched, and it was then that the chief disadvantage of the law—its requirement that billboard owner and landowner be paid—began to make itself felt.
>
> Moreover, California state laws modeled on the federal one have widened the principle of compensation so that, today, it almost always takes cash to get a billboard down, even on nonfederal roads.
>
> Unquestionably, California billboards are fewer and somewhat less obtrusive than they were in the middle 1960s. But any further improvement will be achieved in spite of—not with the help of—the current state and federal laws.

WILLIAM BRONSON   1967

Ear Pollution

While we have watched through tear-filled eyes the brown poisons of photochemical smog corrupt California's urban skies over the last 20-odd years, an unseen but perhaps equally destructive pollution has grown with it. Noise levels in our cities and on our highways are today high enough to constitute a major physical and mental health hazard.

Dr. Vern O. Knudsen, former chancellor of the University of California at Los Angeles and a distinguished physicist who has spent 40 years studying sound, describes noise as "one of the waste products of the 20th century—as unwanted and unnecessary as smog, polluted water or littered streets."

Noise impairs hearing, impedes convalescence, hinders concentrated mental effort, interferes with relaxation and sleep ("If it did nothing else but interfere with sleep, noise would be a menace to good health," says Dr. Knudsen), and perhaps most important, causes stress and nervousness and thus the troubles that are associated with tension— irritability, insomnia, accident proneness, and cardiovascular diseases.

It is no coincidence that ear pollution has grown hand in hand with air pollution. The basic source of each is our ever-increasing consumption of petroleum products: motorcycles, automobiles, trucks, buses, trains, and aircraft together produce an overwhelming share of both the ear- and air-pollutants that contaminate our lives.

More than six million people in the United States suffer serious hearing loss, and although noise is not responsible for it all, it is a major cause. Industrial noise has long been recognized as a major health hazard. It has been estimated that absenteeism and lowered working efficiency resulting from excessive industrial noise cost the nation $4 million to $5 million per day. Yearly claims for industrial hearing loss are greater than $2 billion. And industrial noise is but a drop in the cacophonic bucket.

The human hearing mechanism is a fascinating thing. A young adult with good hearing can discern sounds measured at less than one decibel. Hearing, of course, is stimulated by changes in air pressure created by the noise source. Technically speaking, a sound pressure of one decibel is equal to 0.0002 dyne per square centimeter. (A dyne is the force that, if exerted for one second, will move a gram one centimeter.) As one writer notes: "When acoustics professors are trying to wake up sleepy students, they like to say that the softest sound the human ear can hear is that of a baby mouse urinating on a dry blotter three feet away—roughly one decibel."

For the sake of mathematical convenience, the decibel scale was made logarithmic rather than linear, which means for every increase of 10 decibels, loudness is increased by 10 times. Sounds of 120 decibels, the level where the assault on the ear becomes painful, are one trillion times greater than one-decibel sounds. At the upper end of the noise spectrum, the Apollo rocket will generate 210 decibels on take-off and the astronauts inside the capsule will have to endure 190 decibels for a brief period. (Try to imagine the sound of 10,000,000,000,000,000,000 baby mice wetting a dry blotter three feet from your ear.) During the brief moments of exposure, the astronauts' vision will blur and their skin will heat. Prolonged exposure to noise at this level would kill a man.

With the advent of the steam engine, then the internal combustion engine and now the jet, the Noise Age has become a strident reality. It is generally accepted that community sound levels have increased one decibel a year for the last 30 years, and there is no end in sight. Dr. Knudsen commented on our prospects: "Noise, like smog, is a slow agent of death. If it continues to increase for the next 30 years as it has for the past 30 it could become lethal."

The case against noise is solid, but what have we done about it? The answer is that we haven't done a thing that means much. Aside from quieting the worst industrial noise sources in order to reduce severe hearing damage and the attending compensation claims, we have at best merely played at the game of noise control.

Take the performance of the California legislature. After more than 25 years of study, it has given us our first noise control law: motorcycle and truck (over 6,000 pounds in gross weight rating) noise must not exceed 92 decibels and all other vehicles are limited to 86 decibels, each measured from a distance of 50 feet. Ninety-two decibels at 50 feet is equivalent to 96 at 25 feet and 110 at five feet!

In 1961, the California Highway Patrol hired the sound-consulting firm of Bolt, Beranek and Newman to study motor vehicle noise and to recommend limits that might be imposed. Their job was not to find levels that would protect the human ear, but to define the lowest levels practicable within existing practice and technology. They recommended upper limits equivalent to 87 decibels for trucks and motorcycles and 77 decibels for other motor vehicles, including sports cars. With our new laws, however, our legislature has codified noise levels for sports cars, motorcycles and diesel trucks far above desirable and achievable maximum limits.

And so the tyranny of the special interests who profit one way or another in noisemaking still reigns.

Perhaps we should consider laws that will progressively decrease noise limits over a period long enough to allow the necessary equipment to be developed. A more radical alternative to this would be to phase out the diesel engine for public highway use. There is, after all, no earthly reason why we must tolerate trucks as large as the ones that now crowd our highways.

But in the meantime, here you are, driving up the center lane of the lower deck of the San Francisco-Oakland Bay Bridge—five lanes of freeway with the acoustic qualities of an echo chamber. In front of you and behind you, moving at identical speeds, are rows of monster diesel trucks laboring up the grade. On your right and on your left are two more diesels, each legally muffled, but because of their distance from you, you're receiving 110 decibels from each; and beside them there are two more. Add to their noise the noise of the cars and trucks and motorcycles jammed in back and in front, all echoing back their roar from the deck above. Overhead a squadron of jet fighters from the Alameda Naval Air Base screams across the bridge tops.

Suddenly you notice your vision beginning to blur and your skin feels like it is burning. And in an instant there they are before your eyes—ten thousand trillion baby mice.

- For a sort of ultimate combination pollution experience, T. H. Watkins puts us in the middle of a desert motorcycle race.

T. H. WATKINS   1969

Impressions: The Barstow-to-Las Vegas Motorcycle Race

Silence is perhaps the most impressive thing the desert has to offer. There are sounds, of course—the chattering of birds, the muted rattling of mesquite and needlegrass touched by the wind, the rustling of small animals. Yet these sounds only serve to emphasize the vastness of the desert's essential silence—a stillness that emphasizes the enormity of the space that surrounds you. It is beautiful, this delicate collaboration between space and silence; you do not shout, for fear the sound will shatter the balance and go sweeping across the bleak country like fire in a tinder-dry forest.

Suddenly, you hear a low rumbling. You look to the mountains, but there are no clouds to indicate a distant storm. The birds have stopped singing. A scrubby little desert rabbit skitters from behind a clump of mesquite and heads off across the desert floor. He is followed by several others. A terrified coyote joins them. The rumble has by now become a dull, steady thundering.

And then, on the crest of the horizon, you see them.

Motorcyclists, hundreds of them, too many to count, too many to estimate, too many to believe. They are strung across the landscape like some grotesque reenactment of the Oklahoma land rush, bounding over rocks, grinding through sand washes, flattening mesquite, leaping arroyos, challenging the cracks and lumps and dangers of the land in a frenzied game of hares and hounds. Behind them, a dust cloud a mile wide and a hundred feet high billows into the flat blue sky. As they reach and pass you, the sound is a scream and bellow that pummels your eardrums and shakes the ground beneath your feet. Helmeted and goggled, their faces begrimed, they race remorselessly on, until they are dimmed by the dust and distance, and their sound declines once again to a rumble, a whisper, and finally to nothing.

The air reeks of gasoline, oil, burned rubber, and the heavy smell of exhaust fumes. You walk across the path the motorcycles have taken and note what they have left behind: shrubs and grass and cacti mutilated, the earth itself maimed and rutted by hundreds of tire tracks. In an hour or so, the wind will clean the air of the dust and the stench, but nothing can be done to repair the earth, or to muffle the pounding roar that continues to echo in your mind.

- *Update:* The 140-mile Barstow-to-Las Vegas race was first run in 1967. During the next few years, protest mounted over what the race was doing to the desert landscape. Finally, in 1975, the federal Bureau of Land Management (the agency responsible for the affected public land) suspended the event. But in 1983, under the Reagan administration, the decision was reversed; the motorcycles ran again.

3 *The Bad News from Lake Tahoe*

• Lake Tahoe, that rift in the mountains full of shining water, clear as the air, deep as a sea—Tahoe, the national park that should have been, that never was—was on California Tomorrow's agenda from the beginning.

It was partly a personal matter. For Alfred Heller, the lake was the landscape of childhood. His great-grandfather had built the big house on Sugar Pine Point that is now a tourist attraction at the state park there. The third president of California Tomorrow, Weyman Lundquist, had Tahoe roots almost as deep.

But beyond that the things that have happened to Lake Tahoe and its basin were, and are, a scandal—a shame to California, to Nevada, to the nation. California Tomorrow's was among the first voices raised, in anger and alarm, to make this clear.

In the autumn of 1965, Heller issued the following call for action in a speech before the Lake Tahoe Area Council (predecessor of the League to Save Lake Tahoe). It's a remarkable statement, revealing as much about the speaker and his motivations as about the Tahoe problem itself.

ALFRED HELLER   1965

Time for Tough Federal Action

Lake Tahoe burns images deep in the mind. To one who has traveled at the lake summer and winter for many years, Tahoe is a memory and a promise, a lasting object of love.

One remembers meeting the overnight sleeper train early in the morning on the long pier at the Tavern; the old *Tahoe* rounding the point between Meeks Bay and Rubicon, with the mail and its daily complement of sightseers, and its phonograph playing "Lady of Spain"; a child—my father, or I, or my child—sitting in the sand at the edge of the water, reaching for a pebble under the smooth and brilliant lake surface, reaching down and down through that purity that glorifies the pebble and magnifies the hand; the Indians who used to weave baskets and sell their wares along the west shore; a hike up to Mt. Tallac in the snow; a kayak ride into waves and thunder; balm of Gilead turning gold in the fall; clouds and rain and calm, smooth, clear, pure water.

The loss of Tahoe's purity is connected in my mind with the loss of my youth, the loss of America's youth too. This is an unreasonable association but perhaps it explains why I and so many others are so furious at what is happening at Lake Tahoe today. We can't fight baldness or an irregular heartbeat, but we can fight and reverse the uglification of Lake Tahoe and somehow in the process restore a part of ourselves and our proud heritage.

Last summer on a threatening afternoon, I took a hike, as I have many times before, up a lovely canyon behind Incline Village. Three or four years ago it was unspoiled. Beaver had built dams along the stream. You could hike up and around that canyon for a day without seeing a sign of this generation of men. Now they have torn out the beaver dam; I can't figure out why. They have made tremendous cuts and fills that are now eroding badly. Almost nobody uses the road that has been laid down. Where this great highway-to-nowhere ends, near a tiny meadow the bulldozer missed, a lesser road continues up the canyon.

For some reason I got angry and decided I would try to out-hike this smaller road. I would out-hike the bulldozer and the blasting cap. I must have gone a mile or a mile and a half. Every time I thought the road was petering out I would round a bend and find it going on, senselessly, destructively, steeply, maddeningly. I walked faster and faster. I wanted to climb beyond it and above it. It was raining; I had no time for the rain or the glistening mountain.

Suddenly everything turned yellow, my heart was beating too fast, my legs felt like soft rubber. I couldn't find enough air to breathe. I sat down and put my head low. I felt very weak and alone on that cold mountain. I even wondered vaguely if I were going to die. But I knew this was unlikely—few of us are given to die in such flattering symbolic circumstances, seeking to outdistance and somehow overcome the careless works of man on a road leading through clouded forests toward the stars.

As I wandered down the mountain a few minutes later I found myself singing Blake's lines:

Bring me my bow of burning gold!
Bring me my arrows of desire!
Bring me my spear, O clouds unfold!
Bring me my chariot of fire!

I will not cease from mental fight,
Nor shall my sword sleep in my hand,
Till we have built Jerusalem
In England's green and pleasant land.

So now here we are, grappling with the practical problem: how? By way of answering that question, let's go over again, as many of us have so many times before, three or four of the hard truths about Lake Tahoe.

Truth number one: Tahoe is not as clear as it used to be and it is becoming an algae pond; development around the lake basin is inadequately controlled to prevent an accelerating pattern of landscape desecration, and further lake and stream pollution.

What you see with your eyes, the experts will confirm with facts and statistics. At no time last summer were the waters along the north shore of Tahoe clear. When it blew in the afternoons, bottles and papers and pieces of plastic and clumps of algae-like stuff and worse inevitably floated by.

The experts and their studies have been perfectly clear about the pollution problem facing the lake. The problem is here today, right now, aggravated by the seeping into the lake of sewage effluent containing algae-producing nutrients. Tahoe is not going to be polluted: *Tahoe is polluted* and becoming more so. It has reached or is reaching the critical point of no return, after which the conversion of its water from clarity to opaque green becomes irreversible. And don't let anybody tell you that algae is not a public health menace. The stuff may be drinkable but I for one get sick to my stomach when I see what is happening—see it with my own eyes.

The scarring, the slashing, the stripping-off of ground cover around the shores continue worse than ever. They destroy the beauty of the land and they contribute directly to the pollution of the lake. I was appalled to see the black mud rolling down in torrents in the Incline area this summer. A good summer storm such as we had can produce a roily stream in that area, but only the folly and ignorance of the developers could produce the floods that the developers themselves as well as the rest of us suffered. The relationship between development and drainage is obviously very close, yet the local agencies who can control these things by and large are not doing so.

New and worse development schemes pop up every day. We are up to our ears in variances to weak zoning codes, but the flood of new applications continues to pour in—for apartment skyscrapers where there should be none, pollution-causing earth fills, quarries, flashing signs.

Mark Twain called Lake Tahoe "the fairest picture the whole earth affords." But today a visitor to Lake Tahoe coming from just about any direction is met first by the *ugliest* picture the whole earth affords: the dismal visual cacophony of strip commercial cities, the slurbs. This is what our much-revered local control has brought us. It has been weak home rule and it has brought us home ruin.

Truth number two: A number of groups and agencies are working hard to solve the problems of pollution and uncontrolled development at Lake Tahoe, but the effort has not been adequate and gives little sign that it will be.

Two years ago, the governors of California and Nevada agreed that treated sewage must be exported from the lake basin. The South Tahoe Public Utility District is, in fact, working on the problem, and districts on the north end seem to be wrenching into gear. Yet without a region-wide sewage-collection system, there will continue to be too much dumping of effluents into the basin. We need a basinwide authority to collect, treat and export sewage, but we aren't getting it.

I am quite certain that any number of state, local and federal agencies, working together and operating within their authority, could force the action that is needed. We all know, however, what happened to the edict that emanated from the State of Nevada, suspending develop-ment until the sewage problem was solved: the edict remained in effect one week. California state and regional health agencies working with a newly courageous Nevada could well step in and close down develop-ment—and then wouldn't that "impossible" basin-wide authority spring into being! But they aren't going to do it and I for one don't want to waste my time wishing they would.

The story of uncontrolled development above the rim of the lake is a similar one. All of the five counties bordering on the lake have standards for development, all have planning agencies, all have the police power to control development, to prevent hillside scarring, to limit billboards strictly, to impose architectural controls where needed, to protect the forest and the forest cover, to control drainage, to limit building heights, to maintain optimum population densities, to control timber practices, to create scenic roadsides, to require orderly and attractive patterns of development. But one need only take a ride around the lake to see that local government, which has control over the use of the land, is contributing through its weakness to the uglification of Tahoe.

The respective state governments of California and Nevada could work wonders at Lake Tahoe if they created a joint regional authority. In fact they have joined to create a study commission to come up with regional recommendations—in two years. Another study. Supposing, by some thread of luck, that commission comes up recommending that California and Nevada create a regional authority over the disposal of sewage and over all development in the Lake Tahoe basin. Will the two legislatures then rush to put this proposal into effect?

Meanwhile that effluent continues to seep into the lake. Our technology brings ever faster destruction to the shores of the lake. I think we can hope for miracles and continue to work for miracles but I don't think we can afford to depend on their happening.

Truth number three: If the purity and beauty of Tahoe are to be saved, we must have an agency powerful enough to knock heads together and get the job done. I would suggest there is such an agency in existence and it is the only one that will be available soon enough to do the job while it can be done. It is the federal government.

The federal government was created by us in order, among other things, to promote the general welfare, and secure the blessings of liberty to ourselves and our posterity. It's time that all Californians and Nevadans and Americans who are concerned about the deteriorating environment at Lake Tahoe called upon the federal government to fulfill its reponsibilities here. We must make this appeal because there is no basinwide crisis program to solve a basinwide problem and none is in sight. Such a program must be launched now, immediately, for time and the land spoilers are bidding to outrun us.

Must we continue to heed the perennial plea of local government: give us time, just leave us alone, we can do the job? No. Local government has failed at Lake Tahoe; there is no time for one more chance.

The disarray of governmental authority in this basin and its results must be brought to the attention of the President of the United States. The governors of California and Nevada can take this action. The governor of California could do it alone; the governor of Nevada could do it alone; the Lake Tahoe Area Council could do it, the Sierra Club could; any number of government agencies, private organizations or individuals from Hawaii to Maine could do it.

President Johnson has pledged himself to fight for the natural beauty of America. At Lake Tahoe, as an immediate step, he could take the pollution situation firmly in hand. In the absence of timely and adequate state programs, he could direct existing federal agencies to adopt a coordinated federal program *to prevent the further pollution of Lake Tahoe*. I am speaking of such agencies as the Department of Health, Education and Welfare, the Fish and Wildlife Service, the Forest Service, and the Army Corps of Engineers: all have significant authority and responsibility in the Lake Tahoe basin. I am convinced that the Department of Health, Education and Welfare alone, today, could close off existing and future sources of pollution, if it had a mind to.

As a second step, the President could submit to Congress legislation creating a commission empowered to prevent the future pollution of the land and water of Lake Tahoe. Such a commission would have to have the power to plan and administer land use within the basin. Whether it would use that power would depend on the willingness and ability of existing local agencies to assume that responsibility.

It would seem logical to me that while supporting and encouraging every worthwhile local, regional and state effort at solving the dilemma of Lake Tahoe, organizations like the Tahoe Area Council should climb to the top of Mt. Tallac and call for such federal action—or any similar program that would be *truly* effective. For we see that now even those agencies with strong will and great resources can do little more than build a house in the jungle. It will look pretty for a while and they will be proud of it. But the surrounding tangle of authority and responsibility and conflicting interests will grow around and strangle the house and them and all of us. Progress here and achievement there is not enough.

The final hard truth about Lake Tahoe, it seems to me, is that without tough federal action and the leadership to bring it about, we will proceed to corrupt Tahoe beyond the economic and technical ability of this generation to redeem it. What is happening here is a stark reflection of the extent of our own corruption, yet I think we have it in us to cast off the pall that hangs over us and over our beloved lake.

- Since 1958 limnologist Charles R. Goldman has been studying Lake Tahoe. He has probed it, sampled it, taken its tempera-

81

ture at every depth, drunk it, sailed on it, and submerged himself in it: 1,000 feet down in an underwater capsule called the Pioneer I. And he has fought for it. From the beginning, Goldman feared that the lake was in the process of losing its famous clarity—that clarity, as Heller put it, that "glorifies the pebble and magnifies the hand"—as development spread in the watershed, dribbling sewage and sediment into the luminous water. It took years of patient observation to prove beyond doubt that this deterioration was taking place. But as early as 1962, Goldman was instrumental in persuading sewer districts that their effluent, however elaborately treated, must not enter the lake at all but rather must be piped clear out of the Tahoe watershed.

In 1967, Goldman shared some of his findings—and his fears—with the readers of *Cry California*.

CHARLES R. GOLDMAN 1967

The Bad News from Lake Tahoe

Lake Tahoe is being polluted. To deny this fact is comparable to saying that a man receiving a daily dose of arsenic in his breakfast coffee is not being slowly poisoned. If the poisoning continues, the steady accumulation in the man's system will eventually kill him. If the pollution of Lake Tahoe is not stopped now, the pollutants will continue to accumulate in the lake, and in time, the lake will turn from clear blue to turbid green.

> Goldman explains the difference between water pollution in the public health sense—the buildup of substances and organisms that make water unsafe to drink—and pollution in a larger sense: over-fertilization by the nutrients in sediments and sewage. This latter type is the threat at Tahoe.

In the natural geologic aging process, lakes tend to become more fertile, and their basins gradually fill with the material eroded from their watersheds and with the remains of dead aquatic plants and animals. Tahoe has a small watershed and, left to nature, would remain for thousands of years to come as crystal-clear as it was in 1883 when John

LeConte recorded in the *Overland Monthly* that he could observe a white dinner plate at a depth well over 100 feet.

But every disturbance of the watershed has its influence on the lake. It began with fire, lumbering, and road building, which increased the exposure of mineral soil to the leaching out of nutrients that then flow into the lake by way of tributary streams. The erosion rate of many stream valleys has been accelerated and continues to increase with land disturbance, as well as with human and domestic-animal habitation.

We can think of the primeval lake as existing on a balanced nutrient budget, like a lean man on a balanced diet. If his diet becomes too rich, he will put on weight. The lake's youthful vigor, by this analogy, is being sapped by the tons of nutrients trucked daily into the watershed, to end up in the myriad garbage dumps, septic tanks, and sewage-disposal systems in the basin.

A comprehensive study of the Lake Tahoe basin in 1962 concluded that the best solution would be to export the sewage to a point outside the basin. At this stage in the development of sewage-treatment systems, exportation is certainly the correct solution and some steps are being taken to proceed with it. But what of the numerous inhabited areas that have only septic tanks, too often of inadequate capacity and with insufficient leaching fields? When the spring runoff occurs, these make their annual contribution to the ever-increasing fertility of the lake. The amount of nutrient from septic tanks that moves directly through the porous soil into the lake is difficult to determine, but may prove of grave long-term importance.

Land disturbance remains a problem with dimensions difficult to define. It increases the exposure of mineral soil, which greatly increases the leaching of nutrients directly into the runoff water. These nutrients, like those from sewage, accelerate the growth of algae. Additionally, the actual transport of soil particles to the lake by surface runoff not only increases turbidity of the lake, but as time passes, some of the mineral and organic components of these particles go into solution, thereby further adding to the plant nutrient supply.

The most effective means of soil conservation is to keep the ground covered with vegetation. Almost any construction activity, be it the building of roads, the development of subdivisions, or management of ski areas, will usually remove the protective cover of vegetation from the soil. Among the "eyesores" in the basin are the innumerable road systems that etch their way up the slopes. Because of their lack of vegetation, the road cuts, often visible from the other side of the lake, form a new and very erosive drainage system that moves tons of soil to the lake each spring. Serious mud flows have developed at North Tahoe, and extensive deltas are developing at the mouths of some streams, while the lighter material is carried far out in the lake. Fingers of muddy water from Incline and Third creeks on the north shore were easily visible last spring.

Because of the steepness of the terrain and the necessity of clearing trees from the runs, ski slopes are usually areas of high erosion. This fact is well hidden by the snow during the season, but when the lift lines have stopped and the spring melt begins, gullies and barren slopes in many Lake Tahoe ski areas bear witness to the problem. Once again, cessation of unnecessary soil disturbance and the provision for revegetation offer the best solutions.

To understand how precarious is Lake Tahoe's future as a remarkable aquatic resource, one must look beneath Tahoe's blue surface to the myriad of aquatic organisms whose life and death affect the lake's future. These range from microscopic one-celled plants only a few thousandths of a millimeter in size, through a variety of larger plants and the tiny animal plankton that feed a portion of the fish population. Crayfish, sculpins, worms, and insect larvae inhabit the lake bottom to considerable depths. The Lake Tahoe "food web" is completed by the landlocked red salmon (Kokanee) and the predatory lake, brown, and rainbow trout that are occasionally dragged from its depths by fortunate anglers. These biological elements of the food web ultimately derive almost all their energy from the sun, which can penetrate so far through the clear water that attached plants can exist to about 300 feet beneath the surface. These beds of mosses and algae are important to the economy of the lake, as they provide food and cover for fish in much the same manner that kelp beds do along the seacoast. As soon as the water becomes cloudy from silt, sewage, or growth of plankton algae, these plant beds no longer derive enough light energy to live. Their death in several areas of the lake this spring brought floating mats of the plants to decay along the beaches.

Nine years ago, when I began studying Lake Tahoe, the rocks along the shore showed only a slight growth of attached algae. Last spring one could collect handsful almost anywhere in the shallows, and waves piled up mats of the detached material along the shore. Marina owners looked into green weed beds from their docks during the entire summer, and the hulls of boats left in the water for long periods developed a slimy coating of attached algae. To the limnologist these are unmistakable signs of pollution, but there are also more subtle changes to be measured farther offshore.

Variation in the fertility of the lake water from pollution was first documented in 1962 from eight different places around the lake. We were able to measure photosynthesis in the lake with carbon-14 to a depth of 60 meters (197 feet). The highest productivity in July was in areas receiving nutrients from the Upper Truckee River and from Incline Creek.

Because of its great volume, Lake Tahoe stores enough heat during the summer so that it never freezes in winter. As the water cools in the fall and winter, it mixes almost continuously, and nutrients added at the lake's margin rapidly become a near-permanent component of the whole volume. The unusual permanence of the water mass in Tahoe is illustrated when one considers that, if the lake were emptied, the inflow (less the evaporation loss) would take over 600 years to refill it. This means that once pollutants are in the lake, except for the small nutrient removal in the form of fish caught, the Truckee River outflow, and the very slow accumulation of sediments on the lake bottom, they are essentially there to stay. There is not enough water coming into the basin to have any significant flushing action in the lake. The pollution of today is already a sad legacy for many generations to come.

Decisive action must now be taken if Tahoe's water quality is to be preserved in anything approaching its present state. California has already laid legal groundwork for attacking the staggering problem of nutrient discharge, and Nevada may soon follow suit. California's legislation was greeted hopefully, but we have not yet seen the creation of a regional administrative agency that has the power and uses it to establish and enforce strong controls on sewage and solid waste disposal and on the appalling erosion of the watershed.

Until that time, we can look forward to acceleration of the pollution. Without swift and firm action, the clear blue waters of the lake will soon be only a matter of historical interest in California and Nevada—and the rest of the world.

- As both Heller and Goldman noted in their early articles, the machinery of government was churning even then to salvage something of the Tahoe marvel. But what machinery! The watershed was split among five counties, the usual double handful of towns and special districts, and—the core of the problem—between two states with very different outlooks.

Here if anywhere was a case where a strong regional authority—whether imposed from above as Heller urged, or built up
from below—was the only possible solution. What developed,
after years of hassles, was a regional authority indeed, but an
untenably weak one.

Ten years after *Cry California* first brought attention to the
Tahoe issue, Walt Anderson briefed a Tahoe situation that had
changed to some degree but had not, on balance, improved. All
sewage was now being sent out of the basin, but it had become
obvious that sediment from the watershed was, if anything, the
greater problem; the lake continued its slide from clear blue
toward turbid green. Only strict development controls could
even slow the process now. Meanwhile, the continuing population boom had brought with it chronic air pollution and acid
rain. Anderson's bottom line: another call for federal action,
this time in the form of a National Scenic Area.

WALTER TRUETT ANDERSON   1978

The Tahoe Troubles

If you fly over Lake Tahoe, or drive along its shore, you see what
appears to be basically one thing: a high mountain lake basin, a single
ecosystem. It doesn't seem entirely logical that the basin is actually in
two states, divided by an invisible boundary line that zips down in a
straight line from the north, angles off to the left somewhere on the lake,
and heads off southeasterly toward Hoover Dam. But the boundary is
there, logical or not, and everything that goes on in the basin has to
contend with it.

Tahoe, thus divided, poses a question suitable for a political science
midterm: How do two states work together to maintain a natural ecosystem divided by a state border? The answer: Not very well.

The problem is not only that the Tahoe basin is governed by two
states; they also happen to be two rather dissimilar states. The most
obvious difference is that Nevada has legalized gambling and California
hasn't. But there are other differences no less significant: California is
the country's most populous state; Nevada, although rapidly urbanizing
in the Reno-Carson area that adjoins Tahoe, is still sparsely populated

and largely rural. California has a vociferous environmental movement and has grown accustomed to the continual wrestling match between environmentalists and developers over land-use issues. Nevada is generally more laissez-faire about letting people build any damn thing they want as long as they can raise the money for it—see Las Vegas— and its citizens are highly resistant to anything that might look like government interference.

So Tahoe is in trouble, and the troubles have been growing through-out the post-World War II baby boom and building boom decades: more permanent residents, more visitors, more pollution (smog in the moun-tain air, sewage in the once-pure water), more and bigger casinos. South Lake Tahoe has become Las-Vegas-by-the-Lake, a gaudy/sleazy eye-sore of casinos on the Nevada side and motels on the California side.

The largely ineffectual efforts to deal with all this, to regulate growth in the area and treat the Tahoe basin like the unique and priceless resource it is, have been documented in *Cry California*. There have been, God knows, plenty of governments and agencies involved: the states, the local governments, two regional planning agencies—the one-state California Tahoe Regional Planning Agency and the bistate Tahoe Regional Planning Agency (TRPA)—and of course the federal government. The U.S. Forest Service owns about 62 percent of the land in the basin, Congress ratified the bistate compact that created TRPA, and federal environmental regulations—especially regarding air quality—are an increasingly important factor in the whole process.

Since all this gets kind of complicated, let us keep our attention fixed on the central issue, which is gambling—or, as they prefer to call it on the Nevada side, gaming. Gambling is not the *only* source of trouble at Tahoe, but it is far and away the main one. Nor is the problem exactly gambling, but the big casinos, the mass-merchandised kind of gambling that has grown up around Tahoe. Nobody complained much when there were only a few modest-sized casinos at the lake, but they have grown into garish monstrosities that are visited daily by hundreds of thousands of people who go there for the action and not for the scenery. This has in turn brought in other businesses, more permanent residents, and lots of traffic.

The gambling is all on the Nevada side, of course, but the problems created by it know no state boundaries: This is why there has been so much interest on the California side in regulating growth on the Nevada side. And this is also why the whole process has been from the start a rather touchy one, since it involves state sovereignty and has moral overtones: good-guy California versus bad-guy Nevada.

This irritates Nevadans and intensifies the atmosphere of border warfare. Nevada State Senator Thomas C. "Spike" Wilson, a legislator who has been involved with the Tahoe issue for several years, told me, "Nobody on the western slope trusts anybody on the eastern slope on this issue, and vice versa. Californians, I suppose, feel the Nevada gaming interests run the show. People in Nevada feel the only real interest in California is to shoot up the gaming and nobody gives a damn about the lake, and besides that the Californians ruined it first. These are the things you get in hearings. And our hearings are never hearings, they're rallies. We've never had a hearing on a TRPA bill in a normal committee hearing room—we've had to use an auditorium."

This brings us back to TRPA. The Tahoe Regional Planning Agency was created as an act of interstate diplomacy; its bistate compact was negotiated in many meetings between Nevada and California officials, then passed by the two legislatures and approved by Congress. As an adventure in interstate planning the compact was, I suppose, better than nothing—but not much. It created a single planning agency made up of representatives from the two states and—in an obvious effort to back away from anything that might actually give one state's representatives some say over what went on in the other state—incorporated a dual-majority provision. In order for the board to disapprove a development proposal, a majority of *each state*'s delegation has to vote against it. The compact created another masterpiece of governmental evasiveness known as the 60-day rule. This says that whenever the TRPA members fail to arrive at a decision on a project within 60 days of the time of application, it is "deemed approved." To further load the dice in favor of developers, the compact provided that each state's delegation to the board would be made up of two "public members" appointed by its governor and three members appointed by each local government, thus giving a definite edge to the more business-oriented locals.

TRPA has got to be one of the most criticized agencies in the whole history of land-use planning. The League to Save Lake Tahoe, which originally supported the move to create TRPA, has since condemned its "dismal record." Some of the details of that record, as enumerated by the league, include approval of 96 percent of the units submitted for approval from 1971 through 1977—major subdivisions, hotel and casino expansions, and infrastructure to make it possible for the basin population to keep increasing.

Various efforts to amend the TRPA compact have originated on each side of the border. The general pattern of these efforts has been that Nevada didn't like the California proposals and California didn't like the Nevada proposals.

Anderson goes on to describe the latest campaign to strengthen TRPA, which—like its predecessors—was doomed to fail.

Over the past year there has been a definite change of pace in the Tahoe situation, a growing sense of crisis—and an increasingly evident conviction on the part of many of Tahoe's defenders that any real solution to the problem would have to come not from Sacramento or Carson City but from Washington, D.C.

In August 1977, California Resources Secretary Huey Johnson, in a speech to the League to Save Lake Tahoe, made this proposal: "Give basic land-management control in the basin to the Forest Service under a concept similar to that of a national recreation area."

This was not an entirely new idea; many people believe that Tahoe should have been made a national park a long time ago and that, if it's too late to do that, some other arrangement should be made for dealing with it as a national resource rather than as an enticing backdrop for the projects of local developers. Various schemes for an increased federal role had been proposed before. But Johnson was speaking from a position of some stature, and persuasively argued that similar solutions had worked in other parts of the country.

Some months after Johnson made his proposal, the league's board of directors voted unanimously to support it. By this time the proposal had undergone a subtle but significant metamorphosis from "national recreation area"—the term used for comparable projects such as the Cuyahoga Valley NRA in Ohio, the Sawtooth NRA in Idaho and the Golden Gate NRA in California—into "national scenic area."

If the various parties on both sides of the border can come to some agreement about fixing up TRPA, it will certainly be an improvement in the Tahoe situation. But the National Scenic Area proposal will not be abandoned. It shouldn't be. It is clearly the best solution to the problem.

TRPA—even a strengthened and reformed TRPA—would still be a regional planning agency, a suitable arrangement for an urbanizing region. But Tahoe should not be dealt with as an urbanizing region; it should be dealt with as a natural resource. So far TRPA has been distinguished mainly by its capacity to say "yes" to proposals for developing Tahoe. Even if its vocabulary is now expanded to include "no," it will still be in the business of guiding development and *not* in the business of managing the Tahoe basin as a unique scenic resource.

This is the appeal of the National Scenic Area proposal. The mandate to the Forest Service would have to be not simply to stalemate development and keep things from getting much worse, but to develop and manage Tahoe in the direction of making it a *better* place for people to visit—meaning clean air and water, and more open space.

It has become fashionable in recent years to say that you can't solve all problems by throwing money at them. As a general proposition this is probably true, but there remain a few problems that need to get some money thrown at them. Tahoe is one. The legislation to create a national scenic area should be backed up with appropriations to allow the Forest Service to acquire more property in the basin.

What would Tahoe look like as a national scenic area? For some time to come it would look about as it does now. The Forest Service would undoubtedly put the lid on casino building and slow down other kinds of development, but everything there will stay there and business, scenic or not, will go on as usual. Some move to do something about improving public transportation in the basin is a likely high-priority item, but it will take a long while to get traffic under control and finally lick the air-pollution problem at Tahoe. Two likely efforts would be: a new study of the basin's carrying capacity, leading toward development of a new plan for its management, and a systematic program of acquiring undeveloped, privately owned land. There are thousands of lots around Tahoe, whose owners cannot build on them, that might logically be purchased. Johnson reckons that, since it would cost taxpayers some $300 million to build the necessary water-service and sewage-treatment infrastructure for some of the buildable lots—about $13,000 per housing unit—it would make more sense to go ahead and buy the land.

Undoubtedly this issue will play an important part in determining whether the National Scenic Area proposal gets anywhere. The prospect of the government coming in and buying up undeveloped land—especially land that because of zoning and/or other constraints can't be developed anyway—should have some appeal to thousands of Tahoe landowners who might not otherwise thrill to the idea of federal management of the basin.

It is (at the very least) 20 years too late to take care of Tahoe without delays and problems. Much damage has been done, and for many years to come we are going to have to live with it. It is a priceless resource that has, through carelessness and greed and political shortsightedness, been allowed to deteriorate badly. The blame for that belongs on both sides of the invisible border; so will the credit if things improve. No "federal solution"—whether a new TRPA compact, a national scenic area or anything else—is going to be forcefully imposed on Tahoe without the consent of the states. There will be no peaceful and permanent solution to the Tahoe problem unless both states make it happen.

- *Update:* At the end of the 1970s, hopes for a Lake Tahoe National Scenic Area were high. The Carter administration supported the idea, and in 1978 the President signed an executive order directing all federal agencies involved in the Tahoe region to modify their plans and expenditures so as to discourage further growth around the lake. But November 1980 marked the end of this promising trend. President Reagan soon rescinded Carter's order, and the prospects for national scenic area legislation have been poor ever since.

STEVEN M. JOHNSON   1977

Lake Tahoe 1977

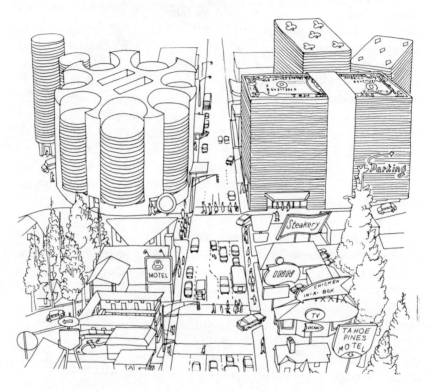

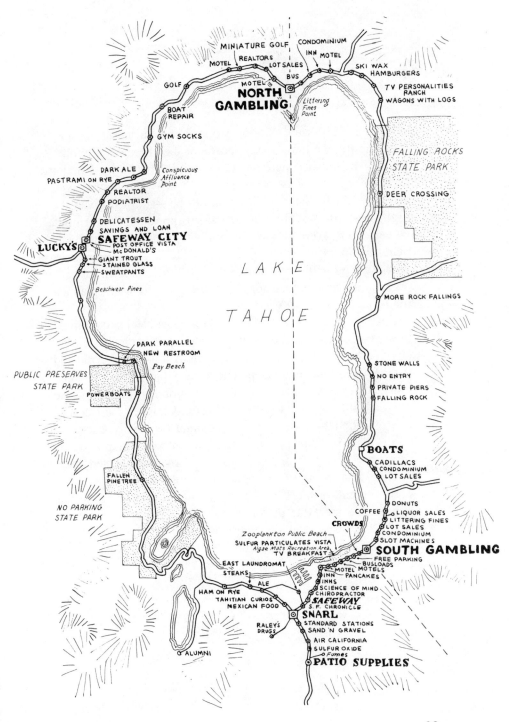

4 *Home Is a Freeway*

• Even as California Tomorrow opened for business, the state
was entering the tumultuous decade of the "Freeway Revolt."
The legislature had determined to build a network of major
high-speed highways—we forget just how vast that system is,
and how much vaster it was meant to be—and had given the
highway-building bureaucracy correspondingly enormous
powers. But even as the commitment was made, highway
planners found themselves facing people in place after place
who were unwilling to see parks shattered, coastlines bulldozed, city centers torn apart by the big and often ill-planned
roads.

In *California Going, Going . . .*, Wood and Heller examined
these issues as part of the statewide development picture. Going
beyond the usual debate about routing details, they criticized
the methods of the highway planners and deplored Californians'
lopsided dependence on the private automobile. Throughout the
1960s, California Tomorrow publications tracked the freeway
debate. Though cause and effect cannot be simply traced, it
seems plain that this prominent, persistent voice helped transform the "revolt" from an assortment of unconnected local
holding actions into a statewide and national phenomenon.

By the end of the 1960s, the protesters had won numerous
points. We are grateful for that today. But our automobile-
centered transportation system was more firmly in place than
ever, and had given to California, city and country, a pattern
that will endure.

SAMUEL E. WOOD and ALFRED HELLER 1961

The Auto:
The Most Voracious Land-Consumer

From *California Going, Going . . .*

Of all the creatures of our society, the automobile, which allows us to move from slurb to slurb, from home to job, from job to shopping center and back home again—the automobile is most like a locust, a plague on the bright land.

Almost every family in California needs or wants one or two or more cars. The car has been accepted as the *sine qua non* of transportation. People want cars. Cars need space. People try to see to it that cars get the space they need, in the form of roads and parking areas and garages and driveways.

That is why the state legislature in 1959 approved a 20-year plan for a statewide freeway-expressway system consisting of 12,400 miles of controlled access highways to cost $10.5 billion. That mileage is the distance between California and Afghanistan. The system will use up almost one-half million acres of California land. The 17 million cars in California in 1980 will consume over two million acres of land for parking, for driveways and garages, for roads, highways and freeways. Thus in 20 years 2 percent of all the land in California will be signed, sealed and delivered to the exclusive use of cars.

Still the freeways are crowded. Plans are being revised and will continue to be revised. Even more of the bright land will disappear, for the number of cars and trucks is increasing faster than we can provide road space for safe and economical movement.

The freeway is better suited to transporting cars than people. A California car, no matter how long or wide, today carries an average of 1.7 persons. Take a given point on a freeway lane: you will seldom see more than 2,500 people pass that point in an hour's time. Take a point on a rapid transit track: 40,000 to 60,000 people can pass by in an hour. But there is no rapid transit in California, and the use of public transportation is declining.

The freeways are dumping so many people into downtown areas that more and more land is being used for parking space. In the Los Angeles central business district one-third of the buildable land is devoted to parking. And some of the parking areas are multi-level garages. Even now California's major downtown areas are unable to handle the traffic dumped into them by existing freeways. What will the situation be by 1980?

It is small wonder that people are pushing out into the open bright lands of California, building their slurbs and shopping centers, and forsaking the old worn-out, traffic-glutted downtown areas. We can expect, too, that as present slurban centers become glutted with traffic, people will abandon them, and push out once again into the bright land, driving their cars, on new freeways, in search of new parking, new slurbs, new lives under smoggy skies.

The Department of Public Works, Division of Highways, has the responsibility for planning and building the highways that will take care of the California motorist's needs in the years to come. The division employs 15,600 people. Its 1961–62 budget is $632 million. The division's talented staff of engineers and specialists has a high esprit and is noted around the world for its efficiency. As an agency of state government, the division has a major job to do, and it has the budget, the equipment, the brains and the authority to do the job and do it well.

Yet the division has been perpetually under fire—not because its engineers lack ability, but because in locating and designing freeways, the division itself, *lacking strong state policy direction,* and sustained by the constitutionally provided gas-tax fund, has too often failed to respect the plans of other agencies for the use of California lands; in building freeways it has too often failed to respect the legitimate economic interests of farmers and merchants and others; it has too often failed to respect the aesthetic and social ill-effects of its freeway locations.

Some of the best examples of the state's single-agency, single-interest method of planning the use of California's lands may be found in the division's record of failure to coordinate its highway construction programs with park and recreation demands.

Beginning in 1939, provisions have been added to the highway code allowing the division to buy parkland beside state highways, to buy beach properties adjoining freeway rights-of-way, and to buy easements to beaches. The division never used this authority. It has never used federal funds available for these purposes. It also has evaded entirely the issue of controlling outdoor advertising along highways.

Worse, freeways have run through major priceless park areas in the state and local systems. A survey by an Assembly committee in 1957 indicated that over a ten-year period, freeway construction would have removed approximately 1,000 acres of park land. The division has fought against those who would defend parks against freeway intrusion in Los Angeles and Chico. Loss of substantial redwood park areas to highways was narrowly averted. So was a plan to invade Bliss State Park at Lake Tahoe and bridge Emerald Bay with a new road.

The division's attitude is based on the state highway code, which allows the highway commission to take over any property "dedicated to park purposes, however it may have been dedicated."

Anyone who has sat through local hearings in which state highway engineers explain to irate citizens why the division favors particular freeway routings must wonder at the doubletalk he has heard.

Of all the arguments favored by the division, perhaps the most used—and the most inadequate—is the argument that cites "driver benefit" or "user benefit" as a justification for the choice of one freeway route over another.

This formula translates into dollar values the savings in distance and time and safety to be gained by a driver over the proposed new route. The division claims that the formula helps it to obtain the greatest possible return to the driver-taxpayer for dollars invested. These returns accrue to the individual driver in the form of pennies saved per mile.

However, the formula is inadequate because it fails to take into account the full economic, social, and aesthetic effects of freeway routings. It disregards the fact that a highway "user" is not only a driver but also a human being and a member of a community.

He may be a farmer whose holding is reduced to a marginal operation by a freeway that bisects it. He may be a merchant, or an ordinary Joe who is happy to be able to drive 60 miles an hour instead of 50 over a two-mile stretch, but who is not so happy when he sees that this opportunity may also reduce his town to a slum by taking out part of its business section, some of its historical buildings, and limited developable areas as could happen in Nevada City; or deface a skyline as in San Francisco, erode a major portion of a beautiful park where he and his children can play as in Los Angeles, defile a most breathtaking natural charm as a highway would do at the mouth of Emerald Bay, separate a great city from its commercially valuable and potentially beautiful river front as in Sacramento; or—in short—reduce community values.

Community values could in great part be translated into dollar values just as user benefits are, if responsible agencies would get out their slide rules and devise the formulae.

The inadequate driver-benefit formula is both a cause and a reflection of the division's traditional don't-care attitude toward communities through or near which its freeways pass, and toward the overall best use of California's lands.

District offices of the division continue to exert a variety of pressures, in the form of subtle threats, upon communities to gain acceptance of freeway locations they favor. For example, communities often "get the word" that funds for a particular highway project may be lost to the locality for years if the route favored by the division is not accepted.

In spite of the so-called community value section added to the state highway code in 1956, the division has successfully fought all legislative attempts to specify the exact procedures it should follow when it wants to put a freeway somewhere: procedures that would require the division to fully inform affected communities of their responsibilities, rights and recourses in the process of freeway location.

There is no state policy that takes into account the fact that freeway location influences the ways in which California is developing. Like water projects, freeways—depending on their design and location—help to determine where new communities will or won't spring up, whether old communities will or won't grow, how people will or won't enjoy their leisure hours, what kind of life they will or won't be able to lead on the California land.

CURT GENTRY   1968

Iron Heel on the California Coast

As you read this, California's greatest natural resource is being systematically mutilated. The state's unique shoreline—more than 1,000 miles long—is being carved and battered by the state government in its rush to cover the coast from Oregon to Mexico with steel and concrete freeways. These roads, built to big-truck standards, exact a heavy price from this unique strip—a price far too high for us to continue to pay.

It might be pertinent to start with an area that has thus far managed to escape its intended fate. For, traveling down the California coastline, such examples are few and far between.

In 1963 the Division of Highways (DOH) announced that in order to meet future traffic requirements, and to link existing roads, as called for in the state freeway master plan, a freeway would have to be built through Prairie Creek State Redwoods Park. Three alternate routes were proposed: the first, following but widening the present highway through the park; the second, along the top of Gold Bluffs, overlooking the ocean; the third, along Gold Bluffs Beach itself.

There were certain unpleasant features to each. To accomplish the first would mean chopping down many of the great trees the park was established to preserve. The route along the top of the bluffs would destroy one of two remaining spots in the world where old-growth redwoods sweep down to a spectacularly scenic confrontation with bluffs and beach. And the third would almost totally obliterate the beautiful semiwilderness beach itself.

Thus far the pattern was typical. The DOH would propose a number of freeway routes, all with objectionable features, none taking into consideration the special attributes of the land. Inevitably, public opposition would split into warring factions, each group defending the route it deemed least objectionable. Finally, after the fighting had died down, and the most vocal combatants had dropped out (for you can't spend your life fighting a freeway), the DOH would move in and begin construction on a "compromise" route.

Only this time the inevitable didn't happen. Conservationists found each of the choices so destructive that, contrary to precedent, they united to fight all three. While the Save-The-Redwoods League began collecting funds to buy beach and bluff areas, the Sierra Club pushed for a new eastern route that would bypass the park. Early in 1966, the State Highway Commission, prodded by Governor Brown, passed a resolution requesting division engineers "to find and study a route that would avoid the boundaries of Prairie Creek State Park entirely."

> But going on down the coast, Gentry reports, the prospects for more such successes were not good.

At Eureka, several routes for a new freeway were recently proposed. Of the two most discussed, the "blue route" or Marina freeway would separate Eureka from its waterfront, while the second, a bridge across Humboldt Bay, would not only cut off Arcata but split the bay into sections.

In Marin County, battle lines are forming over what is to be done to the marvelously scenic Stinson Beach road. It would be difficult to imagine a more fragile piece of coastline, or one where the heavy grade called for in current freeway standards would wreak more damage.

99

San Francisco is known as "the home of the freeway revolt." Plans thus far fought to a standstill include uprooting portions of Golden Gate Park and separating the city from its north waterfront: At present the city is standing firm in opposition not only to new freeways but also to further extension of that view-destroying monstrosity, the Embarcadero Freeway. But each day, as traffic congestion increases, pressure builds and the cry "Do something, do anything!" becomes louder. One receptive board of supervisors is all it would take.

Not even the one-time mission town of Santa Cruz is immune to freeway devastation. In fact, the DOH would appear to have gone out of its way to ignore the natural attractions of this coastside community.

In 1967 the DOH offered Santa Cruz several alternate routes for a freeway extension of Highway 1. As this is written, the battle still rages, each advocate so busy championing his lesser evil that no one any longer reacts with horror to the prospect of a concrete monolith running through the Santa Cruz area. The real question is, why build a freeway at all in Santa Cruz? If, as is now clearly evident, the town is perched on too fragile a section of coastline to be able to absorb the trauma of a full-size freeway, other alternatives can and surely must be found.

In Monterey and Carmel, the battle has already been fought, and lost. Carmel now has its massive freeway interchange, while construction is well underway on the Monterey "can of worms."

By way of contrast to Santa Cruz, picturesque Santa Barbara was offered no choice: The Division of Highways designed an elevated freeway, not unlike the one astride San Francisco's Embarcadero, that would divide the city from its waterfront. But in abandoning the multiple-choice tactic, the DOH lost its chance to divide and conquer. Thanks to a legal technicality and a great deal of determination, Santa Barbara still holds out against the elevated structure after eight years of struggle.

What is proposed for Santa Monica is so fantastic as to stun the imagination. The plan—approved by both the city of Santa Monica and the county of Los Angeles—calls for leveling huge portions of the Santa Monica Mountains, thus amassing 120 million cubic yards of fill, this in turn to be dumped into the ocean a mile off Santa Monica and Will Rogers state beaches, to serve as base for a six-mile-long offshore landfill causeway stretching from Topanga Canyon to Santa Monica Municipal Pier.

Gentry next discusses in detail the scale, history, and probable impact of the amazing causeway plan, and tells us just how close it came to being carried out:

In 1965 a bill authorizing the planning, development, and operation of the Santa Monica causeway was introduced in the legislature. It passed both houses, only to be vetoed by Governor Brown. Resubmitted in 1967, it passed again, this time to be signed by Governor Reagan.

The bill—AB 1084—called for a Joint Powers Agreement among the City of Santa Monica, the County of Los Angeles, and the City of Los Angeles. Despite growing concern about the engineering feasibility of the project, and the horrendous changes it would impose on one of California's most colorful bays, the first two granted their approval. Richard H. Ball of the Angeles Chapter, Sierra Club, led the opposition on presentation of the agreement to the Los Angeles City Council in May, 1968. Despite the urging of Mayor Samuel Yorty that the agreement be adopted, the council voted 10 to 0 against it, citing lack of proof of engineering feasibility as its primary concern.

Farther south, another ancient freeway battle rages. Newport Beach wants a freeway inland, through Costa Mesa; Costa Mesa also wants it inland, but through Newport Beach; while the Division of Highways wants it along the beach.

But enough examples have been cited to indicate just how extensive the threat is.

California's greatest natural resource is its coastline. But it is a fragile resource, this meeting of ocean and land, whose delicate balance may easily be altered. There is no area on the California coastline—whether on its beaches, along its bluffs, or through its seaside communities—that can support, without extensive destruction, the massive freeways demanded by current highway standards.

The State Division of Highways is not an evil villain. It is simply single-minded; its primary concern is to move as much traffic as rapidly as possible over the shortest distance between two points. There may be areas where such an approach would not adversely affect the land. The California coastline is not one of them.

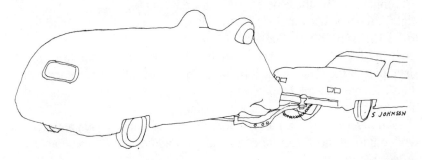

WILLIAM BRONSON   1966

Home Is a Freeway

"It was by chance," Bill Bronson writes, "that *Cry California* learned of Frank and Merilee Ferrier, who live a rather unusual life. The Ferriers spend most of their free hours—when not at work or asleep—driving on the Los Angeles freeway system." Fascinated, Bronson arranged an interview.

The Ferriers, it seems, had faced a choice between keeping up the payments on their house and those on their camper. After long consideration, they chose to keep the camper. And because they held, between them, three jobs in widely separated parts of the metropolitan area, that vehicle was almost constantly in motion. The interview proceeds:

WILLIAM BRONSON: *Would you describe a typical day during the work week?*

FRANK FERRIER: Sure. The weekdays have settled down to a very smooth routine.

At about 7 o'clock in the morning, Lee gets up, changes and feeds the baby, fixes my lunch, starts the run from downtown on the Hollywood Freeway, and doesn't waken me until we pass the Cahuenga off-ramp. When we get to the Lockheed plant, we eat a light breakfast and then she takes the Golden State and San Bernardino freeways back to her mother's place in El Monte, leaves the baby, and then goes to her half-day job in a small department store in West Covina. When she's through with her shift at 3 o'clock, she goes back to her mother's, picks up the baby, and prepares our dinner. Then she reverses her tracks to Burbank to pick me up. On the way back to downtown L.A., I warm up the dinner, and by the time we get to the parking lot where we spend the night, dinner's ready and we eat together. I go to work at 6:30 and work to 2:30 in the morning. The parking lot where I work is about four blocks from the lot where we have arrangements to park. Fortunately, I can sleep part of the time on the job, or I wouldn't be able to make it. When the shift ends, I walk back to our motor home, go to bed, and then the next morning, it's off to Burbank again.

All together, it's about 128 miles of driving a day, which happens to work out to about 10 gallons of gas a day. If you figure 22 working days,

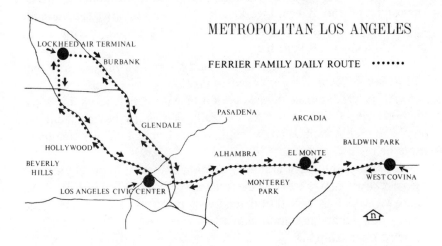

METROPOLITAN LOS ANGELES

FERRIER FAMILY DAILY ROUTE ·······

LOCKHEED AIR TERMINAL
BURBANK
PASADENA
ARCADIA
GLENDALE
HOLLYWOOD
BALDWIN PARK
BEVERLY HILLS
ALHAMBRA
EL MONTE
WEST COVINA
LOS ANGELES CIVIC CENTER
MONTEREY PARK

that means we spend about $75 a month on gas for commuting, which really isn't so bad. We spend more than that, of course, because we go to the beach or the mountains or the desert every weekend.

WB: *How do you take care of things like bathing, laundry, and storage?*

FF: Well, that's really quite simple. I have time to shower and dress between the time Lee wakes me and the time we arrive at the plant. Lee showers at her mother's when she gets there in the morning, and she either bathes the baby in our sink or at her mother's.

One of the first things you learn living in a motor home is to carry an absolute minimum of baggage of one sort or another with you. As soon as you let it become cluttered, you feel trapped. We store most of our clothes at Lee's mother's place, and long ago we sold all of our furniture and appliances. It's really quite a relief to travel as lightly as we do.

Lee's mother does the baby's diapers every day, but we don't feel we can ask her to do more than that. So Lee goes to the laundromat on Tuesday and Friday and she manages very nicely.

She goes to the bank once a week to make our deposit and we keep a post office box right next to where Lee works. We have to avoid imposing as much as possible on her mother, but as you can see, life would be a lot more difficult for us if she didn't live in the area.

WB: *Isn't it a lot more expensive to live on the freeways as you do than to live in a house?*

FF: No. Our payments are $192 and it averages out a little under

103

$200 a month additional for gasoline, tires, routine maintenance, insurance and registration fees. I worked this all out for my own satisfaction, and it's actually a lot cheaper than owning a house *and* driving a car, even if the car is all paid for.

WB: *Life must be somewhat different for you despite the fact that you've got it down to a fairly pat routine.*

FF: Oh, yes. For one thing, you don't have any neighbors, but since we both have friends at work, we really don't miss having them too much. Actually, we had a few neighbors in Tujunga we were happy to leave behind.

Another point is that although we didn't notice it in the beginning, we've really begun to feel that the freeways, particularly the Hollywood Freeway, which is a beautiful road, belong to us. It's not the same feeling you get about a house and a lot, of course, but it's definitely a sense of ownership.

And then, every so often something very funny will happen. For instance, whenever there is a tie-up on the freeway that lasts more than half an hour, one or more people will leave their cars and come up to ask to use our bathroom, and of course you really can't turn a person down.

WB: *Well, that brings up another point. How do you manage to keep your unit serviced?*

FF: Well, to begin with, Lee picks up water twice a day. I use up almost a full tank with my shower and she needs another tankful to take care of washing dishes, hands and faces, and so on. We drain the toilet tank whenever it's necessary. Frankly, we use the toilet as little as possible, because it's kind of a pain in the neck. For heating and cooking we get a new 20-pound bottle as often as twice a week when it's cold. In summer we can get three weeks out of a bottle. Since we can carry 40 gallons of gasoline, Lee only has to fill up twice a week. We give all our gasoline trade to one station in exchange for our night parking space.

WB: *What do you plan to do when you've paid off the motor home?*

FF: We've thought a lot about that. With the baby growing up, we obviously can't live all our lives on the road, and we've considered a number of possibilities. We'll have this paid off before Christmas of 1967, and we have pretty well decided to buy a 40-foot Chinese junk, with a diesel engine, and berth it at Marina Del Rey, you know, just south of Venice. The style we have our eye on has three staterooms, a galley and what they call a saloon, which is really a living room. I must say that although things have worked out all right, it will be good to have our home in one place again.

- Bronson's interview of Frank Ferrier, backed up with sometimes poignant photographs, drew more than a little attention. A couple of issues later, the editor told all: it was a hoax. The "Ferriers" were borrowed friends of photographer Baron Wolman, posing in a rented motor home. "What was designed as a satire," Bronson noted, "was too close to the truth."

BOB SIMMONS   1968

The Freeway Establishment

An informal but extremely powerful alliance of special-interest groups, fattened by the massive California highway program, is effectively preventing the development of alternatives to freeway travel.

The Freeway Establishment stands guard over a sacrosanct fountain of money that each year bubbles out more than 800 million gasoline-tax dollars. The money is collected by the state and federal governments and these funds are used by the state to build and maintain highways alone. The use of the state gas-tax revenues is limited to highway construction and maintenance by a provision of the state constitution; the federal funds are not similarly protected by the federal constitution, but they are almost as inviolate.

The superhighways generate more traffic, which in turn generates need for more superhighways, which generate still more vehicle miles and more gasoline-tax revenues, the source of the magic fountain. The Freeway Establishment is made up of those groups in business and government who benefit financially and professionally from the cycle. They include:

the trucking industry
the auto clubs (AAA, etc.)
the petroleum industry
heavy-equipment manufacturers
auto manufacturers and dealers

concrete producers
general contractors
the lumber industry
rock and aggregate producers
and, of course, the California Division of Highways.

They rally behind the prestigious banner of the California State Chamber of Commerce and in the legislature they work very closely with the pervasively influential Senate Transportation Committee

Chairman Randolph Collier, Democrat of Yreka. The most active and effective lobbyists of the group—those representing the truckers, auto clubs, and petroleum interests—are known affectionately in the Capitol corridors as Randy's Rat Pack.

The interests are allied, not in a sinister conspiracy to destroy California, but in a mutually profitable advocacy of a system they consider to be progressive. Business success and professional prestige are primary to them. The secondary goal is what they define as the public interest. The destruction of California is a side effect.

The "highway users' tax fund" is the fountain of money that can be used only for highway building and maintenance. The deceptive title helps to promote the false idea that the freeway program supports itself from the $800-million-plus yearly state and federal gasoline-tax levies. In truth, virtually all California taxpayers put money into the road system. The League of California Cities estimates that general-property taxpayers subsidize the road system by $440 million each year spent on city streets and county road systems, without which the freeways would be useless.

The freeways would be worse than useless without urban parking facilities now costing as much as $10,000 per stall on surface areas close to the core of cities such as San Francisco.

The 60 percent of downtown Los Angeles now given over to automobiles, for streets and parking, represents a staggering loss from the tax rolls when the alternative uses for that land are considered.

And there are many other tangible and intangible costs—economic, social, historic, scenic—that no one bothers to quantify.

Clearly there is a pressing need for creation of balanced transportation systems in and between our cities. How public money is spent for transportation is the legitimate business of every Californian. But in reality, the members of the Freeway Establishment call the shots.

Legislative proposals that would create new gasoline-tax revenues for alternate transportation systems are branded by the Establishment as "raids on the highway fund." They are dealt with promptly and efficiently by what veteran Assemblyman Frank Lanterman, Republican of La Cañada, calls "the best-coordinated lobbying alliance in Sacramento."

Simmons goes on to describe the different interests that make up the Freeway Establishment and how they work to kill unfavorable bills. The key player, though, is the Division of Highways itself.

For its thousands of engineers, highway building is alpha and omega, and a freeway—any freeway—is a thing of beauty and joy.

Division engineers, viewing the smog-and-traffic-choked Los Angeles basin, can barely contain their emotions while envisioning the entire county cross-hatched with concrete.

"The challenge to men and machines to move mountains is here. We have a vast area for construction; we have the money and what's planned for the area mostly lies ahead. We've only scratched the surface."

So preaches Robert D. Zaniboni, highway administrative officer of District Seven, in an imaginative Division of Highways publication called *How Los Angeles Was Unified by Freeways*.

"Population means money," he continues. "We're doing things in a big way, money-wise. Look at the construction schedule. Every couple of weeks, it seems, we let a contract for $6 million, $7 million, $5 million. Here's one for $14 million. That takes a lot of engineering of varied kinds. It's the big time!"

At the Capitol, big-time evangelists help to drown out every whisper of dissent from the concrete catechism. The division's lobby is one of the most potent in Sacramento, although as a state agency it is not to be found in the roster of registered lobbyists. During debate on bills, members of the Department of Public Works' Legal Division—the Division of Highways lobby, prominently Emerson Rhyner, Robert Williams and Thomas Carroll—actively work the corridors and the legislative offices, as well as making formal committee appearances.

These men have the resources to produce compelling arguments and the impressive backing of a huge administrative branch of government that has a remarkably broad political base touching every county in the state. District engineers and other public-works officials can bring very significant pressure to bear on a legislator within his home district.

The salaries of division personnel are paid from the gas tax. Thus the idea of using revenue derived from gasoline for any nonhighway purpose not only is sacrilegious but threatens the sinecures of division personnel. Its district engineers dominate the setting of priorities at the local level. Its Sacramento staff dominates the Highway Commission, which has no staff of its own to evaluate recommendations submitted to it by the division. Its lawyers operate effectively to protect the division in both legislative and executive branches. Any diversion of money that might someday be used for highways is viewed as an intolerable threat.

As chairman of the Senate committee that gives life or death to all transportation bills, Randolph Collier is the keystone of the structure of legislative control relied upon by the Freeway Establishment. Legislative in-fighters hold him in awe as the "fastest gavel in the West" when it comes to killing bills opposed by the truckers, auto clubs, oil interests or the Division of Highways.

Senator Collier is one of the few legislators in California to achieve public status as chairman of his own lobby. This happened when freeway interests formed a "public education" association known as Californians for Modern Highways, incorporated on June 29, 1964. It served at least one excellent educational function in helping to identify the interest-group alliance that perpetuates the state's superhighway syndrome. On the incorporation papers, Senator Collier is listed as president. The other officers were Wade Sherrard of the California Truckers Association, William R. MacDougall of the County Supervisors Association, Richard Robison of the Auto Club of Southern California, and Robert McClure, Santa Monica publisher, former highway commissioner, and promoter of the famous Santa Monica Causeway scheme to build a freeway over the water off the Santa Monica beaches.

Californians for Modern Highways is now defunct. Its work is being done more effectively and much more elegantly by the California State Chamber of Commerce and its Freeway Support Committee headed by consulting engineer Herbert Hoover, Jr., of Los Angeles.

The State Chamber not only spreads the freeway gospel with fervor, it plays an active, quasi-governmental role in helping the Division of Highways make decisions on route priorities. As explained by Barry Smith, director of the Chamber's Transportation and Highway Department, the local chambers of commerce in 48 counties plan local "Grass Routes" meetings at which the businesses and industries voice their desires for completion and improvement of city, county, state and interstate roads. Then, on whirlwind, statewide trips the Chamber's transportation and highways director visits each of the 48 counties, in the company of Division of Highway officials. They receive the priority proposals of the local interests. The Chamber then makes its presentation to the State Highway Commission as to which road projects should be assigned immediate, intermediate, or long-range priority.

According to Smith, the Highway Commission attaches great importance to the Chamber's recommendations. "We usually have about 90 percent of our program adopted," he said. "One year it was as high as 97 percent.

"We haven't taken a position on the idea of mass transportation. We're neutral on it. But we opposed the diversion of highway fund money. We've got to preserve even the potential highway money for highways. So we want to head off any diversion of money that might someday be available for roads, even if it isn't now."

Most legislators will concede that state transportation financing has been taken far beyond the control of the taxpayers, yet few have been willing to take the initiative in attempting to reclaim some control on behalf of their constituents.

California legislators justifiably pride themselves on being the most independent in the nation, the least reliant on either the administrative branch or the lobbyists to supply them with answers. Backed by the best legislative research staff in the country, the legislature could ignore the influence of the Freeway Establishment if it chose to recognize the pressing need for balanced transportation systems.

The Reagan administration has an opportunity to meet the same challenge. The response to date has been less than emphatic.

What our leadership must at long last insist upon is that the revenue from gasoline and vehicle taxes is transportation money, not freeway-only money—the property of all Californians, not of a dozen or so favored interest groups.

• California Tomorrow had an observer, so to speak, in the heart of the Freeway Establishment—Joseph Houghteling, a member of the California Highway Commission. Houghteling, a most unusual highwayman, had been chairman of the California Park Commission; was appointed to the highway board by Governor Pat Brown; and was also a member of the California Tomorrow advisory board.

JOSEPH C. HOUGHTELING   1966

Confessions of a Highway Commissioner

There have been claims that the Deity alone stands above the California Highway Commission. Let heaven and the critics rest assured—the reality differs from the reputation.

In great part, the commission, good at opening freeways and participating in self-congratulatory events, is as ceremonial as the modern

109

English monarchy. But, unlike Queen Elizabeth, the commission does have the legal power to act far more vigorously, independently, and imaginatively than it now does.

However, the present commission feels that meeting one day a month (occasionally more) between 10 a.m. and 5 p.m. with time out for a two-hour lunch is sufficient to:

Pass upon, within broad limits set by the legislature, the State Highway budget (available in the 1966–67 fiscal year for maintenance, administration, and capital expenditures: $730 million);

Decide every detailed highway routing in California (158 miles of new freeway routing adopted in 1965);

Authorize preliminary surveys to determine advisability of including or excluding from the State Highway System any highway;

Relinquish or abandon portions of superseded state highways;

Approve condemnations for acquisition of rights-of-way;

Pass upon local requests for connection to freeways;

Dispose of, by bid or negotiation, excess parcels of rights-of-way;

Review annually every city and county "select system" of roads on which state-apportioned funds can be spent;

Listen to delegations on any of these matters.

And so forth. The Highway Code is a gold mine of powers. But the key power given the commission is its control over the Division of Highways budget; no other lay authority passes upon its development and detail. Unlike other state activities, the budget of the highway program becomes part of the state budget without the usual gubernatorial-legislative scrutiny and alteration—a procedure even the Regents of the University of California can envy.

If the legislature and people of California believe the commission engages in much serious budget evaluation or that it directs the Division of Highways, let them no longer be deceived. *What actually exists is a condition wherein the inmates run the asylum, with the Chief Inmate serving also as Chairman of the Board of Visitors.*

As I write this, I can sense the hackles rising on certain bureaucratic backs, so let me add quickly that I am not impugning anyone's financial honesty, parentage, patriotism and the like. I simply am saying that things operate in quite a different way than they have been made out to.

My first insight into the realities of commission procedure came shortly after I was appointed by Governor Edmund G. Brown at Thanksgiving, 1964. I inquired of Transportation Agency Administrator

Robert B. Bradford, who also serves *ex officio* as chairman of the Highway Commission, how actual costs of highway projects compared with the estimates on which the commission in part bases its route decisions and from which the division weaves its cost to user-benefit ratios. The chairman's prompt reply was that this information hadn't been compiled so far, and while a special report could be prepared for me, this seemed unnecessary since the estimates of the Division of Highways "are the highest in quality and integrity I've seen in 30 years of public service."

I persisted and got the answer. Actual costs were an average of 32 percent above estimates, most of the increment coming from additional right-of-way costs.

What this means, at first glance, is that a route alternative involving a higher proportion of right-of-way costs than another could end up more expensive to build even though in the estimate stage it appeared cheaper over all.

A more general and more important conclusion is that no matter how many slide rules and computers are used in developing estimates, there are likely to be as many subjective judgments put into the cost equation as go into the *community values* aspect of freeway route selection. And those who find it hard to give an exact economic figure to these community values should have sympathy for the engineers who have the same difficulty in their field.

Finally, I gathered the clear impression that commissioners weren't really expected to ask such questions, an impression that has been reinforced since then. Another example: during the 1965 general legislative session, I asked the chairman to have copies sent me of bills affecting the commission and the division. Months later, having obtained the measures from other sources, I learned why I had received no answer from the chairman's office. An assistant told me, in a candid moment, he had been forwarded my request but had decided not to fulfill it since the information was, in a few more words than I use here, "none of your business."

On the other hand, I've seldom lacked for information from the

State Highway Engineer and his subordinates, although I have become most careful to ask very specific questions; otherwise I'm apt to be mailed a haystack of material in which to find the needle.

Let me add that I've been impressed with the devotion and conviction the engineers bring to their assignments. The rising debate over the highway program is far more an indication of the challenges of the present and future in constructing freeways than it is a broad attack on the system of highways and freeways that have been built in the past.

Enough reflection, now to reform. The first change clearly needed in the Highway Commission organization is to remove the Transportation Agency Administrator from chairmanship of the commission. As it stands now, it's much as if the president of the Pacific Gas and Electric Company were *ex officio* chairman of the Public Utilities Commission.

I believe the commission should have a small staff of its own, responsible only to the commission itself. To continue the Public Utilities analogy, the commission exists in the manner the PUC would if only PG&E engineers served on its staff developing utility rate recommendations. A commissioner questioning portions of the state engineer's route recommendation or budget proposal or even property disposal finds the answer developed by the same people who originally made the presentation. It would be strange if their replies did anything else than explain and sustain what they've already concluded.

I impugn no one's professional integrity; but I have found, when I question engineering-slide-rule-computer conclusions, my inquiries are interpreted almost to be ethical challenges. I'm not an engineer, which may explain why I believe there are far fewer facts in this world than points of view. For the commission to seek out other opinions on various proposals from a staff of its own should not be construed as an assault on anyone's expertise.

Another change I suggest is that the State Park Commission be given powers to participate effectively on routes affecting state parks. There is no reason why state parks should not exist on the same level of importance as the highway program instead of the latter having, as it does now, a priority. (In my four years as a member of the Park Commission, I always had the feeling our dealings with Highways had the friendly, powerless relationship one has when negotiating with the Bureau of Internal Revenue.)

It was only because of Governor Pat Brown's influence that the commission passed its recent, well-publicized resolution asking the highway engineer to study the Jedediah Smith and Prairie Creek state

112

parks highway routings, even though in the latter instance there already existed an alternate, the Ridge Route, acceptable to park people.

Governor Brown's attitude is a splendid asset to those concerned about California's natural beauty, yet the governor as the state's first citizen can only influence, not control, the commission. Only the legislature that created the commission and delegated powers to it can.

In my less naive moments, I sometimes suspect the commission as it now stands is perfectly satisfactory to the legislature, or at least a good part of it. Under the existing Highway Code, the legislature, any time it's in session, may reassume all the powers delegated to the commission. It has shown little desire to do so directly. But any time Senator Randolph Collier, properly called "The Father of the California Freeway System," has a cold, I suspect the amount of sneezing in the offices of the chairman and division is prodigious. Thus the commission can be left in the role of taking bows or brickbats when it doesn't always conduct the performance.

At the bottom of his formal letter appointing me to the Highway Commission, Governor Brown wrote, "Think of California twenty years from now." In my mind, the verb "think" implies activity, curiosity, imagination, and independence. The commission ought to be doing more of this sort of thinking and ought to have the means to do so.

• *Cry California,* for all its skepticism about freeways as commonly planned and executed, could not resist publishing an article that might tend to make a case for freeways—if the piece were good enough. Nobody who ever had to take a car through California's capital city, in the days before the big roads came, can read without a chuckle the jargony item Van Herbert called "Some Psychological Aspects of Driving Through Sacramento."

Herbert details the "elements or mechanisms" involved: six major federal and state highways, five railroad lines ("a single slow-moving freight train bisects the city with the implacability of a Berlin Wall"), two rivers ("one with two drawbridges, frequently drawn"); traffic signals always on red, signs announcing radar speed control, and "an ingeniously intimidating system of routing . . . going west you first go south, then east, then south, then west, then north, then west, etc.

He goes on to tell us how to approach the situation.

113

VAN HERBERT   1965

How to Drive through Sacramento

Palliative measures, even scrupulously applied, will never eliminate the effect of driving through Sacramento. They will, however,
diminish the intensity, duration and accumulation of the aftereffects.
They apply specifically to the driver but are also useful for most
passengers.

A. *General preparations*

1. *Practice hygiene:* Vigorous physical condition is your single
greatest asset.

2. *Do not drink alcohol* for twenty-four hours before leaving. Your
mind must be absolutely clear.

3. *Talk out problem* with anyone who will listen. Admit your fear.
Virtually everyone who has ever driven through Sacramento will under-
stand. Do not believe them if they say they know an easy way through.
They are delusional.

4. *Never look down* if you happen to fly over Sacramento. It will
break your heart to see how easily the whole problem could have been
avoided.

5. *Bring into order* all personal affairs, such as wills, social obligations, etc.

6. *Ruthlessly exploit passengers* who have never been exposed or
who are expendable. Develop a sick headache a mile or so before the
approach and insist that someone else drive. They will welcome your
recovery on the other side of town.

7. *Close your mind* to the problem from the time of departure until
you have reached the approach distance.

B. *Making the approach*

1. *Eat chocolate bar* or other source of quick energy. You have
about twenty minutes before your stomach will clamp down.

2. *Alert passengers*. They are no longer to communicate with you
or with each other (especially children).

3. *Move children and pets* to back of car.

4. *Crack out emergency supplies*. These should consist of cold fruit

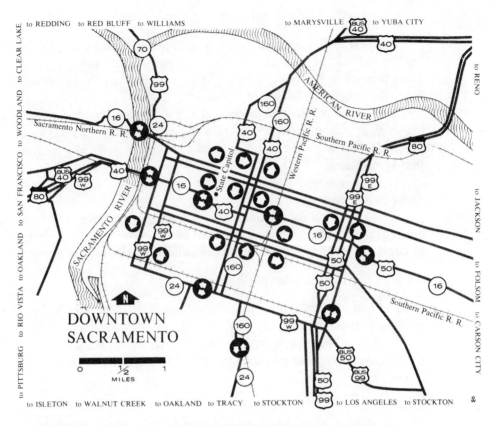

juice, coffee, cold wet towel, plenty of cigarettes, etc. (Never use alcohol.)

5. *Remind yourself* that it will be worse than you expect.

6. *Sing a song* from childhood or college days or a patriotic song such as "The Halls of Montezuma" or "The Star Spangled Banner." Songs involving "Rolling Along" or "Wild Blue Yonder" are totally inappropriate.

7. *Loosen neck* and shoulder muscles by gently rotating head in circles. Practice isometric exercise. (See author's monograph entitled "Isometric Exercises for Driving Through Sacramento.")

8. *Prepare to curse* by rehearsing the particular sequence of epithets that suits your mood at the time. Anticipate the necessity of back-up sequences suited to a more vicious mood should these fail. If persons of tender years or sensibilities are present, seek pungent substitutes for hard-core blasphemy.

9. *Gird up* your loins.

115

C. *The trip through the city.*

1. *Curse.* The importance of cursing to preserve sanity while driving through Sacramento cannot be overemphasized. If you seek religious counsel on this point, be sure your counsellor has driven through Sacramento before you accept his advice.

2. *Be humble.* Remind yourself that you are dealing with a force bigger than yourself. Accept your feeling of impotence.

3. *Do not believe it* if things seem to be going well. You will be thrown off guard.

4. *Do not blame* yourself because you took the "wrong" route. There is no better route.

5. *Do not stop* for anything except traffic signs. Once you have entered Sacramento your sole purpose in life is to get all the way through. Stopping saps the will and consumes crucially needed energy.

D. *Once safely beyond.*

1. *Make amends* to other passengers. Buy milkshakes for children, promise wife an extravagant gift, etc.

2. *Renew vow* never, never again to drive through Sacramento. Even though you know you will, the fantasy will lighten the remainder of your trip.

> • California's reliance on the gasoline-burning automobile has had another troublesome side effect: petrochemical smog. In a landmark *Cry California* article, Frank M. Stead, then chief of the Division of Environmental Sanitation in the State Department of Public Health, recounted the history of pollution control and the reluctant recognition that, even if all other sources were controlled, automobile exhausts alone would be more than enough to keep our air gray and our eyes stinging. He then made a modest proposal.

FRANK M. STEAD   1966

How to Get Rid of Smog

Stripping away all of the fine points of the technical debate, one conclusion is inescapable. If we are to have clean, transparent, and nonirritating air in our basins, we must control the number of gasoline-powered motor vehicles that operate in them. Can we do it?

It is idle to plan that Californians are going to give up their individual automobiles. They simply aren't. I think it is possible to make a bargain with many of them to leave their "horses" at the perimeter of congested urban areas if we can build public urban transportation systems that base their appeal not only on comfort and economy, but on speed, novelty, and exhilaration of the ride. But while the creation of such systems may partially reduce smog, at least temporarily, they will not solve the problem no matter how fervently we wish they might.

It is clearly evident, therefore, that between now and 1980 the gasoline-powered engine must be phased out and replaced with an electrical power package or at least one that does not emit hydrocarbons and oxides of nitrogen. This is far too fast a changeover to be accomplished by private enterprise on a voluntary basis. One reason is the massive capital investment that must be "suddenly" written off. A more formidable obstacle is the high cost of a crash program to develop a new power source. An even greater deterrent is the risk that for the first few years the new power source may lack some of the performance possessed by the gasoline engine and prized by drivers, so that the innovator would be at a competitive disadvantage.

The only realistic way to bring about this historic kind of changeover on schedule is to demand it by law in the public interest; that is, to serve legal notice that after 1980 no gasoline-powered motor vehicles will be permitted to operate in California.

This idea, in turn, raises the question of public understanding and support, without which no such law could be passed or enforced.

So we are back where we started—with the people. What will it cost them and is it worth it? It is not unreasonable to assume that a new type of power plant, including its developmental costs, would increase the average cost of motor vehicles during the changeover period by $500 per car. If the people knew this, how would they react? I believe that if the question were properly presented, the people would say "yes." The

$500 extra car cost, spread over a five-year vehicle life, amounts to $100 per year per car, or $100 per year per working adult (in California there is roughly one car per person of wage-earning age). It will cost each responsible adult citizen of California 28 cents a day over a 10-year period to eliminate once and for all the murky skies and choking smog that now typify what once was the Golden State. Surely, in this land of affluence, that's a bargain.

As a last-ditch plea for delay, someone is sure to ask, "How do we know a new exhaust-free power package can be developed on a crash schedule?" The answer is that it's merely a matter of hardware that can be produced on demand if we are willing to pay a modest premium. No new principles of energy conversion are involved. The new power source can be far more efficient and, ultimately, it will give us a horse under the hood that will bring back the thrill of that first car.

> Was Stead's idea the plan of an impractical radical? Not according to John T. Middleton, director of the Statewide Pollution Research Center at the University of California, Riverside.

"Frank Stead has stated the smog issue clearly, and his conclusions are inescapable. California can no longer tolerate the destruction of its air resource by the gasoline-powered motor vehicle. The importance of the motor vehicle and petroleum industries to the economy and wealth of California requires that their manufacturing and production ingenuity be exploited for the development of propulsion systems that do not pollute the air. The issue is not so much removing the motor vehicle but rather having a power plant that produces no pollutants, a clean propulsion system for the motor vehicle. Therefore, the state must stipulate emission standards or requirements that prohibit the sale and use of gasoline-powered vehicles as we know them today."

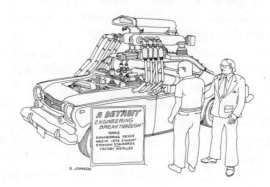

118

5   *Home Rule or Home Ruin?*

• When California Tomorrow surveyed the local planning scene in the 1960s, it found little to cheer about. As things stood, Wood and Heller insisted, "home rule" could almost be equated with "home ruin." In *Cry California,* Bill Bronson published a sequence of expert testimonies suggesting the same thing.

Let's begin with the story of the transformation of the Santa Clara Valley from superlative farmbelt to troubled city, as witnessed by Karl Belser, longtime planning director of Santa Clara County.

KARL BELSER   1970

The Making of Slurban America

The story I am about to unfold is that of the ruination of the Santa Clara Valley, one of the most remarkable agricultural areas in the world, and the substitution of a completely irrelevant urban development of massive size and questionable quality that could have been placed almost anywhere else and most certainly on more appropriate land. It is also, by example, the story of California and many other parts of the nation in the years following World War II. Perhaps, by pausing a moment to find how this magnificent place got into the fix it's in, we might learn how to act more rationally in the decades ahead.

Santa Clara County lies at the southern tip of San Francisco Bay. Its urban focus is the city of San Jose, which is approximately 50 miles southeast of San Francisco. The county is 1,300 square miles in size and may be best described as a fertile valley flanked by low mountains of the coastal range on either side.

Here was nature's handsome gift: soils second to none in the state and perhaps the world, indigenous water enough, if properly used, to serve that soil, and a mild climate with a year-round growing season.

By 1940, the Santa Clara Valley was a fully integrated agricultural

119

community. San Jose, with a population of about 50,000, was the county seat and the center of the food-processing industry and related industrial development. Stanford University, seated on its magnificent 6,000-acre farm with Palo Alto, a town of about 20,000, nestling up to it, was the focus of the northern end of the valley. The other six towns were distributed around the valley, enclaves in a vast matrix of green.

These towns were the service centers for the roughly 100,000 acres of orchards and 8,000 acres of vegetable crops. At the high point of development there were over 200 food-processing plants of various kinds in the valley.

At this time Santa Clara County called itself the "Valley of Heart's Delight." It was beautiful, it was a wholesome place to live, and it was one of the 15 most productive agricultural counties in the United States.

After World War II it became apparent that things were going to change in major ways. Many of those who had passed through the area on their way to the Pacific theater of war began to return to make the valley their home. Population began to grow. In certain ways, Santa Clara County began to gird for the struggle. In 1950 a charter was presented to the electorate and adopted. It called for a strong executive officer with power to appoint most of the traditionally elected county officers. This was a wise move directed at putting local government in a better position to cope with the many new kinds of problems it was beginning to face.

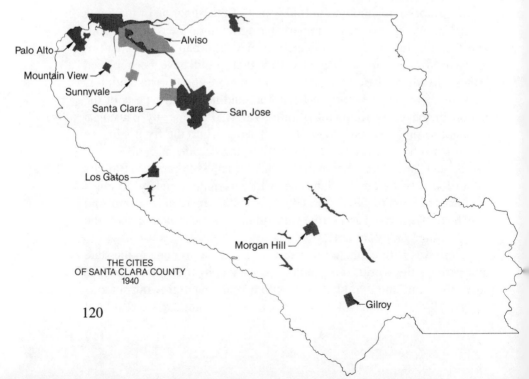

Palo Alto

Mountain View

Sunnyvale

Santa Clara

Alviso

San Jose

Los Gatos

Morgan Hill

THE CITIES
OF SANTA CLARA COUNTY
1940

Gilroy

But it was also in 1950 that the city of San Jose came under a new, aggressive administration that made no bones about its goal of making San Jose the Los Angeles of the North. It formulated definite goals for expansion and growth without any limits or qualifications.

When the inevitability of change became clear, the options the community had as to future growth should have been evaluated. Instead, speculators took over and pushed the county into uncontrolled development. The behavior of all elements of the community during the time from 1950 to 1965 can best be described as pandemonium.

During the critical period of change, the pressure on farmers was immense. The choice was to sell out and take a large gain on the price of the land, or to hang on and replant in the hope that a viable climate for continued agriculture would be maintained.

By 1953, the idea emerged that the urban explosion was a real threat to the farming community. At this time the leadership of the resisting farmers made an appeal to county government to provide some kind of protection against indiscriminate urbanization. The answer to this demand took the form of a new classification of land called "exclusive agriculture" within the framework of the zoning ordinance.

This amendment to the zoning ordinance, adopted in 1954, produced a strong negative reaction from city governments. They viewed it as a move to slow down municipal growth and they visualized themselves as being strangled by the protected agricultural areas tightly

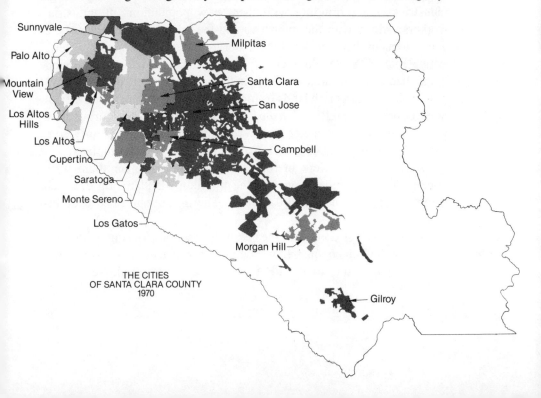

THE CITIES
OF SANTA CLARA COUNTY
1970

surrounding them. In reaction, the cities began to annex property wherever they could, by any means available to them. They took in schools that did not object, and county roads in dazzling patterns of confusion approaching chaos.

The resisting farmers turned to the legislature. Amid great controversy, the legislature passed the "Agricultural Exclusion Act" in the spring of 1955. This law provided that land zoned for exclusive agriculture in a county could not be annexed to a city without the consent of the owner, and that no longer could a city annex more than 500 feet of county road without taking in the property abutting it.

This act really frightened the city officials. It seemed to them that the control of their growth was being placed in the hands of the farmers. This spelled disaster in their view. In the 90 days between the closing of the legislature and the effective date of the law, the cities set about wildly extending their boundaries. At one time the city of San Jose had a boundary over 200 miles in length enclosing less than 20 square miles.

As the cities annexed in frantic patterns, many of the small unincorporated communities became frightened. This set off an orgy of "home-rule" town formation. Where there had been nine incorporated cities in 1950, in a few years seven new cities were formed. In this way, most of the northern valley floor became incorporated into cities. The pattern of city boundaries was chaotic.

Slowly the growth of the county transformed the economy. Large industries came, bringing with them new populations of industrial workers. Along with the industries and the new development came a water demand that overtaxed the underground supply, making water a critical matter. As development proceeded, the very elements of amenity that had made the area attractive in the first place were eroded away.

As the taking of rich lands from agriculture rushed on, the quality of home construction fell, and in the late 1950's it hit bottom. During these years, thousands of cracker boxes were thrown up, all so poorly constructed that they began to fall apart before they were completed.

Building codes were in force, but the abuses under them were unbelievable. The cities pioneered the minimum-standard house, which naturally became substandard at once. The instant slum had been invented.

All of this was done with the aid of the Federal Housing Authority. It was not the homeowner, in whose interest the agency was originally founded, who came to the FHA office with a proposal, but a tract developer who wished to take advantage of the attractive interest rate, the insured mortgage, the built-in opportunity for a no-risk profit. He wished to build hundreds of look-alike homes in rows of 50- by 100-foot lots to be sold to a market in desperate need and with very little choice.

The Veterans Administration was even more lax than the FHA. The VA underwrote marginal developments and allowed them to be built in what were historically known to be floodplains. It was a certainty that they would be flooded. They were, and at one time there were over 400 units in the county that were abandoned by their purchasers, all of which reverted to the government for rehabilitation and resale.

Although the federally insured mortgage program was a fine idea as originally conceived, an idea that envisioned a nation of householders living in modest but quality housing, it was misused and abused by a development system it was not designed to accommodate.

Projections of growth indicate that the entire valley will be completely urbanized within the next 20 years. It will have been given over to uncontrolled, wasteful urban growth with all its attendant miseries. Its land will have been covered with an unsightly urban mess. Because of the character of the air-drainage basin, which receives the accumulated discharge of the entire San Francisco Bay region under its impenetrable inversion layer, the air-pollution problem is bound to become progressively worse. Roads and freeways already overtaxed will unquestionably become nightmares of traffic. Yet the random development pattern defies solution of its transportation needs by systems of mass and rapid transit. Most important of all for people trapped in this net is the steady erosion of most of the qualities of the environment that only a few years ago made the area an exceedingly attractive place to live. Finally, the monstrous debt, bad as it is today, will become larger and more unbearable in the years to come.

While the responsibility for what happened to the Santa Clara Valley (and to almost every growing urban community across the nation) is laid at the door of local governments and special interests, surely both the state of California and the federal government must share some of the blame. Federal programs—housing, highways, defense contracts, etc.—speeded, not hindered, the destruction. And the state, lacking and never seeking any clear notion of how the lands of California should be utilized, stood by idly, apparently powerless to check the onslaught. Other countries where land and its use are all-important to the national interest allow none of the wasteful practices followed in our

123

country; Holland, Israel, the Republic of China and many others impose the kinds of controls by which each step of the urbanizing process can be weighed for its environmental implications. If they can do it, so can we.

- In another widely noticed article, Belser had spoken with bitterness and inside knowledge of the factors that prevented the system from working better.

KARL BELSER   1967

The Planning Fiasco in California

Very few people have any idea of the vicissitudes of the public planner—his frustrations and anxieties. He is consistently counter-manded in his recommendations by elected officials and seldom re-ceives a word of support as he bloodies his head ramming it against the stone wall of political expediency day after day. Yet just as consistently he is blamed for mistakes that are made, even though he has advised properly only to have his advice overridden. He is constantly mystified by the favorite rebuttal—"I know it's bad planning, but . . ." The hypocrisy permeating the entire process is so gross that it is shocking to witness an official decision based on principle alone.

If planning is, as we believe, the true doctrine, it is constantly defending itself against a monumental preponderance of sin.

The planner is only human. He is confronted with an extremely difficult set of alternatives. If he insists on maintaining his integrity and honestly strives for an ethical position, he runs the hazard of falling into the disfavor of his employer and, in that event, finds himself searching for a basket for his head to fall into. If, on the other hand, he elects to play the game, he loses his self-respect and becomes a virtual prostitute to the system. Besides, he can still be fired.

In California, there is a seemingly endless list of agencies, institu-tions and units of local government that dabble in the planning business. Federal, state and local levels engage in madly competitive programs, all trying their very best to undermine the work of the others. Thus we find planning groups without enforcement authority or with only partial jurisdiction muddying the waters and obscuring the vision of the future in a welter of fragmented plans.

This completely confusing and inept condition is costing the tax-payers millions of dollars each year. As an example, the San Francisco Bay Area has federal, state and local planning on such a broad scale that it is difficult to conceive—special planning for roads, water resources, air pollution, rapid transit, bridges, ports, etc., *ad nauseam*. On top of this, there is general planning at state, regional and local levels involving more than 100 jurisdictions.

But in spite of all this planning for conservation and orderly development, the bay is being filled in, air and water are being polluted, hillsides are being mutilated and prime cropland is being paved over. Public and private efforts to halt this kind of defacement of the natural environment are to no avail.

All this planning money is expended ostensibly in the quest for a more ideal urban living situation. The public pays for it, but in place of the "Golden Ring" it deserves, it gets Joe Blatz's service station exactly where everyone agrees it should not be. That is, everyone except Joe.

The prime movers of the community are the economic elite. They include the landowners, the money controllers—the activists in manipulating the use and development of land—and the mass communication media. Generally speaking, the rank and file of the community submit to the rules dictated by an adopted local government plan. They do so, not because they necessarily agree, but rather because they know that they do not have the influence to override them. The power structure, on the contrary, alters the rules almost at will.

Thus the breakdown of valid, approved public plans is achieved by the big operators in the field of urban development. These interests have an inside track to the areas where plans may be manipulated to accommodate their selfish ends. Their schemes, be they slaughterhouses or munition-testing facilities, are always presented as progressive. A great arsenal of technical experts, including private planners, economists and attorneys, is marshaled to bombard the plan. Many times there is no rebuttal, save that of the professional public planner. When his voice has been stemmed by loud shouting and flag-waving and the plan has been reduced to a pulp, the substitution of the exploitive private scheme is officially blessed.

Local authorities, accustomed as they are to identifying with the power structure (which many times is responsible for the outcome of elections), seem to be fair game for the suave presentations made by professionals who have been selected because of their proved effectiveness in breaking public plans.

125

To aggravate the situation still further, we have to consider the competitive jealousy arising out of a myriad of local government jurisdictions. Competing cities are no longer solely concerned with their own proper development, but their leaders seem to spend sleepless nights figuring out how to throw the gig into their neighbors. This completely irresponsible and undisciplined behavior has convinced the private sector that local government has gone out of its mind. Imagine, if you can, a county with 17 building codes, 17 subdivision regulations, 17 zoning ordinances, 17 sets of development standards, 17 planning commissions, etc. With this kind of weakness, the probing of the opportunist is sure to be rewarded.

Along with the confusion created by divided jurisdiction, we find a primitive mythology regarding the urbanizing process. For instance:

"Home rule is good."

"Bigger is better."

"City is superior to county."

"Industrial development pays the taxes."

"Annexation is good."

"Freeways will solve the traffic problem."

"All areas require sanitary sewers."

On the basis of this brand of logic, communities have been led into irrational and ruinous fiscal programs. Some have mortgaged the future for things that will be worn out long before they are paid for and have purchased things they will not need for years to come or may never need. Just how long this fiscal waste can continue without undermining the solvency of the community is a serious question. Contrary to the mythology, growth is expensive, and haphazard growth can be fatal.

- Then there was the case of San Diego, where the city council took the unusual step of submitting a proposed general plan to the voters for their approval. Journalist Harold Keen describes what happened the first time around.

HAROLD KEEN   1966 and 1968

The Trials of
the San Diego General Plan

On the weekend before San Diego's municipal primary election, September 21, 1965, "Eviction Notices," bearing what appeared to be the seal of the city, were posted on the doors of thousands of homes.

"You are hereby ordered to vacate your home by September 22, 1965," the notices read. "Your home has been selected by the Urban Renewal Authority under the Federal Experimental Housing program to improve racial relations. . . . Your house will be occupied by an underprivileged minority-race family now living in a slum area. . . . In a recent survey of your area it was found that there are no Negro families living within 300 feet of your property, therefore 'racial discrimination' is presumed to exist and the San Diego Urban Renewal Authority has determined that you are living in a blighted area and your house is subject to condemnation and seizure."

A close reading revealed the "Eviction Notice" from a nonexistent "Urban Renewal Authority" for what it was—a vicious propaganda leaflet aimed at scaring voters into rejecting San Diego's General Plan at the polls the following Tuesday. Property owners were warned that unless they voted down "this Urban Renewal method of condemning and confiscating private property" on September 21, the machinery of expropriation would be grinding into action September 22.

Ridiculous? An insult to the voters' intelligence? One would think so, yet this dirty weapon was one of the tools the opposition used in their highly successful battle against the General Plan. The count was 66,000 to 39,000, and in this landslide defeat San Diego became the first city in the United States to reject a long-range plan by vote of the people.

The vote was a tremendous embarrassment to San Diego. Community leaders vowed to try again, this time making a much stronger effort to sell the general plan. In November 1967 the plan won a convincing victory. Or did it? Within months it became clear that the city council, for its part, did not feel bound to honor the hard-won plan at all. The document, like all such general plans of the day, was in fact binding on no one. Keen reports in a follow-up article:

The first major test of the general plan was a rezoning sought by one of California's wealthiest entrepreneurs, C. Arnholt Smith. His holdings range from the Yellow Cab Company of San Francisco to the Westgate-California (Breast of Chicken) tuna cannery, from the U.S. National Banks to the San Diego Padres baseball team. Smith had no further need this year for his Westgate Park baseball stadium in Mission Valley, having moved his team into the new municipally owned San Diego Stadium. He was determined to convert his property into a shopping center that would overshadow all others in San Diego County. But the general plan calls for the region in Mission Valley west of Highway 395 (where Westgate Park is located) to Morena Boulevard to be developed for commercial recreation, in harmony with the present Hotel Circle there.

Upshot? Both the city planning commission and the council rejected the planning department's recommendations against rezoning, thus creating the first major breach in the general plan. Only time will tell whether Mission Valley, San Diego's onetime principal greenbelt, will be the better for it. Other enterprises will inevitably seek the same privileges given Smith, creating a possible hodgepodge of business activity along a valuable strip of land ideally suited for recreation.

The Westgate Park rezoning points to the bitter reality that idealism melts under the heat of expediency, and that planning can be subverted by the pressure of strong economic forces. The easy decision is to accept the principle of good planning. But the moment of truth occurs when the political agencies are called on to convert plans into meaningful results.

- When a local government actually tries to guide development (instead of merely speeding it along), the same question continually arises: "How can you take away an owner's right to do as he likes with his land?" In an influential article—reprints of which were sold by the thousand—Ira Michael Heyman, then a professor of law and of planning at the University of California, Berkeley, offered a clear answer.

IRA MICHAEL HEYMAN   1968

The Great
"Property Rights" Fallacy

The planning commission meets. Under consideration is a proposed ordinance that will strictly regulate commercial signs and prohibit billboards within the city limits. A realtor testifies for local commercial interests. He concludes by stating it is an American constitutional principle that ". . . a man can do what he wants with his property. No government can tell him that he can only have a small sign on his store."

This laissez-faire proposition is a popular view. A subtitle to this article might ask: "How far can land regulation legally go?" The answer, as we shall see, is, "A hell of a lot farther than the realtor realizes."

After a thorough review of the cases that have shaped the scope of local government powers over land use, Heyman sums up:

Property rights consist of powers of an owner to dispose of and use his land. The extent of these powers is not static. They can and have been adjusted over time by both courts and legislatures as there have been changes in population, technology and social goals. The Constitution has not been a serious obstacle to these adjustments. A good example of this is land-use regulation. At one time regulation was imposed only against nuisances. Later legislatures were permitted to prohibit nuisance-like activities. This increased the scope of justified objectives for the exercise of public power and concomitantly reduced the scope of property rights. Lately there has been a further progression so that positive enhancement of the general welfare is a permissible basis for regulating private use of land.

The excerpts from the cases that have been quoted indicate that while the permissible goals of regulation are broad indeed, regulations nevertheless must be reasonable as applied to particular parcels of land. We must explore the meaning of "reasonable," for that vague word, in the last analysis, indicates the extent to which property owners may look to constitutions for protection of their argued rights.

The concept of "reasonableness" embraces four interrelated ideas. The first we already have examined—does the regulation reasonably relate to a proper legislative goal? We noted that the scope of proper goals is wide and that courts (especially in California) defer substantially

129

to legislative identifications of goals and means to achieve them. Should the state legislature determine to prohibit filling of San Francisco Bay, a court would undoubtedly say that the objectives of such legislation are valid.

A second idea embraced in the term "reasonable" is that regulations must not unfairly discriminate against similarly situated property owners. Suppose, for instance, that a zoning regulation restricted to residential use a relatively small parcel that was surrounded by business and public uses. The regulation would be suspect and would be found unreasonable, as in the California case of *Reynolds* v. *Barrett,* unless a very good basis was shown for the different treatment. Similarly, courts are often disturbed when a zoning amendment, or a variance or conditional-use permit, is granted that allows the successful applicant to carry on a profitable activity denied to his neighbors.

In both these instances the courts seek to determine whether the regulating agency's decision is based upon a sound and demonstrable public policy. For instance, a number of cases have involved rezoning a relatively small parcel in a residential zone to commercial use. Generally these have been upheld when the city has shown that its action was consistent with a previously stated policy and program for establishing neighborhood shopping centers. When such proofs are absent the courts understandably believe that the development was allowed simply to favor the desires of the applicant and thus invalidly discriminated in his favor. An intelligently prepared general plan with consistent regulation guards against the prohibited type of discrimination.

A third idea that finds considerable mention in judicial discussions of "reasonableness" is the impact of a regulation on the market value of the land to which it is being applied. A consistent series of California cases indicates that it is constitutionally irrelevant that a contested regulation substantially lowers the potential market value of the objector's parcel, so long as the regulation is otherwise reasonable.

It has been usual, however, for courts to say that a regulation that so restricts property that it can be used for no reasonable purpose is confiscatory and thus invalid. Generally, these statements have been made in cases involving regulations that appear to permit profitable uses but that, as applied to an individual parcel, preclude any economic use for either of two reasons. First, the regulation may permit only uses for which there is no present market at the location. Overzoning for exclusive industrial uses is an example. Second, the regulation may preclude development because of special topographical conditions on the subject

130

parcel, or because adjacent activities (e.g., manufacturing) render the subject parcel unusable as restricted (e.g., residential).

The fourth idea implicit in the notion of reasonableness involves the idea of spreading to the public the costs of acquiring public benefits. The California Constitution requires the payment of "just compensation" upon the "taking or damaging" of private property. The effect of this provision, and a similar one in the United States Constitution, is to impose the land cost of a public improvement on the general tax base rather than to have it absorbed by the owner whose land happens to be needed for the government project.

Normally, a "taking" occurs only when the government acquires the title to the land in question. "Damaging" is a broader concept and can occur, for instance, where a road-building project results in undermining the stability of adjacent land.

Regulation, technically, does not involve either "taking" or "damaging." Nevertheless, courts on occasion have struck down regulations on the ground that they seek to accomplish purposes for which eminent domain (with payment) should have been used.

Here Heyman reviews recent cases in which even this limitation on the planning police-power appeared to be eroding, and concludes:

The realtor's statement quoted in the beginning of this article symbolized a 19th-century nostalgia that, while understandable, simply has *no basis in law*. Rights in property have been defined and protected by courts only to the extent that such rights and protections are consistent with social, economic and political realities. How far regulation can go is basically a political question. It is safe to predict that California courts will intervene only in cases of clear discrimination—either because similarly situated owners are being treated unequally, or because demonstrable costs are imposed on just a few landowners while others, quite similarly situated, are tangibly benefited by the regulation.

• How could the local planning system be made to work better? Marion Clawson of Resources for the Future and California Tomorrow's own Sam Wood had two pungent ideas to propose: that zone changes be offered for sale, and that local planning commissions be abolished.

MARION CLAWSON   1966

Why Not Sell Zoning and Rezoning? (Legally, That Is)

Why should the zoning of land for intensive development, or rezoning to a higher use, not be openly sold in competitive bidding?

Much is made, in zoning cases, of possible deprivation of property values to persons whose property is adversely affected. But seldom do we recognize that zoning and rezoning often confer values, sometimes very large values, on some property owners. Owners gain when a tract is zoned commercial, for a new shopping center, or when it is zoned for high-rise apartments.

These gifts in property value come *not* from anything their owner has done. They arise from public action—in the building of streets and highways, water and sewer lines, schools, and other improvements. They are created because other individuals have built and bought houses in the area, or because other businesses have provided jobs and income to prospective tenants.

I deny the contention that property owners have an inherent right to major gifts in property values at public expense. The public that creates these values now recovers relatively little of them. Indeed, the more the public spends for public land improvements, the more values it creates in the land, and the smaller the proportion of its outlay does it recover.

Property owners are fully aware of the potential capital gains from zoning and rezoning. In some cases, something of tangible value accrues to planning and zoning officials when they act in certain ways. Outright bribery is not unknown but is less prevalent than might be expected in view of the sums involved. But payment for insurance, or loans, or legal services can provide fully legal and more or less respectable avenues to the same end. As long as present zoning methods continue, suspicion of improper action will persist.

This might all be changed by open, competitive sale of zoning and rezoning classifications. The zoning authority might offer to sell, at open competitive bid, the rezoning of (say) any 20 acres located within a given one-mile square. Conditions to be met by the buyer should be specified and made part of the contract (and later enforced). Owners of land or of options on land would bid cash sums for the rezoning. While the zoning authority should retain the right to reject any and all bids, normally the reclassification would be awarded to the highest bidder.

If adopted, competitive sale of zoning classification would yield several major advantages. It would bring into the open the value-creation process that now takes place behind the scenes. It would remove most political pressure on zoning boards; the latter would not be denying the applicant, but rather this would fall to rivals who might bid more. The comparative value of one site against others could be determined more accurately by the market than by any planning process.

Finally, competitive bids would produce for the public treasury some of the values created by public actions.

Competitive sales are not without their problems, but they do have major virtues. There will certainly be opposition to this proposal from those who think they can get the rezoning they want more cheaply by the present process, as well as from those planners whose pride will be wounded at the suggestion that the market may do better than they can. But think it over.

S A M U E L   E .   W O O D   1967

Let's Abolish the Planning Commissions

When local planning first became a function of city and county government, it was generally accepted that the planners needed protection by a citizens' commission from the wrath of the public on the one hand, and the contamination of politics on the other. As the years have passed, however, it has become clear that the planning commission concept has not only failed to produce good local planning, it has also led to subversion of the public interest.

The time has come for planning to function along with other established responsibilities of local government. Our planning commissions should be abolished and the planners and their works should be subjected to the same political heat and administrative overview that is faced by other government programs.

For a number of years, planners, sophisticated developers, *ad hoc* groups and grand juries have decried the personal financial gain—direct or indirect—that planning commissioners and other local public officials can derive from the granting of variances and special-use permits

133

and other land-use decisions. Conflict of interest is manifest throughout the state. Evidence of fraud and bribery has been found in many California cities and counties. The recent charge of corruption directed at members of the Los Angeles City Planning Commission is merely the latest in a long series of such scandals.

In fairness, I must say I do not believe that planning commissions on the whole are corrupt. But I do believe that they are particularly vulnerable to corruption because of the huge sums of money to be gained or lost according to the land-use decisions they make. And because planning commissioners are not under the intense public scrutiny to which elected officials are subjected, this vulnerability is compounded.

Even more important, however, is the fact that their existence almost assures political irresponsibility on the part of our elected city councils and boards of supervisors. This is true because the councils and boards are not directly responsible for the major land-use decisions made by the planning commissions they appoint. Thus the all-important environmental decisions of local government do not become election issues. The voters have no effective recourse at the polls.

How can a candidate for county supervisor, for example, campaign on the slogan that "the incumbent was on the board of supervisors that appointed a planning commission that made poor decisions?" There is just no political sex appeal in such a platform. But if the board of supervisors had direct responsibility for local planning, the candidate might campaign as follows: "The incumbent voted to destroy our regional park with a freeway, to destroy a beautiful residential area by zoning critical points commercial, and to permit a subdivision in the middle of our last orange grove. He is destroying the county. A vote for me is a vote to preserve the economy and beauty of our community."

Of course, as things stand today, parties affected by planning commission decisions can, and often do, appeal them to the elected council or board. But our elected officials claim political responsibility when they want to, and deny responsibility when it is politically expedient to do so. Their responsibility for land-use decisions is not clearly visible to the voter.

Strangely enough, professional planners, who should be interested in an effective planning process, seem to regard the commission system as some kind of elixir. Why? I can only conclude that the planners find safety in the system, with its blurred lines of responsibility and consequent isolation from an effective political process. I know a great many professional planners who believe that the political process is too messy for them, who think their planning commissions protect them from the dirt of politics. The fact is that planning commissions provide no immunity from politics, only from responsible political action.

Right now, both the planners and the politicians are dodging full responsibility for land-use decisions made by local government. In this vacuum of responsibility, the developers take over, and the land suffers. Local government continues to insist upon keeping the authority to control land use as a "home rule" prerogative. Let us now demand that local leaders assume, at long last, the responsibility for this control—or give it back to the state from whence it came.

• At the end of the 1960s, California's rural counties faced a sudden new development challenge: the spread of ill-planned "recreational subdivisions." Harold Berliner, then district attorney of Nevada County and a member of California Tomorrow's board of directors, explored the problem in an influential article.

HAROLD A. BERLINER   1970

Plague on the Land

Rural California is being carved up and committed to unneeded urban development for the short-term gain of a handful of corporate subdividers. In the long term, the state and its people are the losers.

Speculative subdivision isn't new in California—it's been going on for more than 120 years. But the coming of new giant corporations to the field has accelerated the process to staggering proportions in the last two or three years.

The new breed of developers appears more respectable than the type that sold desert land, underwater properties and other similar values by mail and at a distance. However, the harm today's land merchants do to the land is a matter of urgent concern; for with their roadbuilding and other "improvements" they permanently commit the land to unneeded development, while the alkali flats and swamps peddled by yesterday's con men still lie as nature left them.

Nevada County is but one of many California counties afflicted with

135

galloping subdivision, but it's a good example of the problems that accompany the overcommitment of land as "recreational" lots.

The county, which has elevations ranging from about 1,000 feet in the foothills to the 7,000-foot level in alpine areas, is typical of California's recreation areas. After 120 years, its population is hardly larger than it was during the Gold Rush.

In 1964 the county decided to develop a general plan to help chart its development to 1990. After a great deal of effort and controversy, one was adopted in early 1967. This plan predicted that the population would grow from 25,100 in 1965 to 45,000 in 1980 and 62,500 by 1990.

> But soon after the plan was adopted, Berliner reports, the recreational subdividers moved in. By 1970, enough lots had been approved to serve more than three times the existing population—if houses were ever built on them.

In addition to ignoring the general plan's population recommendations, the board of supervisors has largely ignored the plan's urban-location recommendations. Just about all the lots authorized since the adoption of the plan have been placed in spots not contemplated by the plan for subdivision development. When public objection to this procedure started to grow strong, the supervisors simply modified the general plan to fit the needs of the promoters, on their request.

Why do these "undeveloped developments" continue to grow? Because they make great sums of money for the developer.

The total price of lots in one of these promotions may reach $50 million, and they can be sold out in a year or two. Representative promotional developers have stated that of this sum, one third is spent for the land, engineering, streets, water supply, sewers if required, country clubs, lakes, etc. Another third is spent on advertising and sales. *The last third is profit.* And there aren't many ventures that offer the huge percentage of return in such a small time, on such a small investment. Because the promoter doesn't *really* invest even the first third.

A typical scheme is this: the developer sends out scouts to buy up options on all the land needed, for relatively small sums, offering the original owner, if the project goes through, a better price than he ever hoped for his acreage. When all the options are in, the developer can safely invest in preliminary engineering, the drawing of maps, and the preparation of large colored illustrations for the planning commission.

If any opposition is seen at the planning commission level or at the board of supervisors, the promoter goes to the local businessmen, claiming that the development is still a marginal operation, and if overstrict requirements are made the whole thing will be abandoned, in favor of an alternate site, in some other county, for the benefit of the other community and its merchants. In smaller counties this tactic never seems to fail.

When the local agencies agree to the plan, it is quick and simple to borrow more money if needed, or if not, just to start in. At this point, the developers work on a close timetable, so the lots can be placed on the official record *after* March 1, when the taxes would shift from open land to land approved for lots, and before the short green-selling season, which is best in late spring and early summer.

A smart developer does not pay for his land outright, but through "release clauses" is able to buy from the original owner gradually, as he sells lots.

The main support for the whole scheme comes from the lack of state or local law that would recognize the community's need for intelligent land use. Today state and local governments proceed on the premise that if the developer can sell his lots, even to obvious suckers, with no use in mind, there is no public interest in preventing him from doing so.

In the early stages of a subdivision there is hope in abundance. The developer promises a golf course, a country club, many new customers for the local merchants and general prosperity. But the main promise is plenty of new taxes; land formerly used by the cows bringing only pasture taxes will soon be high-priced recreation lots, bringing taxes at a rate undreamed of. This portion of the promise paid off at Lake of the Pines, where in a typical area the assessor changed his view of market value from $88.20 per acre to over $40,000 per acre in a year and a half.

But there is another part to the promise: the developer tells the county officials that this income will be virtually cost-free to the county. He explains that these are "second home" or "recreational" lots, and the users will educate their children and use government services in the area where their primary homes are. This promise has been found to be a snare and a delusion.

In the first place, people who build are quite likely to make the subdivision their first home. In Lake of the Pines more than a third of the houses now built are occupied by permanent residents, and of those who intend to build, 60 percent indicate they intend to build their main homes on the property.

Building a subdivision the size of Lake of the Pines is really the planning of a new city of 5,400 people. To imagine that the city won't need all the normal services is ridiculous. Although the building rate is pitifully slow, responsibility must be accepted for the fact that a city has been planned and well may come into being. In any event, it will not be "cost free" to the county. It could become a real burden.

When things go wrong with a rural development, they go wrong badly. In 1965, Humboldt County approved Shelter Cove, a "recreational" subdivision. When the lots were all sold the county supervisors found that something had gone wrong with the roads, drainage, etc., installed by the promoters. Early this year the supervisors added up what it would cost to get the place back in shape. They now know that someone is going to have to come up with nearly $2 million to repair the deficiencies.

Huge acreages are going into speculative subdivisions—more every year. Boise Cascade claims 29 projects as of March 10, 18 of them in California totalling 71,000 acres, and they are now attempting to get permission to cut up thousands of acres more. In addition to the adverse effects these subdivisions may have on buyers, communities and adjoining landowners, the greatest harm done is to the land itself.

In the past it was thought that requiring expensive "improvements" would slow down unneeded development. It is now clear that there is a seller's market at almost any price. The more the consumer is "protected" (by the requirements for sewers, water systems, long-lasting streets, etc.), the more the land is harmed.

When we really need the land for proper lot development or other, better uses, the best of it will be gone. And meanwhile, our open space decreases every year. The intrusion of the "recreational" subdivision changes patterns of wildlife, alters the course of streams. Even though there is little building or use, the cut and fill construction, interference with normal drainage patterns and devastation of natural ground cover permanently alter the environment. They affect hunting, fishing, hiking, and all the pleasures people take in the land. They preclude future cultivation, grazing, timbering. The land as a resource is gone.

The answer to the problem is state legislation that will protect the land from plunder.

Local government must be made to recognize that it is creating a city when it authorizes a 4,000-lot project. Before it can approve, it must know that the area needs a city, and that it is located in the right place, and will have all the facilities a city needs, in keeping with local, regional and state goals.

138

State law must take the initiative and insist that planning commissions and boards of supervisors distinguish good development from poor development. So far they have shown they consider *any* development desirable. They must be told that they can and must deny permission to divide land and sell lots when there is no real *use* in view.

One remedy that has been suggested is to place the burden on the subdivider to prove his promotion will be 50-percent built upon in five years after it begins. It is clear that this would stop almost any unneeded rural subdivision planned.

Although stopgap legislation could bring a halt to this depredation and give us time to take a look at what is happening, more is needed. Only comprehensive planning will help permanently; the kind of planning that will assess and husband California's ultimate resource—its land—and decide how it can best be used for the general welfare.

• *Update:* The foregoing article led to passage, in 1971, of a bill by State Senator Leo McCarthy known simply as the McCarthy Act. This law required subdividers in sparsely-populated areas to make provision in advance for the services the new communities would require. This demand for serious commitment helped to halt the rural subdivision boom almost overnight. But the action came too late to spare Nevada County (and many other counties in California and the West) the burden of servicing many square miles of crumbling rural "estates."

RICHARD D. HEDMAN   1958

Planning in Action

Gentlemen: my chief concern is to make planning **relevant** to our city problems, therefore instead of fighting among ourselves to see who can get the most dollars! I propose applying **rational planning** methods in determining priorities uh - as I see it - what is needed is a coordinated program of action directed toward a set of common goals, herumph, ah .....

Are there irrational planning methods?

hm yes / sounds swell

good idea!

Speaking for Transportation I want to say that we wholeheartedly agree that *rational planning* methods should be applied. I think you all realize that our transit system is in a state of acute **crisis!** Without new equip- -ment **NOW** we won't be able to operate, in fact I have here.. a recent report

AHEM!

141

6   The Impossible City: Views of Los Angeles

• Greater Los Angeles fascinates Californians—even the minority of them who do not already live somewhere in the Southern California metropolitan belt—and it fascinates the world. Confronted with its vastness, its vigor, its apparent shapelessness, we variously gape or cringe. And the mere mention of Los Angeles seems enough to make the professional planners roll up their sleeves and reach for their drawing boards.

The problems (and the triumphs) of Los Angeles are not by any means unique. They are those of any sprawling urban region in the later 20th century. But Los Angeles, having gotten there first, commands our attention in a special way.

Under Bill Bronson, *Cry California* conducted a virtual running symposium of authoritative views on the faults and future of this amazing urban complex. We begin with a very positive piece by Allan Temko, who was and is Architectural and Urban Critic for the *San Francisco Chronicle*. In this 1966 piece, Temko faces the challenge of Los Angeles with an unmistakable zest.

ALLAN TEMKO   1966

Reshaping Super-City: The Problem of Los Angeles

The future of Southern California is potentially magnificent; and by many standards, not necessarily those of the Los Angeles Chamber of Commerce, it is already one of the most civilized places on earth.

In spite of its undeniable virtues, however, Southern California represents a deeply disturbing phase in urban history. Never before has so far-flung a pattern of random, low-density settlement erupted so swiftly, ruthlessly, and senselessly, chopping away hills, spreading

143

over the fertile plain like an oozing Camembert. We may be delighted by the Super-City's cultural strongholds, but between them extends a scene of environmental devastation that is made doubly tragic because of the splendor of the site.

More serious still, individual man has found his basic need for urbane social intercourse thwarted by excessive diffusion of cultural resources. Over hundreds of square miles, there are few places to walk, few occasions for the civilized surprise, the beautiful chance meetings, the freshly discovered, unique thing, which are almost birthrights for citizens of richly venerable cities such as London and Rome. The only discernible urban structure, on the scale that the Super-City requires, is the freeway network. To make this a truly great city, rather than simply a mammoth one, all sorts of new structures must be interwoven logically in a strengthened urban tissue. And because the Super-City itself is unprecedented, these must be unprecedented and revolutionary structures. Old solutions do not exist for this exhilarating problem.

> New solutions, Temko says, will require, among other things, vast joint efforts between private enterprises and public agencies—not at random, as when publicly developed water spurs private development in what may be the wrong place, but according to plan.

Only if we do coordinate large public and private undertakings on this scale can an authentic regional order arise amidst the inchoate settlement patterns of Southern California. The existence of huge private landholdings, of which the Irvine Ranch is the hugest, is potentially a tremendous advantage.

Thus far Irvine departs only in minor features from smaller-scale developments. But surely these large projects *can* be built in such a way that they solve more problems than they create. Surely they *can* be integrated with an overall regional infrastructure of unparalleled comeliness and efficiency. Surely a much higher level of civic design *can* be achieved in the projects themselves, incorporating fresh advances in technology such as microtransportation systems that will dispense with Detroit-style vehicles. Surely some equitable relationship *can* be established between public interest and private profit *on this scale,* where the developers have the financial staying power to see projects through to the end.

One of the greatest myths perpetrated by the enemies of Los Angeles is that it has no urban core. Los Angeles' downtown never disappeared, never was eviscerated, as the traditional urban theorists apparently believe. Not one first-class building, so far as I know, was demolished.

While it is true that a large number of aging buildings, few of them higher than two or three stories, were destroyed to make room for parking lots, this was certainly not harmful to the city in the long run. The market in this case simply cleared land more rapidly than government-sponsored redevelopment ever could have, and provided downtown with a substantial reserve of open land for imminent development. All of these parking lots will be built on before another generation has passed; and the new structures will be decisively superior in every way to the gimcrack little buildings that were destroyed. But will they be good enough? Will they be part of an admirably reorganized downtown, served by both regional and subregional transportation systems, freed from the tyranny of the automobile and yet accessible to it? This is the real question.

If the central business district were to be plunked down in San Francisco, its imposing office blocks, department stores, and public buildings would appear very formidable indeed. Yet in Southern California, because of the scale of settlement, it appears weak; and thus it provides an insight into the nature of the Super-City's evolving form.

For the central business district, augmented by the apartments,

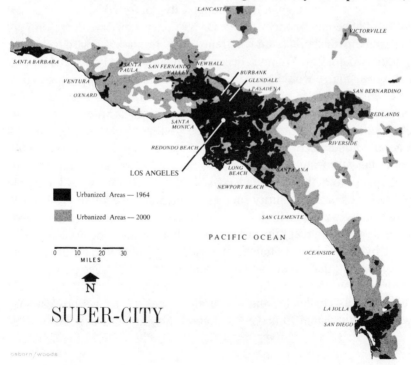

Urbanized Areas — 1964

Urbanized Areas — 2000

0 10 20 30
MILES

N

SUPER-CITY

hotels, stores, restaurants, plazas, and subsurface road system of the $500-million Bunker Hill project, is only one of the great regional components from which the new civic order must be fashioned. Shooting westward from this concentration, something like the tube of a thermometer fourteen miles long, the towers of Wilshire Boulevard present an altogether new kind of urban profile, broadening to join Alcoa's Century City in West Los Angeles, and, a few miles further along, the academic city, studded with high-rise towers, that has arisen around UCLA. At its best, this sumptuous urban passage through Beverly Hills, Brentwood, Bel Air, Westwood and Pacific Palisades is surely one of the most gracious environments yet created in America. At the end of Wilshire, Santa Monica is still another element of this far-flung urban configuration.

If each of these developments were linked with other massive additions to the Super-City, such as the high-rise complex of office buildings, banks, and hotels that now surrounds the International Airport, and further connected, on a larger scale, with the nuclei of San Diego, Santa Barbara, and San Bernardino; and if at the same time gray areas such as Watts were renewed, and integrated, on the same scale, an urban civilization of unprecedented force and graciousness would appear.

There is room enough in the Super-City not for 20 but for 30 or 40 millions of people, if only we have the wisdom to conserve the resources that remain unspoiled, and to renew the resources that have been wantonly damaged. We must decide where we should build, and where the wisest course would be to leave land undeveloped, according to the full scope of future needs. Not the pathetic 8,000 or so acres now planned, but the full panoply of the Santa Monica Mountains would constitute a true regional park on the civilized scale of the future. Literally hundreds of other recreational spaces, some large, some intimate, but all meaningful in terms of human needs, would have to be reclaimed from the degraded coastal plain. All this would require political and social maturity such as Americans have yet to prove they possess, as well as efficient management—of combined water and recreational resources, for instance—such as we have never achieved.

Obviously there is much, at this still primitive stage of human development, that we do not know, that we cannot do. The only way to learn is to accept the reality of the new scale of urban civilization, to rejoice in its challenge, and above all to realize that we possess the wealth and strength to make it the good thing it can easily become.

146

• A few years later, Mark von Wodtke, a professor in the Department of Environmental Design at California State Polytechnic College at Pomona, offered a much less optimistic view. Far from welcoming a greater population, von Wodtke argues that the Los Angeles Basin can safely hold only a limited number of people.

MARK VON WODTKE   1970

The Carrying Capacity
of the Los Angeles Basin

The population of California's South Coastal Area—including Ventura, Los Angeles, Orange, San Diego, and the western parts of Riverside and San Bernardino counties—is expected to grow from its present 11.8 million to about 20 million by the turn of the century. This projection, by the California Department of Finance, is accepted by many as inevitable and, implicitly, as desirable. It has become the foundation for much of the long-term planning done in California. The State Water Plan is committed, at great expense to the citizens and the environment of the state, to bringing water to Southern California for these projected millions. The State Division of Highways plans to pave the way for millions of additional cars and trucks. Investors and banks, speculating on this projection, put out glittering market analyses to spur development in Southern California. The Los Angeles Department of City Planning is accepting this projection in its new "Concept Los Angeles" study, despite its purported concern with the quality of life.

But there is a massive flaw in all these plans, in that natural environmental constraints on development—the finite limitations of air, water and land resources—have not been measured.

Several factors might eventually limit the growth of the Los Angeles area, including water, land, and food supply. The known and obvious limiting factor today, Von Wodtke reminds us, is air.

According to Department of Public Health air-pollution standards, we have *already* passed the safe carrying capacity of the Los Angeles Basin with regard to our air resources. Optimistically, under the present and planned auto-emission control programs, we might be able to return to the emission levels of the 1940s, with regard to unburned hydrocarbons, by 1980. Emissions of carbon monoxide and oxides of nitrogen are expected to round off at a considerably higher level. While still speculative, however, it should be noted that even with emission controls, the level of offending pollutants will climb again after 1980 unless the population in the air basin is limited, or there is a drastic change in our consumption of fossil fuels for energy production, both in power stations and in moving vehicles.

If we are to accept the 1940s as a standard of desirable air quality (which is questionable), it can be estimated that the carrying capacity of the South Coastal Air Basin would be about *14 million* people, assuming that the per-capita pollution rate is reduced as much as the emission-control plans indicate.

There has been no real technological breakthrough in air-pollution control, despite the promises of industry and the efforts of Congress and the state legislature. Yet there is nothing on the agenda that will slow the ever-increasing burning of petroleum products, and nothing in the way of planning for a transportation system that will replace dependence on the auto—which, of course, is mainly responsible for the present frightening air-pollution crisis. The limitations imposed by the air resource alone are so severe that any planning for the region that anticipates a population in excess of 14 million resource consumers—living as they do today—is gullible at best and criminal at worst.

Would planning and legislation based on natural limitations be considered too much of a constraint on our system of "free enterprise?" Would the costs of comprehensive planning, of inventorying our resources, of developing good resource-consumption models based on a steady state in each natural area, of implementing plans that would maximize the benefits of the resources in each area—would these costs be more, in terms of money and energy spent, than the costs of crisis if we continue on our present course? Or are we really such a primitive society that our only option is to foul the nest, then flee?

- The problems of Los Angeles area parks—the stingy ones it has and the generous ones it needs—were another focus of comment. *Cry California* covered from the beginning the (even now unfinished) campaign to set aside adequate open spaces in the Santa Monica Mountains, evoked here by George Barrios.

148

GEORGE BARRIOS   1970

The Santa Monica Mountains

A mountain range rises in the brown air of the heart of Los Angeles and marches westward and higher and into steadily cleaner air for 50 miles before it plunges abruptly into the flat Camarillo-Oxnard plain in Ventura County and into the sea.

The range is the Santa Monica Mountains. From the air its eastern tip looks as if it is foundering, literally drowning under a tide of urbanization rising up from the Los Angeles plain on the south and from the San Fernando Valley on the north. By contrast, the bulk of the range—west of the great gash of the San Diego Freeway—seems progressively more proud and free.

The Santa Monicas jut up from the sea on the south and from gentle valleys and rolling hills on the north. Here are secret valleys, quiet lakes and ponds, suddenly dramatic gorges and bold sandstone outcrops. The views are long—south and west to the Channel Islands, north and east (when the air clears) across valleys and hills to the high San Gabriels.

Here, ten miles from the center of California's largest city, horses still graze behind whitewashed rail fences, and in this remnant of rural California the city child may see a herd of Aberdeen Angus, dark against a golden hillside.

In the spring the white trunks and new leaves of sycamores reflect in bubbling creeks, and over on the south slope—up where speeding coast-highway motorists never think to look—a lofty waterfall splashes. In the spring the sea tang of the air will mix with the scent of lilac.

West of the San Diego Freeway, the Santa Monicas have attracted few residents because slopes are steep and difficult for development and road access so far has been limited. These mountains inspire a deep love of place that the great Nowheresville creeping up on them from three sides does not inspire.

All this is about to change.

The change will be massive, and the taxpayers of California will be paying for it, as we have in the past. Our money will buy the particular kind of hell for these mountains that their first new residents will come thinking they have escaped. . . .

After describing the many threats to the Santa Monicas and the latest move to protect them—through a special agency modeled on the Bay Conservation and Development Commission—Barrios concludes:

The issue in the Santa Monicas is not only regional, it is state- and nationwide. A regional commission is needed, and quickly, for these mountains constitute one of the finest remaining open-space islands in California's urban seas. It seems incredible that local governments are out to destroy that which they should be fighting to protect, but nothing has been done by the growth addicts who now sit on the city and county legislative bodies or by those who preside in the mayor's offices. Nor has the state itself taken any action. No public body in California is committed to the protection of the Santa Monica Mountains as a whole, as a great open-space resource. In fact, nobody sees them as a whole.

The need to save the Santa Monica Mountains was great in 1965. In 1970 it has become compelling.

• In 1966, *Cry California* reviewed an important document called the Urban-Metropolitan Open Space Study. Prepared by the firm of Eckbo, Dean, Austin and Williams as one contribution to the slowly progressing State Development Plan, this study proposed a statewide drive to preserve more than 9 million acres near cities as permanent open landscape. It also suggested that California should move to hew out new parks in existing urban areas that lack them. Bill Bronson asked Garrett Eckbo, a member of the firm that did the study and a leading landscape architect, to explore this last idea.

GARRETT ECKBO   1966

Parklands in the Urban Desert

One of the most striking characteristics of the Los Angeles Basin is its shocking shortage of parkland. No comparable urban region in the nation even remotely approaches the basin's inadequacy in this respect. While professionals in park management and urban planning have set a standard of 30 acres of local and regional parks per 1,000 population, the basin's average is no more than three or four acres per 1,000.

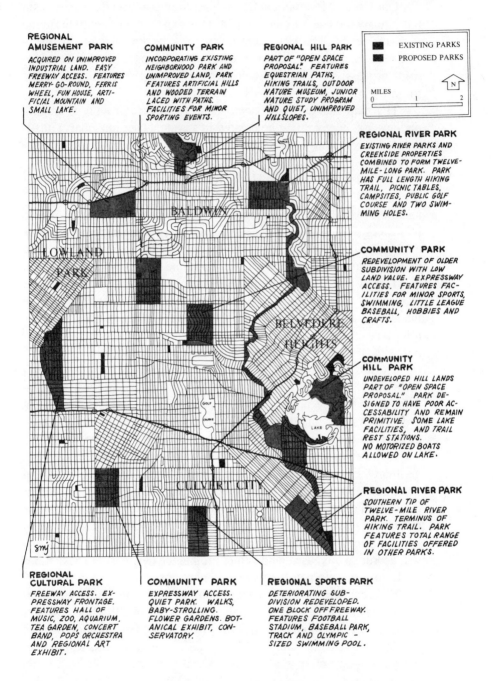

REGIONAL AMUSEMENT PARK

ACQUIRED ON UNIMPROVED INDUSTRIAL LAND. EASY FREEWAY ACCESS. FEATURES MERRY-GO-ROUND, FERRIS WHEEL, FUN HOUSE, ARTIFICIAL MOUNTAIN AND SMALL LAKE.

COMMUNITY PARK

INCORPORATING EXISTING NEIGHBORHOOD PARK AND UNIMPROVED LAND, PARK FEATURES ARTIFICIAL HILLS AND WOODED TERRAIN LACED WITH PATHS. FACILITIES FOR MINOR SPORTING EVENTS.

REGIONAL HILL PARK

PART OF "OPEN SPACE PROPOSAL." FEATURES EQUESTRIAN PATHS, HIKING TRAILS, OUTDOOR NATURE MUSEUM, JUNIOR NATURE STUDY PROGRAM AND QUIET, UNIMPROVED HILLSLOPES.

EXISTING PARKS
PROPOSED PARKS

MILES
0   1   2

N

REGIONAL RIVER PARK

EXISTING RIVER PARKS AND CREEKSIDE PROPERTIES COMBINED TO FORM TWELVE-MILE-LONG PARK. PARK HAS FULL LENGTH HIKING TRAIL, PICNIC TABLES, CAMPSITES, PUBLIC GOLF COURSE AND TWO SWIMMING HOLES.

COMMUNITY PARK

REDEVELOPMENT OF OLDER SUBDIVISION WITH LOW LAND VALUE. EXPRESSWAY ACCESS. FEATURES FACILITIES FOR MINOR SPORTS, SWIMMING, LITTLE LEAGUE BASEBALL, HOBBIES AND CRAFTS.

COMMUNITY HILL PARK

UNDEVELOPED HILL LANDS PART OF "OPEN SPACE PROPOSAL." PARK DESIGNED TO HAVE POOR ACCESSABILITY AND REMAIN PRIMITIVE. SOME LAKE FACILITIES, AND TRAIL REST STATIONS. NO MOTORIZED BOATS ALLOWED ON LAKE.

REGIONAL RIVER PARK

SOUTHERN TIP OF TWELVE-MILE RIVER PARK. TERMINUS OF HIKING TRAIL. PARK FEATURES TOTAL RANGE OF FACILITIES OFFERED IN OTHER PARKS.

REGIONAL CULTURAL PARK

FREEWAY ACCESS. EXPRESSWAY FRONTAGE. FEATURES HALL OF MUSIC, ZOO, AQUARIUM, TEA GARDEN, CONCERT BAND, POPS ORCHESTRA AND REGIONAL ART EXHIBIT.

COMMUNITY PARK

EXPRESSWAY ACCESS. QUIET PARK. WALKS, BABY-STROLLING. FLOWER GARDENS. BOTANICAL EXHIBIT, CONSERVATORY.

REGIONAL SPORTS PARK

DETERIORATING SUBDIVISION REDEVELOPED. ONE BLOCK OFF FREEWAY. FEATURES FOOTBALL STADIUM, BASEBALL PARK, TRACK AND OLYMPIC-SIZED SWIMMING POOL.

151

Our Urban-Metropolitan Open Space study showed that in the basin it is already too late for mere protection of existing open space to fill the regional needs. The only way to create a healthy balance between developed and open lands is to create new open space by the redevelopment process; i.e., by the removal of existing construction to make room for parks.

The map suggests how open space for parks, in units averaging perhaps 500 acres, might be created in a typical (but imaginary) quadrangle by removing considerable existing construction through redevelopment and renewal, and by using existing open land and parks.

Obviously this idea has all the makings of a political hot potato. It involves the relocation of up to perhaps 10 percent of the population, and the construction of new higher-density housing to absorb it. These relocatees would not be only the typical low-income residents of blighted areas. They would range from low-income through middle-income brackets, and might even encroach upon the upper.

This is a major metropolitan problem that will involve all of the residents of the area in a common effort. Redevelopment would involve intensive, detailed study and adjustment to local conditions. *But the total acreage needed is undeniable. Attempts to water this fact down will only return us to the problem we are trying to solve.*

Those relocated could be compensated, not only by a fair market price for their property, but by priority access to the best housing fronting on the new parks. Not only could the living be better for all, but property values and tax returns would surely go up substantially throughout the basin.

Redevelopment should probably encompass an area somewhat larger than the actual parks. By including peripheral construction around these new parks in the redevelopment program, it would be possible for the community to avoid the motel-jungle result that has destroyed the setting of Disneyland. In addition, control of the periphery would allow communities to recapture at least part of the unearned increments that will accrue in increased land values around the new parks. These funds could in turn help pay the redevelopment costs.

How can we do it? Obviously, both the problem and the solutions are beyond the scale of our normal, comfortable, small-minded ways of doing things. Regional organization will be needed to consider regional problems such as this, and the state and federal governments will have to provide strong policy guidance and fiscal support.

What would the program cost? An educated but horseback guess

152

would put the total at $7 billion to $9 billion for the entire region—a staggering sum by any standard.

But the benefits will be incalculably greater. The time has already arrived for our society to embark upon long-range community projects that will provide pride-giving and remunerative employment for the growing number who are and will be left aside in the automation revolution. But the justification for this park-building program rests not on the need for jobs, but upon the needs of our entire society. If both are served, all the better.

It is inevitable that renewal of much of the development in the basin will occur in the next 40 or 50 years. What we need today is clearly stated policy and a blueprint of what is required to bring the region's park resources up to civilized standards. With these, we can then proceed to seek the ways to bring into being an inspiring park system in a fair and orderly fashion.

• Finally, two strong statements on the problems of cities in general, one upbeat, one darker in tone. Both are based on speeches made in 1967. The late Barbara Ward, a distinguished British economist and authority on urban affairs, addressed a planning conference in San Francisco (sponsored by California Tomorrow); Victor Palmieri, a member of the California Tomorrow Advisory Board, was speaking at the Center for the Study of Democratic Institutions in Santa Barbara. "His thesis," editor Bronson noted, "has been praised and cursed . . . and has become a focal point for discussion of the future of our metropolitan regions."

VICTOR H. PALMIERI   1967

Hard Facts about the Future of Our Cities

Much nonsense has been written and spoken of late about our cities, and a great deal more about the future. To talk about both of these subjects creates a splendid opportunity to compound the confusion.

To defeat this prospect, I am going to state three propositions about our cities and their future that I believe are grounded in objective fact.

These propositions concern, first, the racial ghetto and its relationship to the deterioration of the central, or core, city; second, the politics of the metropolitan city; and, third, the source and dimension of the financial resources required for urban needs.

First, as to the ghetto and the core city: within the next two decades, probably by 1980, the core area of almost every major metropolitan city of the United States will be a racial—predominantly black—island. This is not speculation. It is already very largely a fact in Washington, Chicago, and New York City. It is rapidly becoming a fact in Detroit, Philadelphia, and Los Angeles. Three established factors—the rate of population growth among minority groups (almost three times that of the white population in the city of Los Angeles); the increasing income level and mobility of middle-class white families; and the resulting domino effect on racially impacted school districts—will maintain the velocity of the trend and virtually guarantee its ultimate outcome.

Second, as to the politics of the metropolitan city: the fragmented, crazy-quilt pattern of government within the metropolitan region is a familiar fact of urban life. The essential point here is that it is not likely to change. Effective regional government is simply not in the cards.

Third, as to financial resources, often referred to in the city as "money": the fact is that the major metropolitan cities are bankrupt. New York's annual deficit is almost half a billion, Boston is even worse off relative to its size, and Los Angeles' turn has arrived. With tax rates uniformly at or about the $10-per-100 level, a point that students of taxation have traditionally regarded as one of negative return because of the effect on local economic growth, it is clear that the primary revenue base of local government has been exhausted.

This, then, is the city of the future—the very near future. A black island spreading over the heart of a metropolis that is bankrupt financially and paralyzed politically.

These conclusions make up a hard reality that will not yield to rapid-transit systems, or urban renewal projects, or community action programs, or property tax reform, or open housing laws, or police review boards, or compensatory educational programs.

The basic requirements for effective action are clear:

First, there must be a commitment in terms of national policy sufficient in strength to establish priority for the effort over all other domestic goals.

Second, there must be institutions built capable of deploying human and material resources effectively within the core city.

154

Third, there must be concert of action among all agencies of government aimed at shattering the racial hegemony of the ghetto.

The priority commitment at the national level must be definitive. Without a substantial allocation of national resources over the long term, ranging probably from a minimum of 10 percent to a maximum of 20 percent of the national budget, even the most critical needs of the cities cannot and will not be met. Only the incentive of large-scale federal grants can overcome the political paralysis of state and local government in the field of urban problems.

But money, obviously, is only part of the answer. Human competence is just as important, and almost as scarce, at the local level. The fact is that there are no institutions in our major urban areas with the competence that can make it possible to spend large amounts of money effectively in the tricky environment of the core city.

The kind of institution that is needed must have the operational management capabilities of a major defense contractor along with the capacity to exploit social research, to establish and maintain communication with a wide spectrum of groups, and to organize its efforts in such a way that community action and participation become the sustaining source of energy for all programs over the long term. The institution must be, in short, a system manager in the field of social engineering, a combination of Hull House and the Rand Corporation, so to speak, functioning as the primary agent for deploying federal funds in major programs within the city.

Without institutions of high competence operating as prime contracting agencies at the local level, the task cannot be accomplished. Indeed, it should not be attempted.

Finally, the most important point. The monolithic racial structure of the ghetto must be shattered. The black island is, very simply, a menace to the urban culture of our nation. Its degrading effects are not limited to those who live within its creeping boundaries. They reach every one of us who shares the responsibility for its existence. The enforced segregation of the ghetto is as much a cause as an effect of the caste system that a century after Appomattox still dominates the relationship between white and black Americans.

We cannot wait for the Negro adult to be retrained, for the Negro child to be educated, for the Negro family to be reunited.

The notion that dispersal of Negroes will occur gradually through the impact of anti-discrimination measures is nonsense. It fails to take account of the economic and cultural moat that seals off the black island

155

just as effectively as restrictive covenants. Gradualism is simply impractical, given the velocity of this urban crisis.

A radically different strategy is needed, one that marshals all the available forces of public investment, one that couples all the planning apparatus of government to a single objective: to establish within the ghetto new centers of activity—government office buildings, educational installations, medical complexes, major concentrations of public employment—that will bring an ethnic mix to the streets of the ghetto.

Once the community commits itself to this strategy, a whole range of regenerative possibilities will come into view. There will be a prime opportunity to integrate the federal, state, and local health and welfare and anti-poverty programs. Most important, there will be a confrontation on the issue of the drastic changes that must be made in the quality of the ghetto schools.

When the quality of the schools begins to change, when diverse human activity brings a new beat to the pulse of the ghetto, there will be hope for the city. This will mean also new hope for the Negro, the Mexican-American, the Puerto Rican, for the poor and the aged, for all Americans who have missed the last train to suburbia.

BARBARA WARD   1968

"A Great City Program . . ."

In a shift as sudden and seismic as an earthquake, man is moving from the fields to the streets. Only a little over 150 years ago, 80 percent of America's 10 million inhabitants still lived in communities of less than 5,000. By the year 2000, 80 percent will live in urban concentrations and there will be 250 million inhabitants.

The same process is at work everywhere. Cities grow twice as fast as population, big cities twice as fast again. Moreover, it is not only a problem of people. Urban man likes to take a ton of moving metal with him, park it, ride in it, commute in it, escape in it. Even the austere Russians have given way.

By ringing every old concentrated city—London, Paris, Rome, New York—with sprawling suburbs, we overload and run down the center with a congestion of commuting traffic and with the poverty of those who are not rich enough—or, in America, white enough—to move. By building new spread cities on the Los Angeles model, we eliminate any definable city and the values of urban stimulus, concentration and variety vanish in a community in which, between freeways and car parks, 70 percent of the "center" is under asphalt.

Meanwhile, both the overloaded traditional city and the new "un-cities" carry such a freight of dirt, pollution, ugliness and frustration that, at the extremes, their inhabitants riot and burn them down, and in the grey center all too often live lives of discomfort and unease.

The general crisis has occurred largely because it caught mankind unaware. Both the population explosion and the new technology have been dumped on top of preindustrial state and city structures and pretechnological, static systems of government. The rethinking of policies and institutions has not taken place while the reshaping of almost everything else has gone ahead.

> Ward says that a consensus is beginning to form about needs at two levels: the neighborhood, and the metropolitan region.

The neighborhood, where the child learns to live, needs to be safe, culturally rich and diverse, and easily "plugged in" by appropriate transport to the city's wider choices. If it is a neighborhood in the center city, it needs to go *up,* but this does not mean barrack-like slabs of high-rise apartments without schools, shops, amenities, playing areas and greenness.

Naturally, in America, the new neighborhoods deserve the highest priority wherever in fact it is ghettos they must replace. It should not need 34 dead and $40 million in destruction to learn that Watts had no good hospital for 87,000 people, no modern school for 30,000 children, no cinema, one swimming pool and such poor transport to reach employment elsewhere that 30 percent of the labor force was unemployed.

Neighborhoods are cells in a greater organism. That too is in trouble as undifferentiated "slurb" slops over the countryside, denying access to the natural non-urban world without providing many of the stimulants and delights of an urban culture—especially for the marooned chauffeur-housewife.

What can be done to check this sprawl that threatens to cover most of Southern England and turn Belgium into a "spread nation" and engulf America's seaboards? One approach is to see whole regions as gravitational "fields of force" in which a number of urban centers take the strain off each other, mitigate the lemming-like commuter surges and produce a more rational use of transport systems.

157

In Southern England, the "new towns" have failed by being too small to withstand London's "sucking pull." Now the plan is for a new metropolitan center at Southampton and new cities at Swindon and Milton Keynes. These will be built of rich and diverse neighborhoods with multiple centers of high density; they will be linked with London by rapid transit; and they will, it is hoped, provide enough attraction to prevent Southern England's next 20 million people from settling in and around London.

One of the most systematic approaches to this "gravitational field" approach is in Detroit, where a study by the power company determined that continuing with present land use, present transportation patterns and present population growth would result in complete destruction of the center of Detroit, wipe out every major recreation area, create so much blight that movement to the countryside would be irresistible, and pose a transportation problem that would be insoluble. What the metropolitan region plan now suggests is a new twin city at Lake Huron to take the pressure off troubled Detroit, with another thrust of controlled growth reaching out to Toledo later.

Drift creates the impossible city. Discipline and direction alone can cure it. Europe is better off in some ways than America, because the concept of regional government and regional planning is more easily accepted. Greater London and the Paris region are already facts, while the New York region still struggles with over a thousand separate hostile and competing authorities. Yet a purposive overall plan can help.

Planning is essential. So is the discipline of not permitting people to take out of the urban situation far more than they put in. The worst offenders are the landowners who have taken a 15 percent annual increase (compounded) in their gains from values created solely by others. Public purchase at existing prices, different tax procedures, a sharp distinction between property taxes on unused land, which should be high, and on valuable development, which should be less—these are a number of procedures for insuring that the community gets back the value it alone creates. When, 140 years ago, the crucial Erie Canal was built, it was largely financed by a specially assessed tax on the lands whose value its construction had very greatly enhanced. I have seen estimates that the windfall gain to property owners around the Bay Area Rapid Transit scheme's 30 stations would, if recovered in taxes, pay off the cost of the scheme.

But there are other offenders—the industries that dump dirt in the air and pay none of the cleaning bill, the municipalities that dump untreated sewage in rivers and streams, the commuters who expect a subsidy for the use of the inner cities' scarcest commodity—space, and the suburbs that cash out of the big city's problems but live on its work.

This is not simply an issue in morals. It is one of resources as well. Over the next 20 years, over $100 billion a year will be spent in any case on urban growth. But it can be spent to produce ever more uninhabitable cities. Or it can be well spent, to end ghettos, to create genuine neighborhoods, to give richness and variety and choice. Provided land values are not hopelessly inflated, the building of whole neighborhoods and even cities can be profitable. Every one of Britain's new towns is paying a normal commercial return.

A new pattern of public-private cooperation for urban regeneration—as in arms or the space race—is perfectly possible, especially if the cities insist on getting their share of federal tax money. A great city program, comparable to the space race, would provide the technological edge and economic stabilizing factor that today comes from armaments and should, in a sane world, come from the works of peace.

The first nation to produce a beautiful, dignified, and successful city system will do as much for its prestige as the first man on the moon, and perhaps 50 times more for mankind's true well-being. Nowhere yet is there a good model. There are experiments, there are exciting new starts—why not in California? Any kind of working model would bring all mankind to your door. First on the moon is fine; reaching out to the planets is splendid—I'm for it. But I think in the next 50 years, the first person who gives man a safe landfall in the city will be the one who makes the breakthrough to what the world really needs.

7 *Losing the Water Battle*

- In water issues, as with freeway issues, California Tomorrow came on the scene at an historic moment. In 1960, the voters approved the billion-dollar bond issue that launched the State Water Project, the latest in a series of major water developments by local, state, and federal agencies that shaped the California water-delivery system we have today. Since the water picture has not changed in any fundamental way since the construction mandated in 1960 was completed, we can begin, by way of orientation, with a survey of that system written in 1982.

JOHN HART   1982

The Water System Today

As a piece of plumbing, the California water-supply system is awesome.

In a typical rainfall year, almost a third of all the water that runs from the mountains of California is diverted to cities and farms. Some of our longest "rivers" are aqueducts; some of our largest "lakes" are the fluctuating pools that extend behind dams. A drop of water that falls as snow in the Trinity Alps may wind up in a San Diego swimming pool.

We take more than half of our water from the watershed of the great Central Valley: from the Sacramento, the San Joaquin, the Kings, the Kern, the Kaweah and their tributaries. About one sixth comes from the Colorado. The remainder comes from the east slopes of the Sierra and from various coastal streams. In fact, *every* significant river system in California is giving us about all the water it can—with the possible exception of the upper Sacramento, and the clear exception of the North Coast rivers. These streams—the Eel, the Van Dusen, the Trinity, the Salmon, the Scott, the tremendous Klamath and the wild Smith—are little tapped as yet, though not quite so free of dams and diversions as people imagine.

Less visible than dams and aqueducts, but almost as important to the

to
Southern
California

to
East
Bay
cities

Long
Distance
Water

to San
Francisco &
South Bay
cities

to
Los
Angeles

to
Southern
California
cities

to San
Diego

state's water future, are vast hidden stocks of underground water that currently contribute over a fifth of our supply.

Who brings this water to us? Almost a third of the total is self-serve: landowners pump it out of their own ground, or skim it from rivers their property touches. Another 36 percent is collected and distributed by the federal Bureau of Reclamation, largely through its Central Valley Project, but also from the Colorado and the upper Klamath. About 7 percent is currently provided by the state through the State Water Project. The rest is captured by the waterworks of innumerable local water agencies, including San Francisco's Hetch Hetchy Water and Power Department, the East Bay Municipal Utilities District, and the Los Angeles Department of Water and Power.

Where is the water consumed? Overwhelmingly, on farms: about 85 percent goes to produce food and fiber. In water terms, California is not an urban state but an agricultural one.

In important ways, the "real" water consumers—the basic clients of the water system—are not individual households, factories or farms, but rather intermediary districts of various types. There are about 1,000 of these in all. The biggest are primary suppliers as well as distributors.

161

The Metropolitan Water District of Southern California, for instance, is a producer district (drawing its own supply from the Colorado) and a consumer district as well (buying from the State Water Project).

Water consumed does not, of course, disappear; it turns into sewage and salty irrigation waste. In the past we have spent billions trying to get rid of this polluted stream. With advances in treatment, however, more and more wastewater can be purified and used again. The former nuisance is becoming a resource—perhaps the best "new" source of water we will ever find.

- California Tomorrow was critical of the State Water Project from the start. At first the main complaint was that no proper planning was being done to guide the growth the new supply would bring. As the decade went on, however, other issues emerged.

  First concern was the fate of the great California Delta, that universe of waterways where the Sacramento and San Joaquin rivers empty into the San Francisco Bay system. Most of the water projects in the state draw from this vast watershed, and the amount of water permitted to flow out through the delta in the natural pattern has been steadily declining. The State Water Project, when it came on line, depleted the outflow further. Why did this matter? Again, we reproduce a recent look at a situation that has not greatly changed in 20 years.

JOHN HART   1982

The Bay and the Delta in Trouble

At the crossroads of California's artificial water system lies one of our greatest natural assets: the bay-delta estuarine system. That's an unlucky place for so fragile a piece of the Creation to be.

San Francisco Bay, San Pablo Bay, Suisun Bay and Suisun Marsh, and the labyrinthine channels of the Sacramento-San Joaquin River Delta—together they make up the largest estuary on the west coast of the Americas. Like all estuaries, this one is a rich producer of life: fish, local and anadromous; birds, resident and migratory; and all the plants and animals on which they feed. Like all estuaries, this one depends on the continual mixing of fresh river-water with ocean brine. Research around the world suggests that estuaries begin to suffer when more than one third of their freshwater inflow is removed.

Unfortunately for bay and delta, they share their watershed with California's greatest water projects. Each dam, each aqueduct, each new withdrawal from the Central Valley water bank has weakened the rivers that feed the bay. Today, average annual inflow is less than half what it used to be.

The exact effects of this starvation are not yet known. Has a critical point been reached already? There are ominous signs, including a sharp and sustained drop in numbers of striped bass.

But assuming the bay's present freshwater income is enough to maintain its present (already curtailed) richness, any further cut in income could be another matter entirely. And both the Central Valley Project and the State Water Project plan to increase their exports from Central Valley streams.

If this happens, scientists fear these effects:

— The fertile "mixing zone," the contact zone between salt and brackish water, will shift inland. Right now the zone hovers around Suisun Bay, where mudflats, marshes and shallow waters make a perfect nursery for aquatic life. But as river currents weaken further, this contact zone could migrate up into the channel of the lower Sacramento. There deeper water and constricted banks would make it far less fertile.

— Suisun Bay will become saltier. This could threaten Suisun Marsh, one of the finest brackish-water wetlands in the nation. Nobody knows whether it can survive, or will gradually convert to the less-productive type found around coastal bays.

— South San Francisco Bay will lose another portion of the heavy winter flows that help to circulate its waters. Are these floods necessary to the health of that reach of the system? Most biologists now seem to think so.

The bottom line for the bay and the delta is that they are about to lose some more of their sustaining water supplies. No technical fixes seem likely to lessen, much less reverse, the resulting damage. Barring a stunning policy reversal, the outlook is poor for the greatest estuary of them all.

• California's expanding water system threatened (and threatens today) another resource on which people place great value: the almost dam-free rivers of the North Coast, compel-

163

ling in their grandeur, precious for the fish they produce for sport and commerce, and endlessly annoying, to any right-minded engineer, for the water they are "wasting" to the sea. If the water yield of the Sacramento River watershed isn't enough to meet agricultural and urban demand and keep the delta healthy, too—well, the water engineers remark, they know where they can find more.

The battle came to an early climax in 1967, when the Army Corps of Engineers proposed to build the first major dam on the wild Eel River at a spot called Dos Rios. In a piece that had quite a bit to do with the eventual outcome, reporter Lou Cannon (later chief White House correspondent for the *Washington Post*) took after the corps.

LOU CANNON   1968

High Dam in the Valley of the Tall Grass

The road from Longvale at Highway 101 leads along the twisting route of the Eel River's middle fork, where clusters of the crimson-blossomed tree called redbud line either side of the bank and hawk shadows hover against the canyon walls. The road winds back on itself for more than 25 miles along the course of this gray-green river, then ascends without warning to a dusty ridge overlooking a green checker-board of pasture land and descends as abruptly into the valley, cutting ruler-sharp across a landscape dotted by red barns and cows and a white dog running alone through a field of alfalfa. This is Round Valley, the site of a few hundred farms and the remnants of an Indian tribe that may be 9,000 years old. The Indians called this valley "Meshakai," the Valley of the Tall Grass.

It is under a sentence of death.

The U.S. Army Corps of Engineers proposes to drown Round Valley, together with more than 400 archeological sites of the Yuki Tribe, beneath some 300 feet of water. Aided by other federal agencies and by the State Department of Water Resources, the corps intends to carry out this sentence in the name of water supply, flood control, and recreation, using the traditional high dam as the chosen instrument of

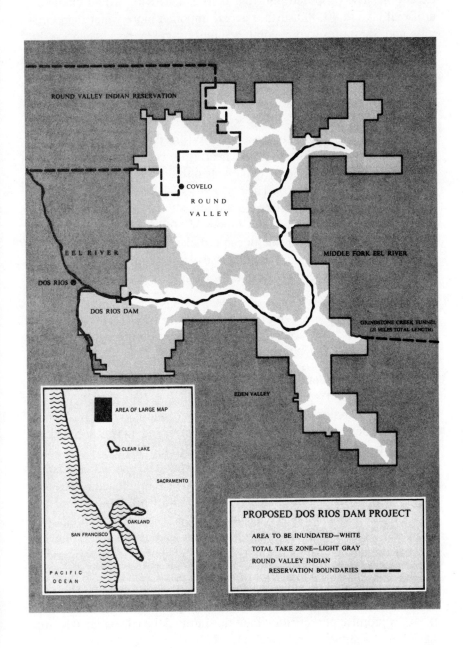

ROUND VALLEY INDIAN RESERVATION

COVELO

R O U N D
V A L L E Y

E E L   R I V E R

MIDDLE FORK EEL RIVER

DOS RIOS

DOS RIOS DAM

GRINDSTONE CREEK TUNNEL
(21 MILES TOTAL LENGTH)

EDEN VALLEY

AREA OF LARGE MAP

CLEAR LAKE

SACRAMENTO

OAKLAND

SAN FRANCISCO

PACIFIC
OCEAN

PROPOSED DOS RIOS DAM PROJECT

AREA TO BE INUNDATED—WHITE

TOTAL TAKE ZONE—LIGHT GRAY

ROUND VALLEY INDIAN
    RESERVATION BOUNDARIES ▬ ▬ ▬

165

execution. The proposed 730-foot dam at Dos Rios would create an artificial lake of 40,000 surface acres, impound more water than Oroville and Shasta reservoirs combined and provide a beachhead for the corps on the wild rivers of California's still-preservable North Coast. The project deserves the close attention of Californians and more public scrutiny than it has thus far received.

In November 1967, a Corps of Engineers report concluded that a high dam was "needed" at Dos Rios, and six weeks later the corps produced a public hearing in the town of Willits that supposedly ratified its own conclusion. Actually, the hearing—according to newspaper accounts—was dominated by opponents of the project, but this proved no deterrent to the engineers. The corps knows that residents of any area about to be flooded don't like it, and since there are only some 950 people in Round Valley, including about 350 Indians on the reservation there, the public opposition doesn't make much difference. Says Colonel Frank C. Boerger, San Francisco district engineer for the corps: "It's a question of the greatest good for the greatest number."

> The corps proposed to relocate the Indians to new lands in the hills above Round Valley, giving them two acres for each one held before.
> A good deal? Not according to a group of anthropologists and archeologists, Cannon reports:

Writing in a recent issue of *The Indian Historian*, this group of experts (Adan E. Treganza, Thomas F. King, Robert E. Schenk and Michael G. Mannion) discusses the history of the native Yuki Tribe, which was "decimated" by whites, and the other Indian tribes that were uprooted from their lands and exported to Round Valley.

"The displacement again of these Indians will be another chapter in a book of callous exploitation that should, in an enlightened nation, be long-closed. Any idea of exchanging flatland for hill land, no matter what the rate of increase of acreage might be, is completely unthinkable. These are flatland dwellers, not hill dwellers, and it should be pointed out that the adjacent hills are not suitable for any type of habitation, white or Indian.

"The idea of relocating the town of Covelo is nothing short of ridiculous. The town of Covelo exists only because Round Valley exists. A promise of recreation facilities (around the lake created by the dam) is no substitute for a farmer who plows the soil, milks cows, raises sheep and cattle. Farmers whose fathers settled the valley are not going to adapt to renting rowboats and selling hotdogs."

166

Perhaps it is too much to expect that at this late date the U.S. Army will come out on the side of the Indians. But surely any citizen, in a day when the cry of "economy" can kill or cripple the most necessary of programs, would agree that the corps should at least be able to justify economically the benefits that a Dos Rios high dam would confer on those fortunate enough not to own property in Round Valley. Their justification appears questionable on some grounds and totally unbelievable on others.

The economic cornerstone of any proposal supported by the corps is the "cost-benefit ratio," the reputed relationship between the cost of building a project and the benefits derived from it. The corps maintains that the Dos Rios Dam, upon which it puts a price tag of $398 million, has a cost-benefit ratio of 1.6 to 1, meaning, of course, that it will confer $1.60 of benefits for every $1 spent on construction. In the final report forwarded to the Board of Engineers for Rivers and Harbors in Washington, the corps more or less arbitrarily upped this cost-benefit ratio to 1.9 to 1, characteristically increasing the estimate of benefits while leaving the costs unchanged.

A 36-page review of the corps report prepared by Gardner Brown, Jr., a resource economist for the University of Washington, found otherwise. The Brown report, which was commissioned by a Round Valley group formed to fight the dam, used federal and state data and arrived at a money-wasting .7 to 1 cost-benefit ratio.

Brown, however, raises a more serious question about the Dos Rios project than corps participation in the familiar government game of rosy economic estimation. His analysis shows that the corps, in the manner of Army establishments thoroughly grounded in fighting the last war, has arrived at its cost-benefit conclusion by ignoring developments in the desalting of sea water while at the same time using the lowest cost estimates for transporting Dos Rios water to Southern California.

The California Water Plan, with its firm commitment to the technology of yesterday, is gospel for the engineers of the State Department of Water Resources. Yet, the Dos Rios Dam is planned for a 100-year life, and even spokesmen for the department recognize that water desalting will long before then be cheaper than transporting Northern California water to Southern California.

"Someplace the costs of desalting and water transportation are going to meet, and I think the place is going to be on the Klamath River," says Dean Thompson, the department's able public information officer. The difficulty with that view, in the opinion of one experienced survey

167

and design engineer who declined to be identified, is that the state will have long been committed to high dams on the North Coast by the time the Klamath is reached. Already, a mammoth 765-foot dam is envisioned on the Klamath, the major river of the North Coast and one of the most important sport fisheries in the state.

"The place for the people who want to defend the North Coast is on that ridge where they propose to build Dos Rios," the engineer said. "Once the state has made the investment in the Grindstone Tunnel, the other dam building will follow."

This tunnel, a major element of the Dos Rios project, would carry Dos Rios water 21 miles through the mountains to the east to Grindstone Creek in Glenn County and then into a reservoir for conveyance south. Since the tunnel would have considerable unused capacity, its existence would inevitably be used to promote additional dams on the North Coast.

> Cannon goes on to discuss the other benefits the dam was supposed to produce—flood control and recreation—and finds little reason to credit either. He notes:

A strong case can be made that the Dos Rios project would destroy some of the best recreation remaining in the state, substituting power-boat recreation for the quality experience of a wild river that is one of the few in California that boasts a summer steelhead run. The corps project plans a hatchery to compensate for the loss of eight million Chinook salmon eggs and two million steelhead eggs, but the record of previous hatcheries and previous high dams suggests that fishing would never be the same again.

Perhaps Professor Treganza, chairman of the Department of Anthropology at San Francisco State College, put it best in his discussion of the effect of the Dos Rios high dam on the culture of the Yuki Indians and the world of Round Valley.

"The study of Man's past," Treganza wrote, "teaches us that we are an integrated part of an ecological system—that each natural region functions in such a way as to strike a balance among all its constituents. The Corps of Engineers proposes to drastically upset this balance in the North Coast ranges, with no idea of possible effects on the total ecosystem, in order to provide water necessary for Southern California to further destroy its own environment with sprawling cities and polluted air. This cycle—the destruction of the north to permit the destruction of the south—is, in the long view of society and history, based on false premises and must be altered."

168

The altering of these premises is one of the urgent tasks confronting those who would save the resources of the North Coast and of America. Time is running out—and not only for Round Valley.

- In early 1969, Governor Ronald Reagan withdrew the state's support for the Dos Rios high dam. Since the Army Corps defers to state policy, that killed the project for the time being. Reagan was swayed partly by public outcry but more, quite probably, by the fact that the Dos Rios project simply did not make good economic sense. (The Cannon article—much noted, much reprinted—certainly did no harm.)

  The issue has never died, however. The water establishment is as convinced as ever that the development of all the North Coast rivers is going to come—that it is only a matter of time.

  Meanwhile, California Tomorrow was mounting a systematic critique of the entire State Water Plan. In a landmark article, environmental engineer Frank Stead addressed himself to the water problem in both its aspects: water supply on the one hand, and water pollution on the other. Then, in an influential followup piece, he proposed a dramatic revision of the water plan.

FRANK M. STEAD   1968

Losing the Water Battle

California is rapidly losing the water battle.

We are striving at Lake Tahoe to preserve the highest level of water purity ever seen in this state in a natural body of surface water, and at the same time are proceeding with all haste to construct the San Luis Drain, an agricultural sewer that will empty damaging waste waters from the San Joaquin Valley into the very headwaters of San Francisco Bay. We are spending $2 billion to transport water from our own matchless Sierra to the Southern California coastal areas where daily we pour into the ocean one billion gallons of water of better chemical quality than the water now imported from the Colorado River for use in the same area. And in this process, we are writing off as expendable the water wonderland of the delta, while the very areas in whose behalf we are perpetuat-

169

ing this ecological blunder lie alongside an inexhaustible supply of water. Finally, we are making the mistake that has destroyed every civilization in history that has attempted to build an irrigated agriculture on an imported water supply: not providing for the exportation of minerals equal to those in the incoming water to maintain a "salt balance."

How did we lose our way? We lost it because we did not realize that "winning the West" was but one short, exciting chapter in our history and that it had to be followed by responsible and thoughtful management of the great land mass. But the colorful years of ruthless exploitation of natural resources never ended, and today it is as though we had set in motion a process that we cannot stop or control.

Let us trace briefly the events that laid the groundwork for the present crisis. First, the mountain streams were tapped and brought to the southern valleys for storage. Then it was discovered that the inland valleys south of the Sierra Madre and San Gabriel mountains were, in effect, vast natural water reservoirs filled to the brim over the centuries, and overflowing into similar reservoirs on the Coastal Plain. In some areas, the rare phenomenon of artesian water occurred and wells would actually flow under pressure, without the need for pumps. Furthermore this water was not just for the riparian owners on the banks of streams; this water was for all for the taking.

Out of this set of circumstances came a concept still firmly held by most Californians: namely, that as fast as water needs develop they will be quickly and easily satisfied.

As the early decades of the 20th century wore on, there was repeated evidence that this vision might be a delusion, but the faith in California's capacity to control the environment never faltered.

Stead describes the major early water projects, including San Francisco's reach to the Sierra and the tapping of the Owens River and the Colorado by Los Angeles.

The primary demand for water was and is for irrigation. First to be dealt with was the great Imperial Valley, where the construction of the All American Canal shortly after the turn of the century brought in Colorado River water and, virtually overnight, turned what had looked like barren desert into the truck garden of the West. Then the plan for construction of Shasta Dam and Friant Dam by the U.S. Bureau of Reclamation gave assurance of water to double the irrigation acreage of the great San Joaquin Valley without further depletion of the overdrawn groundwater basins.

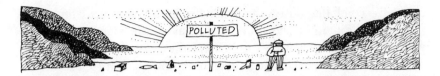

As we reached 1940 with a population of 9,000,000, it seemed that the boundless optimism of Californians was indeed justified and that there would always be a plentiful supply of high-quality water; that everyone would be a winner; that there would be no losers; that the Golden Age was here to stay.

The Gathering Clouds

As California embarked upon its second great period of development under the impetus of World War II, unmistakable signs began to appear that the waters of the state were threatened by pollution. First to show was pollution of the saltwater bays. Santa Monica Bay became so polluted by sewage that the State Board of Public Health in 1941 quarantined 14 miles of the West's most popular beach.

In the San Francisco Bay Area, the discharge into the bay of raw sewage by all of the cities produced unsightliness and intense odors. The proud citizens of the Bay Area tolerated these conditions until the taunts of the visitors to the International Exposition at Treasure Island exceeded their endurance and finally they demanded action.

Furthermore, the groundwaters of the state were showing signs of irreversible damage.

There occurred in the spring of 1947 the dramatic "Montebello Incident." A small distributor of weedicide in Alhambra flushed a few barrels of 2,4,D down his floor drain. Within days this material passed unchanged through the most advanced sewage-treatment plant in the state (the Tri-Cities activated sludge plant in Pasadena), entered the Rio Hondo and was carried by this river to the vicinity of Montebello (a distance of six miles) where it reached the natural groundwater replenishment area for the Coastal Plain, dropped underground, reached six domestic wells and rendered their water unpotable. This was such a dramatic illustration that industrial liquid wastes could destroy water quality that it triggered the California water pollution program.

The result, two years later, was the Dickey Water Pollution Act, fascinating in the complexity of the governmental machinery it established, and based on three simple assumptions: first, that if sewage and industrial wastes were properly handled, water-quality preservation was assured; second, that wastes can be handled in large part by assimilation (that is, by dilution); and third, that liquid-waste management and water-resource management can be treated as separate problems.

In the years since the inauguration of this program in 1950, with its built-in rivalry between one state and nine regional water-pollution control boards and its arbitrary distinction between "contamination" (hazard to health), which was prohibited, and "pollution" (hazard to all other aspects of the water quality), control of which was entrusted to the regional boards, it has worked reasonably well within the constraints of its basic assumptions. But it is now clear for all to see that *the basic assumptions are wrong*.

Management of sewage and industrial wastes alone will not preserve water quality in California. The basic problem of water quality in the long run is rising mineral content. The greatest use of water is for irrigation. In the irrigation process, evaporation directly from the ground surface and through the leaves of plants concentrates a large share of the minerals originally present in the applied water in the top layers of the soil. If the soil is flushed by deliberate overirrigation so that the water not used by the crops percolates downward through the soil (as was done early in the Imperial Valley), the drainage water contains not only these stranded minerals, but also salts dissolved from the soil itself.

The underground aquifers in the coastal plains all terminate in the ocean, and if ground-water levels are lowered, salt water moves into these aquifers unless "hydraulic dams" (ground-water mounds produced by injecting water through wells) are maintained.

Finally, the prinicipal water-resource system of the state—namely, the Sacramento and San Joaquin river system—is directly connected to the ocean through San Francisco Bay, and here tidal action will serve as a gigantic pump to thrust a wedge of heavy salt water far up into the delta itself, unless fresh water is used to hold back this threatening salt-water flood. So it should be clear that a program dealing only with sewage and industrial waste cannot do the big job.

The second and third assumptions are also unsound. The idea of disposal of wastes by dilution presupposes a stream 40 to 50 times as large as the waste. In California we once had such a system for the communities on the Sacramento River, but this concept is completely brushed aside by the California Water Plan. Under this scheme, virtually the entire flow of the Sacramento and San Joaquin river system will be taken into arid regions where there are no perennial streams running to the ocean. This water will be converted to sewage, industrial waste, and

172

agricultural drainage water that must be discharged on land (or in the ocean) with its high mineral and organic content undiluted.

From the foregoing, it should be clear that water-resource management and waste management are really but phases of the same "closed" system and that to attempt separate management of these two phases is the road to disaster.

With the uncomfortable and slightly guilty suspicion that we may have "painted ourselves into a corner," thoughtful Californians are now beginning to take a fresh look at the entire water-resource picture in California and some sobering facts of life are beginning to come into clear focus.

The California Water Plan

The California Water Plan has two basic and fundamental flaws: it is, in reality, only "half a system," and it ruthlessly transforms the ecology of vast areas of the state.

The California Water Plan provides the facilities to bring water into the San Joaquin Valley and the Southern California coastal areas, but provides no parallel facilities to remove waste water, and these basins are devoid of natural rivers to remove water pollution without polluting the groundwaters. Each form of "use" (agricultural, domestic and industrial) actually consumes only a small portion of the water and converts the remainder into "waste water," which contains not only the chemicals present before the "use" but also a great *increment* of chemicals as a result of the use. This increment ranges from about 200 ppm (parts of chemical per million parts of water) in domestic sewage, to several thousand ppm in agricultural drainage, and in the case of industrial waste waters may amount to tens of thousands of ppm. Unless these increments of chemical loadings are removed in some way, the chemical content of the surface and groundwaters of the basin will increase until the water becomes unusable. This phenomenon is already occurring in parts of Ventura and Orange counties where groundwater is today so highly mineralized it approaches the point of unusability, for either agriculture or domestic use. It is the threat of the same situation in the San Joaquin Valley that has prompted the proposal for the San Luis Drain, which if constructed will carry the valley's polluting wastes into the delta and San Francisco Bay systems.

But the State Water Plan contains no *comprehensive* statewide system for removal of the chemical loadings in waste waters, and because of this fatal flaw must be considered as but "half a system."

173

In regard to ecological damage, not only does the State Water Plan write off the delta as expendable, but it threatens to eliminate one of the most valuable estuaries in the world—the San Francisco Bay system. An estuary is not a bay, filled with saltwater from the ocean, but a transition zone between saltwater and freshwater. The gradations of salinity in such a zone support a wide, interdependent spectrum of biologic forms, as well as the necessary means for anadromous fish (striped bass, salmon, steelhead, etc.) to go from the sea to freshwater spawning grounds. The "disconnecting" of the San Francisco Bay from the Sacramento and San Joaquin rivers that is implicit in the peripheral canal plan (which will detour the Sacramento River around the delta) will convert San Francisco Bay into an ocean-water cul-de-sac.

An even greater tragedy will result in the North Coastal area if the full California Water Plan is carried out, because here centuries-old wild river environments will be virtually dried up in their lower reaches and in their upper reaches be filled with a tame succession of end-to-end reservoirs whose water levels fluctuate, leaving broad muddy strips around their shrunken shorelines in dry seasons (or dry years).

The Way Out

But two new sources of supply are available near points of need. The first is high-quality water reclaimed from waste water. From the coastal cities of Southern California and the Bay Area, there is discharged to the ocean or the bays approximately 4 million acre-feet of water per year in the form of treated sewage. For the most part, this water is of chemical quality suitable for almost all direct uses and is more than enough to hold salt water back from the delta. It is virtually equivalent to California's full rights to water from the Colorado River.

The techniques of reclaiming water from domestic sewage have been demonstrated in Southern California at both Santee in San Diego County and Whittier Narrows in Los Angeles County. At Whittier Narrows, the reclaimed water is used to recharge groundwater. At Santee it is used to create recreational lakes and will soon have other uses. The costs in either case are in the competitive range for existing supplies.

Agricultural drainage represents a different problem. Reclamation of the water calls for demineralization as well as removal of organic materials. Two methods of demineralization, electrodialysis and reverse osmosis, are being currently tested at Coalinga. The costs are relatively high, but much lower than the present cost of distillation.

But even with waste-water reclamation, we still fall far short of meeting our ultimate needs unless an entirely new and massive water source is found. That source of course is the ocean itself, the only source upon which at this time we can responsibly stake our future.

The technology of seawater conversion is well known. The costs at the present time are admittedly high ($1.00 per 1,000 gallons), but by no means out of the range of economic feasibility for urban areas, and these costs are sure to come down dramatically.

So there is a way out of the dilemma of the State Water Plan; a way that not only preserves the integrity of California's unique environment, but also has the inherent fairness that no area of the state advances at the expense of another area. It is a way we can well afford. It is the way we should go! California now stands with the California Water Plan at the halfway mark. The first half has produced water badly needed and at reasonable cost, and at this writing has not seriously impaired the state's scenic resources.

The crux of the matter is how we produce the second half of the needed 30 million acre-feet. If we follow the original concept we will do irreparable damage to the state's environment. There is an alternative. We should have the maturity to admit our error in time and immediately develop a new California Water Plan that conforms to state policy as expressed in a general plan for the development of the state. Until such a plan is adopted, the state should not embark on any new interbasin water development and transport programs.

FRANK M. STEAD   1969

A New California Water Plan

The New California Water Plan that emerges is simple in its bold outline. It is based on five key principles:

1. A new comprehensive and binding state development plan should insure that new urban developments to accommodate the second 20 million Californians will be *dispersed* and located in new cities in areas where terrain and climate are best suited to enjoyable living.

2. Waste water from cities, industries and agriculture should be reclaimed, demineralized, reused or recycled, rather than discharged to the ocean, or to bays and estuaries, where it is lost as a water resource.

3. Each region of the state—the Coastal Region, the Desert and Plateau Region and the Great Central Valley—from here on out should meet its water needs from its own resources.

4. Coastal areas should meet their ultimate needs by a combination of wastewater reclamation and seawater conversion.

5. The Central Valley should meet its ultimate needs by transferring a portion of *winter flood flows* of the Sacramento River to the San Joaquin Valley in a peripheral canal and using underground storage in the San Joaquin Valley to smooth out cycles of wet and dry years.

Points two, four and five are by no means entirely new. The state has long acknowledged that reclamation of wastewater should be practiced to a degree, and that seawater conversion will be needed at some future time. The state intends to transfer some winter flood water from the Sacramento River to the San Luis Reservoir in the San Joaquin Valley, and has long recognized the necessity of utilizing the groundwater reservoirs of the valley conjunctively with surface reservoirs. The point is that the state, considering itself bound by decisions already made, proposes an utterly inadequate application of these principles.

One important problem remains to be considered: what do we do with the facilities already completed to deliver water from the Central Valley to the Central Coast sector and Southern California? This question, with all its legal and financial implications, must be decided by the legislature at the soonest possible date. Even though, as contended in this article, the long-range solution to the water problems of this area lies in other directions, it may prove necessary to permit some use of these conveyance facilities during the next ten years, as long as a certain and sure termination date is established.

Deep policy issues are at stake here. The matter is too urgent to be further delayed. The whole question of the concepts to be followed in the solution of California's water problems should be reexamined in depth. The California legislature should tackle this problem in the most dedicated and penetrating study of its 120-year history. Californians can't *live* with anything less!

• Frank Stead's engineering ideas for the future of California—bold, informed, unconventional—were prominent in *Cry California* for many years.

His suggestions concerning water management cannot be said to have caught on. For one thing, they involved the desalting of seawater and wastewater in very large quantities; and the technology to do this at acceptable cost has not come along as rapidly as conservationists were hoping in the 1960s. Everybody assumed, back then, that nuclear power (cheap, safe and plentiful) would drive the energy-hungry desalting plants. This vision proved a mirage. The great age of desalinization, if there is to be one, is still in our future.

A controversial feature of the Stead plan was the peripheral canal he wanted built around the delta to siphon off water from the Sacramento River for storage in the groundwater basins of the San Joaquin Valley. The state was already proposing such a canal, to be used year-round; Stead called for a still larger one, to be used, however, only in winter, when the withdrawal of water would be less damaging to the bay and delta downstream. But the fear grew that any peripheral canal would eventually be used to its full capacity—that promises to limit the "take" of water or to stop the pumping in summer would last, at best, until the next drought. So the super-canal proposal brought little echo.

During the 1970s, the hopes of would-be reformers were to focus on another package, one emphasizing the more efficient use of existing water supplies.

But other features of Frank Stead's water philosophy—his insistence that pollution control and water supply are one problem, not two; his demand for fuller use of groundwater reservoirs; his emphasis on the value of regional self-sufficiency in water; and his recognition that water planning must be one part of general planning for human settlement—demand our attention today no less than the day they were written.

The water establishment, in the face of criticism from California Tomorrow and many others, was not silent. In 1970, Bill Bronson pulled together a lively anthology of counterattacks.

177

WILLIAM BRONSON, Editor   1970

Piercing the Quagmire Trap
of Chicken Little Emotionalists
with the Laser Beam of Truth:

The Water Establishment Speaks

" 'A cloud-nine brainchild potentially harmful to all Californians' was the way California Water Resources Association President Doyle F. Boen described a proposed new California Water Plan, authored by Frank M. Stead and published in the preservationist magazine *Cry California,* which advocated shutdown of the California Aqueduct south of the Tehachapi after 1980. . . .

"We believe the Stead article is typical of the flood of misinformation being given the public concerning water development and should be exposed for what it is—a concept unsupported by any sound or proofed engineering data,' Boen said."

California Water Resources Association *Newsletter,* January 6, 1970.

"In our haste to develop this land, we have overdeveloped it so much in many areas that we have polluted our air and our water. Should we go to the other extreme with protection of our natural resources, we may very well complete the destruction through lack of use."

William R. Gianelli, director, State Department of Water Resources, speaking to the Eureka Rotary Club on November 3, 1969.

"Preservation as 'wild' rivers of the Eel, Trinity and Klamath Rivers is the goal of a newly formed 'Committee of Two Million,' a fish-oriented northern group which doesn't speak for 18 million recreation-minded Californians who don't fish."

California Water Resources Association *Newsletter,* December 2, 1969.

"The water supplies we have today and which will be the heritage for the next generation are largely the result of blood, sweat, tears, and some gun play, and much money."

Herbert W. Greydanus, division engineer, State Department of Water Resources, talking to the Lodi Adult School Spring Forum, March 17, 1970.

"Now that people have discovered 'environment' and 'ecology' —and I do not mean to sound facetious—let us welcome their interest in maintaining a program which will allow us to conserve, to use, and still to protect all of our valuable resources. But, let us not fall into the quagmire trap of Chicken Little emotionalists who tell us we have to bring development to a full stop in this state because we're desecrating our environment. . . ."

William R. Gianelli, director, State Department of Water Resources, speaking to the 1969 Fall Convention of the Irrigation Districts Association of California on December 4, 1969.

"For the past four months, many of you have been doing an outstanding job of delivering that [the California Water Establishment's] message. No one knows better than I how many 'dragons' have had to be slain . . . how much misinformation we each had to wade through . . . or, how many half-truths we must have climbed over. But our labors are bearing the fruit of reason and are opening the minds of men.

"You have used truth as an intellectual laser beam, to cut through the lies, pierce the lack of knowledge, and open the whole field of water problems and solutions. . . .

"When it comes to the environment, the truth of the matter is that the State Water Project has accomplished more overall good for the environment of this State than is possible to measure."

William R. Gianelli, speaking to the general session of the Irrigation Districts Association of California Spring Convention, April 10, 1970.

8 *The Desert Pupfish*

- In 1970, as the "ecology" movement swelled across America, *Cry California* broke away from its usual emphasis on problems connected in one way or another with urban growth, and devoted most of an issue to what might have seemed the farthest-afield of subjects: the plight of a tiny aquatic creature, minor in size but major in scientific meaning, called the desert pupfish. "The pupfish feature," Heller recalls wryly, "shocked some of our friends." It did more than that. Though not quite the first discussion of the pupfish problem in print, this was the first to attract wide attention. Partly as a result of this coverage, the situation was to improve.

   Three stories, each excerpted here, make up the special pupfish report. The first, by Sterling Bunnell, explains the reasons for caring about this little-known creature. In the second, Bunnell and James Deacon, a professor of biology at the University of Nevada, Las Vegas, discuss the threats to the survival of the various pupfish species. Finally, Martin Litton, a noted conservationist, sets out what had to be done if the fish were to be saved.

STERLING BUNNELL   1970

The Fish

If Charles Darwin had known of the pupfish of the Death Valley region, he would have been enthralled. They are as remarkable as the Galapagos finches that inspired him to form his theory of evolution.

Thousands of years ago, the pupfish were divided into separate populations as the Death Valley region dried following the last ice age, and in the process they evolved adaptations to a variety of unbelievably extreme physical conditions. They now live in perhaps three dozen widely separated hot springs and saline creeks.

They represent one of the most striking examples of evolutionary change now to be found on our planet. Their research potential in genetics and evolutionary studies is enormous and still scarcely touched. Yet these marvelous little fish and their habitats are now being thoughtlessly wiped out by man. Several species or subspecies have already been exterminated, and the remaining ones are threatened.

During the last glacial advance, which began about 50,000 years ago, the Death Valley region received much rain. A system of interconnected lakes and streams developed.

These waterways were inhabited by relatively few varieties of fish, mainly members of the killifish (of which today's pupfish is a member) and minnow families. The land bordering these streams was well vegetated and supported mastodon, ground sloths, sabre-tooth tigers, dire wolves, camels, horses, elk, deer, and many smaller creatures.

As the glaciers began to recede about 20,000 years ago, the Southwest slowly began to dry and true deserts appeared in the lowlands. The large mammals vanished and the fish were isolated in smaller and ever more separated waterways. About 4,000 years ago the present severe desert conditions were fully established, and in most of the region the only waters remaining as habitats for fish were volcanic hot springs and their outflow streams. The minnows, with few exceptions, failed to adapt to hot water or extreme alkalinity, but the killifish somehow did, and did so in a remarkably short period of geologic time—only a few thousand years. Two genera of killifish persisted in the desert springs, the pupfish *(Cyprinodon),* represented by four species and a number of subspecies, and the closely related poolfish *(Empetrichthys),* only one species of which now survives in a single spring.

Among the pupfish species, the most divergent is the small (one inch long), dark, Devil's Hole species *(C. diabolis).* These fish were isolated at least 20,000 years ago and have since been confined in the steep-sided pool at the bottom of Devil's Hole. Here the population fluctuates from about 700 in summer when the sun is overhead and stimulates algae growth, to 200 in winter when food is more restricted. Breeding occurs mainly on a small ledge about three feet underwater. Precarious as their situation may be, they have survived in this way for thousands of years.

The Salt Creek pupfish *(C. salinus)* inhabit the upper reaches of a saline creek in the floor of Death Valley and show many distinct anatomical and physiological characteristics. About five miles south of Salt Creek is Cottonball Marsh, where an as yet unidentified species of pupfish recently has been found. These Cottonball Marsh fish appear to have been separated from the Salt Creek population for no more than

2,000 years, a remarkably short time for a new species to emerge.

The *C. nevadensis* subspecies separated only a few thousand years ago and are still diverging. Their pattern and form vary considerably from one spring to another, even within the same subspecies.

The Owens pupfish *(C. radiosus)* has been isolated for a long time, perhaps 15,000 years. It displays much less difference in appearance between the sexes than do the other species.

All pupfish have physical characteristics and vitality that are fascinating. They dart about their pools, feeding or defending territory or pursuing mates, with the speed and vigor of hummingbirds. They are very aggressive toward each other, especially when breeding, which in hot springs is a year-round affair. The males become very colorful, with iridescent blues and purples on their backs and sides, black bars on their sides and also on their fin edges, and sometimes yellow on their heads. The females tend to be slimmer, and mottled with brown.

Pupfish are omnivorous, feeding on algae, aquatic insects, crustaceans, plankton, flying insects that fall into the water, even the dead bodies of their own kind. Much of their feeding is done in shallow marshy areas immediately adjoining the spring pools.

Pupfish are able to get about in flooded vegetation where the water is less than an inch deep, or over muddy ground puddled by animal hooves. They flip about actively between bits of water, feeding as they go. While the temperature of the hot springs is more or less constant, the temperature of these marshy or puddled zones fluctuates widely, and it is in this kind of environment that the pupfish probably evolved their ability to withstand abrupt changes in temperature to which most fish are very vulnerable. Adaptation to salinity may also occur in similar areas. The pupfish of Death Valley's Cottonball Marsh spend much of their time in small, evaporating puddles of saline water. In experiments they have been found to tolerate saline concentrations up to *six* times that of sea water.

In the Ash Meadows region, habitat temperatures range from 72 to 93 degrees Fahrenheit, and in at least one steaming spring in California, pupfish have been observed in water up to 112 degrees. Other pupfish are able to hibernate, buried in the mud in freezing weather.

It is impossible to review the tremendous adaptive ability of the pupfish without wonder; the little creature is a veritable powerhouse of evolutionary change.

How the pupfish are able to evolve so fast is, Bunnell explains, "a fascinating question, not yet fully understood."

One way that evolution could have accelerated is through an increase in the mutation rate. Since most mutations are unfavorable, dominants are quickly lost, but many recessive mutations are retained and serve as new material for evolutionary change. Experiments indicate that when a stock of pupfish is bred in captivity from a single pair, they do well at first, but gradually die out over several generations. This indicates that the pupfish swim a very thin line between the Scylla of rapidly changing environment and the Charybdis of extinction through inbreeding. An understanding of how they have survived the high rate of genetic variation within the severe inbreeding situations that prevail in almost all pupfish habitats could be of immense scientific value.

While we can only speculate on the pupfish's extraordinary adaptability at this point, existing and yet-to-be developed scientific techniques will reveal many of the genetic secrets that have contributed to its survival. And what we can learn may be of far more than theoretical interest to mankind.

For instance, many geneticists have warned that the radiation dosages to which we are increasingly exposed (and which would be vastly magnified in any nuclear conflict) can raise the number of mutations the average individual carries, perhaps to the level where our species would die out in a few generations as the lethal genes combine. How the pupfish have managed to survive what appears to be a fairly high mutation load may thus be of vital importance to us.

Other practical benefits to be derived from pupfish research could be knowledge of how they withstand high temperatures, low oxygen concentration, and salinity—all of which could be of great value in medicine and space research.

The clearer understanding of evolution they offer may be of tremendous help in guiding evolutionary processes in domestic animals—and perhaps, as some have proposed, even in ourselves.

JAMES DEACON and STERLING BUNNELL 1970

The Threat

Of the six known species in the Death Valley region, the hand of man has wiped out one *(Empetrichthys merriami)*, another is almost gone *(E. latos)*, and a third *(Cyprinodon radiosus)*, thought to be extinct in 1942, appears to have been saved from extermination following the discovery of a remnant population in 1964. Several subspecies *(E. latos concavus, E. l. pahrump, C. nevadensis shoshone,* and probably *C. n. calidæ)* have also been lost.

There are three—or perhaps four—ways in which man has exterminated pupfish species and subspecies. The first is through the introduction of exotic, that is non-native, species to the pupfish habitats; the second is by the disturbance of the habitat itself; the third is by underground pumping; and the fourth way is accidental poisoning.

> After surveying the damage done to the pupfish by exotic fish, by land disturbance, and by poisoning, the authors turn to the latest and most dangerous threat: the uncontrolled pumping of groundwater from an aquifer in the Amargosa Desert just east of Death Valley proper, across the Nevada line. This pumping threatened to lower the water table over huge areas and dry up almost all the springs and ponds the pupfish live in. Most immediately threatened was the richest cluster of pupfish habitats, the area around Ash Meadows, Nevada, which the fish shared with a farm enterprise called Spring Meadows, Inc.

In Ash Meadows, there are perhaps 20 springs with pupfish

populations, including Devil's Hole, which is the only habitat of the *C. diabolis,* the Devil's Hole pupfish.

Spring Meadows, Inc., now owns or controls nearly all surface water in Ash Meadows and has diverted much of it through their extensive irrigation system. It has also developed a number of wells, and plans to put three to five thousand acres into alfalfa production to support a large cattle feed lot.

Recently, Spring Meadows drilled a well about 15 feet away from the boundary of Devil's Hole—which sits in a crevice in a detached 40-acre section of Death Valley National Monument. A U.S. Geological Survey report indicates that any well within a mile of Devil's Hole is likely to cause a decline of pool level within a year after it is put into operation. Since virtually all breeding and feeding by Devil's Hole pupfish occur on a rocky ledge no more than three feet underwater any drop in pool level is serious and a three-foot drop may be catastrophic.

A pump has been installed at the adjacent well but to date has not been used, and according to company spokesmen it will not be used—an agreement reached under pressure of The Bureau of Land Management and the National Park Service. But Spring Meadows has prepared large tracts of land near the well for cultivation and has at least seven other wells within a three-and-a-half-mile radius of Devil's Hole, all of which may prove to be the end of the Devil's Hole pupfish.

MARTIN LITTON   1970

The Answer

It's a safe guess that no matter what we do, all the killifish populations of the Death Valley region are going to become extinct anyway. Countless organisms, countless animate creatures that were never subject to human influences, have vanished with the passing of time. If we believe our own science, we must expect time alone to extinguish *Cyprinodon* and *Empetrichthys*—and us.

But how much time?

We are just beginning to acknowledge that our own foolishness can drastically shorten human tenure on earth. Whether study of the adaptation of the beautiful little pupfish to crowding, competition, anoxia, salinity, starvation, and extreme heat will produce keys to human survival is not the point. That scientists are fascinated by pupfish purely as pupfish is not quite the point either. The point is that pupfish are important to and in themselves, and to the whole scheme of creation, whether they are destined to survive for a million years or a century. As things are going, they haven't a decade.

There is not enough money or talent in the civilized world to produce a single pupfish; for a pittance (but not for nothing) we can save the remaining species in the Amargosa basin from man-wrought oblivion in our time. The obliteration of habitat by bulldozer and plow must be stopped at once. That may take some doing: Spring Meadows, Inc., is in the process of bringing thousands of acres of desert land under cultivation in Ash Meadows. Last fall the corporation claimed to have sunk $3.5 million in the ranching operation; ransoming the pupfish today could take $4 million, plus extraordinary application of government guts and muscle.

An alternative to buying Spring Meadows, Inc., might be to find legal bases for banning all pumping. Wishful thinking will not keep springs flowing or natural pools standing while electric pumps suck down the water table they depend on, and without the natural flow, the Ash Meadows pupfish will vanish.

Second only to pumping as a threat to pupfish habitat—and to the renowned water-related scenery of Death Valley National Monument—is irrigation by the surface flow of the springs. In nature, the final resting place for waters of the Amargosa basin is Death Valley. Some of the water gets into Death Valley by way of the surface channels of the Amargosa River; more goes underground, by various routes, to percolate into the valley's water table or emerge as springs. Spreading any of the waters of the upper Amargosa basin on alfalfa fields means almost total loss to the atmosphere of water so used. It cannot be emphasized too strongly that extreme danger of drying up threatens not only the pupfish sanctuaries of the lower Amargosa River and great Saratoga Springs of Death Valley, but also such familiar and cherished phenomena as Badwater, the Salt Pools, Devil's Golf Course, and the valley's primary source of fresh water in Furnace Creek. By the time Death Valley feels the upstream depletion of its water supply, years may have passed; then even full restoration of the native upstream flows—an unlikely prospect—might never rebuild the valley's water table, and in any event not do so in time to forestall ecological disaster.

Litton calls for a number of federal actions to protect the pupfish, closing with this call on President Nixon:

In view of all we now know, it would seem clearly the duty of, and within the power of, the President to proclaim the pupfish collectively a national biological treasure—to declare that government policy henceforth will be to protect them forever. The declaration will take little time or thought away from other things, but it will serve notice to Congress to respond with its own resolutions—and it is no longer politic for legislators (or administrators or bureaucrats) to snicker at such things.

The President should create a new agency—or empower an existing one, perhaps the Bureau of Sport Fisheries and Wildlife—to regulate land use by whatever measures are necessary to limit practices to those that will not adversely affect pupfish habitats; this could mean the end of cultivation along the Amargosa. The federal agency must have ample money allotted for restoration of habitat. It must have the administrative power to control earth-moving, pumping, and use of pesticides; to eliminate exotic species; to seek suitable new habitats affording at least temporary sanctuary; and to carry out whatever management programs prove to be necessary—not to guarantee survival of the pupfish for all time but to make sure that civilized man is not their killer.

The pupfish may seem merely a drop in the biological bucket, but we cannot afford to let them go. Rallying to their survival is as pure, clean, and moral a thing as we can do. It will show that as a people we are growing up, achieving reverence for life itself, and accepting guardianship of living things for which we have no material use whatsoever. Pupfish provide us no food or fertilizer or sport; they don't lend themselves to sentimental caricaturing in the Disney or Smokey Bear traditions, and certainly they don't know or care that as a life form they are endangered. That is for *us* to know, and to care.

After millennia of gradual change, time has suddenly run out for the pupfish. The manner in which we respond to this circumstance, so isolated and simple in comparison with present and imminent perils to other creatures not excepting ourselves, can be a model for our approaches to weightier tasks ahead.

• *Update:* Since 1970, the outlook for the desert pupfish has improved dramatically—but only after some close calls. First, the Interior Department went to court to limit the agricultural pumping that was causing the water to sink in Devils Hole; the case went all the way to the Supreme Court, which in 1976 ruled for the fish. Next, Spring Valley, Inc., offered to sell out to the

Fish and Wildlife Service—and got, incredibly, a turndown. So the land was sold instead to Preferred Equities Corporation, a development concern that promptly proposed a subdivision of some 15,000 lots. The Supreme Court decision had said nothing, it seems, about limiting pumping for *residential* use! The new plan endangered not just the pupfish but the entire Ash Meadows oasis, home to a whole community of rare and specialized animals and plants. Consternation.

But once again the government moved in, securing emergency action under the Endangered Species Act to block development. (This was one of the very few aggressive conservation actions carried out under Interior Secretary James Watt.) Meanwhile, Congress had appropriated money—not quite enough—for the purchase of Ash Meadows. In February 1984, after prolonged negotiation, Preferred Equities sold its entire 12,663 acres to The Nature Conservancy for transfer to the Fish and Wildlife Service. Ash Meadows will be a National Wildlife Refuge at last.

9   *The Lesson of a Garden*

- In 1969, California Tomorrow focused on a matter it had, until then, considered only in passing: the problem of pesticides in agriculture and in homes and gardens. "The emphasis," Bill Bronson wrote in the introduction to a special issue of *Cry California,* "is on the garden. The hard pesticides can disappear from our backyards. And the word that they must be banished— that they can be, without disturbing much of anything except the poison industry—will trickle up to our legislatures. They can act to make the world a poison-free garden. We hope that they will."

The special issue seemed to have quite an impact. After it was published, *Sunset* magazine decided to stop accepting advertisements for chlorinated hydrocarbon pesticides, and lost the Ortho account for a time.

A year later, Bill Bronson's "The Lesson of a Garden," about the student garden project at the University of California at Santa Cruz, attracted wide attention. The coverage gave a boost to the emerging movement for an "alternative" agriculture based on less use of commercial chemicals and large-scale machinery, on more understanding of what makes a seminatural system like a garden work, and (admittedly) on a great deal of human time and labor.

Before turning to some exemplary gardens, the *Cry California* special issue examines the poisons and the problems they pose.

WILLIAM BRONSON   1969

Pesticides and Politics

1969 will surely be remembered as the year the roof finally fell on the pesticide industry and its allies in agribusiness.

By spring, Sweden had called a two-year moratorium on the use of DDT, aldrin, and dieldrin in agriculture, and on DDT and lindane for home and garden use; a major legal test case against DDT and dieldrin was under way in Wisconsin; Congress was considering several bills that would outlaw DDT; Michigan and Arizona had suspended the use of DDT; and the California legislature was studying bills that would outlaw or severely curb the use of the compound.

It's about time California took up the subject. Some of the most dramatic evidence against DDT and other chlorinated hydrocarbons has been gathered in California—the Clear Lake and California brown pelican disasters, the long history of fish and game kills, and then, late in the spring of 1969, news of a study that indicates DDT may be responsible for the sad decline of the Dungeness crab.

But it should surprise no one that the state has dragged its feet. California, as the nation's leading agricultural and home-gardening state, accounts for about 20 percent of the pesticides consumed in the country, which in 1968 amounted to about a billion pounds. This is big business. At the beginning of 1969, the industry anticipated retail sales of $1.7 billion, which would put California's share at something close to $350 million.

About half of the pesticides produced in the country are insecticides (another third are herbicides and the balance, about a sixth, are fungicides). Of the half-billion pounds of insecticides, roughly half are the insidious chlorinated hydrocarbons, and it is this quarter-billion pounds of poison per year with which we are here concerned.

It is now impossible to find out how much of what pesticide is being used where on what crop in California. You can't even find out how much of any poison is sold for any purpose on a statewide basis. It isn't that the figures would be hard to gather, but rather that the regulatory agencies that oversee the use of pesticides feel that to make public what they term "trade secrets" would not be in the interest of the poison manufacturers.

Here we have a pollution problem of enormous scale, and yet no quantitative data are available to the research community. The State Department of Agriculture does publish a summary of the acres treated with pest controls, but the only breakdown is by aircraft and ground equipment; by spray, dust and "other"; and by crops. They supply no breakdown of what chemicals in what quantities are used. The summary isn't worth a farthing.

One of the simplest moves the legislature could make would be to create a pesticide-monitoring office that could take the data gathered by the counties and do whatever further investigating is necessary to create monthly and annual profiles of the who, what, when, where, why, and how of all pesticide applications in the state. The data would prove of great value not only to public health and fish and wildlife agencies, but to agriculture and the poison industry itself.

Pesticides have unquestionably saved millions of lives around the world by killing insects that carry such diseases as malaria, equine encephalitis, dengue fever, yellow fever, bubonic plague and others. DDT and other pesticides have helped to increase harvest yields dramatically. No one is suggesting that we stop using all pesticides. But the case against DDT is compelling. By pouring billions of pounds into the environment, we have corrupted the world ecosystem.

How did we get into this mess?

Until about 130 years ago the control of pests was in the hands of the gods, but with the advent of lime-sulphur spray for the control of mildew, the age of chemical pest control had arrived. In the latter half of the 19th century, simple compounds that controlled a wide range of insects and fungi, including Bordeaux mixture, Paris green, London purple, calcium arsenate and natural botanical poisons, were in use. It wasn't until 1942, the year DDT was patented, that the age of synthetic organic pesticides burst forth with the promise that famine and pestilence might finally be vanquished. For 20 years DDT was generally regarded as one of mankind's great blessings. But in 1962, Rachel Carson's *Silent Spring* gave the lie to the promise. While her position against poisons may have been biased and a few of her scientific claims unsupportable, her general thesis has been fully vindicated in the intervening years. Numerous scientific studies have provided the irrefutable scientific facts that DDT is disrupting the world food chain, that it has gravely endangered several bird species, that it interferes with reproduction and metabolic processes and has produced genetic effects in laboratory mammals, indeed that it can be carcinogenic in humans.

The weight of informed world opinion against the continued indiscriminate use of DDT is so overwhelming that policymakers in the industry are certainly now planning what they can sell in its place when the ban is imposed.

> But, Bronson goes on, the industry is fighting bitterly against the regulation of DDT or any other pesticide.

It is clear that the industry's opposition to anti-DDT legislation is not merely concern for the future of DDT itself. Most likely, it is recognition of the fact that if DDT goes, the public will not allow other persistent chlorinated hydrocarbons that are just as bad or worse to be used in its place. There is ample evidence that if chlordane, lindane, aldrin, endrin, dieldrin, methoxychlor, heptachlor, toxaphene, to name the best-known and most-used of the other chlorinated hydrocarbons, had been poured into the world's air, soils and waters in quantities equal to the DDT that has been spread, the resulting ecological impact would have been as devastating as that produced by DDT, or perhaps worse.

Therefore, it will not be enough to outlaw or severely restrict the use of DDT unless similar prohibitions are placed on the others. To control DDT and not the others would be something like having a gun-control law that prohibited the sale of .38-caliber pistols but placed no restrictions on .22s and .45s.

California, as the nation's leading agricultural state, should, on the basis of overwhelming evidence against the chlorinated hydrocarbons, lead the world in banning their use in agriculture and industry and in the home and garden. This prohibition should not begin merely with DDT, but with *all* the hard poisons.

While details of the legislation and the administrative machinery necessary are matters for the legislature to work out, the necessity of such a ban is beyond question. For California to wait any longer to assert leadership in this field is unconscionable. Our preeminence in agriculture and our emerging awareness of the great dangers of environmental contamination demand it.

- If not pesticides, what? Some home gardeners, like the one featured in the following piece, feel they can afford simply to let the bugs (and the birds) take a share of what they grow.

WHAT DID YOU PUT
IN THAT PLANKTON, MAN ?

RICHARD REINHARDT   1969

Miss Tilly's Garden

The flower garden, as a basis for moral parables, used to be an item
in the imagery of every well-trained poet, orator and minister in America. Recently, the symbol has fallen out of fashion. The fault, apparently, is with our gardens, not our gurus. Even the most resolute moralist is
disheartened by a few square yards of brushed aggregate, a corrugated
plastic wind screen, a fenced plot of drought-resistant shrubbery and a
shelf of chemicals compounded for the purpose of exterminating weeds,
annihilating insects, obliterating bacteria, eradicating fungi, alienating
dogs, estranging deer, strangling gophers and stimulating plants to put
forth supernatural quantities of leaf and flower.

A notable exception to the general run of clean-cut, ruthlessly
fumigated gardens is Dorothy Tilly's hillside acre in Marin County, just
north of the Golden Gate. Miss Tilly's garden is a rarity: a large,
diverse, luxurious, venturesome garden that thrives without the intrusion of poisonous chemicals.

Perhaps a poison-free garden is no oddity in your neighborhood, but
it is in most parts of California. One approaches it with curiosity
bordering on suspicion. Isn't the whole place overrun with creatures that
look as if they had been pressed out of a plastic monster mold? What
about mildew, gophers, leaf miners, beagles and other enemies of
mankind? What is this gardener trying to prove? Is she a Nature Girl who
handpicks aphids off the rose buds so she won't have to kill them? Or is
she one of those darty-eyed paranoiacs who thinks that everything we
eat and drink is lethal?

Seen from a distance, Miss Tilly's garden shows no obvious peculiarities. Trees enclose the cottage; hedges enclose the trees. Inside the
hedge, some silver birches toss.

From the gate, you peer into a soft, pea-green catacomb. Later, you
realize that this tunnel is formed by a pyracantha bush that arches above
the path; but the first impression is confused by an onslaught of rioting
dogs, leaping and whooping, completely ignoring a female voice that is
patiently asking everyone to please calm down. The dogs turn out to be a
Hungarian pouly called Buda and a cross-pollinated shepherd-Airedale
named Binky. They are only two in number, but assertive.

And this, of course, would be Miss Tilly: whitehaired and spare, wearing a gold corduroy dress, a beige cardigan sweater and a pair of canvas sneakers, and carrying in her right hand the universal scepter of the master gardener, a pair of sharp pruning shears. She leads the way inside—not inside the house, inside the garden—past the gold-tipped fringes of a deodar, around some redwood boxes packed with immense, coral-colored tulips, under an exuberant clematis vine.

It is a mediocre day for looking at gardens—one of those pale-pewter, north bay mornings in late spring, when a veil of clouds is over the Tiburon Peninsula and winds are rollicking down the slope toward Richardson Bay. But the temper of the weather seems exactly suited to the spirit of this garden, with its untamed abundance of weeds and blossoms, birds and animals, insects and fragrance. Many gardens vibrate with life; this one bursts with it. The clematis vine looks as if it is about to devour the cottage and then tackle the dogs, the visitor and even Miss Tilly, if it can first disarm her. Herbs are crowding the path; lilacs are locked in combat with advancing roses; and Binky is snorting and plunging shoulder-deep through a bed of azaleas to scratch her back on the lower branches of a rhododendron.

"Gardens and dogs don't mix," Miss Tilly murmurs, without rancor. "Unfortunately, I happen to like both."

Like many suburban homes in this part of Marin County, Miss Tilly's place started as a family weekend retreat in the 1920s, when one used to cross the Golden Gate from San Francisco to Sausalito in a ferry boat. The cottage had one room. The Tillys added a cubicle now and then, a lot here and there, until finally the property extended more than an acre and the cottage became a low-slung badger burrow of interconnecting chambers, bright with potted succulents, tea roses and the dust-jackets of books.

For many years, Miss Tilly was only a parttime weeder and waterer, helping out during her visits from Detroit, where she headed the music and drama departments of the public library. A decade ago, she retired and moved into the cottage, thereby increasing her work to a 16-hour day, seven days a week. To help maintain discipline, a handyman comes in for half a day every week, and another gardener spends a full day every other week. They yank weeds, haul manure, clean fish ponds and carry out armloads of rubbish. Once a year, a tree service sends up a crew to head back the hedges, prune the peaches and Comice pears, top out the silver birches and cart away any fallen trees or branches. The rest of the chores—potting, pinching, weeding, watering—fall on Miss Tilly and her family; but if sections of the garden sometimes resemble the forest around Sleeping Beauty's castle, that is all right with Miss Tilly. She likes the lower section of the garden best when it is " . . .all lost in the tall, wild oats—magnificently overgrown, just jungle. I'm all for things that take kindly to neglect."

In the beginning, the hillside was quite bare, except for those wild plants that grow in the red earth of the Bay Area: lupine, coyote bush, foxtails, monkey flowers. The soil was a shallow layer of gardener's despair, heavy and sticky as plum pudding in winter, hard as burnt brick in summer. But Miss Tilly's mother was a gardener of the sort that works outdoors from dawn until darkness, then carries a flashlight while finishing up a few essentials. It was she who established the garden on plain principles of sunshine and water, plenty of care and plenty of compost.

Miss Tilly's compost bins, waist-high and ten or 12 feet square, stand around the edges of the service yard, quietly digesting layer after layer of vegetable matter (grass clippings, carrot tops, weeds), cow manure and garden soil. From time to time, Miss Tilly or the handyman waters the pile; but they have given up turning the contents. In five or six months, turned or unturned, the refuse decays into crumbly, blackish-brown compost, just right for mulching rose bushes, forking into the flower beds and enriching the thin, red soil under the shade trees.

The results make other gardeners grind their teeth in envy. A Japanese maple that Miss Tilly's mother planted 43 years ago as a seedling towers 40 feet above the cottage, to the astonishment of visiting arborists. A subtropical jacaranda (which prefers warmer climates) spreads blue parasols in a sheltered corner. White lilacs (which prefer chillier winters) carry spikes of flowers thicker than a man's arm. Raspberries and red currants (which like deeper soil), lemons and peaches (which like more summer heat), strawberries and cherries (which are vulnerable to pests) flourish in the terraces. Pink dogwood flowers at the door; and, ten yards away, desert succulents bloom so splendidly in the lathhouse that Miss Tilly admits to being "rather chesty" about the display.

Through the midst of the garden fly hundreds of birds, which are the beneficiaries of Miss Tilly's poison-free regime; thrushes, finches, sparrows and jays, mostly, joined occasionally by a nuthatch, titmouse or chickadee. Linnets and juncos pick kernels of grain from the four feeding platforms; robins and cedar waxwings swarm the pyracantha bush; white-crown sparrows splash in the bird baths; and now and then a sparrow hawk casts his minatory shadow over the east lawn.

195

To protect the lives of these and other small animals, Miss Tilly rigidly excludes from her garden such toxic compounds as DDT, lindane, chlordane and arsenic. Her warfare against aphids is limited to spraying the leaves and buds of her rose bushes with a little water—if she finds time—and luring in birds to take care of the residue. She brings in a tree service to spray the birches and fruit trees with an oil-copper mixture when the trees are leafless in the winter.

"They think we're quite mad because we won't have any of the new poisons," Miss Tilly says. In truth, she dislikes the *old* poisons, too. She scatters around a few handfuls of Corry's, a metaldehyde snail and slug bait that does not contain arsenic; but she would rather have a duck to eat the night crawling pests. ("It's a lot less trouble than going around with snail bait all the time.") As for gophers, they are put off by a bed of low-growing spurge, which exudes a caustic, milky sap. (The juice, Miss Tilly warns, is painfully caustic to eyes and hands. Antidote: fresh goat's milk.)

As her only fertilizer, Miss Tilly uses cow manure, straight from the farm. She has little use for weed-free, sterilized manures in paper sacks.

"I'm not so keen on all these processed things. I would get weeds, anyway, even using dried manure. Weeds make good compost."

In defense of poison-free gardening, it would be pleasant to report that Miss Tilly's mild protective measures have produced an Eden where leaves are never chewed or curled, where boughs never break, fruit never falls and ripeness is all. This is not the case. There is decay, damage and a struggle for life. Aphids *do* attack the roses. Snails and slugs *do* come in. So do gophers. And the dogs and birds cause a good deal of damage. Although Miss Tilly has strung wire fences around her dwarf Korean peach tree, her plum trees and her beds of strawberries, parsley and primroses, the birds still gorge on apricots and cherries, the dogs still prance among the pelargoniums. A family of raccoons, residents of the basement, are adept in vandalism. They dig in the lawn, which, as a result, " . . .looks as though archeologists have been around"; they throw all-night parties in the apricot tree; and they killed and ate Miss Tilly's mallard drake, who had given six months of service rousting snails and slugs.

But none of these acts of aggression has converted Miss Tilly to the principle of massive retaliation. She belongs to the same school as E. B. White, who once wrote, in regard to a raccoon that was eating the sweet corn on his farm in Maine: "In the country a man has to weigh everything against everything else, balance his pleasures and indulgences one

196

against another. I find that I can't shoot this coon, and I continue to plant corn—some for her, what's left for me and mine—surrounding the patch with all sorts of coon baffles. It is an arrangement that works out well enough."

Miss Tilly's arrangement also is one that works out well enough. She prefers to allow nature to blemish her garden once in a while rather than permit chemicals to poison it forever.

"If the birds will eat the bugs," she says, "we'll spare them a little fruit. When this garden was started, we didn't hear about all these chemicals, yet the garden grew. I'd rather have a few bugs in the garden than to have the garden full of poisons."

- Other gardeners take a harder line. One such is Harold Swanton, whose garden in the San Fernando Valley town of Northridge is a showcase.

JOHN SEGINSKI   1969

Mr. Swanton's Garden

While Miss Tilly lives with almost all the insects that inhabit her garden, Swanton uses whatever chemical controls are necessary to make sure that pest invasions don't harm his plants.

Swanton's formula is basically that of any successful gardener:

> He waters regularly and often.
> He feeds often.
> He janitors often.
> He makes and plants in good soil.
> He knows his pests and what to do them in with.

The garden has a great variety of plants, some of which are quite prone to pest infestations. But Swanton, who, incidentally, is a zoologist by training and a screenwriter by profession, draws one very significant line in the use of pesticides: *he will not use any of the hard poisons in his garden.* Because of his awareness of the ecological havoc wrought by the chlorinated hydrocarbon insecticides, he has abandoned the use of all of them, as a matter of principle. But this has meant no compromise in the garden. The simple fact is that *nobody* needs these destructive compounds to make his garden grow straight and true.

Swanton doesn't have to deal with all the pest species that infest California gardens (*no* single gardener does); however, a look at his specific problems and how he deals with them can be instructive.

In the first few years of gardening, he mastered the really simple (and overrated) skill of recognizing garden pests and diagnosing pest damage. He also learned what kinds of controls were required to solve each problem. When chemical controls are called for, he does not use any more than absolutely necessary. And what is necessary, in truth, is surprisingly little.

Basically, there are three types of problems he must contend with: weeds, harmful insects or other small creatures, and squirrels.

To control weeds in the orchard and other places, Swanton sprays them with diesel oil. The oil blocks the pores of the leaves, and the weeds die in a few days. To keep weeds out of the dichondra lawns, he feeds them with a fertilizer (Scott's Bonus) that contains a weed-control agent. If tufts of Bermuda grass insist on sprouting in the dichondra, he uses dalapon to destroy them. And the weeds that sprout in the flower beds are pulled by hand.

Every garden, no matter how well managed, has an abundance of insects and other small pests, some harmful and some beneficial to plants. Some beneficial insects pollinate the flowers and others parasitize or feed upon the harmful insects. Because some of the harmful insects are controlled by their natural enemies, Swanton is very careful when it comes to selection and use of poisons. And before using any chemical, he'll wait to see if nature can take care of the problem for him. If he sees aphids on the leaves of an orange tree, for example, he lets them alone for several days, because ladybugs or other predators may show up and eat them. If help doesn't arrive, Swanton sprays with nicotine sulfate to destroy the bugs before much damage is done.

For scale insects that, for example, attack the many species of holly that grow in the garden, he uses Volck, an oil mixture that smothers the insects within their shells.

The snails and slugs, a constant problem in most California gardens, are controlled by metaldehyde bait. (Swanton doesn't use bait containing arsenic because it is highly toxic and persists in the soil.)

The rose garden is prized for the beauty of its blossoms, and to control the aphids and other sucking insects that stunt the growth of buds and tender shoots, he uses a systemic poison, Di-syston. These poisons are absorbed by roots or leaves and make a plant itself poisonous to the sucking pests. And if the systemic fails, he uses a nicotine-sulfate spray.

And finally, for the nematodes that infest the roots of his chrysanthemums, he fumigates the soil in that plot with ethylene dibromide capsules.

If there are those who might doubt that Swanton is really tough on pests, what with his personal embargo on the chlorinated hydrocarbons, they should consider his solution to the squirrel problem. Everybody likes squirrels, and the Swantons are no exception. When they saw the first eastern fox squirrel in their garden, they were delighted. (This species was first introduced to the San Fernando Valley via Texas about ten years ago.) But as time went on, the squirrels became so numerous that they became a threat to the health of the garden and to sanity. They girdle the avocado tree, clean out the almonds, lop off the new shoots on the walnut trees, eat the citrus fruits as they mature, eat camellia buds "like they were ice-cream cones," and do other mischief.

Swanton was not about to turn his garden over to the squirrels. He bought traps from the local agricultural agent. By setting these walnut-baited, quick-death snares in his trees, he has the neighborhood squirrels on the defensive. In 1969 alone, as of May 26th, 47 squirrels had been interred in the Swanton garden.

So long as the soil is rich, well-mulched and watered, pest control takes but a tiny fraction of Swanton's gardening time.

• Can the ideas implicit in these garden stories be applied on a larger scale? William Bronson went to Santa Cruz and found that, indeed, they could.

WILLIAM BRONSON   1970

The Lesson of a Garden

There is a student-run garden on the campus of the University of California at Santa Cruz that puts forth flowers and vegetables in an abundance and with a vigor that simply must be seen to be fully comprehended.

The word "revolutionary" is both easy and dangerous to throw about these days, but it is surely appropriate to use it in this context, for the dedicated young people who are responsible for the garden have not only succeeded in producing flowers and vegetables on a four-acre hillside plot in quantities many times—at the very least, four times—greater than are realized in commercial agriculture, they have created an institution with a sense of purpose, a sense of hope, a sense of community, and a pervading sense of sanity that today so many of our institutions and activities lack.

The garden began in the conversations of two faculty members who, early in 1967, shared a temporary office and a long-range concern: what sort of shape and character would the raw new Santa Cruz campus develop? One of the men was Paul Lee, a professor of philosophy; the other was Donald Nicholl, a visiting historian from England. Nicholl, in Lee's words, "mourned the institutional imposition on a great landscape and wondered how we could ever develop a sense of *place* here." The two broached to Chancellor Dean McHenry the notion of a garden as a partial answer, and McHenry gave the project his active backing.

But who would run the garden? Through a friend Lee heard that an English gardening authority, Alan Chadwick, was soon to come to Santa Cruz. Chadwick was an advocate of what he called the French Intensive school of organic agriculture. His approach to the art was philosophical, almost religious, and when he arrived he warmed immediately to the idea of a garden as a means to "redeem the landscape." He was hired.

Chadwick bought a shovel, selected the site, recruited a student "cadre," and set about transforming a rugged hillside into the beautiful garden it is today.

The garden is located on what seems an unlikely spot—a very steep slope above the embankment of the main entrance road to the campus. A mixed forest once stood here—redwood, Douglas fir, madrone, tanbark oak, hazel, huckleberry, fern and oxalis. Almost 300 years ago a severe fire burned through, but the great trees survived, only to fall to the logger's ax in the late 19th century. Today, a couple of fine second-growth redwood rings and scattered madrone and Douglas fir remain as evidence of the original fog-nourished stand. The soil at the garden site was thought by the campus landscape architect to be poor.

Of the four-acre plot, about half an acre is planted in vegetables, another acre and a half in flowers for cutting, perhaps another acre in other flowering plants, and the balance is either densely tree-shaded or used for such things as the nursery, compost piles, and chicken yards.

The Method and the Place

There are some basic observations about the French Intensive Method that are central to the garden's success.

First off, the soils in the garden are constantly enriched. Initially, nitrogenous crops such as fava beans were set out, and the planting beds were dressed between each crop with two-year-old composted manure—untreated and right from the farm, quite different from the bagged product you get at the supermarket. Bone meal is added to each bed, but in smaller quantities than during the first two years. Wood ash was and is used for many vegetables. As much compost as could be acquired or made was worked into the beds initially, and composting remains a regular and important part of the soil-conditioning process. Each time a bed is reworked for sowing or planting, the soil is improved.

One of the striking differences between commercial agriculture and the French Intensive Method is the absence of row planting in the latter. Row planting facilitates large-scale irrigation and machine cultivation, but in terms of production it is very wasteful.

As a student, Steve Kaffka was president of the garden project; today he is one of four paid staff members. He writes: "Because the plants are set close enough to each other so that as they mature they touch or nearly touch, the ground is shaded and protected from direct sunlight; naturally, the roots are quite close, as are the stems and stalks. In the spaces between there exists a greater evenness of temperature and moisture than it is possible to attain by row planting, and each plant, because of the proximity of its sister plant, seems able to create a climate around itself that it prefers."

To make the most of the sunlight available, most of the vegetable planting beds run up and down the hill to maximize the southern exposure. The first question that came to my mind was how they kept the hillside from washing away. The secret lies in careful watering practices and in a very simple soil-conservation technique. The little soil that is washed into the paths at the foot of the beds is either wheelbarrowed up to the top of the bed or spread on the compost piles.

There is no off-season for the garden. As soon as a vegetable bed has been harvested or a flower bed ceases to yield sufficient blooms, it is reworked and a new planting is made. Visually the garden is a carpet of color and texture, and during the day hums with insects and birds. The variety of species planted is extraordinary, although certain favorites—dahlias and lettuce, for example—occupy more space than many others.

201

Work in the garden begins shortly after sunrise and ends as darkness falls. The staff works all through the day, and the students come and go as their academic schedules allow. At 9:15, a half-hour is taken for breakfast at an airy, one-room decked cabin that serves as kitchen, dining room, office and gathering place. During breakfast, which anywhere from 6 to 20 students and staff will join, plans for the day's work are often discussed. After breakfast, the gardeners spend the rest of their long day planting, weeding, harvesting, watering, feeding the chickens and attending to all the other needs appropriate to the day and the season. A big lunch is set out at one o'clock and tea (or high tea, if garden business is to be discussed) is served at 4:30. After tea, the work goes on till dark.

Mealtime is about as unplastic an eating experience as you can find in this country today. The students do the cooking, which includes baking their own bread, and camaraderie prevails. Much of the food served at the chalet, but not all, is grown in the garden.

Pest control is pursued entirely without synthetic chemical tinkering. Occasionally, the aphid population may get out of hand on certain crops, such as Brussels sprouts, and if the natural predators fail to move in, nicotine sulphate (a highly toxic, plant-derived, nonpersistent insecticide) is sprayed on the plants. Other than this, and the control of snails and slugs by hand, pest control is left to nature. These are Steve Kaffka's thoughts on the subject of letting nature work and helping nature work to achieve the optimum garden:

"The word 'pest' needs redefining. In nature, there's no such thing. There are balances in nature that work to maintain healthy plant life—insects, birds, animals, each has its place. The gardener following the principle of simulating nature seeks to preserve the balance. If this is done, the word 'pest' doesn't enter the picture. Our garden is a bird sanctuary, we have more birds this year than ever before, they increase every year. To encourage the birds to come and stay, we allow weeds such as groundsel and dandelion to remain and go to seed, then the birds eat the seeds. Many birds, such as juncos and canary warblers, are both seed and insect eaters. We provide birdbaths and water troughs and let them drink unmolested. We also discourage cats.

"When you don't use pesticides and poisons, you frequently have insects such as mantis and ladybugs, which prey on destructive insects. Each year, the harmless insects increase in number, as do the birds that feed upon them. Each year without poisons makes life more possible and plentiful for all."

202

Sowing is always done on the inclination of the moon—that is, the seeds are put into the ground at the time of the new moon, or perhaps even a few days before, in order to take advantage of the growing brilliance of the moon during the two weeks it takes for the full moon to arrive. (How the light gets through the soil to hasten germination eludes me, but the world is full of mysteries.) Transplanting, on the other hand, is done in the evenings during the declination of the moon—that is, the two-week period between the full moon and the new moon. Project members are quick to tell you that sowing and transplanting by the moon were ritually practiced in much of the world for millennia prior to the 20th century.

The Garden in Our Future

So successful has the project been that the university administration has granted 20 acres to the students, along with $15,000 seed (no pun) money, to found a model farm.

We often speak of relevance these days, and question the purpose and meaning of existing educational programs. If the garden project and the proposed model farm are not relevant, purposeful and meaningful in terms of the development of our young, then nothing in this world is. In approaching the National Science Foundation for the funds necessary to get the model farm in operation, Dan McGuire, a sophomore and current president of the Student Garden Project, wrote: "To be in affinity with their environment and to produce part of what they consume will give students a perception of life they often do not discover in the usual university curriculum."

One of the great things the Santa Cruz program could do would be to train an army of inspiring teachers who could help spread the garden concept across the state and nation. I strongly believe that the state, with the university leading the way, should bring the garden-project idea to every community within its borders, and I suggest that the program contain the following elements:

— Every grammar-school district should have a garden that could be visited and *worked in* at least once a week by every child in the school.

— Every college campus and every high school in the state should have a garden project that would function not as a sop or a distraction but as a retreat and a locus of learning. While classes should be given for credit, participation should be open to all.

203

— University Extension should begin garden projects for the hundreds of thousands of older people who, given the chance, would throw themselves into intensive gardening. The demand for this has already been established in the Santa Cruz experience. So many townspeople came to work in the campus project that the original rules allowing outsiders to work in the garden had to be changed.

The change in American life that could result from such a program is great. The possibilities include a renascence in urban gardening and home food production that might, among other things, contribute to the solution of our anticipated "leisure-time" problem. (It could, at the same time, go far in redeeming part of the prime agricultural land we have squandered on urban development, by returning the soil to the use for which it is best suited: growing food.) It clearly suggests the possibility of reestablishing, to some degree at least, a Jeffersonian rural lifestyle, that of the small freeholder living on the fruits of the land and his labor, which has virtually vanished from American life. Even the implications for commercial agriculture can't be dismissed, although how the French Intensive Method, with its strong demand for hand labor, could fit into present-day agriculture is not at all clear.

There are a lot of young people out there, walking through our nights looking for the pill that will make manifest the fantasy world of their childhood, that world promised by television, by Zorro, Disney, Superman, and the rest of the fascinating trash we let them feed on. Lives are being wasted in the search. I can only speculate on what today's lost young people might have been doing if they had had the opportunity to work with their hands in the soil and to learn the way the earth puts forth its bounty.

If we can teach mathematics and woodworking and music, surely we can give the young the opportunity to discover the earth that nurtures them. Perhaps it is wishful thinking to believe that the world might be changed for the better thereby, but God knows no harm could come from such a program.

• *Update:* Since 1970, the Student Garden Project at Santa Cruz has had its ups and downs. In 1971, the project added the hoped-for 17-acre farm. But in 1973, Alan Chadwick departed, along with most of the original group of volunteers, and the project floundered for a time. (One year the plantings survived only because four faculty members made time to do the watering.) Later in the decade, though, the operation got back on track. Today, the garden and farm are used and valued more than ever. The project is now formally a part of College 8, whose provost is conservationist Raymond Dasmann. The university, meanwhile, has set up a program in "agroecology," with the farm and garden as its research center. Purpose: to show how ecologically sound methods can be applied to agricultural production. Santa Cruz thus emerges as a small counter-influence to the several University of California campuses that specialize in research on mechanization and chemicals as solutions to agricultural problems.

———————

At about the time of the garden stories, California Tomorrow got into related but much more controversial territory. In 1970, after the U.S. invasion of Cambodia and the months of protest that followed, it published a report written by the Stanford Biology Study Group and titled *The Destruction of Indochina*. (One of the group was Professor Donald Kennedy, later head of the Food and Drug Administration and currently president of Stanford.) *Destruction* deals with those American military measures that were aimed not directly at combatants, or even at other human beings, but at the land itself. While attacks on the enemy's environment are less new to warfare than the Stanford authors seemed to believe, never before had such attacks been carried out remotely on this scale.

Chief among the novelties of Vietnam was the massive use of herbicides, which were sprayed on some five million acres to defoliate or kill off the forests under which enemy forces hid, and to damage both standing crops and future production in enemy-held farm areas. The Stanford report explores the various chemicals in use, including the now-infamous Agent Orange (key ingredient: 2,4,5-T, a potent mutation-producer, often contaminated with the furiously toxic dioxin). It discusses reports of resulting birth defects in Vietnam. Later the document turns to the problems caused by the destruction, by whatever means, of tropical vegetation—an issue that was to be recognized in ensuing years as crucial not only in this war-torn country but in many a peaceful but land-hungry one. A portion of this section follows.

205

STANFORD BIOLOGY STUDY GROUP   1970

From *The Destruction of Indochina*

Tropical forests and soils are very different from those in the temperate zone. To understand the long-term effects of the war in Southeast Asia it is necessary to describe certain characteristics of these forests and soils.

One feature is the intricate interdependence of the plants and animals. For instance, the trees of tropical forests depend entirely upon insects, birds, and bats (rather than wind) for pollination. Birds, bats, and ground-dwelling mammals are responsible for dispersing seeds from the parent plants to new clearings. These complex plant-animal relations have reached their greatest intricacy in tropical forests because of the mild and predictable climate. Animals can be active the year round because many flowering and fruiting trees provide food continuously. Massive defoliation means an end to this reliable food supply and death for those animals that are most important to the survival of the forest plants.

A second important characteristic of humid tropical forests is that most of the plant nutrients, including nitrates, phosphates, calcium, potassium, magnesium, sulphur and other elements required in smaller amounts, are tied up in the vegetation. Nutrients not contained in the vegetation itself are continuously washed from the soil by heavy rainfall. Under normal conditions, the nutrients released by decaying vegetation are rapidly recaptured and transferred to the roots of the living plants by certain fungi. But large-scale defoliation disrupts this efficient process, and the vital nutrients are quickly lost into streams. Fishing in these streams may temporarily improve because of increased aquatic plant growth due to the higher nutrient levels, but this effect is short term and is gained at the expense of soil fertility. As a direct result of lower fertility and the lack of seeds of the natural colonizing plants, pest species, such as giant bamboo, take over and spread. Once established, bamboo forms an impenetrable thicket that prevents normal forest regeneration and makes future use of the land for agriculture nearly impossible. This bamboo is very resistant to defoliants, and because it reproduces vegetatively from tough underground stems, it cannot be eliminated by burning or cutting once it is established.

From 30 to 50 percent of Vietnamese soils are of a type that have the potential to turn into a bricklike substance known as laterite if they are deprived of the organic covering that protects them from exposure to severe weathering. The potential for laterization is greatest in areas that were already disturbed before herbicide application. Cropland, as well as bombed and bulldozed areas along roadways, fall into this category. The permanence of laterite is well illustrated by the Khmer ruins around Angkor Wat in Cambodia where many of the temples were constructed primarily of this rock nearly ten centuries ago. Obviously, laterized land is useless for agriculture.

Along lowland rivers and waterways in the tropics, rich forests grade into pure stands of mangrove trees. These plants extend stilt-roots into shallow, brackish water; the silt they trap plays an important role in delta formation. They also provide a special habitat for key stages in the life cycles of economically important fish and shellfish. The intensive defoliation program along waterways in Vietnam has killed mile upon mile of this living border. There will undoubtedly be a drastic and long-lasting effect upon river fishing and upon the natural process of delta formation along Vietnamese rivers.

The destruction of crop and forest land fertility by herbicides, the alteration of forest composition, and the formation of laterite soil will all result in long-term damage to the agriculture and ecology of Vietnam.

This war has two time scales. There is the immediacy of bombs and battles and of instant destruction and death, and there is the prolonged suffering and hardship that will face all survivors for generations. When the fighting has finally ended, the suffering and hardship will have only begun, for our actions in Vietnam have severely upset the environment and greatly reduced the ability of the land to support its people.

- The publication of this critique under the California Tomorrow imprint drew wide attention, not all of it favorable. It may or may not have been coincidental that, some weeks after the appearance of *The Destruction of Indochina*, California Tomorrow was audited by the Internal Revenue Service—for the second time within the space of a few months.

10 *The Life and Death of State Planning in California*

• When California Tomorrow was founded, we recall, a State Office of Planning had just been created by the legislature and instructed to prepare a comprehensive State Development Plan. Though the resulting document was not intended to have binding authority, many observers hoped it would be a powerful guide and a truly useful model. As Wood and Heller wrote in *California Going, Going . . .,* "A State Development Plan . . . could stand as a guidepost on the road toward a comprehensive planning and development program, and thus substantially help to fill many of the planning and development gaps in our state."

The work went on fitfully for many years. Most of it was paid for by grants from the federal government; most of it was performed by outside consultants, some of them excellent, rather than by the state's own small planning staff. (One truly pioneering piece of work, done for the project but thereafter officially ignored, was the Urban-Metropolitan Open Space Study by Eckbo, Dean, Austin and Williams. Its bold proposal for metropolitan greenbelts had been brought to public attention by a 1966 review in *Cry California.*)

Finally, in 1968, there appeared what was called *The California State Development Plan Program Phase II Report.*

It was, in certain ways, an impressive document. Certainly it had weight and volume. And it contained masses of information, much of it new or newly pulled together (though difficult to locate in a hurry). It even communicated some urgency about the situation the state was facing. What it did not offer—and California Tomorrow was the first to point it out—was any very definite policy on anything.

Reactions did vary. A spokesman for the League of California Cities praised it as "exceptional." But William R. Mac-Dougall, then general manager of the County Supervisors Association of California, remembers the report as "one of the giant ostrich eggs of all time. . . . greeted with two things, monumental sighs and almost total silence."

Whatever else the ill-fated report did, it produced a lively exchange in the pages of *Cry California,* most of which follows in this chapter. Alfred Heller took the plan apart in his editorial "The Life and Death of State Planning in California"; Willie Brown, then an assemblyman but not yet Assembly speaker, attacked it from a slightly different angle; and Caspar Weinberger, at that time Governor Reagan's director of finance (and thus head of the department in which the planning office was located) came back with an angry defense.

The debacle did have two additional, and very significant, results. One was the abolition of the State Planning Office and its replacement, in 1970, by an Office of Planning and Research in the governor's office. Though no immediate change was apparent, OPR had more potential power than the planning office: power waiting for a governor who wished to take advantage of it.

The second significant result of the whole exercise was that it led to the formulation of *The California Tomorrow Plan.*

ALFRED HELLER   1968

The Life and Death of State Planning in California

We have waited all these years—since 1959 when the state legislature said we need and we will have a State Development Plan for California—a plan that must include "recommendations for the most desirable general pattern of land use and circulation within the state and for the most desirable use and development of land resources of the state . . . recommendations concerning the need for, and the proposed general location of, major public and private works and facilities."

And now we have spent almost $4 million for the plan and Lo! it is not a plan at all. It is called "State Development Plan Program Phase II Report." It is a Non-Plan that has the effect of precluding the creation of a State Development Plan.

Over and over again, this document, which should itself be the major State Development Plan authorized by the legislature, merely calls for bits and pieces of planning, to be undertaken sometime in the future. For example, it calls for the creation of a state land-use policy. After $4 million and all this effort, what was to have been the State Development Plan, presumably based on an explicit state land-use policy, now turns around and calls for that policy. What was to have been the State Development Plan calls for the creation of a state urban policy instead of setting out that policy along with a plan for the urban development of California. What was to have been the State Development Plan calls for a state resources development plan and all sorts of little additional plans, a state watershed planning program, a state master plan for ocean resources, a comprehensive recreation plan, and so on. It calls for the kind of thing we have had—single-interest plans, one piled on the other, instead of what it should be itself, a *State Development Plan* that could shepherd all these little plans.

Oh, hell, that's nothing. What was to have been the State Development Plan actually looks you in the eye and says, "There exists an urgent need for comprehensive state land-use planning to be undertaken as early as possible."

This pile of mush is clearly intended as a barricade against the future. There is no State Development Plan; there will be none, for this report says that from now on, the State Office of Planning is to concern itself with "up-dating of information; improvement of inter-program relationships; improvement of inter-governmental relationships."

And the State Office of Planning just sank slowly in the west.

This California Non-Plan comes to absolutely no conclusions regarding what lands specifically should be preserved for open space purposes, which land should be parks, which should be used for cities, where our cities should be, how big they should be, what they should look like, where our transportation corridors should go and what vehicles should fill them, or how we might live our lives on the land now and in the future. (By contrast, Hawaii's new General Plan, in six volumes, sets forth a cogent set of planning goals; reaffirms the value of the state land-use law under which statewide zoning is administered; shows with maps the zoning of the islands into state land-use districts; lists public facilities requirements by 1985; points the way toward balanced transportation planning; and recommends a hugely expanded comprehensive planning program for the Hawaiian Islands.)

The California Non-Plan pays lip service to everything from beautiful cities to good health for everyone. However, it is obvious and ludicrous in the way it avoids recommending any comprehensive program to achieve these goals. Take, for example, the subject of open space. One of the "input" studies made for the state planning program, the Urban-Metropolitan Open Space Study, recommended that California should spend about $4 billion for the outright purchase of key open space areas or for the purchase of development rights to open spaces that could not be protected through state zoning. The study recommended that California protect 9.4 million acres of open space, all within a 40-mile radius of our metropolitan centers, before 1975—7.4 million acres by means of state zoning, 1.1 million acres by less-than-fee purchase, and 789,000 acres by outright purchase.

The California Non-Plan says that "state government is strongly in favor of open space . . . the need is urgent and the time is short." But then, in referring to the recommendations of the open space study, it says: "A direct recommendation that the state spend $4 billion over the next eight years for purchase of open space is not within the ken of this report." The report does come out foursquare for "completion and maintenance of a statewide inventory of open space."

Or take another example. As I mentioned, one of the recommendations of the Non-Plan is the preparation of a state resources-management plan. So let us assume this project goes forward. Then, when it is finished, how will the state's resources-management plan be carried out when, to quote the Non-Plan itself, "decisions at the local level may be at variance with over-all State policy"? Here is the answer: local government will " . . . cooperate with over-all State policy" once it is "informed" about the policy and "shown" that everyone's best interests would be served in the process. Of course.

But the report looks good, I guess. It is "designed." On slick paper. And it is illustrated—a kid on a surfboard, a view above the fruited plain, black and white children in nursery school. There are graphs and charts.

The book is unreadable, incidentally—because of the black sans serif type that swims across three columns on shiny pages and because of the writing. An example: "The issues and problems discussed in the previous Section will require that the State utilize a diverse mixture of policy postures, and policy and program innovations in its efforts to respond to the challenges posed by California's urban growth."

It is extremely difficult to find anything in the report. There is no index. There is no summary of recommendations (there *are* some useful ones, especially in one chapter that proposes changes in laws affecting state development). There are subsummaries (but incomplete) of plan recommendations, but no consolidated summaries. The bibliography is a catchall that does not list separately the resource documents prepared for the State Office of Planning as it struggled to produce what was supposed to be the State Development Plan. But then I suppose that is an irrelevant point. The state has not published one of these documents, so even if you knew their titles, you couldn't get hold of them.

What is closing in on this state is ecological disaster. Even the Non-Plan makes that clear enough—it is willing to list problems. Yet it says, in effect, *too bad, but never mind: the state will not use its brain and its authority to meet the situation.* Oh, yes, we'll have an inventory here, a new law and a departmental program there, statements of good intentions everywhere, but no real action. No real program for action. No planning except as some sort of abstract function carried on to mollify the conservationists, but with no relation to what is going on in the state.

The easy thing, I suppose, would be to blame the Reagan administration for this state of affairs. Obviously, the present administration is mainly responsible. And indeed, on occasion in this report, the administration shows as much interest in encouraging exploiters of natural resources as in controlling them. The report proposes, for example, that the word "conservation" be dropped from the state's lexicon and replaced by the term "resource management." Or—perhaps a more clear-cut example—it says that the *first* goal for the management of resources in California should be " . . . to seek an optimum balance between economic and social benefits to be derived from the State's natural resources." To say the least, that is a funny way of describing resource-management goals. Are social and economic benefits to be considered antithetical? If so, then we are not talking here about economic benefits, we are talking about the exploitation of resources without regard to the social consequences.

But Pat Brown's administration is also responsible. It was in the Brown administration that the state planners, bedazzled by one or two experts in the relatively new "systems" approach to planning, began to conclude that the State Development Plan did not need to be specific about the future of California. There would be no maps, for example, establishing or proposing desirable land uses. The State Development Plan was to contain statements of policy controlling land use. It was to set up "methods" of planning for the future. It was to offer "alternatives," about a dozen of them at any given moment. There would be methods of developing alternatives and methods of evaluating alternatives. Everything would be set forth except a course of action for protecting the California environment.

Now you can see what happened to this already-doubtful Brown administration heritage when it got into the hands of the Reagan administration with its built-in indifference to planning. The proposed statements of policy, the methods for determining and evaluating alternatives, quickly became a bunch of platitudes written in bureaucratese— the oatmeal we have before us.

A decade ago, when our environmental problems in California were smaller, we were breathing life into state planning. We declared for a State Development Plan. Now, with problems greater than ever, we have a Non-Plan designed to give us all tired blood.

What is left for us but to subside into destruction-as-usual in California? Well, there is always hope, and new blood. The politician in this state who sets his sights on the environmental issue—the complete failure of previous political administrations to avert the disaster creeping up on us; the fantastic price the taxpayers are paying for the slurbanization of the California landscape; the social costs, the social disruption, the lives lost or maimed, the beauty that we are allowing to slip from our grasp, the beautiful life Californians could lead if . . . the first politician to grab this issue as the major issue just might be able to command the respect of Californians and of their children after them.

In the interim, the legislature could well reject the Non-Plan as a subversion of its will, and demand that a State Development Plan be produced forthwith.

WILLIE L. BROWN, JR.   1969

State Planning: The Cities and the Deprived

To the extent that California's planning program, as expressed in the long-awaited State Development Plan Program Report released early this year, pertains to problems of the poor and of our cities, it is worthless by any measure. A few examples will do to illustrate the total irrelevance of the so-called program.

First, you should know that California has no state housing and community development policy. No goals of financial assistance to individuals or local governments, of houses to build, of neighborhoods to be improved, or of run-down dwellings to be rehabilitated, have been adopted so that state action can be planned and executed. More damning, nobody in state government and nobody in state planning evidently thinks there should be any advocacy of such goals in the so-called state planning program.

Second, there is the question of urban education. The report does take note of the generally low achievement of disadvantaged children in the public schools. It then merely recommends that the "Department of Education and the Department of Finance prepare a program for fully meeting the needs of the low-achieving pupils of the state, including alternative means for implementing such a program."

Well, even so enlightened an educator as Max Rafferty [the controversial state schools chief of the day] knows what is needed—money. His recommendation for 1969 was $325 million more in state aid; the Governor requested $105 million. The state's planners recommend *more study*. There is *nothing* in the state's program report about the real failure of the current system to reflect the desperate plight of many urban parents—poor, confused, often poorly educated in southern school systems, but desiring that their kids get a better break. Such a break is going to take more teachers, better trained teachers, smaller classes, better equipment, and whole new approaches in teaching methods.

The greatest failure of the state's planning program—and the classic case of its irrelevance—is its effort on behalf of the disadvantaged. The report puts it this way: "The number of the disadvantaged in our society has assumed significant proportions. . . . It is imperative that the problem be adequately understood and that efforts be clearly directed towards realistic goals and objectives which will assure that the funds now spent will achieve both maximum impact and lasting benefits. . . ."

All this results in four recommendations for state action: (1) that the state study, develop and declare general and specific social and economic goals for state government with respect to the problems of the disadvantaged; (2) that the state study current programs that deal with the disadvantaged; (3) that the state study the feasibility of developing a pragmatic approach to handling the problems of disadvantagement; and (4) that the state establish a manpower center using computer technology to match men with jobs or training.

Now, all this is good, fine and repetitious, but it doesn't say anything about the problem. I challenge Governor Reagan to get one idea for solid policy out of the report's section on the disadvantaged.

214

Why, planners were talking—and talking more sense—about these problems ten years ago. Where is the commitment to end discrimination with state law and enforcement of equal education, job and housing provisions? Where is the call for state action to rebuild our cities and create the new cities that must be built to house 20 million new Californians by the year 2000? Where are the plans to create whole new industries using state funds, if necessary, for job development and training?

Our state plans should contain such bold proposals. They don't.

CASPAR W. WEINBERGER   1969

Rebuttal

Those who worked diligently to prepare and make available the state report cannot help but be deeply disappointed in the tone and content of "The Life and Death of State Planning in California." Personally, I was particularly disappointed because the article revealed to me how shallow, superficial and headline-hunting *Cry California* can be. As a member of long standing of the California Tomorrow advisory board, and as an enthusiastic supporter of the magazine, I had expected far more intelligent treatment of this important subject.

The State Development Plan Program is more than a single or static instrument. It certainly is not a physical planning document, nor was it ever intended to be. It is rather a combination of relevant information and processes directed toward identifying goals and marshalling the resources necessary to solve problems that confront the people of California now and for many years into the future. State development planning must continuously move forward in time to provide a focus and a sound foundation for the formulation and review of broad development policy.

The idea that a large state such as California, with its several departments in state government, many with development-related programs, along with 58 counties, over 400 cities, and almost 3,700 special districts—each of the latter with varying responsibilities in the area of development—could undertake the "blueprinting" of statewide development and planning for all of these vastly different governmental organizations is patently absurd. Such a theory ignores the basic physical, social, economic, and political facts that are inherent in such complicated inter- and intragovernmental relationships. It also fails to consider the interests and capabilities of the independent and private sectors who have much to contribute. Yet, apparently *Cry California* expected a blueprint telling everyone what to do far into the future.

Comparisons to Hawaii are misleading. The State of Hawaii is unique, as well as beautiful. Statehood came to this group of islands at a very recent date and, consequently, the framers of its constitution, its state organization, and public policies and the interrelationship of its governmental units differ totally from California and from most other states. A comparison between California and Hawaii ought to contrast the differences in size, population, geography, and isolated position. Hawaii, with a land area of 6,424 square miles, is about the size of Siskiyou County, and its population is 786,000. Five of California's counties (Alameda, Los Angeles, Orange, San Diego and Santa Clara) are more populous than the whole state of Hawaii. At Hawaii's scale, and without any significant prior planning by its component parts, it is agreed that statewide planning and programming is not only feasible, it is probably desirable indeed. To attempt, however, similar centralized direction of detailed planning and programming for a state as large as California from Sacramento, in the face of our vast regional, physical and economic differences, is unworkable and unrealistic, to put it mildly. We have neither the legal authority nor the philosophical inclination to centralize in the state government this type of process in California. To do so would be to cut off the creativity of the jurisdictions within the state.

In recognition of the many positive and constructive suggestions in the State Development Plan Report, comments were received from leading planners, conservationists, and those whose life work is saving California's great resources for the future. These favorable reactions from experts and officials well recognized in the field of planning and development were expressed in such comments as: "an important fundamental instrument for sound growth," "exciting in its bold concepts and intentionally challenging, offer(ing) an unprecedented opportunity for the creative planning necessary to solve the multifarious . . . problems . . . facing the state," and "broad in its vision." Indeed, the *Cry California* article, and a few newspaper articles based on quotes from it, constitute the only really adverse reaction to the report.

The California Development Plan Program Report does present a program for action—not simplistic, single-purpose advocacy of good causes, but a program that stresses the urgency of the many issues facing

216

our state and the interrelations between issues. It sets forth various types of policy and program decisions that must be made by the decision-makers of California as we work to enhance our environment and provide a better life for our citizens, and it suggests a process through which these are achievable. It demonstrates the need for sophisticated intelligence gathering, which can do much to ensure that those decisions will be wisely made.

The section on transportation outlines major changes in transportation policy as well as essential alterations in state and local financing and organization. Integrated planning for all modes of transportation, and proposed action steps by the state in improving decision making at state and local levels are specified. Economic development, use of resources, and issues of urban development are only a few of the major areas addressed. The policy alternatives raised in the report, like those in the transportation section, have an impact on state policy in California.

State planning in California is not dead, though such a phrase has an attraction for writers who prefer headlines to solid accomplishment.

We are well aware that the problems are great, that our knowledge is inadequate and our resources are limited. The state administration shares *Cry California's* commitment to the cause of conservation, to the mitigation of adverse social consequences of exploitation of resources, and to the need for taking constructive and positive actions regarding the many physical, social and economic challenges our state faces. We have no doubt that the people of California will succeed in meeting these problems, given sufficient accurate information far enough in advance, which is one of the things the state can and should provide.

However, a constructive and creative partnership will have to be maintained between government at all levels, the private sector and individual citizens and citizen groups. Organizations such as California Tomorrow, well recognized for its dedication to the causes of conservation, could help greatly in building that creative relationship. Future policy makers, both legislative and executive, will need all collaboration and help if our approach to the utilization of the state's resources is to proceed more rationally in the future than it has in the past. We urgently invite that collaboration.

There is plenty to criticize in our past and our present. Those who wish to engage in something more practical and helpful than ill-prepared rhetorical exercises will not only be welcomed, they are desperately needed.

217

III   *The California Tomorrow Plan*

11 *The California Tomorrow Plan*

• A few months after denouncing the state's feeble gesture at a State Development Plan, Heller began rounding up a team to put together a plan of California Tomorrow's own.

It might be argued (and was, by some) that this was not the most important step to take at that point. No need, some of Heller's advisors felt, to seek new solutions to the familiar problems: the challenge was rather to put into practice solutions already well known. Heller demurred. "I never bought the notion that the world is full of good ideas, it's just a matter of getting them implemented. I think the world is full of bum ideas—but that, if people would take ten minutes, they could develop good ones." California Tomorrow was going to take the metaphorical ten minutes and come up with something of genuine value—an uncompromised best-we-can-do.

It took, of course, more than ten minutes—or ten months. But considering its scale and ambitiousness, the model state plan was created in very short order indeed. And its budget— about $50,000 in all, almost half of it contributed by California Tomorrow members—was truly austere.

The group that came together to work on the plan was pretty high-powered. One key figure was Harvey Perloff, dean of Architecture and Urban Planning at UCLA. Another was Assemblyman Willie Brown. Bill Roth and Jack Abbott were regulars from California Tomorrow; Heller himself chaired the group. Nat Owings of Skidmore, Owings and Merrill, the architectural firm, was part of the team, and suggested, as main staff person, his associate Marc Goldstein.

Goldstein was not a planner by training. Heller liked that. "I felt that an architect might be better able to come through with a structure that would work. I was also very worried about plan- ners' language." Architects, Heller thought, might talk straighter.

The first challenge was to plan how to plan, to find a rationale. Heller: "The staff did what Marc called a 'systems probe,' which at the time was not widely done in planning, and developed this scheme showing the array of problems besetting our society and the underlying causes for those problems." These causes in turn suggested, or at least gave an order to, a series of proposed solutions.

Heller had been scornful of the 'systems approach' when the state's consultants tried it on the State Development Plan; now he embraced it. The difference, one gathers, was simply that Goldstein and company were doing a better job.

Work proceeded in small meetings and seminars. Often guests were brought in—representatives of labor, for instance, and of minority groups—to brief the planners on their concerns. Willie Brown and Harvey Perloff were particularly insistent that the plan not confine itself to land and structures, but make dramatic proposals for dealing with such social problems as housing shortages and poverty. Out of this grew, among other things, a proposal for a national guaranteed-income floor.

A key question, recognized early, was whether these programs and regulations could be set up without intruding unduly on personal liberties. Here the proposed regional governments emerged as part of the solution, not as part of the problem—only if there are regional legislatures, directly elected, can the voters even begin to control the future of the regional communities they live in. It was partly for this reason that the planning team decided to propose a regional government in every region of the state, not just in the metropolitan areas that California Tomorrow had considered candidates for such government in the past.

New "community councils," sublocal advisory groups to be formed within cities and counties, would be another mechanism to increase people's access to the levers of power. Campaign reform was emphasized for similar reasons.

Early in 1971 a draft of the plan was published—on newsprint, as a tabloid. The modest format, chosen at Bill Roth's suggestion, was meant to show the plan as a work-in-progress, something that its reviewers still could influence.

In April, the plan was presented at a two-day conference at the Palace Hotel in San Francisco. The organizers, veterans of those unprofitable conferences at which the convinced preach to the convinced, were determined to bring out a better cross-section of Californians. They succeeded. The result was a lot of useful criticism, along with general acclaim.

The 600 people who gathered at the Palace seemed to treat the occasion almost as a constitutional convention. They spoke and debated as though the object before them were a plan proposed by a government for early application, not just a prototype. There was a rare feeling of power. Environmental journalist Harold Gilliam summed up the general feeling in his *San Francisco Chronicle* column: "Finally, at last, at last, somebody is beginning to do what needs to be done."

The big conference was followed by many smaller ones around the state (and one in Washington, D.C.). These were aimed at cementing contacts with a variety of interest groups. A particularly lively seminar at UCLA was filmed and broadcast on local television. "I don't know of a group that wasn't supportive, after we got through with all the meetings," Heller recalls.

The revision of the plan took about a year. An elaborate file was set up to match each comment that came in with the exact spot in the plan to which it applied. The decision to change or not to change was Heller's. Though the framework remained the same, there were in fact some shifts and additions. In response to many requests, a lot more was said about the economics of the plan; the section on health care was expanded at the urging of advisory board member Russel Lee. More examples were given of how particular problems might be solved by the proposed government tools. One of the proposals for population control—that an entry fee be charged to persons moving into California to cover the added services they will require—was omitted.

The revised plan, published as a book, was also well received. It was not (as some of its enthusiastic early readers hoped) immediately translated into bills and pushed through in Sacramento. But then the authors had not encouraged such hopes. The plan had proved what it set out to prove: that such a pattern for the state could be designed; that it could be put together fairly quickly; that it could be done relatively cheaply; and that, once done, it could command very wide support.

It was never insisted that *The California Tomorrow Plan* be regarded as *the* answer to California's difficulties, *the* hope for California's future. The fundamental purpose of the effort was to make people think in a way they had not before—and to spur them, if they rejected California Tomorrow's solutions, to offer solutions of their own. "It is a challenge," Alfred Heller wrote in introducing the plan, "both to those who now wield power and to those who are critical of 'the system': are you making a better plan?"

Styles in planning and politics change, but that challenge is permanently valid.

———

Before it gets down to stating its recommendations for future action, *The California Tomorrow Plan* plays the game of alternative futures. It describes California as it appeared at the time of the plan's preparation and labels this picture "California Zero." California Zero looks pretty bad. Then it makes a projection into the future of that California Zero, estimating what things will be like if we do not take hold of our situation in a dramatic new way: this scenario is labeled California One. California One looks worse. Then comes the core of the document: recommendations for a better future, to be produced by new government structures and a coordinated attack on the problems; this the authors call California Two. California Two is the *plan* part of *The California Tomorrow Plan*.

But it is out of California Zero that the analysis flows. The planners begin by listing the "disruptions" threatening the quality of life and the environment in California, and find 21 of them, ranging from depletion of open space and agricultural land to unemployment and crime. These are first grouped, simply enough, according to who or what is suffering damage: people, land, or physical structures. But a more probing analysis shows that the distruptions can be sorted more usefully according to their causes: and that, behind the immediate causes, more fundamental sources of disorder can be discerned. The *Plan* summarizes the elaborate process by which Goldstein and the others arrived at four major "underlying causes" of what ails us. Each cause suggests an equally fundamental approach to solution.

1. *Lack of individual political strength.* (Government institutions are neither as efficient nor as democratic as they need to be. Too often they push people around while failing to get the

Four underlying causes of disruption emerge from the matrix of direct causes

A PARTIAL LIST OF CAUSES

A. Obsolete governmental institutions
B. Inaccessibility to effective individual control
C. Overcontrol of individual action
D. Distribution pattern of income, goods, and services
E. Effect of tax structure
F. Lack of finance
G. Little public control of destructive activities
H. Infrastructure location
I. Population growth
J. Consumption practices
K. Limited resource supply
L. Effect of market system

DISRUPTIONS

LAND/AIR/WATER
1. Energy resources
2. Water sources
3. Wild lands & open spaces
4. Agricultural land
5. Species
6. Air quality
7. Water quality
8. Noise
9. Visual order

STRUCTURES
10. Transportation
11. Energy distribution & communications
12. Solid waste
13. Disaster-prone structures
14. Housing
15. Community facilities

PEOPLE
16. Employment
17. Education
18. Health
19. Recreation
20. Civil order
21. Security

1 LACK OF INDIVIDUAL POLITICAL STRENGTH
2 LACK OF INDIVIDUAL ECONOMIC STRENGTH
3 DAMAGING DISTRIBUTION OF POPULATION
4 DAMAGING PATTERNS OF RESOURCE CONSUMPTION

225

real job done.) *Policy:* "Provide political strength" by revising government structures for greater effectiveness and for easier citizen control.

2. *Lack of individual economic strength.* (Wealth is unequally divided, and the tax structure and the inadequacy of some government services tend to magnify and perpetuate the inequity.) *Policy:* "Provide economic strength" through employment programs, public works projects, improved services, and federal income supports.

3. *Damaging distribution of population.* (People are settling in the wrong places; the destructive effects of overgrowth and misplaced growth are not well controlled.) *Policy:* "Guide settlement" through statewide land-use zoning and other means.

4. *Damaging patterns of resource use.* (We are using limited resources wastefully; the "free" market system as now constituted tends to encourage waste; rising population makes all problems worse.) *Policy:* "Guide resource use" through taxes and subsidies, and by working to stabilize population.

These four policies can be rolled up into one sweeping statement of purpose: "To provide for personal fulfillment within an amenable environment."

In *The California Tomorrow Plan,* the four proposed "driving policies" organize the discussion of the alternate future called California Two. The state is seen as adopting these policies, which then pervade its planning. Ideas and proposals are grouped according to the policy they serve.

To summarize the nuts and bolts of the proposed system, here is a piece by Alfred Heller based on remarks introducing the tabloid version to the San Francisco conference in April, 1971. As modified here, it reflects the *Plan* in its final form.

ALFRED HELLER   1971

The Plan in Brief

Driving Policy One:
Provide Political Strength

Driving Policy One provides for direct public control over state development policy at virtually every level. This central policy (as well as the other three) is served largely by new or refurbished governmental mechanisms.

First of all, the state's planning and budgeting functions are combined and placed in one strong agency, the state planning agency. This agency is supervised by an 11-member State Planning Council, four members of which are the governor, who is chairman, and three cabinet members. Seven representatives of the general public are appointed by the governor to four-year, staggered terms, and confirmed by the legislature. Public members receive salaries equal to those of the highest-paid cabinet members. This council has the job of guiding and directing the state planning agency in the preparation every year of the California State Plan.

The California State Plan is a state plan *and coordinated state budget* with long-term and short-term features. It has three sections—a Land section, a Structures section, and a People section. It is built upon four central policies and contains a state zoning plan, a state infrastructure plan, and a number of California standards insuring environmental amenity and social well-being. In other words, in the California Two we imagine, the state plan happens to be organized along the lines of *The California Tomorrow Plan*.

The state planning council submits the annual plan and budget to the governor. Guided by them, the governor then submits to the legislature for adoption his plan and budget, with appropriate explanation of any changes he has made in the original version. Then every year the legislature adopts an annually up-dated version of the state plan and the coordinated state budget. If the public does not like the results, it can vote in a new governor or new legislators. The new governor will immediately control four of the eleven members of the planning council (three agency heads and himself) and will gain majority control in due course. However, the holdover public members of the council from the

227

previous administration protect the council and its staff arm, the state planning agency, from rash changes of direction.

Driving Policy One also establishes regional governments for every region of the state. For the first time, the public is enfranchised to deal with major issues that heretofore had been either ignored by local governments or aggravated by the actions or inactions of local government and the operations of a multiplicity of single-purpose regional agencies. Open space, housing, air and water pollution, transportation, waste disposal, tax equalization, health-care facilities and other matters of regional concern are now dealt with in a regional context.

In addition, existing counties become full municipal governments, like the cities able to provide a full range of services. Through these established local governments, "community councils" are established to bring public decision-making from every neighborhood to all aspects of planning within the region.

Finally, policy one includes public subsidies of political campaigns, limitations on the length of campaigns, and other measures to prevent elections from being taken over completely by special, powerful, economic interests.

Thus, in California Two the public has stronger and more direct control over the shape and character and the life of its cities and regions than it has ever had before.

Driving Policy Two:
Provide Economic Strength

Driving Policy Two aims to protect the economic interests of individuals, and the ability of society to pay for its conservation and development goals. Its purposes are served by truly massive state and regional building and rebuilding programs that provide major job opportunities. The regional improvement programs are financed largely by the federal government through a Federal Conservation and Development Bank. The *Plan,* in fact, offers a fairly detailed proposal for a state and regional system of planning, budgeting and financing that translates an extremely broad range of popular goals into achievement.

In addition, under policy two, the state calls for and helps to obtain a federal program providing not a bare survival income, but sufficient means, through an income floor, for each family or individual to live modestly in healthful surroundings. An income floor is established, for example, at $6,000 a year for a family of four.

228

Regions of California

Planning districts as adopted
by the Council on Intergovernmental Relations

1
Del Norte
Humboldt
Mendocino
Lake

2
Siskiyou   Tehama
Modoc   Plumas
Trinity   Glenn
Shasta   Butte
Lassen   Colusa

3
Sierra   Placer
Nevada   El Dorado
Yuba   Yolo
Sutter   Sacramento

4
Sonoma
Napa
Solano
Marin
San Francisco
Contra Costa
Alameda
San Mateo
Santa Clara

5
Alpine   San Joaquin
Amador   Stanislaus
Calaveras   Merced
Tuolumne

10
Mono
Inyo

6
Mariposa
Madera
Fresno
Kings
Tulare
Kern

7
Santa Cruz
San Benito
Monterey
San Luis Obispo
Santa Barbara

8
Ventura
Los Angeles
San Bernardino
Orange
Riverside
Imperial

9
San Diego

Driving Policy Three:
Guide Settlement

Under Driving Policy Three, state zones are established. They define in general which areas may be built upon and which may not be (these zones also serve driving policy four, "guide resource use," by protecting the state's most valuable open lands, including agricultural lands). There are four state zones:

Agricultural, including all Classes 1 and 2 and some Class 3 soils;

Conservation, including lands of ecological, scenic, and historical importance;

Urban, including essentially only lands that have already become urban; and

Regional reserves, including lands not in the other categories.

Driving Policy Three also includes specific California standards having to do with amenity—air quality standards, for example; water quality standards; extremely tough regulations concerning the use of pesticides; and minimum open space standards for populated areas. It includes maximum noise levels. It includes performance standards for the development of transportation facilities.

It includes a "state infrastructure plan," a plan for the movement network of people, goods, water, wastes, energy, and information.

It establishes regulations that must be met by the regions regarding health-care facilities, educational and cultural facilities, employment centers, correctional facilities, industrial locations, and other established facilities and services.

That is policy three, "to develop a framework for settlement."

Driving Policy Four:
Guide Resource Use

Driving Policy Four includes a state population policy that aims for a stable population, or zero growth. This is brought about by policies such as limiting the number of children eligible for income-tax exemptions to two, leaving abortion as a medical matter to be decided entirely between a woman and her physician, and setting up new, constitutional controls over in-migration.

While population policy limits the number of consumers, a system of taxes, fees, fines, and other measures works directly to limit excessive consumption of valuable, limited resources. It includes the assess-

California's four state zones

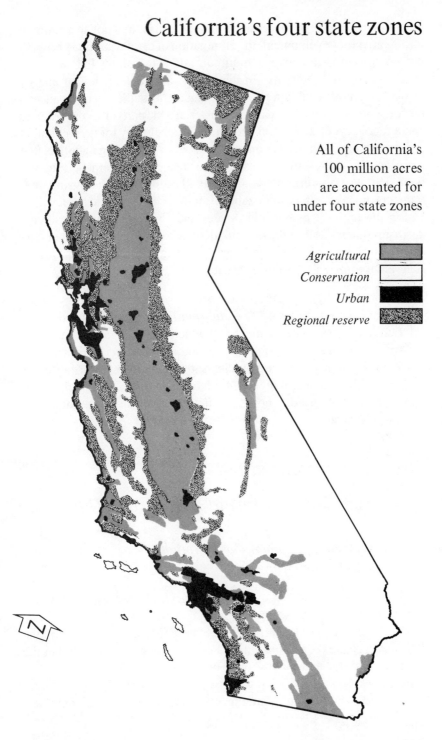

All of California's
100 million acres
are accounted for
under four state zones

Agricultural

Conservation

Urban

Regional reserve

ment of land for tax purposes according to its use, and not according to its potential for development; the elimination of capital gains tax relief; a tax on horsepower above a minimum standard of 65 hp; taxes on excessive use of electricity, to discourage undue depletion of energy resources; an oil-depletion tax rather than an oil-depletion allowance; a tax on containers and packaging materials as part of a program to encourage recycling; a tax on automobiles to help pay for their eventual removal and recycling; a tax on redwood or other building materials that represent limited resources; a tax on the "unearned increment"; regulations that severely discourage and virtually eliminate interbasin water transfers in favor of desalinization, total reclamation, and recycling within the regions; a schedule of fees and fines automatically levied against polluters. All of these regulations require a commitment and an ability on the part of the state to apply strong enforcement, through a state environmental protection agency.

• Three key sections of *The California Tomorrow Plan* follow: first, a discussion of the means by which regional governments would finance their programs; second, a "tour" of California Two, including two case studies showing how regions might deal with particular nagging problems; and third, the concluding section suggesting how the whole *Plan* apparatus might be put in place.

ALFRED HELLER, Editor   1972

From *The California Tomorrow Plan*

*Paying for Regional Conservation
and Development*

In brief, here is a step-by-step summary of how the regional programs are put together and paid for:

First, the regional plan identifies the particular problems of the region in each area of responsibility. For example, the plan examines the location, supply, and quality of housing in the region and identifies deficiencies.

Second, within state planning guidelines, the regional plan sets

232

forth for each problem area a program to meet the deficiencies, using all resources available, private and public. In the case of housing, existing programs and procedures—involving, for example, FHA-guaranteed construction, ordinary privately financed housing, public housing, and various types of subsidized housing—would be applied to meet the identified needs, and coordinated with the overall financing provided by the Conservation and Development Bank.

Third, economic evaluations are conducted for each area of responsibility. The economic evaluation includes a benefit-cost study. This is a balance sheet that shows the full costs of a program as against the full benefits.

In addition to a benefit-cost study, the economic evaluation includes a study of financial feasibility that shows to what extent the program can pay for itself. This study lists and compares all expected public and private expenditure for the program and anticipated income in connection with it. Thus, a study might take into account federal and state grants and loans; income from sources such as the sale of services; taxes generated by the program; and the major and essential participation of the private sector.

Fourth, economic evaluations for all areas of responsibility are then combined, rationalized and totaled, to arrive at a comprehensive analysis for the total regional conservation and development program.

In other words, a total program is prepared to meet the major problems of a total region, and demonstrated on balance to be economically justified and feasible.

Traditionally, large public works have been financed through single-purpose bond issues (schools, rapid transit, water systems), or single-purpose loans (dams). Some public works, such as strategically placed bridges, are very profitable, while others, like public housing, operate at a loss. In California Two, comprehensive, low-interest financing is used to underwrite all aspects of regional development. Revenue-producing investments are included with nonrevenue-producing investments in one economic package.

By this procedure, for example, strong revenue-producing elements of the regional program, such as water development and distribution, can help carry drug rehabilitation programs.

Fifth, the regional government adopts its conservation and development program and accompanying financing proposals. These include yearly performance budgets in each area of responsibility, and a listing of projects by priority.

233

The total regional program, the analyses supporting it, and the financing arrangements are covered in a comprehensive authorizing document prepared by the region.

Sixth, the State Planning Council must certify that the program is within the guides of the California State Plan. The governor then submits the total program to the Congress and asks for authorization of the federally guaranteed and funded parts of the program.

The Congress considers a full regional program, perhaps involving several billion dollars of public funds, before authorizing the federal features of it. This employs, on a large scale, procedures similar to those used in the past for area resource-development programs prepared by the Department of Agriculture.

After federal authorization, the regional program receives yearly funding through the budgets of the regional, state and federal agencies involved and from the Federal Conservation and Development Bank.

The regional government makes an annual report on the progress of the total program and recommends changes as necessary. Its conclusions are transmitted to the appropriate congressional committees and the federal agencies involved, and reflected in the annually adopted regional plan and budget and the budgets of local government.

Property Taxes

State assessment policy enables the regional government to assess all property taxes in the region. The region uses a portion of these monies for its own support, and allocates the remainder to the cities, municipal counties and other governmental agencies in the region on the basis of local needs reflected in the regional budget. This is a major tool to help the region coordinate the activities of other agencies, in carrying out its conservation and development program. It is a means for equalizing the tax burden within the region.

Public Corporations

In order to help realize regional plans, the state authorizes regional governments to charter public corporations capable of carrying out large-scale, integrated regional projects from planning to land acquisition through construction and leasing. The New York State Urban Development Corporation, established in 1968, is an example of a public corporation.

An entirely new community might be built by a public corporation, as an example. The corporation operates by the rules of the state and

234

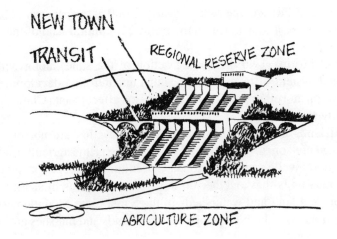

regional plans. No housing is planned in zones subject to hazardous earthquakes, fires, floods, or landslides. State agricultural and conservation zones and amenity requirements are incorporated in all project plans.

Aided by loan guarantees and by grants and loans from the Federal Conservation and Development Bank, the corporation plans the new community and buys the land, through eminent domain if necessary. It may construct and lease the facilities on its own or by contract. It can also lease land to other entities for housing and for commercial purposes. Surplus funds go to support underfinanced but necessary projects in the regional program. The corporation builds parks and schools, and transportation facilities to connect with the regional grid. It does what is necessary to complete its project in every aspect.

Regional renewal programs in established cities are carried out by public corporations in the same way.

California Two in Operation

The driving policies are intended to work together to solve the state's major problems. Will they? How can the California Two framework be applied to critical problems? One way of finding answers to these questions is to take recognized problems and "test out" how well California Two, with its emphasis on regional planning and development, would deal with them. Two examples follow:

1. *How can needed open space be assured in Santa Clara County?* In the 1960s and into the 1970s, the lands of Santa Clara County were

235

urbanizing at the average rate of nearly 4,000 acres per year. Most of this development took place on the prime agricultural land of the Santa Clara Valley.

In California Two the zoning action of the state, along with the reformed system of land taxation, stops uncontrolled development of agricultural and other open-space lands. This affects Santa Clara County as follows:

All lands in the south Santa Clara Valley that are not presently urbanized are zoned "agricultural." Remaining prime agricultural lands in the north valley are also zoned agricultural (except for single or contiguous units that together do not exceed 25 acres in size).

Forested land and watersheds in the Santa Cruz Mountains, steep slopes in the Mt. Hamilton range, and bay lands and marshes are zoned "conservation."

Lands of the Santa Clara Valley that are already urbanized are zoned "urban."

The eastern foothills and plots of open land under 25 acres within urban areas are zoned "regional reserve."

Because open land in California Two is zoned by the state, and only the state can change the agricultural and conservation zones, the land is protected from pressures for development. Speculators are discouraged from buying open lands in the hope of converting them to urban uses. Because all lands are assessed for tax purposes according to their zones, owners of agricultural and other open-space lands are no longer forced to sell out under tax pressures.

The government of Region 4, which includes seven Bay Area counties, is required by law to prepare a regional conservation and development plan and budget, within the guidelines of the California State Plan.

The state zones are incorporated in the regional plan. The regional plan adopts limits for urban development in the regional reserve zone. In its open-space section, the plan specifies how the remaining open spaces in the regional reserve are to be protected.

To meet (or exceed) regional park minimum requirements, there is a program of park land acquisition and maintenance. The open-space section of the regional plan also adheres to other parts of the state plan, such as the minimum requirements for open space in urban neighborhoods. But the exact way that all this is done is decided after give-and-take among the regional planning agency, the cities and counties, their community councils, private owners, and the general public.

To meet local open-space requirements, the plan of the people of one community might propose to convert many of the local streets to green strips, retaining only a bare essential of narrowed streets to allow for bus and other small local transit systems (in 1970, paved streets covered 30,000 acres of land in Santa Clara county).

Another community might convert vacant lots or those with decrepit houses into miniparks. Or a municipal plan could choose to purchase isolated houses in outlying areas, turn the outlying lands into green-space, or even restore them as agricultural land, and concentrate development in the central districts.

The region takes all of these projects into account and makes an economic analysis of the total regional open-space program, and this, along with economic analyses in other action areas (housing, transportation, etc.), is used in drawing up the regional plan and budget. Once the regional government adopts a total program, the Congress authorizes the federal features of it, and the specified funding begins, all of the people of Santa Clara County can be assured of an extensive open-space preservation program, from every residential neighborhood to the surrounding hillsides. They know which open spaces are going to be preserved and for what purposes, when this is going to happen, and where the money is coming from.

2. *How can a pleasing and serviceable transportation system be developed in the Santa Barbara area?* The Santa Barbara basin is subject to air inversions. As the number of automobiles increases, the area becomes very susceptible to smog. U.S. Highway 101, a major north-south route, runs through the west side of the city, as does the Southern Pacific's north-south rail line. The highway is subject to some congestion. It acts as a barrier that separates the downtown from the beach area, and generates noise and air pollution.

U.S. 101 serves as a link between Los Angeles and San Francisco, but a large part of its traffic comes from people traveling locally in the South Coast area. Because of a lack of low-income housing in Santa Barbara, many persons who work in the city live in the Carpinteria area and use U.S. 101 to travel to work. In addition, many faculty members and employees of the UC Santa Barbara campus at Goleta live south of Santa Barbara. There is no rapid bus or rail link between Santa Barbara, Carpinteria, and Goleta. Nor is there a satisfactory public-transit system linking various neighborhoods and outlying areas with the central business district or the beaches.

The state infrastructure plan of California Two would include a

237

section on this area. The government of Region 7 (coastal counties, Santa Cruz to Santa Barbara) is required to include a transportation element in its comprehensive regional plan and budget. In assembling a transportation program, the regional planning agency might first suggest to the Santa Barbara municipalities (city and county) some general, alternative approaches to solving transportation problems.

The municipalities and the community councils would hold public hearings on the alternatives, and express their own planning objectives. In due course a preliminary regional plan, including the transportation section, would be published and subjected to public hearings in the counties. A final plan would be adopted by the regional legislature.

It might retain the old U.S. 101 at four lanes in width, underground in the downtown Santa Barbara area (State, Anacapa, and Santa Barbara streets would pass over the underground portion), and designate a new freeway-bypass route. The north-south Southern Pacific tracks might be designated for commuter train service along the coast. An improved local bus system would connect outlying areas with the city center, in keeping with state access standards.

The proposed system would, of course, be justified in planning and engineering studies. An economic feasibility study would accompany not only the proposed transportation program but the entire regional plan and program. Sources of funds—local, regional, state, federal and private—would all be specified so that regional and local budgets would be geared to the accomplishment of the program. Thus the piecemeal "solutions" of the past, imposed upon Santa Barbara by the state bureaucracy or by one or another local agency, are replaced by a comprehensive regional approach to planning and conservation closely related to the region, its citizens and their needs.

A Tour of California Two

The foregoing examples show how the California Two structure might be capable of helping people solve actual problems in real places. The development of similar studies in all regions for all of the major disruptions would begin to bring into focus a picture of life in California Two, as follows:

A community that, in the early 1970s, was part of an array of aging, run-down central-city homes, has now been largely redeemed in a regional renewal program carried out over more than two decades, step by logical step. Many homes and apartments have been renovated;

238

others have been replaced; some have been removed to create neighbor-hood parks; the installation of new public transportation facilities in the area has permitted some streets to be closed off and turned into play-grounds or gardens. New clusters of offices and stores, churches and meeting places have sprung up around the transit stops. The area is safer and far more pleasant than most communities were in the past.

The old, established cities are still sprawled out, but not much more than they were in the 1970s. They come to a stop at their boundaries, at the edge of the urban zone, and beyond that there is farmland or undeveloped hills.

The shape of a community is determined in a good measure by what people want. The community council has a strong voice in city and county planning. Decisions must be in keeping with the regional plan and the priorities of the regional budget. There are practical considera-tions, such as the financing available from the Federal Conservation and Development Bank and other sources. Nevertheless, local imagination and preference come through. The big-city communities are quite dif-ferent from one another in size, in layout, in architectural appearance, and in other characteristics. All housing has to be within standards set by the California State Plan.

The population has leveled off at about 30 million, an increase of ten million since 1970. New cities have absorbed some of these people, but most of them have been accommodated in existing urban areas. Also, rural assistance programs have encouraged people to stay on the land.

Because of the pattern of concentrated urban development in Cali-fornia Two, government does not have to extend municipal services such as water-supply and waste-disposal facilities into every corner of the far countryside. State conservation and agricultural zones are not open to urban development. Many regional-reserve lands are left open or in low-density housing, by choice of the regions.

A wide choice among residential locations is now available to those who, in the past, could not afford to move out of neighborhoods they did not like. This results from expanded job opportunities, a guaranteed income floor, and new or renewed housing that meets "California Standards" of amenity and availability.

Because of the income floor, people are not locked into dead-end employment, nor do they have to face the specter of prolonged unem-ployment or dependency on relief. They do not need to fight or train for jobs that are not available. At the same time, the income floor is not munificent, and most people want to work and have the opportunity of working. There are a great many jobs offered, year after year, as each additional increment to the major regional development programs is built. These multibillion-dollar programs provide employment directly, and also cause many more jobs to be created in support industries and services. The state encourages other kinds of development in keeping with the goals of the California State Plan. The statewide employment-information network brings early warning to the local schools and training institutions of what skills will be needed.

The schools are centers of year-round study and they inspire all kinds of avocational and recreational activity. Activities formerly considered "hobbies," such as fine craftsmanship or organic gardening, have become full-time pursuits. Under the regional development program, schools at all levels become centers of community life. Their libraries, classes, electronic equipment, their spirit of awakening, serve not only students but all the people of the area.

There is a complete system of health care. Everyone is covered by a national health program. The option of choosing a private doctor is open, but there is a publicly provided health clinic for every community, and a regional system of hospitals and care programs for the aged and mentally ill. The community councils help determine the character of each local clinic. The cost of providing adequate health care is high.

Public transportation forms the skeleton of entire urban regions. Regional transportation systems are based on a combination of rapid-transit lines of various kinds—minirail, computer-controlled jitneys, buses, other feeder vehicles and "people moving" conveyances in commercial centers or neighborhood residential areas. Nonpolluting automobiles are used extensively, but it is not necessary for individuals to own automobiles; there are attractive alternatives.

Transit systems provide good service for entire cities and may include a concentrated grid covering 100 square miles or more in sprawling areas like Los Angeles, with high-speed connectors to other communities in the region. The regional transportation system is an integral part of the regional plan and is used as a basis for areawide renewal. It makes possible, for example, the conversion in large sections of Los Angeles of over half the established street grid, including freeways that existed in California Zero, to greenways of various kinds. The planning possibilities, right down to the residential neighborhood level, are exciting when the established street grid of California Zero can be regarded not simply as a paved-over runway for cars but as a public resource of almost limitless opportunity.

The transit stations become centers of activity—stores, offices, health facilities, some apartments, places of worship, recreational areas, plazas, theaters, meeting places. The land surrounding the transit stations is acquired, as part of the right-of-way purchase, by the public corporation that has been chartered by the regional government to assist in carrying out the regional development program. Income derived from these areas helps to retire the construction loans. In addition, these funds help to create community facilities, such as schools, that are part of the total regional plan.

There is a trend away from the commuting patterns of the past when citizens jammed the freeways to get from their homes in one place to high-rise urban centers in another. Many activities now revolve around local centers. And new or improved forms of electronic communication bring people together sufficiently well so that they do not have to travel to be in proximity with each other.

There is a new ultra-high-speed rail line linking the northern and southern parts of the state. Along this rail line are new cities designed to take the pressure off the urban clusters centering around old city cores.

The infusion of open-space recreational areas into every community, under the state and regional standards, helps to make the city a good place to be, instead of a good place to get away from.

In California Two, some of the most important environmental concerns of past decades have diminished. However, development of new, clean energy sources remains a concern, and the search for them is strongly accelerated. Air and water quality now meet the high California Standards for amenity, polluters having been guided and encouraged by the state consumption policies into new ways of operation. Very few of the old, ecologically destructive interbasin water-diversion proposals have been carried out since the early 1970s. The regions produce much of their own water through recycling, desalinization and judicious tapping of underground supplies.

Systematic collection and disposal of solid wastes are part of each regional development plan and are financed within the total regional development program. Waste facilities can handle completely, efficiently and economically, without pollution and without the depletion involved in extensive landfill, all of the solid wastes of the region through separation into components suitable for direct reuse, recycling, conversion to new materials, or combustion with steam production.

People do not have a great deal of disposable income, and costs are high, partly because of the environmental constraints on manufacturers.

241

Taxes are high. But new buying habits, guaranteed public access to amenities such as public transportation and parks, clean air and water, and health-care services stand in lieu of direct purchasing power. Most people eat better and enjoy better housing than they did years before.

There is still crime, drug abuse, and disorder, but regional programs of rehabilitation in California Two have replaced the primitive approach of the past. Crime and other social disruptions are at more tolerable levels, at least in part because many of the conditions that used to cause them—poverty, hunger, poor housing, and blighted neighborhoods—have been alleviated.

Still, many are discontented—with housing, income, and restrictions on the use of private property. Prejudice, and inequities arising from it, are still on the scene. Nevertheless, the restructuring of the planning process gives citizens a chance to work with the governmental bodies—community, regional, and state—that are actually responsible for solving important problems.

There are widespread complaints about government interference, bureaucratic red tape and waste of money. In actual fact, government exerts strong controls mainly in the areas that are necessary for the protection of the natural environment. In other areas, government helps to establish a framework under which individuals and communities can decide pretty much for themselves how they want to live their lives on the land.

California Two is not to be considered Utopia, but a reasonable, workable conception of how planning can help assure that this state and this nation will be better places for people to live, rather than worse, in the decades ahead.

> One strong and recurring reaction from readers of *The California Tomorrow Plan* was, naturally, "Great—but how do we get there from here?" The authors tried to map out a possible road to California Two.

Phasing In—California Two

Shifting direction toward California Two requires major changes in governmental structures, new levels and patterns of public and private spending, large-scale action programs, some new thinking, even new ways of life. Yet California Two or any other reasonable set of choices about the future can be achieved.

We have approached the achievement of California Two through nine basic "activators," which are listed below. Adoption of the activators, whether all at once through a sweeping legislative change, or more gradually, is simply a prerequisite for achieving the goals of California Two. The activators set up procedures for planning, programming, and budgeting, long-range as well as short-range, by which the vital needs and desires of the public can be attained.

Each California Two activator is of manageable size for political adoption. The adoption of each is in itself desirable and does not depend on the immediate adoption of the others. Furthermore, the activators need not be put into effect in the order listed. They can all be advanced at once, or any one at a time. Nevertheless, together they constitute the essentials of a complete system capable of operating effectively.

It must be emphasized that the full strength and purpose of the activators cannot be compromised. The demands of the political process may require that the activators be broken down into smaller action units. But halfway measures that undermine and defeat any activator are unacceptable. They are worse than no action at all for they preempt the field. For example, the creation, year after year, of new single-purpose regional commissions in California would begin to get in the way of achieving activator four—the creation of multipurpose regional governments for every region in the state. In fact, we must guard against any narrowly conceived "solution" to California's problems. The test should be: "Is this proposal part of a comprehensive plan for solving problems and, if so, what is the plan and where does the proposal fit in?"

The activators are:

1. *Take emergency action* to protect valuable lands of the state that are in critical danger of change or destruction. The procedure involves rapid and complete identification of the endangered areas by the State Office of Planning and Research, and enactment by the legislature of emergency open-space zoning for the endangered lands. Such zoning would remain in effect pending the adoption of a full state zoning plan and other measures reflecting comprehensive state policies for settlement and resource use.

2. *Adopt basic policies.* The legislature can identify and adopt central, driving policies for the state of California. The driving policies would form the basis for developing and coordinating all state policies and programs. (The four driving policies in *The California Tomorrow Plan* could be a good starting point for the legislative discussion.)

3. *Set up state planning and budgeting in one strong agency.* Such

an agency would be required to produce a plan for the future of California—a California State Plan—within 18 months, and the plan would include corresponding long-term and yearly budgets.

4. *Establish regional governments.* Strong regional governments are absolutely essential to the operation of California Two. To give all Californians, residents of metropolitan and outlying areas alike, representation at the regional level, the legislature can establish major regional subdivisions of the state, set up the organization for a multipurpose government for each region, assign responsibilities to regional government, and provide for the necessary funding.

5. *Establish community councils.* The legislature can require the establishment of community councils within the framework of local government in order to give strong voice to neighborhood needs and concerns.

6. *Make new election laws* to prevent the election process from being overwhelmed by special, powerful, economic interests.

7. *Use modern fact-gathering techniques.* The legislature can assure the financing necessary to develop a model of the state's social and economic conditions and resource capabilities, as an essential tool for legislative and executive decision-making. Complete and up-to-date monitoring and fact-gathering tools are required for any responsible state planning operation.

8. *Urge federal action.* We can urge that the federal government design all federal grants and loans to the state and local governments, including "revenue sharing," to serve and encourage strong state planning/budgeting operations, and comprehensive regional plans and budgets backed up by regional governments able to carry them out. Federal aid can thus become a partner in total regional improvement programs, and the federal government and the general public can at long last be assured that tens of billions of dollars collected annually from taxpayers across the nation do not continue to be used in ineffective, disconnected programs.

In addition, Californians can concertedly ask the federal government to institute other programs and policies essential to the well-being of the states. (These include, in the California Two narrative, a national income floor, national health insurance, national policies for settlement, population and resource use, and a variety of tax and fiscal reforms.)

9. *Make the commitment. The California Tomorrow Plan* is an attempt to post clear conditions of passage to survival with amenity. These conditions require that we change some of our ways of living and

switch around some priorities on spending. They suggest that we must take certain risks—that to build the future, we must adjust the towering disparity between our expenditures for defense and those for domestic improvements; or that to protect the bright land of California, we risk inconvenience by forswearing the use of certain machines or products or poisons. They ask, above all, for a broad public commitment to compassionate, systematic, comprehensive planning—the kind that we have tried to exemplify in our picture of California Two. We can, at long last, make such a commitment and, to win the future, we will.

• Of the various critical responses to *The California Tomorrow Plan,* one of the most interesting is this critique by Dr. Robert Jenkins, then director of the Science Department of The Nature Conservancy. He argues that population must not just be stabilized but actually reduced if we are to have a tolerable life in California—or anywhere else in the world.

ROBERT E. JENKINS   1973

!Kung vs. *Utopia*

> I did not read books the first summer; I hoed beans
> Nay, I often did better than this. There were times
> when I could not afford to sacrifice the bloom
> of the present moment to any work, whether of
> head or hands. I love a broad margin to my life.
>
> Henry David Thoreau, *Walden*

California Two has a serious defect—it isn't perfect. Worse, it isn't even optimum. After all, California Two is not a fact, it is a persuasion model. "If you do this, look what you can have." One shouldn't compromise on a persuasion model.

What is wrong with Caifornia Two that would be better in the optimum California? It seems too crowded, too planned, too bureaucratic, too hypercontrolled. It is democratic but restrictive of individual freedoms. When everyone has a voice in what individuals do, then

245

individuals only have a voice in what other people do. The benefits provided by California Two make the controls necessary and fair, but there is a better alternative.

The disruptions described in the California Tomorrow Plan are all reflections of resource shortages, Jenkins says.

There are three ways of dealing with these problems: One can increase the supply by finding or producing more of the resource or substituting another; one can impose controls on various parts of the system; or one can reduce the demand by reducing the need. We have reached this point in our history primarily by employing the first strategy. *The California Tomorrow Plan* suggests that we make much greater use of solution two and, to some extent, solution three. I would like to emphasize the overwhelming advantages of the third, which has practically never been chosen. To use this strategy we have to work on the problem of growth.

Several years ago, Professor Harold Thomas of the Engineering Department of Harvard University gave a seminar on the demography of the !Kung bushmen of Africa. Of an estimated 60,000 !Kung, only a few thousand still escape acculturation and exist by hunting-gathering rather than agriculture. Among these, the group most studied by anthropologists and demographers are the Dobe !Kung. The researchers wanted to know how hard the bushmen work; how much food they are thus able to obtain; and what relationship this may have to the mechanisms of population control, social structure, and so on.

What they appear to have found out seems astonishing. The bushmen usually don't work very hard and at the same time they really enjoy a surprisingly high standard of living. Generally, they have plenty to eat with more food available to them than they need. They manage to capture or gather this food and perform nearly all other necessary maintenance tasks by working an average of only about two to two and one half days a week. How in the world do these "primitive" people, existing in the harsh environment of the Kalahari Desert, manage to order their lives in a way that hasn't even been achieved by modern industrial man?

Most importantly, the !Kung population is stable. Bushmen control their numbers so that their population is almost always well below that which could be accommodated by the carrying capacity of their environment. Only very infrequently does the carrying capacity dip to the limiting point at which the bushmen are caught in the crunch. At all

246

other times, they live in an environment of superabundance with the sort of "broad margin" to their lives that Thoreau enjoyed at Walden.

For those who feel that work is tremendously important, it might be necessary to note that neither the !Kung bushman nor Thoreau was prevented from working by the fact that he had the option not to.

In the same vein, it might be objected by some that the !Kung are not really so well off. After all, they are not going anywhere (presumably); they are not "progressing," they haven't begun to make many of the simplest technological innovations—why, they haven't even invented agriculture! Ah . . . but let's see what happens to those who invent agriculture. One of the results of agriculture is that the production of crops and storage of harvests reduces fluctuation in the carrying capacity of the environment. It also generates the need for labor: it takes helpers to run a farm, and this encourages larger family size. At the same time, the reduction in degree of carrying-capacity fluctuations tends to remove the impact of the periodic crunch, and the net effect of all this is to bring the average population size very much closer to the average carrying capacity. The margin, or the "slack" as it might be called, has been substantially reduced. Additional cultural inventions—improved methods of environmental manipulation, crop production, food storage, industrialization, etc., tend to have the same dampening effect on carrying-capacity fluctuations.

Along with moderating fluctuation, we have vastly elevated carrying capacity and this has been accompanied by a concomitant increase in the total human population. We have reduced slack (free goods) to practically nothing as we have vastly inflated our energy demands, our needs for food, fiber and fuel over that which the environment unresistingly provides. We have created a situation like a stretched rubber band that is kept stretched only by our collective and mightiest efforts to hold it taut and, indeed, to stretch it still further.

No thoughtful person proposes that our society revert to emulate that of the bushmen; but, as we have seen, they do have something going for them. There is no reason to suppose that, if left to their own devices, they would not be carrying on in good style in another hundred years. Will we?

Moreover, as the population increases and the rubber band is pulled tighter and tighter, we have more and more need to extend controls. With the free goods go freedoms. To quote British economist Ezra Mishan, "As the carpet of increased choice is being unrolled before us by the foot, it is simultaneously being rolled up behind us by the yard."

Suppose you were a trout fisherman. As long as the number of streams and trout is large and the number of fishermen and their capacity to take fish are small, the whole procedure can remain unregulated. One can expect the fishing to be tremendous and the enjoyment derived to be huge. One can catch as many fish as desired and with whatever methods, as sporting or unsporting as suits the fancy. However, when the number of fishermen and their capacity to take fish become large relative to the number and rate of increase of fish, then regulation must occur to sustain the stock. Fishing is no longer as much fun. You have to obtain a license, you have to learn the laws, and you probably have to catch fewer fish using different methods than you might otherwise choose.

More serious examples can be given. All of urban America is one giant example. Water is brought from reservoirs hundreds of miles away. It comes out of the tap as long as the reservoir and the entire system function. Food arrives from half a continent away. Work, residences, and recreation are far apart and mechanized transportation is a necessity. Waste products are removed through separate control systems—garbage trucks, smokestacks, and sewers. Land is zoned. As density increases, old systems must be replaced with new to perform the same function. Larger reservoirs must be built and more pumping stations, as well as more generating facilities and more and wider, multilevel and limited-access highways. The system has become more and more vulnerable. Supply systems for water and food generally function fairly well because they are given the high priority they must have. Public transportation and energy utilities are on shaky ground. Corners are cut on waste control—it is in the systems handling garbage, sewage, combustion waste and other effluents that destruction of the environment and system failure are most evident.

Not only should we be anxious about the reliability of these systems, we should be furious with the ways in which they erode our freedoms. Not only are we controlled by these necessities, but more and more, we are enslaved by the growing workloads necessary to make the controls function. Not only do many of our citizens spend their lives engaged in the meaningless work of maintaining these systems, but all of us are tyrannized by the time and resources we must fritter away on license applications, report forms, commutation, and a whole mass of trivia necessary to maintain the systems of control.

Is all of this, then, to suggest that we can do without controls? Most emphatically not. The point is rather that it makes a great deal of difference which elements in the system are controlled.

The element most in need of regulation is population. By analogy, if your boat has a worsening leak, it makes more sense to repair the leak than to take on a bigger crew for bailing. Instead, we have figuratively taken on more crew and added bigger pumps by the year.

If our population decreased, we could reduce the artificially high levels of some of the carrying-capacity factors. We might do away with many uses of pesticides, for example, and let the insects eat more of our crop plants. We would still have enough and we would be removing a potentially very dangerous element from the ecological system. We could leave large wilderness areas undeveloped, and these would sustain the natural ecological systems that are our buffer against environmental management mistakes. Some factors might be completely released from our controlling influences.

Infinite growth is an obvious impossibility, and at some point we are either going to have to choose to halt the growth of our population and our resource utilization or the halt will be forced upon us, perhaps with the catastrophic effects of an overshoot. However, the maximum in misery might result from halting growth just at the threshold point where population and consumption are equal to that which could be sustained by the most inflated carrying capacity conceivable. Such a system, without any slack, would be totally lacking in livability, and yet by a course of continuous accommodation, this is exactly the sort of world we are setting about to create. The earlier we begin to halt growth—in fact, to "ungrow"—the larger will be the remaining supply of resources to be equitably distributed so as to provide what *The California Tomorrow Plan* calls "personal fulfillment within an amenable environment."

A positive national policy of no-growth population, coupled with added inducements to lower the birth rate still further, might well produce a stationary or declining population. This, it seems, is the real hope for the future: to reduce the magnitude of our demands on resources and to restore slack to our system. We will not achieve utopia, since that is impossible, but we might achieve optopia, which is far and away better than simply making the best of a bad job.

IV *Cry California:*
Notes on a Mild Revolution

The Planning Boom

• Looking back at *The California Tomorrow Plan*, we can see it now both as the unique labor it was and as a product of its time—as one of many tenacious efforts made, many eloquent voices raised, during an extraordinary period of government action on behalf of environmental protection. It was, to borrow a phrase from *Cry California* contributor Walt Anderson, "a mild revolution."

Consider what was going on during the genesis of the plan— and what continued to take place through much of the decade of the 1970s:

1969—The San Francisco Bay Conservation and Development Commission, established four years earlier on a temporary basis, is made permanent after a difficult struggle in the legislature. (A *Cry California* article by Gil Bailey, picked up by state and national media, is influential here.)

1970—The lawmakers pass the California Environmental Quality Act, requiring environmental impact assessments on public and private developments alike. Its application to private projects, at first contested, is confirmed in 1972 by the State Supreme Court in the famous *Friends of Mammoth* decision.

1970—The Bay Area gets another powerful single-purpose regional agency: the Metropolitan Transportation Commission, with authority over the allocation of state and federal transportation dollars.

1970—The voluntary Association of Bay Area Governments publishes a remarkable, though unenforceable, blueprint for the future: the *Regional Plan 1970–1990*. It calls for compact, "city-centered" growth and for the setting aside of a metropolitan greenbelt of some 3.5 million acres. Bills to establish a metropolitan open-space authority are offered in the legislature in several succeeding years.

1971—At the same time a movement is underway to reconstitute ABAG as California's first multipurpose regional government. Its champion in the legislature, Assemblyman John

Knox, comes close to achieving passage of a bill this year, on his third try of an eventual seven.

1971—The legislature, which has gradually tightened the laws governing local general plans, now adds the most important requirement of all: that local government boards must adhere to their own adopted plans as they consider proposals for developments.

1972—After years of frustration and stalemate in the legislature, the voters approve Proposition 20 and put in place a strict coastline protection law.

1972—Local bond issues for the purchase of open space pass by the dozen, especially in the San Francisco Bay region.

1972—State Senator Peter Behr shepherds through the legislature—and persuades Governor Reagan to sign—the historic Wild Rivers Act, which now rules out new water-supply dams on the rivers of the North Coast region.

1972—A law authored by State Senator Leo McCarthy cracks down on rural subdivisions of the type attacked by Harold Berliner in *Cry California*. Subdividers must now set money aside to build promised improvements—a requirement that virtually ends the subdivision boom.

1974—The Arab oil embargo spurs the state to act on transportation and energy. A California Energy Resources Commission is created and given power over power-plant siting. At about the same time, the state transportation bureaucracy is reorganized. What had been the single-purpose Division of Highways is now the comprehensive Department of Transportation; it is supposed to give equal weight to all means of getting around.

1974—With the election of Edmund G. Brown, Jr., Californians have a governor who makes improved land-use planning one of four major campaign themes—and who, in at least one campaign speech, promises to look for guidance in *The California Tomorrow Plan*.

1975—The California Land-Use Task Force, a high-level group organized by the Planning and Conservation Foundation and composed equally of business and environmental leaders, proposes major improvements in state planning—again much along the lines of *The California Tomorrow Plan*.

1976—The Coastal Commission, following the path of the

Bay Conservation and Development Commission, is made permanent.

1976—A consensus appears to be building on the need to protect important agricultural land from development. A strong bill by Assemblyman Charles Warren passes the Assembly but dies in the Senate.

1978—The Brown administration promulgates an "Urban Strategy" in which the state—for the first time—makes it an official goal to discourage California's traditional sprawling style of development.

The series ends with another dramatic action taken in 1978: Proposition 13. With one tax-cutting stroke, the voters change the face of state politics and bring an end to the legislature's willingness to tinker with government structure. But at the same time, the property tax rollback has tremendous consequences for the style of California's growth—consequences that may prove to be more good than bad.

12 The Little Boom in Growth Control

- The first half of the 1970s saw a widespread movement to get a handle on growth in California. Not that there was some sweeping statewide policy—the state was as far from that as ever. Rather, the brakes were applied by cities, counties, and special districts—often at the insistence of the voters.

Several strategies were involved. Often the "control" took an indirect form in the setting aside of large blocks of open space. Valuable in themselves, these reserves also had the effect of curbing the horizontal expansion of cities. A somewhat related strategy was the adoption of "urban limit lines" beyond which development would be discouraged. Another technique was to limit the expansion of basic services—roads, sewerage, water supply—on which development depends. Finally, in some jurisdictions—and this was something very new—local government asserted the right to control the rate of development directly by limiting the number of housing units to be built each year.

One of the pioneers in the growth-control field was the city of Palo Alto, where a landmark study, published in 1971, raised the startling suggestion that a city can sometimes be better off financially by keeping land *out* of development.

JAY THORWALDSON   1973

The Palo Alto Experience

"*Open space* vs. *development*." That phrase, overstamped on the cover of a Palo Alto study of its large undeveloped foothill areas, appeared to announce the prizefight of the decade. In a sense, it did.

In one corner: developers, bulldozing and hammering their way across the landscape. In the other: environmentalists throwing themselves in the path of advancing machinery, or using guerrilla-warfare methods in the courts and on the political field.

The first couple of rounds are over now. Environmentalists hold the countryside and the developers are mustering their forces in big-city offices. But is it all that simple? Is it just the good guys against the bad guys?

The story behind Palo Alto's present open-space dilemma goes back a decade or so. Situated midway down the San Francisco Peninsula between San Francisco and San Jose, the city extends from the bay across virtually level lowlands, then climbs over rolling and grassy "lower foothills" to Skyline Boulevard on the Skyline Ridge of the Santa Cruz Mountain range. The flatlands are almost fully developed, occupied by about 56,000 people who live mainly along spacious streets lined with more than 100,000 trees. The foothills, about equal in area to the flatlands, are almost entirely undeveloped, except for a few residences and farms.

As the Palo Alto flatlands filled in during the 1950s with the homes of aerospace and electronics workers and their families, community concern focused on how the foothills should be developed. A mayor's committee of local citizens studied the hills, a city planner projected a capacity of 3,480 dwelling units, and by the mid-1960s, after extended hearings, a prototype development covering more than 600 acres in the lower foothills had won final city approval. But the development, a project of Sunset International Petroleum Co., fell through.

In 1969, the city hired the San Francisco planning firm of Livingston and Blayney to prepare the now-famous "Foothills Environmental Design Study." Ironically, the $144,000 project did not begin as an open-space study, but as a development study—to create an "environmental design" for the development toward which the foothills area appeared to be heading.

During the 20-month period of the study, development alternatives were narrowed by a process of elimination from high- to low-density residential use.

Then came the startling discovery that brought Palo Alto national attention. The report's economic analysis revealed that it would actually be as cheap for the city to buy the foothills outright as to allow them to be developed. The study concluded that if the cost of schools, roads, police and fire facilities, and staff and other municipal items were added (basic utilities had been installed in the early 1960s), the total investment would so far exceed any tax revenues the area could produce that buying

257

the land would be cheaper. Thus, the most economical environmental design would be no design.

Word of the report's conclusions was seized upon by conservationists throughout the country. Many had had hunches along those lines, but lacked hard evidence. Planner Lawrence Livingston quickly qualified the report, pointing out that it would not apply everywhere. The principles could, however, be applied in most areas with extensive undeveloped lands close to surburban or urban development to which existing services would logically be extended—possibly the Santa Monica Mountains region near Los Angeles, where the Palo Alto report has been widely discussed.

The Palo Alto City Council ultimately approved a policy of preserving open space in the hills. It then squeezed out more than $4 million from its next two annual budgets (by deferring some other projects) and set it aside for foothills acquisition, if needed. Simultaneously, the council told its planning and legal staffs to investigate alternative means of preserving open space.

The report's suggestions, along with a strong editorial boost from the *Palo Alto Times,* helped a small group of conservationists conduct a two-year campaign that resulted in the creation in November 1972 of the Midpeninsula Regional Park District. The district's sole responsibility is to acquire and preserve open-space land along Skyline Ridge and in the foothills area, and possibly some in the baylands.

> But not everyone, Thorwaldson notes, was pleased with this outcome. Local minority leaders worried that the open-space program could be, at best, a diversion of energy from other social needs and, at worst, part of a subtle attempt to deny decent housing to minorities. Palo Alto, a leader in providing affordable housing and ambitious social services, was not very vulnerable to such criticism, but the debate pointed up problems highly visible on the national scene.

Nationwide, individual cities and counties have begun seriously to consider limiting their growth, and some have adopted ordinances for that purpose. Simultaneously, there has been statewide and regional reexamination of hitherto widely permissive growth policies, and growth-control measures have appeared in the legislatures of several states and in Congress.

Along with this rising sensitivity to growth have come other changes. The conflict of housing needs with market trends and income levels has come sharply into focus in conjunction with the open-space

258

issue, while various other social concerns are demanding attention, including critical human needs in the urban-core areas. There is growing awareness of the difficulties local communities face in trying to deal with problems that encompass broad, regional areas.

As environmentalists score legal, political and public-opinion victories, some landowners, developers and trade-union groups grow increasingly bitter. There is talk of showdown, with at least some support for the developer/job-seeker side of the controversy coming from spokesmen for urban-core minorities and the poor. So, as the conservationists' open-space push has made itself felt in the broader society, it has caught the attention of other groups in that society that have priorities of their own.

In this context, it is clear that preservation of open space is not enough in itself to meet the needs and concerns of the future. It is not a panacea—does not guarantee the economic health of a community, and cannot solve social, housing or employment problems.

• Palo Alto recognizes this fact, Thorwaldson concludes. Cities that think of following Palo Alto's example had better recognize it, too.

The news from Palo Alto was one of many things that had been reinforcing a drive for a truly vast and systematic program to set aside open space in the San Francisco Bay Area, as the *San Francisco Examiner*'s Gerald Adams reported in the following *Cry California* piece.

GERALD D. ADAMS   1970

The Open Space Explosion

In a Sacramento hearing room one morning this June, a lobbyist for the home-building industry was protesting Senator Milton Marks' bill (SB 1400) to create an open-space commission for the San Francisco Bay Region. It was the first time that he had protested the measure, which had already cleared one Senate subcommittee.

"But why didn't you object when we held the last hearing?" queried Senator Lewis Sherman, chairman of the Senate Committee on Governmental Operations.

"Because," stammered the startled lobbyist, "I didn't think the bill stood a chance."

The people of the San Francisco Bay Region, with the help of the state legislature, may well be on the verge of establishing the first great metropolitan open-space program in the nation. The bill in question failed to pass out of the Senate Finance Committee by a single vote, but the idea of creating an open-space commission, with power to designate vast acreages as a permanent greenbelt in and through the urban complex of the Bay Area, could become a reality next year.

The open-space program promises many things: beauty, the end of unchecked sprawl, the assurance of breathing space for the millions already here and those to come, orchards and vineyards, rolling livestock ranges, recreation areas, wildlife refuges and the like, all woven through the residential-industrial-transportation complex of the region. What it means, simply, is that we will put aside the remarkable legacy that is still left to us and, in so doing, will create greenbelts that will rival the splendid examples of London, Stockholm and other metropolitan regions of the world.

> Some 400,000 acres of existing parks and watershed reserves make a good beginning, Adams observes, but a quantum leap is now required. Several significant planning reports have pointed the way.

In 1965, the State Office of Planning published a remarkable report, "Urban-Metropolitan Open Space Study," prepared by Eckbo, Dean, Austin and Williams, that touched off the present open-space campaign by outlining the needs, the standards, the techniques and the costs for providing open space in California. The plan called for putting aside, by various means, well over half the land of the Bay Region as permanent open space.

In 1968, another important report entitled "Economic Impact of a Regional Open Space Plan" was published, along with a companion summary called "The Case for Open Space," by People for Open Space, a regional citizens' group. The report (funded by the Ford Foundation) was the first study of its kind ever undertaken in the United States.

In 1970, the Association of Bay Area Governments (ABAG) voted overwhelming approval of a general plan for the region that would set aside more than 3.5-million acres as open space and as reserves for controlled urban expansion after 1990. More than 2 million acres, not including the Bay itself, are designated as permanent open space. While this plan is not binding on members of ABAG (it merely calls for

implementation by the cities and counties), it may be considered the best guide for open-space planning yet produced.

These ABAG recommendations for open-space land, which would include major ridges and watercourses, the ocean shore, selected bay and river shorelines and areas of outstanding natural attractions, cover 3,060,000 acres, including lands already protected. An additional 660,000 acres are designated for controlled development, the ultimate disposition of which would be postponed until sometime in the future.

Uses for which the permanent open space would be reserved are described in the plan as follows:

— For resource production, including vineyards, orchards and artichoke fields; for dairy and meat-producing lands; for water supplies and for marine-life production.

— For resource preservation, including forests, tidelands, marshes, grasslands and unique physical features such as cliffs.

— For health, welfare and well-being. This category includes watersheds to protect drinking supplies; airsheds that perform a similar function for the air we breathe; areas for solid-waste disposal; areas for recreation and hiking; protection of scenic panoramas and historic and cultural sites; separations between cities; buffer zones to reduce noise pollution.

— For public safety. This includes maintenance of flood-control reservoirs, floodplains, drainage channels, areas below dams, landslide areas, earthquake fault zones, airport clear-path zones, and firebreaks.

— Corridors for utilities: transportation, canals, aqueducts, power transmission.

Inevitably, the question of financing this immense undertaking arises. It will take money. How much money depends on the method used to acquire the open space. In the economic study conducted for People for Open Space, the following four strategies were put forth:

— Voluntary contracts between owners and county governments to keep lands in their present use.

— Public purchase of all open-space lands.

— Public purchase of some lands and zoning of others.

— Zoning of all lands needed for open-space use, with compensation to owners whose lands lost value as a result, a complex procedure that has yet to find political acceptance here.

The report recommends a combination of these, and calculates that $2 billion (at 1969 prices) will buy all the lands envisioned in its study. By way of comparison, the 75-mile Bay Area Rapid Transit system will have cost over $1.2 billion ($10 billion if it ever is extended to San Jose) by completion; and $1 billion has been spent on highway construction in the Bay Area in the last 10 years.

To repay a $2-billion bond issue over a 30-year period would cost about $10 per person a year, an amount that would be considerably offset by these factors:

— Appreciation of the value of the lands still held in private hands.

— The saving of some $1.5 billion as the result of limiting urban sprawl. Otherwise, future growth at the present rate and pattern would cost the people of the Bay Area an extra $300 million for governmental services and $835 million for gas, electric and telephone services directly attributed to sprawl, according to the economists consulted by People For Open Space.

— Income from agricultural land leased to private ranchers.

In addition, uncalculated savings will accrue from the protection of the region's environment against damage from considerable air pollution, from landslides and floods, and from multimillion-dollar flood-control projects that have been necessitated by previous development on floodplains. The People for Open Space study thereby concludes that the future cost of acquiring all the lands proposed can be brought down to perhaps $2 to $3 per person per year.

Furthermore, if we were merely to purchase a minimum of 350,000 acres outright, and protect the remainder of the lands by means of zoning, the total cost would drop to $1.25 billion. Subtract from this figure the savings realized in utility service costs, government services, recreational use benefits and rent revenue, and the *benefits far outweigh the cost* of an open-space program.

The course for the push toward creation of a Bay Area open-space program is well blocked out. In 1970, a new committee based in San

Francisco and calling itself "Open Space Action" was created solely for the purpose of getting the Bay Area open-space program in gear. The new organization, sparked by the unsinkable Dorothy Erskine, grand lady of Bay Area open space, was the main lobbying force in Sacramento behind SB 1400 and has already laid its plans for 1971.

The legislature can well expect further concerted citizen pressure for the creation of the study commission as envisioned by the Open Space Action people. As Dorothy Erskine says, "Open space is a live issue now, not just a dream or hope."

• These early hopes did not prove justified. But the ABAG open-space plan remains a model, and People for Open Space and other citizen groups are still laboring to see it carried out.

JOHN HART   1976

Petaluma:
The Little City That Could

A few years ago any ambitious city government knew exactly what it had to do to make its reputation. It had to *grow*. Spread faster, spread farther than its neighbors. Colonize the grandest territories. Choke off its rivals. That was the city game as Los Angeles played it, and San Diego, and San Jose.

But today the rules of that game are quickly changing. Not totally, of course, and not everywhere. But these days a city can best attract attention by what it does to *limit* its expansion, by its success in slowing down the growth that few any longer would call "inevitable."

The city of Petaluma, in the green fields of Sonoma County north of San Francisco, has tried both methods. Like many another American farm town on the edge of a metropolis, Petaluma long looked forward to a boom, planned for it, zoned for it. But when that sudden growth began to come, Petaluma found the transformation less pleasant than it sounded in the pages of the general plan. There was alarm—there was even a kind of grief—as an old rural center became a commuter suburb, changing, as the song puts it, "forever, not for better."

Across the freeway from old Petaluma, with its grain elevators and

263

white Victorian halls, a new city appeared—a horizon of similar houses on similar lots along enormous barren streets, the too-familiar image of suburbia badly done. With it came great inconvenience and expense as the town labored to build the schools, the parks, the sewage-treatment facilities its larger population required.

Thus far the story is familiar. But in 1972, Petaluma did what no other American city had yet done. Resolving not to suffer another sudden boom, it put a limit on its rate of growth. A formal limit, a number—a quota. Just 500 new units, the city council declared, would be built in the city each year. To choose just who would build those 500 units, the city would hold a semiannual competition among plans. The best (one hoped) would be chosen, the worst left out.

The notion of slowing growth is, of course, a popular one just now. Controls of one kind or another have been tried in perhaps a hundred American cities. In Boca Raton, Florida, the city council chose an ultimate population. We will grow so far, they said, and no farther. In Ramapo, New York, the plan was subtler. Growth is fine in Ramapo, but proceeds only as fast as the city can reasonably expand its services. And in more than one town exclusive large-lot zoning has had the incidental effect of slowing the rate of building.

But Petaluma has this distinction—it was the first to succeed in setting up an explicit quota. And while that number was not pegged very low, the fact of the quota was something very new.

So this "Petaluma Plan" had an instant national audience. In every forum it was praised and damned. Even among professional planners the reaction was split. And in April 1973, the Construction Industry Association of Sonoma County, together with other plaintiffs, took Petaluma to court. Their wish: to prove the plan a violation of federal law.

Most planning disputes are decided in state courts; but this time the builders, in search of a swift, binding precedent, went instead to the U.S. courts, and found their grounds in the U.S. Constitution. Growth limits, they charged, violate each American's right to travel and to settle where he likes. These grounds were novel—as novel as the plan—and national interest grew.

In January 1974, in a San Francisco courtroom, District Judge Lloyd H. Burke ruled for the construction industry and against Petaluma: "No city can control its population growth numerically." Burke's language was sweeping, and some observers saw a chance that even traditional zoning could be threatened by extensions of the right-to-travel argument as Judge Burke read it. But none of this was to be. In August 1975, the Ninth Appeals Court reversed the decision and restored the Petaluma Plan. Finally, on February 23, 1976, the U.S. Supreme Court refused to take another look at *Petaluma* vs. *Construction Industry Association*. For the moment, at least, it is decided: Local governments *may* work with quotas—a very large precedent.

But no court decision will end the debate about the Petaluma Plan. "I didn't like the approach," one antiquota planner commented after Judge Burke struck down the plan, "even when it was legal." Now that the quotas are once more legal, the critics dislike them all the more.

In fact, the plaintiffs see in the plan a perilous precedent: a threat, most obviously, to their construction trade, but also (or so they claim) a threat to the housing market, to the economy, to the social progress of the entire urban region. In this there is both self-interest and exaggeration. Yet the arguments are worth recalling.

What, exactly, did the plantiffs fear from Petaluma?

They feared, and fear, that Petaluma's example will be imitated widely in the San Francisco Bay Area, in California, in the nation—wherever some pleasant suburb feels the shock of change. From the pleadings: "The Petaluma Plan has the most serious impact throughout the state of California. If the plan is constitutional, cities throughout the state and elsewhere will turn to the plan as the most restrictive permissible form of urban growth control."

If this takes place, the plaintiffs say, fewer new houses and apartments will be built. As a result, they predict, housing prices will rise still faster, if possible, than they have been rising. Thus they claim an injury not to themselves only, as builders, but an injury to anyone who, in coming years, sets out to find a home.

This argument was put into legal terms by Malcolm Misuraca of the Santa Rosa firm of Arata, Misuraca and Clement. But the real author of that argument—its authority, theorist, and most significant witness—was Claude Gruen, economist, of Gruen, Gruen and Associates, San Francisco.

Gruen is by profession a consultant to local governments. Yet he looks beyond them to the regional metropolis of which they are a part. He sees that supercity almost as a biologist sees a living creature, or as an ecologist sees a forest: as a tremendous, intricate mechanism working by definite rules of its own. It is dangerous, he tells us, to interfere too much with the way this organism functions. And growth control, he feels, is interference indeed.

Growth in the metropolis, Gruen reasons, always takes place disproportionately in certain "growth centers." These are the fringe towns where both urban services and plentiful vacant land are found—the San Joses, the Livermores, the Petalumas of any urban region. One after another of these towns will go through a swift, perhaps destructive boom, then grow more quietly as land costs rise and buildable ground grows scarce. To Gruen, this cycle is a natural thing and, in spite of the problems it undeniably brings, a very necessary thing.

The job of the local government, Gruen would say, is not to set itself against growth, but to manage growth gracefully. Petaluma gets no special sympathy from him for having botched the job. "The city did not come up with a plan that charted its destiny; it sought to avoid that destiny." And as lawyer Misuraca puts it, "This is a study in anti-planning, the refusal of a city to come to grips with the fact that it has joined a metropolitan complex . . ."

If one town so abdicates, then others are forced to follow. People will still need housing—somewhere; they will still need services—somewhere. By adopting its plan, Gruen and Misuraca feel, "Petaluma legislates its problems into problems for Vallejo, Napa, or Walnut Creek." But why should any of these volunteer to deal with the problems that Petaluma, allegedly, avoids? Thus arises a "new mercantilism," a competition not for trade or population, but for freedom from the disadvantages of growth.

From the viewpoint of a local government, Gruen concedes, this is only good sense. But if the "growth centers" all refuse to do their job—if they do not accept all comers—there are consequences, complex as Gruen describes them, but in summary quite simple. The stock of housing falls still farther behind the need. Rents and mortgages become still more preposterous. And the poor are still less able to afford that necessity, a roof over their heads.

So goes Claude Gruen's scenario. One part of it, at least, is unmistakably coming true: government after government, in the Bay Area as elsewhere, is considering some type of growth control. A very partial list:

— The county of Napa, some 15 miles east of Petaluma, has resolved to plan for a growth rate of one percent per year, about a third of the growth expected in the unrestricted market.

— Livermore, in the dangerously smoggy Livermore Valley east of Oakland, has chosen a two-percent expansion rate each year.

266

— In the island city of Alameda, the people voted to outlaw the building of apartments. This amounts to a drastic restriction on growth.

— San Jose is hoping to limit the outward sprawl of housing into the fertile farmlands to the south. Numbers aren't the issue here; but Gruen, at least, feels that the new plans assume a pinching off of San Jose's "natural" growth.

— Perhaps the most interesting case is that of Marin County, Petaluma's neighbor to the south. Marin planners were talking quotas well before the Petaluma experiment began. Their progress has been slow because they have been looking for a *countywide* growth-control plan: a system in which the county and the 11 incorporated cities within its border could cooperate. If, almost miraculously, an agreement comes, it will be the first time anywhere that several local governments have joined to manipulate the growth of a large part of an urban region.

Is this, then, the "new mercantilism" Gruen and Misuraca fear? The governments certainly don't see it as such. They are not at this point consciously competing against one another. Rather, each is responding to the discontent of its own present citizens—a somewhat different thing. Nor is there a rush to adopt the particular methods Petaluma has pioneered.

What about the problems the *Petaluma* plaintiffs predict? Above all, what about those housing prices? Will less be built because of *Petaluma?* Will prices rise more swiftly, more inexorably still?

As in any planning debate, the right answer is hard to find. Who knows—who *really* knows—what causes give us what effects? If rents rise insanely, on what shall we blame this? Some experts doubt that growth—or the control of growth—is the key. They point out that much of the price of housing is actually in the interest charged.

In the Bay Area, the quotas have yet to be tested against a real boom. The construction business has been slow for several years. In Petaluma, the first crisis was already over when the plan was adopted. Elsewhere, shortages—of water in Marin, of clean air in the Livermore Valley— have stifled growth more totally than any city council ever could.

And yet the tool is there, to be used perhaps less gently when the building industry picks up vigor again.

Trying to convince the skeptics, the controllers raise one further argument. Perhaps, they say, we *must* limit growth on the fringe where the city invades the open land, not just for the sake of the land but for the

267

sake of the city as well. Perhaps, if our suburbs grow less rapidly, we will turn our attention again to the most neglected landscapes of them all—to the old central cities, becoming year by year less livable.

Does the Petaluma Plan have in it a promise of better days for San Francisco? Gruen is one of many people who label such hopes "naive."

Claude Gruen states, in the language of planning, the elegant case of the moderate economic conservative. Like others of that tradition, he does not deny the failures of the private market; but he still trusts it better than anything governments can do. As always the argument is attractive. And as always it leaves us with huge problems unsolved: the housing shortage itself not least among them.

It seems inconceivable, now, that planners and politicians should return to their old obedience to the market. There is no doubt that suburban sprawl (as its detractors call it) has been more destructive than it need have been. We could have carried out the will of the market much better. But the results of the old ways were so unpleasant, so costly, so socially unsuccessful, that few now seem willing to return to them even part way. The final decision in *Petaluma* vs. *Construction Industry Association* makes the return less likely than ever before.

What it does not do is to solve the problem of dealing with growth, in the San Francisco metropolitan region or in any other.

Rather, it makes that problem more pressing still.

• During 1975, California Tomorrow mounted a series of seven "Town Meetings" across the state to ask and answer the question: How are we doing? Are current mechanisms of planning and government action creating a workable future?

Though the agendas varied, most of these meetings zeroed in on the problems of managing rapid growth. This was especially the case in the September gathering at Cupertino near San Jose. Shocked, in retrospect, by the transformation of the northern Santa Clara Valley into a Los Angeles North, local governments in Santa Clara County were looking for a way to manage their future growth more gracefully. The vehicle: the Local Agency Formation Commission, a body established in Santa Clara County (and in every other county with multiple cities) by a 1963 law.

A partial account of the Town Meeting:

JOHN HART   1975

Can Urban Boundary Lines
Manage Growth?

Today the cult of development is over. Mayor Janet Gray Hayes of San Jose, a morning panelist, recalled her election campaign slogan: "We must make San Jose better before we make it bigger." And Ronald R. James, president of that city's Chamber of Commerce, told the meeting, "We are long past the day of growth for growth's sake."

But however unpopular growth may have become, it is certain that development will go on. The pressures that changed the valley from farmland to supersuburb have not ceased. At Cupertino, one question was asked in many ways: can Santa Clara County choose the kind of future most of its people want? Or will its governments be carried helplessly along as the trends of the past work out their independent, ruthless way?

The Town Meeting heard both some hope and quite a bit of pessimistic doubt.

How much more, after all, *should* Santa Clara grow? There was fairly little comment at Cupertino on this, the fundamental issue. Paul Sagers of the county executive's office was "elated," he said, that the federal court of appeals had upheld Petaluma's plan for growth control. "Local governments must have this power," he added, "because they have the burden of these decisions." But James of the Chamber of Commerce was skeptical. "When we begin to consider a no-growth philosophy, we are approaching a form of social injustice." Joseph Houghteling, of the Bay Conservation and Development Commission, pointed to the sharp decline in freeway construction and suggested that development would be less rapid from now on, but a fourth speaker seemed resigned. "Maybe we just have to let things deteriorate to the point where people will start *leaving* Santa Clara County."

Since about 1970, the county of Santa Clara and the 15 cities within its boundaries have been working out a common plan for managing their growth, but they have left to the future the problem of controlling the *quantity* of new development. For the moment, they are looking only at the problem of *location:* the ordering, the logic of development. And that is challenge enough.

During the expansionist years, subdivisions and commercial

269

developments fanned out across the flatlands like pieces on a chess-board, leaving vacant the squares of doomed farmland in between. Even today a good deal of vacant land remains in the developed zone.

Now, the planners agree, the cities should restrain themselves from pushing farther *out* until they have used up the open land they have already surrounded. And when they need more building land, they should spread out slowly, within concentric bands.

There is in fact only one city in the Santa Clara urban area that has much room for expansion, and that city is San Jose. San Jose now fills the flatland north of the small natural barrier called Tulare Hill. South of that rise lie rich, undisturbed farmlands, still producing food, and the small towns of Morgan Hill and Gilroy. There is wide agreement that development should not spill south over Tulare Hill, at least not yet, and probably not at all.

How do the governments of Santa Clara County plan to contain their growth? The method, based on authorizing state legislation, is fairly simple.

Each city defines for itself an *urban services area*. This is intended to contain enough land for about five years of building, close to existing roads and services. Each city agrees to permit development only inside this boundary, even if its official city limits extend farther.

The county government could easily make nonsense of these volun-tary restrictions by permitting large-scale building outside city limits. But the supervisors have resolved not to do this. "Since 1969," said Supervisor Dominic Cortese, "the county has tried to avoid develop-ment within the unincorporated area. We have tried to make it a *city* issue."

Thus a would-be developer of county land must ordinarily take his plan to the nearest city and ask both for city council approval and for annexation. This brings in a third agency of great importance: LAFCO, the Local Agency Formation Commission. LAFCO is made up of two city councilmen, two supervisors, and a fifth, "public" member chosen by the other four. Its main power is over annexation—it can veto any extension of city limits into land that is *not* considered "ready" for development in terms of the locality's ability to provide supporting services. In other words, LAFCO can enforce the urban-services bound-aries that the cities have agreed to respect.

Many speakers at Cupertino praised this approach. Dave Beatty spoke for the League of California Cities. "We propose that many of the ideas developed in Santa Clara County should be extended statewide."

270

But there were also critics who feared the LAFCO formula is not enough. The commission, some said, has been too ready to approve the generous expansion boundaries that some cities propose for themselves. It is an appointive agency that the voters cannot control. Most important, LAFCO cannot prevent the development of vacant lands the cities annexed long ago, no matter what plans may be upset.

For these and other reasons, the skeptics fear the new controls will fail at the critical point: Tulare Hill, where development threatens the fertile South Valley. They charge that the county of Santa Clara, the city of San Jose, and LAFCO itself have all been weak at the times of crucial decision.

For its part, the board of supervisors had resolved to protect farmland, reserving it for rural uses. Yet political pressure can make such policies hard to carry out.

The cities, too, may find it hard to turn down attractive development outside the agreed-on service boundaries. San Jose has approved construction of an IBM plant on farmland south of Tulare Hill. The land is already inside city limits, so LAFCO cannot intervene. The plant will be a "special case."

• *Update:* These last two growth-control stories—the Petaluma case and the Santa Clara County effort—have contrasting sequels. Petaluma, although it has revised the details of its system repeatedly, has in general stuck to its moderate-growth guns. Local voters have helped. In 1981, when the city council was ready to approve the massive Frates Ranch development southeast of the existing town, violating the spirit if not the

271

letter of the controls, the voters overwhelmingly vetoed the proposed decision.

But in Santa Clara County temptation was not so successfully resisted. San Jose's urban limit policy remained in effect until 1983, when the balance of opinion on the San Jose City Council suddenly tipped in favor of industrial development south of Tulare Hill. The urbanization of the next stretch of valuable farmland—known as the Coyote Valley—was set in motion.

Here is an irony: previously the council, in an admirable effort to produce consistent policy, had persuaded the California Department of Transportation not to construct interchanges on the new freeway it was building through the Coyote Valley. The reason: easy freeway access would add to the pressure for growth. But now that growth has won out anyway, the interchanges will sooner or later have to be added on to the finished freeway—at multiplied expense.

Local governments, beyond a doubt, have become more efficient and more sensitive since California Tomorrow indicted their performance in such early statements as *The Phantom Cities of California*. But the fact remains that consistent local policy is hard to come by. And we have reason to be nervous when fundamental decisions about the future of a region lie entirely in local hands.

What about *state* growth policy? In a sense, there is no such thing. California has come to no coherent conclusion about its carrying capacity—the numbers of people it is able to house or where, in the public interest, it is preferable for them to live. But for all that, there is a powerful state influence on growth. Major public-works projects guide it and encourage it, and so do population projections. Walt Anderson and Elizabeth Dickson show how this occurs.

WALTER TRUETT ANDERSON
and ELIZABETH DICKSON   1976

How We Keep Losing the Numbers Game

Although the term "growth management" is in wide use these days, there is really very little that governments at any level do—at least explicitly—to manage growth. It might be more accurate to say that growth manages government.

Over most of California's history, decision-making has been guided by two assumptions: (1) that growth is good, and (2) that the proper function of government is to encourage growth by providing the public services and infrastructure that will permit growth to take place. And along with this has gone the conviction that, in a free society, it is not the business of government to tell people where to live: people should be able to settle wherever they choose.

In practice, this has meant guessing where growth was likely to take place and then doing whatever was necessary to take care of it: build freeways to it, pump water to it, give it what it needed. This was the process that gave birth to the California Water Plan and the Transportation Master Plan. These mighty undertakings depended on projections of what future populations would be.

It now appears that most of the population projections used in the past to justify our massive freeway-building and water-moving enterprises were far too high. Population analysts are rapidly scaling down their projections of future growth.

Most agencies use the projections of the population research unit of the Department of Finance. Each set of projections the DOF publishes is lower than the previous set, but still they are consistently high.

In order to understand how this happens, let us take a brief plunge into the world of the population analyst.

First, note that there are different ways to project population growth. One way is the "econometric" model, in which economic activities are the main factors taken into account—so that a given area's population is projected in terms of what would be a necessary work force. Another way is a land-use model, which projects population on the basis of effective zoning and an area's holding capacities. These are examples of ways that are *not* used by the Department of Finance. The

273

way that *is* used is a strictly demographic model, based on births, deaths, and migration. Since the death rate has tended to remain fairly stable, the big variables are births and migration.

> Here the authors go into DOF methodology and discuss the most recent projections of the day, those published in 1974. These were lower than previous estimates but still higher than those made by other agencies—and higher than demonstrable current trends.

DOF's demographers apparently prefer to overproject rather than to underproject, and state bureaucracies prefer to overbuild rather than to underbuild. We concede that there are good arguments on both sides of the dispute among demographers over which fertility rates most accurately represent current trends; there are demographers with no vested interest in California policy-making who agree with the projections of the DOF. We are still left with the fact that altogether too many state officials have carelessly and irresponsibly based their decision-making on expectations of future population growth that were little more than wishful thinking.

One consequence is the creation of incentives to overuse resources and energy. Where underbuilding might stimulate conservation—recycling, reclamation, reuse—overbuilding stimulates waste.

Another consequence is the self-fulfilling-prophecy phenomenon. Sewage systems are a prime example. According to a publication by the New Jersey governor's office, "Once sewage treatment plants are constructed and interceptor lines are in the ground, there is an inexorable chain of actions by developers, public officials, entrepreneurs, completely legitimate, that ensure the rapid utilization of the capacity of the sewerage system."

What this means is that much of our past nonpolicy has in fact been a policy—it has encouraged growth generally, and more specifically has encouraged growth in areas such as Southern California that were attractive to developers and potential residents but required massive technological supports in order to sustain population increases.

The alternative to this would be an explicit population policy. Such a policy could—at least theoretically—address itself to any of the factors of growth. Actually, movement across state lines is not subject to state control, and so far nothing of this sort has been done—unless you count former Governor Tom McCall's message to prospective new Oregonians that they were welcome to move—somewhere else. Several states, however, are exploring the possibilities: Hawaii, for one.

274

Another major factor in growth is birth control. While some states have considered adopting explicit birth-control policies as a means of affecting fertility rates, birth control remains an individual decision, only indirectly touched by public policy. And, considering the explosive nature of the subject, this is probably as it should be.

Migration restrictions and/or birth-control policies are, at best, doubtful areas of state involvement. But there are areas in which government's role is already clearly established: provision of public services and infrastructure, and land-use controls.

The most practical approaches to state population policy do not involve regulating or controlling *either* migration or births, but rather influencing the way population is distributed within the state through comprehensive planning involving services or land use. The goal should be to funnel growth into areas that can be developed without environmental disruption and also without high cost for public services and infrastructure.

As a modest interim step in that direction, it would make sense to pay a lot more attention to the political importance of population projections and the role they play in the planning or nonplanning of major state agencies. The population projection research unit should be moved out of the finance department and into the office of the governor (logically under the Office of Planning and Research) and directed to revise its projections downward to conform to the best available demographic realities instead of the wistful hopes of empire-building bureaucrats. Furthermore, once a reasonable series of projections has been made, it should serve uniformly as the planning basis for *all* state agencies.

• Four years later, Walt Anderson took another look at the state's ill-defined population policies and cited the case of a state that has done a good deal more.

WALTER TRUETT ANDERSON   1980

What Hawaii Did

Hawaii is the only state in the union with an explicit and official population policy. This is contained within its basic planning document, the Hawaii State Planning Act of 1978. It does not identify an optimum population for the state, but it does clearly enunciate a controlled-growth policy and prescribes some ways to implement it: by encouraging the federal government to "promote a more balanced distribution of immigration among the states"; by exploring the possibility of state laws or programs to manage immigration; by encouraging firms doing business in the state to hire from within the state; by seeking "to provide for adequate housing to meet the needs of Hawaii's people without encouraging an additional influx of people"; and by encouraging a continued low birth rate. Besides these efforts aimed at statewide population as a whole, there are specified actions regarding growth *within* the state (basically distributing it away from Oahu to the neighbor islands) and also for *intraregional* growth distribution (infilling, and preservation of agricultural land and greenbelts).

Hawaii's population policy has been in place only a short while and it is too early to judge its effectiveness. Undoubtedly some parts of it will prove to be little more than planning-document pieties, and even the more concrete parts may prove hard to carry out—nevertheless it is a far-reaching document that intelligently integrates population with land use and economic planning, and it sets an admirable model for other states—including California—to follow.

13 Energy: "Crisis" and After

- Earth Day 1970: it seemed at the time like a turning point, the start of a permanent new age of environmental sophistication. But that euphoria did not last very long. The case can be made that our more fundamental reeducation began, willy-nilly, in the summer of 1973, when war in the Middle East led the Arab oil-producing nations to embargo oil shipments to much of the Western world.

Who can forget the gas lines, the anger, the appalling sense of a seismic shift in the ground? A resource taken for granted for decades—a resource that seemed almost to grow cheaper as we used it the more lavishly—was suddenly uncertain. And expensive. In retrospect, the shortage seems to have been much less serious than we imagined, and the early price increases rather modest. But the change in the world was real.

Very suddenly, energy was an issue, a preoccupation, a "crisis" at every level of government. And how we all talked about it! Late in 1973, *Cry California* editor John W. Abbott analyzed the babble from the California Tomorrow point of view.

JOHN W. ABBOTT   1973

Ill Fares the Land

The energy crisis finds California and the nation poorly equipped to deal with it, except, as shown by daily news reports, on an oftentimes confusing and contradictory basis.

Unless it is recognized that the disruptions stem primarily from a refusal to face facts, we shall continue to repeat past mistakes, with ever-mounting consequences.

Will we now, in Sacramento and in Washington, give prompt and serious attention to the need for comprehensive national and state planning? The signs are not reassuring.

277

We will not make much progress by cutting the speed limit and turning down the thermostats. The problems are far deeper. But in Sacramento even these mild proposals initially received a "cool" reception. The lieutenant governor voiced anxiety over the danger of increased traffic congestion and injuries if motorists, buses and trucks were held to a speed of 50 miles per hour, but he later concurred in the view that this action should be "recommended" to the legislature.

As to long-range planning, consider the present state situation. The coastal zoning commissions, carrying a heavy load of work arising from numerous requests for permits to develop commercial and residential shore properties, must evaluate immediately requests for approval of energy-plant siting. Obviously, these facilities will have far-reaching consequences, not only for the coast but for the entire state. Yet the commissions, already overburdened and understaffed, must assume this essentially statewide planning function.

The fragmented approach is evident also in the activity of the legislature. Among the measures receiving interim committee attention are proposals to create a state "land-use" commission, a statewide environmental protection agency, a regional planning agency for the San Francisco Bay Area, and others.

Any of these, in varying degree, might be an improvement. Lacking a broad attack on our interrelated economic and environmental problems, however, further enactment of "pieces" will not be adequate. We are down to fundamentals.

The critical factor for the future is that we must deal with problems in their whole dimension, simultaneously. To fail in this will surely mean sacrifice of environmental gains and reckless dissipation of finite resources. The legislature should give coherence and direction to its planning by the adoption of long-range policies for the conservation and development of California. The same approach, of course, should apply with equal or greater force in Washington. These policies must lead to action. "A step in the right direction" will no longer suffice. As a start, there might be a State Planning Council with authority to do more than recommend, whose responsibilities would include planning on a comprehensive scale. Serious as it is, the energy crisis is only surface evidence of a planning crisis—we shall not be saved by gasoline alone.

• A year later, the government's response was clearer. In Washington, President Nixon had proclaimed an impossible

278

goal: to make the United States, in a very few years, absolutely independent of any source of energy outside its borders. This would require a crash program to develop every conventional energy source—oil, coal, synthetic fuels, hydroelectric, nuclear—without regard for the cost in dollars or in environmental damage.

Two major consequences would be an enormous increase in air pollution (since a weakening of pollution controls was also in prospect) and—less widely recognized—an acute competition, all over the West, between the water demands of agriculture and those of the burgeoning energy industry. Indulging the old sport of worst-case projection (pick a trend and see where it would lead if nothing stopped it!) journalist Gil Bailey produced this scenario.

GIL BAILEY   1974

Dateline: Project Independence

Washington—the year is 1990 and Project Independence is a reality.

A commercial airliner takes off from Dulles International Airport and climbs swiftly. Although it is still daylight, the sky is eerily dark. Little can be seen of the ground below, the Capitol dome, or the Potomac River a few miles away. Smoke, heavy and black from the coal-fired power plants, and heavy auto emissions have combined to cast a pall over the area. The pall is not confined to the capital city. It covers most of the metropolitan East Coast, the great megalopolis that stretches down the Atlantic seaboard.

The smog, of course, has destroyed more than esthetic values. The rate of lung cancer has risen in urban regions, as has the death rate from heart disease. Respiratory problems are much more serious, and doctors advise those with heart or lung problems to leave the vicinity, as in the 1960s and 1970s they advised patients with similar ailments to move from the Los Angeles region. There are other side effects. Paint peels off homes located downwind from the power plants. Soot collects on everything and there is no longer such a thing, fashion or no fashion, as a white shirt.

279

Finally above the dark layer, the plane swings west on its flight across what has often been called "America's Heartland," where the "amber waves of grain" provided not only sustenance for the nation, but a surplus for export. Here, also, there are huge clouds of smoke formed, as in the East, by the mixture of auto exhausts and emissions from coal-fired plants. Chicago and Gary are invisible, as later are the twin cities of Minneapolis and St. Paul, and St. Louis.

Over St. Louis, another phenomenon is glimpsed only dimly. The Missouri River is no longer "wide." It is reduced to a thin stream, most of its waters having been preempted for the oil-shale and coal-gas plants upstream. Barges can no longer navigate the river, which puts an additional burden on the rail and highway transport systems. But then, there is less to be carried from the Dakotas and the mountain states, for the same demands that dried up the Missouri—water for coal, lignite and oil shale—have also reduced the water available for cropland irrigation.

Farther west, the plane crosses the Colorado River, now also a small black stream. Its waters too have been turned over to the ever-increasing demand for energy. Already overextended in 1974, the Colorado now is truly a dead river. The salt and acid content of its lower basin is so great that no farmer wishes its waters to wash his fields, and the cost of desalting the river is prohibitive.

The pilot is more than usually careful on this leg of the trip because weather-modification projects in the Upper Colorado River Basin have had unpredicted climatic effects in the Rocky Mountain and Plains states.

The jet lands at San Francisco after flying over Yosemite Valley. The valley is now filling with water, the culmination of a project similar to San Francisco's Hetch Hetchy, which many years ago inundated another scenic valley to supply water for the city of San Francisco. Farther north, huge machines bore giant tunnels to divert Columbia River waters to the Colorado basin, against the outraged protests of Oregon and Washington.

Had the plane been scheduled to land in Los Angeles, its passengers would have observed a skeletal, thinly populated city. The decline was caused by many factors. Introduction of oil and high-sulfur coal to fuel its power plants contributed heavily to the severe smog of 1979. Massive spills from offshore oil fields ruined the beaches and destroyed marine life. The final blow was the shrunken supply of water, which gradually strangled this once basically desert area converted to a

280

metropolis only through the importation of water. The disappearance of their water came as a great shock to the millions who lived here but were unaware of the precarious balance of the natural resources on which the richness of the area depended. The lush fields of the Imperial, Coachella and Gila valleys have meanwhile been destroyed by salt-laden irrigation water, and the diversion of water from the San Joaquin and Sacramento valleys in a desperate effort to save Los Angeles has sharply reduced agricultural production there.

The plane's passengers disembark at San Francisco and buy newspapers at $1.50 for 12 pages. They read of the continuing border wars with Mexico, sparked partly by United States efforts to control Mexico's offshore oil fields, and also by the accumulated impurities in the Colorado River that destroy Mexican cropland.

San Francisco, too, is smog-bound, and respiratory disease has increased sharply because of the use of coal in power plants. A trip to Monterey and Carmel is no longer a pleasure. The sea otter, once a

281

friendly and diverting sight in Monterey Bay, is extinct, victim of oil spills and other man-caused disruptions of the marine environment. There are serious problems caused by radiation leaks from nuclear plants along the coast and inland.

California markets, once filled with fresh produce, are nearly empty because of the curtailment of agriculture brought on by the need for energy. International demands for food aggravate the domestic situation. Several hungry but nuclear-equipped nations back demands for American produce with clear threat of holocaust.

> • California's immediate response to the energy problem was less dramatic than the Federal one but more useful and more enduring. In 1974, the legislature created a California Energy Commission to be the state's lead planning agency in energy matters. The commission had authority in several areas but particularly over the siting of electrical power plants. Its first years were by no means easy.

DOUGLAS FOSTER   1978

The Energy Commission: The Board You Love to Hate

California's Energy Commission—an unprecedented experiment in centralized energy planning that has since served as a model for energy researchers all across the country—is under the gun.

Attorney General Evelle Younger has withdrawn as the commission's attorney, a public vote of no-confidence. Leading to Younger's move was the commission's decision last January *not* to exempt the proposed Sundesert nuclear plant from legal safeguards adopted by the legislature in 1976. In February, seven senators introduced a bill "to abolish the commission and transfer its duties and functions to the Public Utilities Commission."

Most of the Energy commissioners have faced this latest wave of senatorial disapprobation with unflappable cool. "The commission was enacted to make some damn hard decisions," said one commissioner, "and, of course, to provide bayonet practice for everyone."

Nonetheless, if some such bayonet charge ever does wipe out the commission, it will take years to revive any semblance of intelligent energy planning in the state.

Actually, crisis is business-as-usual for the Energy Commission. Its short history has been marked by political battles and flights of rhetorical extremism, and of course it was a crisis—the oil embargo—that launched it into existence.

In 1973 Americans found themselves over a barrel. The Arab oil embargo hit the public by surprise, and there was a sense of panic. Nowhere was this more evident than in California—lines snaking down city streets for blocks and rising tempers around the gas pumps. In this political atmosphere of shock and anger, environmentalist Assemblyman Charles Warren and pronuclear Senator Alfred Alquist teamed up to create the state Energy Resources Conservation and Development Commission.

It was a marriage of convenience at best, for the interests embodied by the original bill were in some cases implicitly opposed. Warren wanted stringent regulation of utility companies and a strong conservation program. Alquist wanted an efficient "one stop" siting procedure for new power plants.

The Warren-Alquist bill was a complicated compromise, with all parties hoping a new high-powered agency might—given enough good leadership, expert staffing, scientific research and perhaps blind luck—figure out some way to solve the state's energy problems. The authors steered the bill through their respective houses of the legislature, and then-Governor Ronald Reagan signed it into law on May 21, 1974.

The commission was given sweeping powers and responsibilities: to regulate the electric power consumption of appliances, to decide on power-plant siting, to set standards for energy-saving features of new buildings, to research and forecast future energy needs, and to speed along the development of "alternative" energy technologies. It was a mammoth task, to be undertaken with deliberate speed.

The five energy commissioners were appointed by newly elected Governor Jerry Brown early in 1975. His original appointees—Richard Maullin, Richard Tuttle, Robert Moretti, Alan Pasternak and Ronald Doctor—were primarily development oriented and, with the exception of Doctor, by and large pronuclear. That did not sit well with the environmentalists.

Just a year after the commission set up shop, Assemblyman Warren was denouncing his brainchild for proutility decisions. "I have no confidence at all in what the commission is doing," he said in May 1976.

Warren charged that a commission report to the legislature, which was based on utility company and PUC statistics, was "giving the utilities a license to steal."

"Damn it," Warren added at the time, "if the commission is always going to side with the utilities, the way the Public Utilities Commission does, I might as well repeal my goddamned act that created the thing." During its first year of operation, it was environmentalists, and not the regulated utilities, who raised howls of protest and demanded that the commission be scrapped.

In 1976 an initiative before California voters would have virtually banned further nuclear development unless it could be *proven* safe. The commission majority—Pasternak, Tuttle and Moretti—publicly opposed Proposition 15 and only Doctor supported its passage. Commission Chairman Maullin and Governor Brown kept a cautious silence on the matter.

At the time, many legislators feared the proposition could pass and nuclear development be curtailed. As a result, pronuclear representatives joined ranks with environmentalists—including Warren again—to author three nuclear safety bills. Although generally less stringent than Proposition 15, the bills do require real safeguards. They require that, before approving new nuclear plant operations, the Energy Commission must determine whether or not the federal government has resolved the problems involved in disposing of nuclear wastes and reprocessing spent fuel. The commission was also ordered to study the feasibility of building nuclear power plants *underground*.

When Proposition 15 was defeated by a margin of two to one, pronuclear legislators expressed regret that they had supported the three "nuclear fuel cycle" bills. But the laws were on the books.

Shortly after he signed the fuel-cycle bills in 1976, Governor Brown began responding to complaints from environmentalists about the pro-development stance of the commission. Richard Tuttle was given a judgeship and replaced on the commission by Emilio Varanini in July 1976.

Varanini proved to be a very energetic energy commissioner—and a highly visible one. According to one former staff member of the commission, it is Varanini—more than any other commissioner—who "determines what the commission says publicly." As an aide to Assemblyman Warren, he had been a chief draftsman of the Warren-Alquist bill and seemed to have definite ideas about what the legislation intended.

Moretti finally quit, after a year of public squabbling that severely damaged the commission's public image. On the way out, he charged that the commission had become unbalanced and narrowly environmentalist. "If the lights ever go out, the price California will pay will be enormous, economically and socially," he warned.

The commission's list of friends and enemies had turned topsyturvy, and Governor Brown did not reassure the proponents of nuclear power when he nominated his own advisor on energy, Suzanne Reed, to replace Moretti.

During these years the commission also built up a staff that worked steadily, behind the scenes, in the areas of energy conservation and the prediction of future energy needs. Among their projects were:

— A plan for attic insulation, automatic night setbacks on thermostats, and more efficient use of water heaters, a voluntary plan that would save Californians $1 billion and avoid the necessity of building from five to seven new power plants.

— An education campaign about "peak demand" of electricity, especially important during the 1976–77 drought when hydroelectric power ebbed, but also crucial for future efficient use of electric power plants.

— A systematic study of "alternative" energy resources—including solar, biomass conversion and photovoltaic cells.

The commission also made headway in the complicated process of distinguishing between "real energy needs" and the raft of predictions put forward by growth-happy utility companies. Although the commission's methodology is at an infant stage, its work has nonetheless raised critical questions that, oddly enough, have not been addressed by government previously. How are the massive additions of high-cost electricity going to be used? And, since large percentages of projected energy needs are for heating air and water, can't we do it much more efficiently and cheaply by using renewable energy resources (sun, wind, etc.) than by relying on oil, gas, coal and nuclear power? And, finally, how much energy can we save by cutting absolutely foolish waste?

As for challenges made about the commission's own predictions, Sy Goldstone, director of the Energy Assessments Division, says: "No forecast is perfect, but we need it as a tool. In fact, the utilities have been somewhat responsive to our work. Pacific Gas and Electric, for example, recently reduced their estimate of future needs by about seven large power plants as a result of our forecast."

The next confrontation, Foster reports, arrived early in 1978, when the commission had to rule on the proposed Sundesert project near Blythe in the Mojave Desert—not a solar plant, as the name might suggest, but a 950-megawatt nuclear unit. Many people expected that Sundesert would slide through the process. Not so.

The commission ruled that "practical alternatives" to this nuclear plant exist, and cited a raft of them: increased conservation, building a conventional coal plant, upgrading existing fossil-fuel plants, developing geothermal energy, using solar power, adopting regional power-pooling, and buying power from the Northwest. Since no overarching need for Sundesert had been proven to its satisfaction, the commission decided not to exempt the project from standards set down by the legislature in 1976.

The utilities were outraged, and so were the seven state senators who, two weeks later, introduced the bill to do away with the Energy Commission. Yet in their outrage the legislators seemed to overlook the complex set of issues the commission had studied so exhaustively. After all, it was not in any way certain that the Sundesert plant could have been built without causing an economic breakdown for San Diego Gas and Electric or colossal rate increases for utility consumers in the area. "All you have to do is look at San Onofre and Diablo Canyon to realize that regulatory approval does not a power plant make," says Commissioner Reed. "The focus of publicity is always on what's called environmental obstructionism. But what about the viability of the plants themselves? What about the finances?"

Part of the steady attack on the Energy Commission, of course, is actually directed at Governor Brown. Perhaps it is appropriate for Brown to bear some of the heat, for it is his shift in attitude that led to the appointments of Varanini and Reed.

It may also have been Brown who tipped the balance on Sundesert. A former staff member of the commission claims that the proposal "was a pipeline project before Brown intervened. Sundesert was going to be the last nuke in California." Apparently events over the past year—whether scientific or political—convinced Brown that it would be foolish to exempt Sundesert from the fuel-cycle laws.

The division in California reflects the Janus-faced chaos of *federal* policy. While President Carter has waved the red flag on plutonium proliferation, his secretary of energy has lobbied for efficient licensing of nuclear plants as though not a single doubt has been raised on safety questions that might slow nuclear development. Such double messages from Washington place the state Energy Commission in a vulnerable front-runner position, treading new paths with no guidance from the national level.

286

Without doubt the Energy Commission has made several major blunders in its front-runner role, but it is a young institution, only 3.5 years old. In its short history it has been a whipping boy, first for environmentalists and now for nuclear power proponents. No one, especially its authors, has been entirely pleased with it.

Nevertheless, abolishing the commission at this juncture would be a giant step backward. Instead of having a somewhat coherent state policy on energy—with which we are free to disagree—the state would once again be plunged into a wholly industry-determined system of energy supply and consumption, a system that has brought us to the edge of disaster.

It is better to have a central energy-planning institution—however ridden with conflict and crisis—than to return to the old myopic faith in never-ending supply.

• As Foster noted, nuclear power in California was already falling out of favor before the 1979 accident at Three Mile Island. That event gave added force to the influential article that follows.

HAL RUBIN   1979

Another Joker in the Nuclear Deck

One oft-ignored fact about nuclear power is that every plant is a temporary structure that begins to wear out from the first moment it is put into operation. The average lifetime is only 30 to 40 years.

When a nuclear plant is no longer safe to operate, it cannot simply be turned off; fuel must be removed, radioactive parts and wastes taken from the site, the whole structure sealed or dismantled. "Decommissioning" is the gently euphemistic term by which the nuclear energy industry describes this complex and expensive task. Although we really don't know yet exactly how to decommission a major plant, we know it will have to be done in decades not too far-off, and in some cases perhaps much sooner.

The critical element governing the life of the facility is the reactor vessel itself. Intense radiation eventually embrittles the steel walls of the

287

vessel that houses the core. After 30 to 40 years of plant operation, the vessel develops stresses that reduce its ability to withstand operational conditions. A secondary limiting factor in the life of a plant is the amount of available storage space for spent fuel.

A tally of the nuclear power facilities that will eventually require decommissioning indicates the scope of the problem. Twenty-two countries now have 220 licensed power reactors and more than 320 reactors are under construction or on order. Despite a definite slowdown recently in nuclear power activity, the United States has 72 power plants in 27 states, and 90 more are being built.

In California, three commercial power reactors are already in operation: Humboldt Bay at Eureka, 63 megawatts; San Onofre near San Diego, 450 megawatts; and Rancho Seco near Sacramento, 913 megawatts. Near Morro Bay, Diablo Canyon 1 has been completed and Diablo Canyon 2 is nearly completed; each facility develops 1,100 megawatts. San Onofre 2 and 3, each 1,300 megawatts, are being built at the site of San Onofre 1. Rancho Seco has 27 more years of operational life if the storage problem is resolved; San Onofre 1 has about 20 years remaining. Humboldt Bay, which was operated for about 14 years of its expected 30-year lifespan, has been shut down since 1977 and is being considered for permanent shut down because of seismic problems. If this happens, the Humboldt Bay facility will become the first commercial reactor in California to require decommissioning.

Ways to Decommission

The Nuclear Regulatory Commission describes four methods for decommissioning spent reactors: dismantlement, entombment, mothballing, and a combination of either entombment or mothballing with subsequent dismantling.

According to the NRC, dismantlement involves the total removal of the facility from the site to radioactive-waste burial grounds. The land is then restored to its original condition and released for unrestricted use. The major problem of immediate dismantlement involves contending with the radiation hazards from large amounts of induced radioactivity. To protect workers engaged in the dismantling activities against excessive doses of radiation, much of the cutting of the reactor parts must be done under water with remotely controlled equipment—a costly and time-consuming process.

Entombment consists of sealing the reactor with concrete or steel

288

after all liquid waste, fuel and easily removed surface contamination have been removed and sent to fuel-storage facilities or burial grounds. The NRC does not require an entombed facility to have security systems to protect against intrusion. However, it does require annual surveillance for possible radiation leaks. Also, periodic maintenance is required to insure the integrity of the entombed structure.

Mothballing is simply removing the fuel and radioactive waste and then placing the facility in protective storage. A mothballed facility requires a security system to prevent intrusion; annual radiological surveys; and periodic maintenance. Both mothballing and entombment permit unlimited amounts of induced radiation and surface contamination to remain on the site.

The fourth method is a combination of either mothballing or entombment with subsequent dismantlement. This method is said to offer the advantage of placing the facility in an entombed or mothballed status for about 65 to 110 years, until the induced radioactivity decays to a level that permits dismantling without undue radiation danger to the workers.

The technology of decommissioning is expected to improve, says D. G. Raasch, chairman of the Sacramento Municipal Utility District committee that is studying the eventual decommissioning of the Rancho Seco plant.

"If I were trying to do this in five years I would be concerned. For any plant that is from 10 to 30 years down the road [from decommissioning] I don't have any personal concerns that they won't have the techniques available. By that time, there will probably be some companies that are pretty good at this business."

Government and nuclear industry studies place the decommissioning and dismantling costs for a large reactor at $25 million to $30 million. Studies made by some of the utility companies that operate nuclear power sites show costs ranging between $90 million and $100 million. Still other estimates, which are based on inflated dollars of the future, put the cost at $1 billion.

Although we are now three decades into the nuclear power era, some vital questions remain unanswered. Who pays for the eventual decommissioning and dismantlement? How and when should the payment be made? What happens if a publicly or a privately owned utility company becomes insolvent before it has met all of its long-term financial obligations for a nuclear facility? Who pays if a facility is shut down prematurely before installation costs have been amortized? What are the implications when costs are calculated in current dollars, but inflation over a 30-year period increases the estimate by a factor of 10?

At present, the NRC requires only that a prospective reactor operator demonstrate to the NRC's satisfaction that it has sufficient financial strength to pay the costs of decommissioning at the time the reactor is retired. According to the NRC, it does not require a plan at the time it licenses a reactor facility because current decommissioning technology will probably be obsolete by the time the facility is retired.

The accident at Three Mile Island occurred while the NRC was trying to decide what to do eventually with dead reactors.

Now that the meltdown threat in Pennsylvania has been averted, some equally serious problems remain. In all likelihood, the plant is no longer usable. Nuclear engineers may be called on to achieve the first decommissioning and dismantling of a full-scale power plant under a staggering array of negative conditions: premature shutdown after a major accident, serious damage to the reactor core, and severe contamination of the containment building. Perhaps half of the 90 tons of uranium-filled fuel rods are damaged.

Neither temporary mothballing nor entombment appears to be feasible unless the fuel is removed first. Can the workers get close enough to enter the containment building? Can the building be breached without releasing dangerous amounts of radioactivity?

Robert Bernero, a senior engineer at NRC, said: "The only politically acceptable solution is to dismantle the reactor and go bury it away from populated areas." Senator Gary Hart (D-Colorado) has called the Three Mile Island plant a "billion dollar mausoleum." Even a high-level team of engineers from Babcock and Wilcox and the NRC isn't sure the dismantling job can be done or how to do it.

Perhaps the lesson of the nuclear power age will be that what has been released from Pandora's Box can never be put back.

• In 1983 Hal Rubin's speculation about the future of the Humboldt Bay nuclear power plant came true. In October, Pacific Gas and Electric ratepayers received notice telling of the company's application to the Public Utilities Commission for a rate increase to cover "Retirement and decommissioning of Humboldt Bay Power Plant, Unit 3." Estimated cost in the first year of the decommissioning effort: $30 million.

Meanwhile, Californians were in fact working out a new kind of energy policy—and not entirely, or even any longer primarily, through the operations of the Energy Commission. The changes begun by the oil shock of 1973 were fitfully, gradually, working their way through the society.

PAT WASHBURN RUBIN   1981

Moving Uncertainly into a New Era

Assessing California's commitment to renewable energy sources is only slightly easier than grabbing a handful of water. The news is both heartening and discouraging, and there is reason to be optimistic as well as wary.

A definite move toward renewable sources is discernible. The question is no longer whether such energy sources are economical, feasible, or acceptable, but how soon the alternatives can become a significant part of California's energy picture.

But the prime movers—the utilities—who have the money and the resources to make the switch a reality continue to drag their feet.

The Good News

Utilities have cut their estimates of demand to less than half of projections made in the early 1970s. The debate of the '70s over proposed new, large power plants (such as the Sundesert nuclear plant) seems to have ended. In fact, no new major power plant has been sited in California in six years. Renewable energy sources are seen as prudent, even essential, investments for at least the next 20 years. California utilities seem to be responding to mounting evidence that the best investment they can make is in discouraging the demand for electricity.

This is a complete about-face from projections during the 1960s. At that time an alarm was sounded that power plants could not be built quickly enough to meet the rapidly growing demand. Energy industries were predicting it would be necessary to build 100 or more nuclear plants in the state.

By reducing their dependency on electricity, California consumers debunked the claim that there was a one-to-one relationship between energy consumption and the gross national product. In the past, energy consumption had been linked to economic growth because for many years the rise in the GNP paralleled the rise in consumption. Energy planners now know that economic growth need not suffer as energy growth slows.

Southern California Edison (SCE) announced last October that it was reorganizing its capital-investment program to include projects to develop renewable resources. A spokesman said renewable sources will provide 30 percent of the company's electricity by 1990.

In 1978 Governor Brown signed into law a state wind-energy bill intended to provide 10 percent of California's projected electricity needs by the year 2000. Two years later customers of SCE began receiving part of their power from a wind-turbine generator. PG&E is planning to have its first large wind-turbine generator (2,500 kilowatts) on line by next year. According to the California Energy Commission, wind-electric energy could save more than 50 million barrels of oil a year.

Cogeneration, which is the generation of electricity by using waste heat from industrial processes to run a turbine, is making a comeback in California. Cogeneration was popular in the United States when electricity was neither widely available nor cheap. Now it contributes about 4 percent of the state's power, and energy planners want to raise that to about 10 percent—6,000 megawatts—by the end of the decade. Cogeneration is 60- to 80-percent efficient in its use of energy, while an oil-fired generating plant is only 30- to 40-percent efficient.

A mandate requiring all new houses to use solar water heating became effective in San Diego County about two years ago. Since then about 20 similar mandates have been passed throughout the state, and approximately 80 more are pending enactment or being seriously considered.

Utilities in Trouble

The bad news is that, at the same time, California's major utility companies are still firmly committed to nuclear power. PG&E is betting its financial health on being able to operate the two nuclear plants at Diablo Canyon, and SCE is anxious to put the two San Onofre plants on line.

While California's utilities are the most forward-looking in the nation, they haven't been progressive very long and still harbor prejudices against alternatives to conventional fuels. Bob Weisenmiller of the California Energy Commission says, "They're not innovative companies. You expect from them a slow, phased approach without much risk-taking."

California's utilities are caught in a trap, and the idle Diablo Canyon reactors symbolize the illness that haunts the entire industry—that the electric utilities are no longer in control of their destinies.

They rushed pell-mell into a high-risk nuclear technology. The utilities and the Nuclear Regulatory Commission never contemplated a debacle like that at Three Mile Island, which happened three months after the plant opened. Just as bad, from a financial standpoint, is the situation at Diablo Canyon and San Onofre where the fate of about $3-billion worth of brand-new equipment hangs in the balance because of unforeseen seismic problems. The possibility of having to absorb a loss of that magnitude has traumatized the directors of PG&E and SCE, and forced them to defend their original decisions to go nuclear.

Utilities have always been growth industries accustomed to doubling their size every 7 to 10 years. But in California, projections of demand are down to an annual increase of 1.44 percent—half the amount predicted as recently as 1974.

The major investor-owned utilities must face the grim fact that they are in serious financial trouble. Marginal costs have increased, demand is uncertain, and the capital constraints are fierce.

Utilities are also losing the monopoly over power generation they have held for so long. The major reason is changes in the Public Utilities Regulatory Policy Act (PURPA) regulations that govern how much utilities are required to pay for the excess electricity they buy from small producers. Utilities must now pay their "avoided cost," which is what it would have cost the utility to produce the extra electricity. The state Public Utilities Commission (PUC) sets the rate for the avoided cost for each utility. That rate is lower than the cost of building new power plants, but higher than the average rate, which makes it lucrative for the small producer.

Small power projects are blooming throughout the state. An example would be a water or irrigation district placing a turbine in a canal or pipe to generate electricity, of which any excess over need would be sold to the local utility company.

"Every month there's a long list of permit applications for small hydro or cogeneration projects in California," says Commissioner Weisenmiller. "These are going on outside the traditional process. The

293

utilities have not been keeping track of small hydro, cogeneration or wind-farm projects in the state, but every month we find another 40 projects being proposed. It's profitable now."

Janice Hamrin, of the Alliance for Renewable Energy, believes the increased competition from small producers will force the utilities to either change the way they do business or be wiped out; to continue on a conventional path would be disastrous for them.

One available option is that the utilities could become energy service companies. Instead of simply producing the electricity or gas to meet demand, they would concern themselves with the end use of the power and select optimum sources of supply. One obvious example of wastefulness is the use of electricity to heat water.

In addition, utilities could develop joint ventures with the private sector, with local governments or with irrigation districts to distribute the excess power generated by small producers where it is needed. Other options would be for the utilities to finance installation of solar water heaters or load-management units. The latter devices enable the company to reduce peak demands by installing a gadget that would temporarily switch off air conditioners, for example, for short periods during hours of peak demand.

Hamrin says, "I really believe the utilities will be wiped out in the long term if they don't switch over to this way of looking at themselves [as energy service companies]. They can fight it every step of the way, but they may end up losing."

The Local Level

Hamrin sees a great deal of interest in renewables at the local level. She cites two main reasons. First, there is concern about energy security should there be a major disruption of Mideast oil. "The real point is that the only place you can do anything significant in a short time is on the local level."

The second reason is economic. As energy and utility prices go up, millions of dollars are leaving the communities and going to the utilities. To counteract that, one community, Oceanside, is thinking of developing a municipal corporation to produce solar energy and promote conservation, which is actually a way to finance and market conservation and renewable energy. Hamrin says the savings in energy expenditures that could result from this program would keep in the community about $1 million that now goes outside to pay for energy.

The concept of municipal solar utilities began in Santa Clara, where it was used to finance and market solar water heating for swimming pools. Since then, six more California cities have obtained funding to develop pilot programs. Four of them have had programs approved by their city councils.

Perhaps the ultimate irony in the confusing energy-politics picture is the fact that, although advocates of renewables are popularly perceived as belonging at the left of the political spectrum, the kind of energy future they describe has strong conservative appeal: it is decentralized and pluralistic, with new opportunities for private enterprise, challenges for the imaginative entrepreneur, healthy competition and a role for local government.

14 *The Diamond Lane*

- A few years into the 1970s, the great freeway controversy began to fade out, for a reason no one, a few years earlier, had reckoned on: the government was simply finding the big roads too costly to build in anything like the abundance originally conceived. In 1974, Joseph C. Houghteling, long the "token conservationist" on the State Highway Commission and at that point a member of the Bay Area's Metropolitan Transportation Commission, read the handwriting on the wall—not without a curious note of regret.

JOSEPH C. HOUGHTELING   1974

Some of Our Freeways Are Missing

There may be those who think this title a bit overblown, something the mid-1920s *New York Graphic* might have displayed in type intended only for the announcement of Doomsday. Actually, it's modest. Of equal validity would be "California's Missing Five Billion Dollars," an eye-catcher that would gain attention even in these days of high crimes and misdemeanors.

In the mid-1960s, when I was on the California Highway Commission, it was believed with justification that there was a perpetual-motion money machine in the back room. This marvelous mechanism cranked out gas-tax revenues that constructed freeways that promoted higher consumption of gasoline that generated more gas-tax revenues to construct more freeways *ad infinitum*. Platoons of surveyors were dotting California's landscape with straight-lined markers, presaging the construction to follow.

During that time, the public issues, disputes, hearings and delegation presentations to the Highway Commission concerned freeway-route adoptions. In 1965 alone, 158 miles of new freeway alignments appeared on California's map. Once the routes were adopted, attention turned to the highway budget that inevitably would transform the line on the map into concrete, asphalt, and opening-day ceremonies.

Communities petitioned and received the blessings of prompt adoption of freeway routes, regardless of the fiscal fact that construction was a task reserved for the next generation. But the early positioning of routes allowed local development planning to proceed, using freeway and interchange locations as base lines; the promise of future freeways became the reality for immediate decisions. Subdivisions, industrial plants and shopping centers came into being long before the freeway; to doubt its ultimate construction was to question tomorrow's sunrise.

Well, the sun continues to rise, but the marvelous perpetual-motion money machine is gone, taking with it, perhaps permanently, many if not most of the freeways of the future. Who took the machine? Certainly the Arabs or stagflation, or both, depending on which economist you believe, are major dismantlers.

Gas taxes for highway purposes are based on gallonage, not price—seven cents per gallon for the state, four cents for the "feds." Thus as gasoline consumption has been lessened by shortages and higher costs, the endless sequence of new freeways resulting in new highway revenues has been broken on the income side.

Not only is gas usage an income factor, but changing allocations from highway trust funds have been significant. Even before the present jolt of gasoline constraints and stagflation, the amounts of funding available for freeway construction have been eroding. Federal interstate and urban highway funds now also go for transit capital outlay.

Were the income squeeze and uncertainties not enough, freeway construction costs are rising at an angle that would challenge an experienced alpinist. In the first three months of 1974, the construction dollar's value eroded 32 cents. Over an even longer span, assuming a larger view of the past tells more of the future, the California construction index is one of the growth shocks of our time. When I left the Highway Commission on January 1, 1967, the index was at 100; seven and a half years later, on May 31, 1974, it was at 219.

What this has already done to freeway planning and construction can more than be imagined. Early in 1973, it was estimated that $7.8 billion would be available for construction of projects in the state highway program over the eight years beginning July 1, 1975.

Then last May, a new forecast, revised in the light of intervening events, showed only $3.9 billion would be available for the same period. And the added factor of inflation lowered the estimate to only

$2.7 billion worth of actual construction during the eight years. $2.7 billion is a considerable sum, unless it was once expected to be $7.8 billion. The $5-billion difference is what made the freeways disappear.

Unlike the ancient emperor who decapitated the bearer of bad tidings, the Highway Commission has confined itself to lopping off adopted freeway routes. Since unpleasant chores are best performed under an agreeable name, the process is called "recycling," a term used more happily in the environmentalist jargon.

One of the significant recyclings does have a cheerful environmental tone. Lake Tahoe's westside freeway, Route 89, has been through the process—the adopted line has been rescinded and the acquired rights-of-way offered for sale. For many, this action recalls the long, heated arguments of the early 1960s over the route's missing link in the unique Emerald Bay area. With Route 89 freeway adoptions to both the north and south of the D. L. Bliss and Emerald Bay state parks, the debate centered on the lower bridge route versus the upper hillside location, with a tunnel sometimes thrown in as a diversion.

Eligible for the recycling process, like Route 89, is any freeway-route adoption for which it is unlikely construction funds will be found in the next two decades. As of August this year, the commission was considering 20 present freeway-route adoptions for recycling, the "bottom line" of the process being disadoption. These represent 177 miles of freeway, mostly rural, that if constructed would cost $770 million at current projections.

In addition, there are 70 more unfinanced freeway-route alignments in the present 20-year Highway Program Guide. These are in limbo, still shown as adopted lines on the planning maps, but lacking any foreseeable funding.

Responding mostly to local concerns, and usually with considerable local publicity, legislative bills have removed various routes from the Freeway and Expressway System. Route 1 along the Los Angeles coast was once to be a freeway; it's now in the more humble highway system in most areas. Two proposed freeways, the causes of San Francisco's "granddaddy" freeway revolt of the mid-sixties, are gone from the higher status, the stub ends of the city's Embarcadero and Central freeways being monuments to this change.

There are 12,333 miles authorized in the California F&E System. As of 1974, only 4,394 miles, a little more than a third, have been constructed or are in future budgets. Ask not which freeway the commission recycles—it may be yours, anywhere in California.

• But if the mighty freeway push was losing momentum, its replacement with a new thrust, a more varied strategy, proved to be no automatic or easy consequence.

Considerable changes were duly made:

— In 1972, Assembly Bill 69 rearranged the transportation bureaucracy and promised a fresh beginning in transportation planning. A new transportation board was set up to do the statewide planning job; advisory councils of government in the various regions were charged with building component regional plans. (In the Bay Area, a more authoritative body—the Metropolitan Transportation Commission—took on this job.)

— Also in 1972, the Legislature placed a sales tax on gasoline for the purpose of funding mass transit.

— In 1974, the voters consented to a very modest "raid" on the hitherto sacrosanct highway trust funds. Proposition 5 of that year provided that up to 25 percent of highway funds allocated to a county could be used for mass transit—but only after a countywide referendum.

As is often the case, it proved much easier to change labels and to shuffle organizations than to change realities. This 1977 article sketches the frustrating course of the new planning process up to that time.

THOMAS H. CRAWFORD   1977

The $60-Million Misunderstanding

For more than four years now, the state government has been planning to have a transportation plan.

The effort dates from 1972, when the state legislature passed AB 69, a law intended to move California away from its heavy emphasis on a single mode of transportation—the private car—and toward a more mixed and energy-efficient system. One part of this was a major reorganization of the state-level transportation bureaucracy: the Department of Public Works became the Department of Transportation (CalTrans), and the State Transportation Board was established.

The new arrangement was supposed to launch a new era in transportation policy. Now, instead of being preoccupied with highway building, the state would turn toward developing what the legislature called "balanced transportation." The details of this new approach were to be contained in a plan "directed at the achievement of a coordinated and balanced transportation system for the state, including but not limited to mass transportation, highways, aviation, and maritime and railroad facilities and services." The plan was to be adopted by the board and submitted to the legislature by January 1, 1976.

CalTrans and regional planning agencies produced an impressive document, replete with colored graphs and maps; it cost a lot of money, and nobody liked it much. Donald Burns, who had become Secretary of Business and Transportation, called it "a veritable wind-tunnel of rhetoric." All it really amounted to, he said, was more highways. Governor Brown called it "the $60 million misunderstanding."

The plan was rejected by the board, and a special planning task force was assembled to have another go at it. The new team produced a new plan—actually, a "policy element" of a plan—with lots of imaginative ideas about how to reduce our dependence on automobiles. The most controversial were the "pricing strategy" mechanisms such as vehicle stickers, regional "smog taxes" on vehicles, tolls on freeways, and transportation stamps based on income. Although these ideas were indeed daring, they violated one of the basic political canons of the Brown administration, which was to avoid tax raises of any kind. As a result, the administration proceeded to disown the plan.

Back to the task force for still another try. After several months' more work, a new basic policy element was produced. The controversial pricing strategy was submerged, and there was more emphasis now on efficient ways of using the present transportation system. The new statement of goals, policies and objectives was forwarded to the legislature this year.

The legislature shows no inclination to accept the new plan, or even touch it with a 10-foot pole. The arguments and justifications for this are fairly complex, but the main reason is simple: when it comes right down to it, the legislature is not ready to go ahead and do the thing it created the planning process for—take California's transportation development in a new direction.

• Despite all this churning, the Brown administration did have some definite ideas about transportation. For one thing, it discouraged new freeway projects even more strongly than the money crunch was already doing. It was now time, the administration reasoned, to focus on the very expensive business of maintaining the vast existing system, rather than increasing the load by expanding it. At the same time, Brown's people sought ways of using that system—the networks of asphalt, the hundreds of buses, the millions of automobiles—a little more efficiently. More than anything else, that meant getting people to join in carpools, rather than traveling always one to a car.

Of various strategies for encouraging formal and informal carpools, the best appeared to be the "diamond-lane" technique. By setting aside an existing freeway lane for buses and multipassenger cars, the engineers could use both carrot and stick. They made life easier for carpoolers, harder for the unaccompanied commuters creeping along in the remaining lanes.

The diamond-lane technique was first tested on the Golden Gate Bridge and Highway 101 in San Francisco and Marin counties, and was judged a great success, postponing for many years a looming congestion crisis. The second experiment—on the Santa Monica Freeway in Los Angeles—was a fiasco. Commuters bitterly resented the special lane and refused to honor it; local press and politicians denounced the state transportation planners; and in the end that effort was abandoned. The same thing happened a little later in Livermore.

In 1977, *Cry California's* Walt Anderson interviewed Adriana Gianturco, Brown's able and controversial Secretary of Transportation, and got her analysis of what went wrong.

ADRIANA GIANTURCO
and WALTER TRUETT ANDERSON   1977

The Diamond Lane: An Interview

ADRIANA GIANTURCO: The Santa Monica Freeway diamond lane was three to four years in the planning stage, and what happened during that period was primarily negotiating with local governments and getting their agreement. Of course, when the going got tough, it was as though none of this had ever happened. The city council of Los Angeles turned right around and took a vote saying it didn't support the project, which really put us in a difficult position.

301

Looking back, of course, it's apparent that the public didn't understand this project—didn't understand what it was supposed to achieve, thought it was all negative and nothing positive. Clearly there ought to have been more public participation. In that particular instance, however, we were working with the regional planning body. I haven't been terribly impressed, to tell you the truth, with the performance of the bodies we already have—the Councils of Government—in that case, the Southern California Association of Governments, which receives money from the state to do comprehensive planning in the Los Angeles area. They had a citizen-advisory committee that dealt with this diamond-lane project, but apparently it never got beyond a small group that discussed it and endorsed it.

I think when you're talking about something that turns out to be as fundamental as a diamond-lane concept in Los Angeles, it has to go way beyond having a small group of people discuss it. Our previous experience with a dedicated lane had been in San Francisco, and although there was some initial opposition, that project has turned out to be highly successful—it works beautifully.

WALT ANDERSON: *What do you think was the difference?*

AG: There seem to be two crucial differences. One is the attitude of local politicians, and in the Marin-101 case they just did not see this as a major issue. There were complaints when the lanes were first instituted, but nobody got on the bandwagon and made it a political issue. Secondly, it's the role of the press. The *Los Angeles Times* wrote something like five editorials in four weeks on it, really incredible editorials. In one they talked about conspiracy on the part of CalTrans in instituting this project, the implication being that it was just sprung on the public after the greatest secrecy. The fact was that the *Times* itself had written editorials in support the year before it was opened.

WA: *Wasn't the diamond-lane program just one part of a general strategy of increasing vehicle occupancy?*

AG: That's the case. The plan involves four major techniques for trying to increase vehicle occupancy. The first technique is the one we applied on the Santa Monica Freeway, which is to take an existing lane out of use and dedicate it to buses and carpools. The second is to build a new lane, and dedicate that to buses and carpools. We tried that on the San Diego Freeway—we constructed an additional lane, meaning that the other lanes would remain the same. That one we were forced to open up to all traffic! The third concept is building a separated facility for buses and carpools. We have done that on the El Monte busway, which runs down the middle of the San Bernardino Freeway. That's been in operation for several years, it's working very well. The fourth technique is to use ramp meters entering the freeways [delaying access during peak periods so that traffic on the freeway itself continues to flow], with bypass lanes for buses and carpools.

In looking at any of these things you have to look at costs as well as benefits. The Santa Monica diamond lane had a much greater impact on increasing bus ridership and carpooling than has the El Monte busway, and the Santa Monica project cost, in capital costs, about $100,000, as compared to $50 million for the El Monte busway.

WA: *So where do you think you'll go from there, as far as that strategy is concerned?*

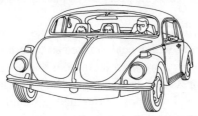

AG: Well, we're in a bind, because we're under a mandate from the federal government to try to improve air quality. There are really three objectives. One is improvement in air quality, which would come from fewer miles being driven by vehicles. The second objective is energy conservation. Clearly, if you have fewer vehicles you're using less gasoline. The third objective is reducing congestion. Those objectives remain the same. There are several ways of meeting those objectives, but only one way seems to meet all three and be financially feasible, and that is increasing vehicle occupancy.

We have estimated that if you can raise vehicle occupancy in Los Angeles from the existing 1.2 persons per car at peak hours, which means practically everybody is traveling alone, to 1.4 persons, you would relieve congestion. And the way to do that is more carpools and more bus ridership. Then the question is, how do you get more carpools and more bus riders? And there are two fundamental approaches to that. One is a transportation-management strategy; the other is a pricing strategy—make it so expensive people can't afford to go out in their own vehicles. Those are the options. I don't know what the answers are. I would tend to favor less restrictive ways of doing things. The question is, do we just let things happen or do we try to get ahead of the game and deal with them positively to avoid a really serious crisis?

- In the following piece, Walt Anderson reviews the record of a decade in which change had been "trying to happen." In 1979, he tells us, a number of pieces at last fell into place.

WALTER TRUETT ANDERSON   1979

Taking a Transfer to Mass Transit

All it took was the right combination of events: a renewed world petroleum crisis, the threat of gasoline rationing, double-digit inflation, a presidential election and the prospect of passage of the Gann "Spirit of 13" amendment.

On May 31, 1979, Governor Brown held a press conference to unveil a new program, which he described as "a serious attempt to come to grips with the energy problem facing our state." This was generally interpreted by the press as a combination of transportation planning and presidential politics. President Carter had responded to the gasoline crisis by calling for a crash program to develop synthetic fuels. Governor Brown was responding by calling for a crash program to develop mass transit. Both were ways of preserving high levels of mobility: Carter would produce new fuels, Brown would give us different ways to come and go. "Californians are not going to give up their mobility," Brown said in his press conference. "That's the essence of our whole way of life."

With remarkable speed, a major portion of the transportation program was enacted into law. Less than a month after the governor's press conference, the legislature had passed (and the governor had signed) Senate Bill 620, which appropriated some $300 million for transit development over the next three years. The bill was, among other things, an unprecedented expression of agreement among transportation policy makers who have often disagreed on basic issues.

A cynic might think that, considering the historically strong bias of California legislators toward highway development, a mass-transit bill would not pass that easily unless there were something in it for the highway builders. A cynic would be right.

Anderson explains that the bill provided a way of sheltering half a billion dollars in gas-tax money—already collected but not yet allocated to specific projects—from the effects of Paul Gann's pending "Spirit-of-13" spending-limit initiative.

As revolutions go, it is rather mild. Nevertheless it is a significant new program. It provides new assistance for local bus and light-rail streetcar systems and for the first time puts the state in the railroad business. Now CalTrans has the authority to sponsor rail lines—contracting with operators to run them—and can also design, acquire and construct new intercity transit systems.

CalTrans Director Gianturco says: "One of the reasons we have a good highway system in this state is because there was a determined effort to get something done and a single agency was given vast authority to do it. One of the problems in the transit area has been that we have fragmented authority; lots of different institutions have partial control over one, and there is no sustained, heavy state role. I think giving the state greater authority in the transit area is a step in the right direction."

SB 620 appropriates $150 million for local transit and $150 million for state projects—commuter and intercity rail, grade separations, fuel research and intermodal facilities. Among the likely results will be:

— Expansion and improvement of service in local transit systems.

— Increased commuter and intercity rail service.

— New light-rail (streetcar) systems in such cities as San Diego and Sacramento.

— More intermodal facilities to make it easier for travelers to make direct connections—for example, from intercity rail to local buses.

— Possible state assistance in developing a new rapid-transit system in Los Angeles—the Wilshire corridor route.

The new state activity in transit development is proceeding—so far—without any new taxes. The funds appropriated in SB 620 will all come from sales taxes on gasoline—*not* the seven-cent special gasoline tax, which can be rerouted only through constitutional amendment.

Does passage of SB 620 mark the high tide of state support for transit development, or will the state go even farther in that direction? Some Sacramento insiders say the legislators think they have done as much as can be expected of them and they will now stand back and wait to see what CalTrans does with its new money and powers. Others are certain that further increases in transit support will be necessary; one way to get this would be to make more gasoline-tax funds available for other-than-highway purposes.

It would seem that, since California has one of the most advanced systems of highways in the world, the easiest and least expensive way to develop mass transit would be to take maximum advantage of that

305

resource—designate more lanes for carpool-only or bus-only traffic. This, too, is politically unlikely at the moment. The Brown administration was burned by the effort to impose a diamond-lane arrangement to encourage carpooling on the Santa Monica Freeway; now the administration's position is that no lanes will be removed from automobile use. Transit-only lanes will come into existence only when added on to existing freeways or included as part of new ones.

We now have a total of 44 miles of exclusive bus and carpool lines in the entire state, a minuscule fragment of our enormous highway system. This will change, but very slowly and at great cost; political "realism" dictates that one of the most sensible approaches toward modifying our transportation system be done in the slowest and most expensive way possible.

There is a lot of power politics connected with transportation policy-making, and there is also a lot of plain demagoguery. Young politicians in Los Angeles launched their careers by shaking their fists at Sacramento over the diamond-lane incident; Governor Brown got a fair amount of publicity out of shaking his fist at Washington, threatening dire things if California did not get its fair share of gasoline; the President and the Vice-President, meanwhile, were busy shaking their fists at OPEC. All of this being done in the name of mobility, which has been elevated to the status of a civic virtue.

A Mild Revolution

We are indeed in the midst of a mild revolution in transportation. It has been coming on for some time, and it may well gather speed. What is going on right now *is* an important change, but we should keep in mind what it *is not:*

First, it is not a shift from the automobile to mass transit. It is a shift from an enormous overdependence on one transportation mode toward a modestly multimodal system in which the automobile continues to dominate. Even with SB 620 in place, transportation spending will favor automobile-related development over other modes by about ten to one.

Second, it is not a serious effort to appraise our real transportation needs and plan for the future. Everything is dominated by the question of how we can preserve present levels of mobility. That is the wrong question, and as long as we keep asking it we are going to keep getting answers irrelevant to the real question. The times call for a hard look at

306

mobility itself, an attempt to sort out how much of it is necessity, how much is luxury, and how much utter gasburning nonsense. We don't even need to look too hard, because we all know that a huge portion of our charging about contributes nothing to the production of useful goods and services and isn't much fun, either.

I had a friend in college who got in his car one Saturday and drove from Berkeley to Los Angeles for a date. She stood him up. He got in his car and drove back to Berkeley. I thought of him when I read Governor Brown's remarks about mobility as the essence of our way of life.

Our current modest tinkering with transportation policy is far short of the thorough reappraisal the times call for. Unless we are willing to take a look at it in a fundamental way and think about what our present needs are and what future conditions are likely to be, we are not really planning, and the impressive new policies being produced now are not apt to look much better 20 years from now than the plans of the 1950s look to us today.

15   *The Peripheral Canal*

- The pages of *Cry California* show us a state working hard in the 1970s to match its plans and policies to a changing world. In some areas change was relatively swift. Energy policy and transportation policy, if hardly revolutionized at decade's end, had certainly moved a long way from the norms of the 1960s. The new reality—that it was no longer possible to build and spend on the old grandiose scale—had sunk in.

In certain other basic areas, though, change came much more slowly. One region of policy where changes were attempted and very largely thwarted was the all-important concern of water.

During the 1970s, two kinds of water planning, an old and a new, were going on at the same time. The first was a search for new water sources, new damsites on new rivers. The second was a pursuit of water *management,* a search for ways of using the present developed supply more efficiently. The advocates of each approach had managed, at the end of the second Brown administration, largely to frustrate the other.

Yet hopes had been very high at the beginning.

DANIEL J. BLACKBURN   1976

New Look, or Business as Usual?

Business conducted at meetings of the California Water Commission during the early seventies was not of a pulse-quickening nature; water and its management share a common bland quality.

But there was tenseness, a tangible edge as the June 1975 meeting was gaveled to a start by chairman Ira J. Chrisman, whose term even then was at an end. Exactly one-half hour later, California's nervous water establishment had a whole new set of rules.

Ronald B. Robie—brash, articulate, confident—took the microphone to address the commission. It would be Robie's first statement as California's newly designated director of water resources, but already his words had been anticipated, rumored, dissected, distributed throughout the state's water world:

"In comparing alternative water-management possibilities, consideration shall be given to capital and annual costs, cost-effectiveness, economic and social benefits, environmental and ecological effects, and energy requirements."

Then: "The least expensive alternative will not necessarily be selected."

Spoken by another, the meaning of the message would have been winked away as mere public-relations dialogue. But the commission was not hearing from Harvey O. Banks, or William Warne, or Bill Gianelli, or John Teerink—all former DWR directors. It was Robie, at 37 the youngest appointee in the business, a lawyer, one-time legislative committee consultant and vice-chairman of the State Water Resources Control Board.

Now, California has never been frugal in its approach to water transfer. No other state in the country—and for that matter, few nations in the world—have matched our willingness to spend lavishly for such purposes. But in the past this spending has always been guided by the rationale of getting water to the customers at the lowest possible price and letting the hidden costs of water projects (such matters as the destruction of fisheries or the damage to the ecology of regions from which water is being removed) be passed on to other agencies or future generations.

Robie was telling the developers that all future water projects would bear the additional cost of environmental protection. This new attention to adverse environmental changes caused by construction and operation of water projects could have but one obvious result: projects would now cost more—in some cases, *much* more.

The betting was that Robie meant to implement what he said. For the state's water resources string-pullers, public and private, the new director's irreverent trampling of the "cheapest project" concept was near heresy and ignited dark misgivings about the future control of California's water.

Others in the audience reacted quite differently to Robie's barrage of policy alterations. To them, an end was in sight to frustrations and political pummeling at the hands of construction-oriented water planners who had been at the controls for so many years. Robie's philosophies would meld well with those of his boss, Claire Dedrick, a Sierra Club vice-president turned Resources Secretary. Optimism grew.

So Robie and Dedrick set out to set the water world ablaze, and everyone sat back to watch.

Today the watching continues.

• Blackburn went on to complain that, for all the brave talk, no sign of a real reexamination of policy had yet appeared. The blame for this he placed on Governor Brown.

The wheels were turning, however; and if the results were slow, it was partly because of the immense complexity of the task Robie faced. On the one hand, his department was supposed to be the water planner, to see the big picture, for the entire state of California—though its actual authorities were limited. On the other hand, DWR was the proprietor of the State Water Project, one of the greatest of the dam-and-ditch systems that lace the state. And it was a signatory of contracts promising to deliver, to irrigation districts and to the Metropolitan Water District of Southern California, an amount about twice as large as its present waterworks could produce.

To simplify, we can say that Brown's DWR was impelled by one of its roles—as statewide water planner—to a new emphasis on conservation, on the efficient use of groundwater, on the reclamation of wastewater, and on other "new look" strategies for matching water use with the available supply. But by its other role—as water supplier with promises to keep—it was driven toward the building of additional dams and canals.

The greatest of these works—and the symbol of the water controversy—was the long-planned Peripheral Canal. It would move Northern California water around the bottleneck of the Sacramento-San Joaquin Delta for export to the thirsty San Joaquin Valley farms and to the Southern California metropolis. To traditional water planners, the canal was an indispensable missing link in the system, which could not work at full capacity without it.

But to people who feared the effects of increased water export, the absence of the canal was reassurance. The very inefficiency of moving water through the labyrinthine channels of the Delta put a limit on how much could be moved. Build the canal, and it would become physically possible to take much more of the Sacramento's water (with resulting damage to the Delta and to San Francisco Bay)—possible, too, to transfer water from the Eel and the other North Coast rivers. True, the legislature had resolved in 1972 not to develop these rivers, and the Brown water planners agreed; but all this could change in a hurry.

Nicholas Arguimbau takes up the story.

NICHOLAS ARGUIMBAU   1979

New Developments
Are Not the Answer

A number of events have brought water politics to the forefront in the last two years. One is the drought of 1976–77. As Ronald Robie, director of the state Department of Water Resources, remarked as California headed in the summer of 1977 toward what could have been a third and disastrous dry winter, "The State has had 40 years without serious drought conditions, and people forget." The people could not immediately forget this time, however, how critical to California's economy its water supplies really are. Another factor bringing matters to a head is that the state has a number of major contracts for water delivery, and the contractual entitlements, regardless of need, are inexorably creeping up to the maximum the State Water Project can currently deliver.

Entitlements to the Metropolitan Water District of Southern California, in particular, are about to take a leap because of a predicted diversion of Colorado River water to the Central Arizona Project.

Ron Robie entered upon the scene bright-eyed and bushy-tailed in 1975, determined to take a fresh look at the State Water Project's basic assumptions.

Central to the new administration's water policy were conservation and reclamation. Director Robie announced a "water management policy," based on the principle that "water resources already developed shall be used to the maximum extent before new sources are developed," and he was not afraid to tell the Association of California Water Agencies what he thought of an expanded State Water Project: "The dinosaur's eloquent lesson is that if some bigness is good, an overabundance of bigness is not necessarily better." A comprehensive look at water conservation was commenced, and DWR began to reassess the need for

311

the Peripheral Canal, which—as Robie had recognized in his white paper—had both environmental significance and "strategic importance" as leverage to persuade the Metropolitan Water District to limit its designs on the northern rivers.

> But when the two studies were completed, Arguimbau reports, they recommended only modest changes in old policies.

Water Conservation in California, the first of the reports, was disappointing to people who had held hopes for the conservation alternative. Its predictions about potential agricultural water conservation in particular were surprisingly conservative. While the report came out in May 1976, it was not until 1978 that a few environmentalists and DWR staffers noticed that its complex formula for "agricultural irrigation efficiency" was totally unrelated to the statistic of primary concern: water consumed per unit of crop yield.

By November 1978, Robie expressed his own doubts about the formula. In short, it is almost official today that the only comprehensive study of agricultural water use cannot be used to estimate conservation potential. (DWR's current projection of 1980 demand shows a *total* saving from conservation of only 200,000 acre-feet.)

How much water *can* be saved? Estimates range from the current DWR projection to a federal General Accounting Office estimate of 40 percent—more than 50 times that amount. There are arguments over the extent to which excess water is necessary to wash salts out of the soil; over the cost of efficient irrigation systems; over the amount of land that is of adequate quality to be converted from highly water-consumptive uses such as irrigated pasture to lower water-consumptive uses such as irrigated orchard crops. There are disputes over the future of the cattle industry, which will have a greater effect on water demand than anything that can happen in the urban sector.

> Despite the disagreements, Arguimbau says, it is clear that vastly more can be accomplished through conservation than the state planners admit—especially if the subsidies that keep the price of irrigation water so very low are reduced and replaced with rewards for those who conserve.

The second long-awaited report, the reassessment of the Peripheral Canal, came out early in 1977. Shortly thereafter, an amusing scene took place in the Sierra Club national headquarters in San Francisco. Governor Brown was there to give a talk on environmental issues: "era of limits," and all that. A reporter caught him in the hall afterward and

312

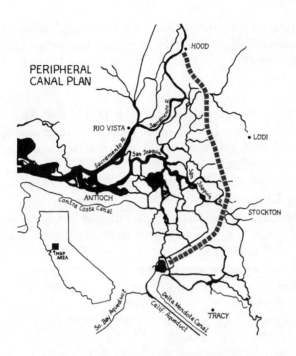

asked, "But what are you doing about employment, Governor?" Brown replied to this effect: "We have the Delta Facility. That'll produce lots of jobs." Confronted by a blank stare, he repeated, "You know, the Delta Facility." An aide pulled aside the still-confused reporter and explained that the Delta Facility had once been known as the Peripheral Canal.

People may disagree about the merits of the Peripheral Canal, but small it isn't. Over 400 feet wide. Deep enough to float a tanker. Big enough to carry over half the average flow of the Sacramento River and its tributaries, the proposed canal could be the largest river south of the Columbia, if anyone wanted to operate it that way.

The Brown administration had come up with a dream package. Among its features:

— The Peripheral Canal, sucking enough water from the Sacramento River to supply southern California's demand to the year 2000 and to douse the southern end of the Delta with fresh water to keep out the salt.

— Glenn Reservoir, a man-made lake on the eastern slope of the Coast Range north of Clear Lake, big enough to dwarf Lake Shasta, designed as a storage point for the spring flood of the Sacramento River, to be sent south in the dry season.

313

— Promises to the dam builders that feasibility studies for Dos Rios, controversial reservoir on the Eel River, would be speeded up.

— Promises to environmentalists that we wouldn't need Dos Rios if we built Glenn.

A dream package indeed: save the Delta, save the North Coast rivers, flush the San Joaquin Valley and Los Angeles with sparkling water from the mountains of Northern California, and generate thousands of construction jobs.

Something for everyone, if it works. There are only two questions: Will it work? Who will pay for it?

Whether or not it works has to do with a variety of safeguards in the Brown administration package: fish screens on the canal, to be approved by Fish and Game before the last segment of the canal is completed; operation in compliance with Delta water-quality standards; joint federal/state operation of the canal to protect the Delta; no need to dam the Eel. All very well, but if you have a ditch in the north that can carry half the Sacramento River, and votes in the south that can take away the safeguards, where are you?

One line of thinking is that if the safeguards are for real, it should be possible to build them into federal law or the state constitution. Some attempts were made along this line in the legislature in 1977 and 1978, such as requiring that North Coast rivers receive federal protection, or amending the state constitution to make the safeguards safe, but the supporters of Brown's package balked. The coalition behind the administration bill began to erode, and the bill failed to pass in either year.

What will come of it all is unclear. What *is* clear is that a program that attempts development and conservation at the same time will be in serious trouble. From the point of view of development, there are dangers of default on bonded indebtedness if water demand is substantially curtailed, since the SWP must pay for itself from water sales. From the standpoint of conservation, the existence of surplus supplies and the commitment elsewhere of the capital needed to convert agricultural land to water-efficient uses can only discourage conservation efforts. Moreover, because the state's water contracts *require* delivery of entitlements if adequate supplies exist, it will be legally difficult to impose limits on water users if the delivery capabilities of the project are expanded without first renegotiating the contracts.

Clearly, alternatives exist that need to be explored. The massive subsidies from federal, state and local taxes funneled into water consumption could be partially eliminated, and partially diverted to subsidize conservation instead. Marginal cost-pricing could be instituted so that expanded water demand would bear its real costs. Water rights could be made transferable on the open market. Few of these steps can be taken, however, without a major change in direction.

Arguimbau borrows the terms used by energy theorist Amory Lovins, who contrasts a high-technology "hard path" in energy development with a "soft path" emphasizing conservation and renewable sources:

The state is thus at a fork in the road. The hard path leads to water development in Northern California on a scale never before seen, with the billions of dollars of capital expenditures to be borne largely by consumers and taxpayers in the Southern California urban area. The alternative route—yet to be fully explored—*may* lead to multibillion-dollar savings, preservation of the North Coast rivers, and a more efficient agriculture. Will we take the soft path? The coming months should bring the answer.

• During this period, groups of experts all over the state seemed to be working on this or that aspect of what Arguimbau called the "soft path" strategy. Perhaps the most notable of these was the Governor's Commission to Review Water Rights Law. Here, Harrison C. Dunning, staff director to the commission, reviews its 1978 conclusions:

HARRISON C. DUNNING   1980

Toward a California Water Policy

Imagine, underlying California's fertile valleys, a series of geologic structures much like sponges. During wet periods the water in these sponges increases, just as it does in surface reservoirs. In dry periods, the sponges provide some 40 percent of the water needed by farmers, cities, and others throughout the state.

Imagine further that at any time anyone can stick a straw in one of the sponges and draw out all the water they want. This can be done in total disregard for harm caused to neighbors. And so many straws can be put in and so much water taken out that in some areas the sponges dry and compact. In other areas the costs of extracting water rise enormously and, along the coast, the ocean invades what once were freshwater perserves.

Impossible? Not so. This is only a statement of California's dependence today on groundwater and of the inadequacy of state law to ensure proper conservation of this important natural resource.

Take another example—imagine a river rising in the mountains to make its way through the valleys to the Pacific. Owners of land along the river have a right to use water from the river for farming or other reasonable beneficial purposes. Others also have rights they obtain from the state allowing them similarly to use water, subject to conditions necessary to protect downstream use for fisheries, recreation or other uses "in the public interest." But no one has ever spelled out, for any given river, what the public interest requires. And those who want water in a river for fisheries or rafting or just plain watching are told they are not entitled to the water rights the farmers are given.

Unlikely? Not so. This is merely a statement of the unbalanced way in which California today deals with competing demands for water in and out of a river.

During the 1976–77 drought, a Governor's Commission to Review California Water Rights Law spent nearly two years in an intensive study of the existing law and of ways it could be improved. The result is a 264-page report documenting the need for effective management of groundwater resources, better protection of instream uses, clearer definition of surface-water rights, and improved efficiency in water use.

For *groundwater,* the report recommends a state policy designed to eventually end most overdraft, the result of regularly taking out more groundwater than nature or people put back each year. This deficit spending of a natural resource now runs at an annual average of some 2.2 million acre-feet.

Instead of suggesting a state program run from Sacramento to implement the state policy, the commission recommends a regional approach that would place the principal responsibility in the hands of the local water agencies. These agencies would be given the fiscal and regulatory tools needed for effective management. Where groundwater problems are now critical and are not being adequately addressed, the agencies would be required to develop and implement a groundwater management plan.

To deal with the *instream* problem, the commission recommends that the State Water Resources Control Boards be authorized to develop instream flow standards. These standards would represent a balancing of instream and offstream needs and equities.

To bring greater clarity to the definition of surface-water rights, the commission emphasizes improvements to and more use of an existing administrative process for determining water rights known as "statutory adjudication." To encourage greater efficiency in water use, recommendations are made to remove barriers to the free transfer of water rights from willing sellers to willing buyers.

Historically, California's answer to water shortages has been to build more dams. But today that solution is not an easy one. Conservationists seek to preserve a few rivers in their wild state and demand that any new water projects be planned and constructed with sensitivity to the impacts on instream uses. Economists point to the skyrocketing costs of water projects, and politicians to the Proposition 13 mood, which suggests that those deriving direct economic benefit from water projects pay their fair share of the costs.

To the disinterested observer, all this may imply that the days of "business as usual" are over—that better water management, including reforms in water rights law, must occur. But political reality may be otherwise. Proponents of reform lack a grass-roots constituency that understands the subtle and somewhat esoteric legal questions, while the opponents are well organized, well financed, and highly sophisticated politically.

- In 1982, as the water controversies of the Brown years neared a climax, *Cry California* devoted an entire issue to water problems and tried to summarize the challenge.

JOHN HART   1982

Seven Steps toward
a Steady-State Water Policy

In the long view, it may not greatly matter which dam goes down in history as California's last. We must deal, soon or late, with the fact of a fixed or slowly growing water supply. What adjustments must we make to live within our means?

It is important to realize that a steady-state water policy need not bring an abrupt end to California's growth. For one thing, there are several means of modestly increasing the physical supply without reaching out for new rivers or further degrading old ones. For another, the California water system contains—as has been recognized for years—enormous amounts of sloppiness, slack and misallocation. Our water institutions are not designed to avoid waste, and often they promote it. Until much of this inefficiency is squeezed out of our present system, we can't very well talk of absolute shortage.

A slowly growing water supply would constrain the growth of urban areas least of all. Cities use a fraction of the amount farms do to begin with, and have the political clout to secure first claim on supplies.

It must be acknowledged, though, that one traditional type of growth cannot continue without new water imports. This is the constant expansion of irrigated acreage that has been typical of California agriculture. Though the very best land is probably under the plow already, there are still millions of acres of lower quality that could be profitably farmed. It cannot be a goal of water policy, in a regime of nearly static supply, to provide irrigation water to everyone who would like some.

There are six or eight key components to a steady-state water strategy. Some would have the effect of increasing usable supply without adding new dams; others would reduce consumption, or slow the rate of its increase; still others would knock down barriers that now prevent efficient management.

Here is the list:

— *A firm statement of policy* committing the state to encourage and require efficient water use. No such policy exists today!

— *The creation of a water market* to permit the easy sale and exchange of water supplies.

— A *thorough reform of state and federal water pricing* on the principle that users should pay the true cost of water they consume.

— To reduce demand, *increased conservation and more sparing use* of water, in cities but most especially on irrigated farms.

— To increase supply, *more purification and reuse* of urban and agricultural wastewater.

— To increase supply, *greater use of aquifers* as storage vessels for the extra runoff available in wet years.

— A long-range *campaign to phase out groundwater mining* and manage all the state's aquifers for perpetual firm yield.

This list is not pulled out of the air. All of these elements have been widely discussed and some are even beginning to be widely practiced. They have been explored in studies by the Rand Corporation (*Efficient Water Use in California*, 1978); the Governor's Commission to Review California Water Rights Law (*Final Report*, 1978); the Assembly Office of Research (*A Marketing Approach for Water Allocation*, 1982); and many more. The Department of Water Resources itself has described a number of the techniques. Bills to encourage reform have begun to appear in the legislature and in Congress. And in other western states, notably Arizona, recent policy transformations show the way California might go.

Another section of the 1982 report summarizes the "water market" strategy that lay at the heart of current reform proposals.

Freeing Up the Water Market

It is often remarked that California has plenty of water, but distributed wrongly in place and time: too much in winter and in the north, too little in summer and in the south. All our dams, our aqueducts, our water-management schemes are designed to correct that imbalance.

But there is another type of maldistribution, not natural but part of the system we have built. Because California water has always been exploited on the principle of seize-and-hold-fast, rules grew up that discourage cooperation to move water from where it is abundant to where it is needed most.

A basic doctrine imbedded in our water-rights system can be paraphrased "use it or lose it." If a right-holder takes less than his authorized amount, it is quite possible for the unused water to be taken out of his

319

control. A survey of Central Valley water-right holders (prepared for the Assembly Office of Research) shows that almost three quarters of them fear losing their rights if they sell, lease or exchange water they do not need themselves.

Many water districts operate under laws that strongly discourage them from selling water outside their boundaries unless every conceivable local need is satisfied first. Similarly, charter provisions may prohibit districts from making a profit—no matter how great the advantages of a possible water deal.

If these and other impediments were removed, there could arise a free-wheeling water market in which water would be shifted to its most profitable use. As one result, temporary surpluses would pass quickly to areas of need.

The 1976–77 drought helped set a number of exemplary transfers in motion. In the most important, the so-called "Metropolitan Exchange," the Metropolitan Water District relinquished 400,000 acre-feet of State Water Project water, replacing it with additional flow then available from the Colorado.

The state is trying now to set up a cooperative arrangement with MWD in regard to Colorado River water. In years when the State Water Project is water-rich, the Met would rely on this and leave its share of the Colorado untouched, piling up in Lake Mead. In dry years, the district could take less from the state and draw on the Lake Mead backlog. Because the Colorado is an interstate river, both Nevada and Arizona would have to consent.

For a water market to be most effective, economists such as Charles Phelps of the Rand Corporation suggest, districts will have to be restructured so that individual users have the right to sell or trade their water.

Once the barriers to such horsetrading are broken down, it will be very much easier for the state's water system to respond to a dry cycle without major hardship. The *effective* water supply will be much greater. And economic gains will be considerable. A recent computer-modeling study of the operation of an interregional water market concluded that "the limited marketlike system . . . would result in savings of up to 2 million acre-feet of water annually and would benefit buyers and sellers of water in an amount of over $70 million" in the first year. The Rand Corporation's 1978 study entitled "Efficient Water Use in California" reached comparable conclusions.

320

• What might have been the turning point came in 1982 when, for the first time in 20 years, the California public was asked to give its verdict on water policy—to do so, in fact, twice.

First, in June, came Proposition 9. Nine embodied the Brown administration's water program, including the Peripheral Canal, several new reservoirs, constitutional protection for the wild rivers, and some modest targets for conservation and wastewater reclamation. The program, cleared by the legislature, had been forced onto the ballot by citizen petition. To the astonishment of many, it lost. The Brown water policy was dead for the time being.

In the campaign against Proposition 9, agricultural interests desiring *more* water development and *fewer* safeguards joined conservationists and others who feared the Peripheral Canal. In the second water campaign of the year, there were no such odd alliances. November's proposition, number 13, was called the Water Resources Conservation and Efficiency Act; it was based on the conclusions of the Governor's Commission to Review California Water Rights Law; it enjoyed the clear backing of conservationists and the united opposition of the farm and water lobbies. This package too went down.

Californians said "no" to business as usual. Then we said "no" to reform. We seem to have asked for the one truly impossible outcome—that the problem should go away.

16 *Growing Food from Money*

- California Tomorrow was one of the first voices in California to raise the alarm about the steady loss of rich agricultural land to "slurban" growth and other factors. As the years went on, *Cry California* turned its attention to other disquieting aspects of the agricultural scene: the escalating use of pesticides; the difficulty of preserving the small-scale "family farm"; the problem of salt buildup in fertile soils; the wasteful use of subsidized water. It explored also the possibilities of alternative styles of agriculture using a minimum of automation and chemical treatment and a maximum of organic methods and elbow grease.

    To represent the many articles covering the problem of agricultural land loss, here is the last of them: a retrospective written in 1983.

STEVEN WITT   1983

The Struggle to Legislate Protection for Agricultural Lands

In 1965, the Williamson Act became the first state law aimed at protecting California's rich agricultural lands from conversion to other uses. In 1983—18 years later—the Williamson Act is still California's only state law designed to protect agricultural lands.

This would not matter, of course, if the Williamson Act actually achieved its intended goal—to prevent California's prime agricultural lands near urban areas from becoming urban areas themselves. But it does not; it never has. And it's easy to understand why.

The Williamson Act is a voluntary program that gives landowners a trade-off. They sign a ten-year contract with their city or county (automatically renewed each year) that prevents them from developing their land or selling it for development. In return, the city or county substantially reduces landowners' property taxes. But the dangling carrot of tax reduction has never attracted many farmers and ranchers on the edge of

town who, above all, do not want to sign away their one chance at the most lucrative harvest of all—selling their land for development.

While the Williamson Act currently protects some 16.2 million acres of California's farm, ranch, and open-space lands, only about 4 percent of these lands, according to state Department of Conservation figures, are prime agricultural lands in and around urban areas.

Since 1965 many legislators have tried to create more effective protection for California's important agricultural lands, but all have failed.

One was Democrat Charles Warren, a Los Angeles assemblyman. Warren had first come to Sacramento in the early 1960s with such notables as Jesse Unruh (now state treasurer) and Henry Waxman (now a U.S. representative). In 1974 Warren traveled to Rome on his own tab to attend the United Nations World Food Conference as an unofficial delegate. He was disappointed by the attitudes of many of the official delegates to the conference, and sensed that "nationally or internationally

323

very little would get done to protect the world's food-producing capabilities." Thus, Warren committed himself to the preservation of California's prime agricultural lands, hoping California would become "an example for others to follow."

In December 1974, Warren introduced the strongest bill to protect agricultural lands ever considered in California. Warren's Assembly Bill 15 (AB 15) would have created a state council much like the Coastal Commission to regulate agricultural land use.

AB 15 was so potent that one assemblyman, Jerry Lewis (R-San Bernardino), issued this statement to the press:

> *"Agriculture—California's number one industry—had better wake up, for the legislature, along with Governor Brown's administration, is about to take over their business . . . AB 15 . . . would vest in the Governor the power to regulate all agricultural land use statewide, taking this authority from local government and the individual farmer."*

In spite of well-organized opposition, AB 15 was passed by the Assembly in January 1976, due in large measure to a gutsy speech in support of Warren's bill by then-freshman Assemblyman John Garamendi (D-Mokelumne Hill).

But Warren's bill died in August 1976 in the Senate Finance Committee. Not since AB 15 has a bill designed to protect California's agricultural lands from conversion to other uses come so close to becoming state law.

"The single most important reason AB 15 failed," according to Warren himself, "was that Rose Bird [then Secretary of Agriculture] opposed it." Second, Brown himself, Warren says, "told me I had too many bills that session and he didn't want to lend a hand."

Another critical factor in the failure of Warren's tough agriculture bill was that the California public and the governor—in that order—had focused their attention on California's coastline. On the same day that A.B. 15 died in the Senate Finance Committee, the Coastal Bill passed, permanently establishing the Coastal Commission. Vivid memories of oil-drenched birds on beaches blackened by oil spills lingered in people's minds. In sharp contrast, no such visible and emotional evidence of an agricultural lands crisis could be found, and cannot to this day.

In January 1977, newly elected President Jimmy Carter invited Charles Warren to Washington, D.C., to serve as chairman of the Council on Environmental Quality. In spite of Warren's absence, the number of bills introduced in the legislature to protect California farmlands actually increased during the following year.

> What hampered the effort most, Witt notes, was a lack of solid supporting information. People could see farmland going under, but they couldn't put numbers to it.

No one yet knew the rate at which California's productive agricultural lands were being lost to urban uses; California still did not have a useful inventory of its prime farmlands. This lack was reflected in the three major bills submitted at the time, AB 1900, SB 1003 and SB 193: Each made substantially different recommendations of the amount of agricultural land that should be legally protected. The acreages were 11.8 million, 15.1 million, and 28.4 million, respectively. Opponents of any farmland protection bill could simply ask to be shown where farmlands were disappearing and at what rate, knowing that such information didn't exist. As a result, most legislation was tabled until substantive figures became available.

In June 1978, the tax-initiative storm—Proposition 13—struck California and demolished the property-tax incentives upon which all such legislation had been constructed. Suddenly landowners could have their cake and eat it too: they got nearly the same break in property taxes that the Williamson Act had provided without having to tie up their land by signing a contract.

Of the many pieces of legislation written since 1978 and introduced by people such as Assemblymen Doug Bosco (D-Occidental), Tom Hannigan (D-Fairfield), Richard Lehman (D-Fresno), Byron Sher (D-Palo Alto), John Thurman (D-Modesto), and Senator John Garamendi (D-Stockton), only two bills stand out.

The first bill was a response to a strict interpretation of the Williamson Act by the California Supreme Court in February 1981. In *Sierra Club* vs. *City of Hayward,* the court upheld the binding nature of Williamson Act contracts. The court stated: "If those with an eye toward developing such [agricultural and open-space] land within a few years are allowed to enroll in contracts, enjoy the tax benefits during their short holding period, then cancel and commence construction on a showing that the land is ripe for needed housing, the act would simply function as a tax shelter for real estate speculators."

This decision prompted landowners, who already felt trammeled by their Williamson Act contracts, to call for legislative relief. Assemblyman Richard Robinson (D-Santa Ana) answered with AB 2074, a bill passed in late 1981. Robinson's bill created a window in the Williamson Act that gave landowners the opportunity to bail out of their contracts during the first five months of 1982 if their reasons for doing so met certain requirements. When this window closed in May 1982, contracts covering 96,000 acres of land—most of it agricultural land on the urban fringe—had been submitted for cancellation. County boards of supervisors will be making final decisions on individual applications for years to come. But the number of acres that will actually be released is not the most important point; what is most significant is that the only major change in the Williamson Act since it was passed 18 years ago moved it further away from its intended goal.

The second noticeable bill was Richard Lehman's AB 966, signed into law on February 2, 1982, by then Governor Jerry Brown. Lehman's bill established in the state Department of Conservation the Farmlands Mapping and Monitoring Program—an ambitious, unique and long overdue effort to inventory and monitor California's agricultural land base.

It works like this: program staff take soil maps produced by the U.S. Soil Conservation Service, field-check their accuracy, and delineate urban and built-up areas. Eventually these maps will be fully computerized and updated each year or two to show exactly where farmland conversion has occurred and where new lands have been brought into production.

California finally will be able to respond authoritatively to the questions that have stifled agricultural land-use debates for more than 25 years: How much farmland is being lost each year to other uses? And to what extent are such losses offset as previously unfarmed lands are brought into production?

> • A second movement to alter past patterns in California agriculture was under way in the late 1970s. This one focused on land ownership, and particularly on enforcement of the venerable act of Congress according to which heavily subsidized federal water should be provided to *small* farms and to small farms only. It was partly to get around this inconvenient law that corporate farm interests had persuaded the state, back in the 1950s, to get into the water supply business itself. But, as the following piece makes clear, even federal agencies were doing little to enforce the small-farm rule.

DANIEL J. BLACKBURN   1977

Those Clouds over Westlands Aren't Rain

Ralph M. Brody, silver-maned manager-chief counsel for the Westlands Water District in Fresno—the man whom *The California Journal* tagged last year as "California's highest-paid public official"—is contemplating retirement. He has duly noted that, in this dry year, more and more people are asking hard questions about Westlands water and the 1902 Reclamation Act.

The Reclamation Act was a deliberate attempt to use federal irrigation projects for a specific social purpose—putting more people on the land. Although a product of the administration of Theodore Roosevelt, it could as easily have been drafted by Thomas Jefferson—it clearly expressed the old American idealistic belief that there is something naturally healthy about a nation of small farmers. The law required that water from federal projects be supplied only to landholdings of not more than 160 acres—320 acres in the case of a husband and wife.

It has been systematically nonenforced ever since it was passed, and Brody has certainly done his part.

With impressive skill and tenacity, Brody has molded, manipulated and exploited the Reclamation Act to the multimillion-dollar advantage of his employers—the owner-irrigators of Westlands. For more years than anyone had thought possible, they have gotten what they wanted and he has earned his ample salary for helping them get it. It, of course, being water.

M. Woodrow Wilson of the governor's Office of Planning and Research: "The reclamation laws intentionally provide subsidies to help their intended beneficiaries, the settler and the small farmer. It is arguable, however, that the subsidies were not intended to reach their present magnitude, and it is unquestionably true that most of those presently receiving reclamation benefits in Westlands are not settlers or small farmers."

That is a remarkable understatement. The subsidies' "present magnitude" is expected to top $2.5 billion when the public's investment is computed. And the recipients are certainly not "settlers or small farmers." More than two-thirds of Westlands' total irrigable acreage is held as "excess land"; that is, more than the 160 acres allowable to qualify for

327

reclamation-project water. Large landowners dominate the district: Southern Pacific has 106,000 acres; Boswell's Boston Ranch, 24,000 acres; and Standard Oil, 11,500 acres.

But the heat is on Westlands, and it seems likely that the district will soon have to conform to at last *part* of the law. And with compliance in Westlands, it may follow that other Bureau of Reclamation operations, in other parts of the country, may be in for some congressional face-lifting.

Undoubtedly the drought is helping call attention to the Westlands situation. The 200 farms that receive water within the district are remarkable water-consumers. Collectively they produced crops with a gross value of $275 million in 1974. To do that, they received and spread 1.08 million acre-feet of water during the same 12-month period. That amounts to 700,000 gallons of water each and every minute pouring onto rich, brown earth that only 20 years ago was dry, dusty, and dirt cheap.

> Blackburn goes into the history of the federal San Luis water project, which draws water from the Sacramento-San Joaquin Delta, stores it in San Luis Reservoir, and distributes it to Westlands and a few other users. For some years after the project was completed, Westlands got water on a temporary basis. In 1976, a long-term contract was about to be signed; but incoming Interior Secretary Cecil B. Andrus held it up, partly out of concern that the acreage limit be enforced. National attention came to focus on the small-farm issue, and Congress began looking into Westlands in particular and the Reclamation Act in general. For a short while it appeared that the law, after some necessary modernization, would at last be enforced.

In the late 1950s, George Ballis was the editor of a small labor newspaper. Today he is head of National Land for People, a Fresno-based public-interest group working for land reform in Westlands.

"Back then, no one cared that this huge federal project was being built to line the pockets of the valley's land barons," Ballis smiles. "Today everyone is sitting up and taking notice." Soon, if all goes according to schedule, National Land for People will begin to help first-time investors buy, and farm, their own land in the San Joaquin Valley.

One of these days, we may see a California version of what the law promised—small farmers happily tilling in the San Joaquin Valley, the boundaries of their property plainly visible on the horizon, their fields irrigated with water from San Luis Reservoir.

One result of that would be higher agricultural productivity. That's right—despite the agribusiness myth that larger farms are more efficient and the small farmer can't make it, research from several sources (including the University of California and the U.S. Department of Agriculture) shows clearly that small family farms operated by resident owners are more productive.

There would also be secondary payoffs to the Westlands area. Whereas today it is mainly a place of rich land and poor people, vast fields with few buildings except equipment sheds and workers' barracks, the change to significant numbers of small farms would undoubtedly stimulate construction of farm houses and buildings. In place of the rather bleak and semifeudal Westlands that exists today, there could be an area of stable and prosperous rural communities. Perhaps, after 75 years, we will get a chance to see what kinds of social and economic benefits the Reclamation Act can provide.

- These hopes were not realized. The Reclamation Act was revised in 1982, but not in the manner the reformers had intended. The chief result was that owners of very large properties had to pay a modestly higher price for water; no real pressure to break up the major holdings came to bear. "We lost," said George Ballis of National Land for People, "because what we advocated is against the warp of our time."

The use and abuse of pesticides was a third major farm issue tracked by *Cry California* in these years. The situation had changed somewhat since the days when California Tomorrow was a leader in the attack on "hard" chlorinated hydrocarbon pesticides; the worst of these—including DDT—had indeed been banned. But the chemical menu remained huge, the quantities applied immense, and the controls very weak indeed.

WALTER TRUETT ANDERSON   1979

Pesticide Politics

Pesticides have become a political issue. They started out as a scientific revolution that swept American agriculture a few decades ago when potent new compounds—DDT, the organophosphates, the carbamates—first became available for use against farm pests. A new era in agricultural science was born, and so was a new industry. In California, where 15 to 20 percent of the nation's pesticide production is used, it is a billion-dollar industry.

Inevitably there are problems when millions of pounds of such highly toxic chemicals are sprayed, dusted and otherwise deposited on open fields. Some of the problems:

— Dangers to people exposed to pesticides during their manufacture, transportation or application. In 1977, a typical year, more than 1,500 cases of illness from pesticide exposure were reported in California. No one knows how accurate this reporting system is—state officials estimate that it accounts for about 80 percent of the actual poisonings; a reputable scientist testified some years ago that it accounts for about one percent.

— Dangers to nonpest animal life. Honeybees, for example, are commonly wiped out by pesticides. Sometimes a pesticide is passed along the food chain and poisons animals far from the fields.

— Damage to crops and other plant life. This often results from aerial application of herbicides, some 20 to 60 percent of which commonly drift to neighboring fields.

— Pollution of streams, rivers, surface runoff or underground water supplies. The most recent case was the discovery in well water of DBCP, the chemical that caused sterility among workers at an Occidental Chemical Company plant in California; it is also a known carcinogen.

— Ecological mishaps of various kinds: Pest resurgence, also known as "bug backlash," results from application of a chemical that is lethal to all forms of insect life, including the main pest's natural predators; the pest population diminishes temporarily, then explodes. Secondary-pest outbreaks result when the biotic vacuum is filled by an explosion in the population of *another* pest. Another such mishap is pest resistance, which results when a pest species develops strains that are immune to the pesticide. Some 400 major pests in the United States are now resistant to one or more poisons. In California, the strain of mosquito that carries encephalitis cannot be killed by any registered pesticide.

— Harm to consumers of pesticide-treated food products. The U.S. Environmental Protection Agency and the California Department of Food and Agriculture (DFA) set tolerance levels that determine the "safe" amounts of pesticides that may be present on foods. These have

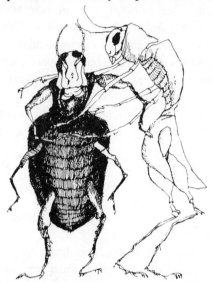

been much criticized lately because they are calculated on the assumption that people eat limited amounts of the foods in question—but many Californians eat far more than the 7.5 ounces per year set as the standard for such products as artichokes, avocadoes, eggplant and mushrooms.

Two things can be said about California's regulatory program. First, it is probably the best in the country. Second, it is not nearly good enough.

California, under the DFA, has its own system of registering and classifying pesticides, and it has a system for licensing applicators and requiring permits in certain cases. It requires pesticide-related illnesses to be reported, and has regulations governing the disposal of pesticide residues and containers in special hazardous-waste disposal sites.

However, the system is rather less impressive when viewed more closely. Of the nearly 11,000 pesticides registered for use in California, only about one third contain materials that are in the "restricted" category and are therefore subject to the licensing and permit procedures. Other products, including some highly lethal ones, may be used much more freely. DBCP was banned in 1977, but before that it was a nonrestricted pesticide and quite widely used. There are many other such gaps in the system, pesticide uses that escape regulation and reporting. Also, there is as yet no reliable way of monitoring the effects of pesticide use and obtaining concrete data on its long-range impacts.

Nobody is quite certain how much good is being done by all the chemicals being used, and nobody is quite sure how much harm.

The officials responsible for enforcing regulations on pesticide use are the county agricultural commissioners—local officials chosen by the county boards of supervisors. Their policies vary greatly from county to county, according to their personal capabilities and convictions. They are responsible for both promoting agriculture and protecting farmworkers. Then there are the licensed pesticide advisors, who give farmers advice on how and when to use pesticides; about 90 percent of them are employed by pesticide manufacturers.

The fact is that California's pesticide regulatory system is not really protecting workers, consumers or farmers.

Pesticide politics is not partisan politics; you can't get far by identifying the antagonists in terms of party labels. It divides along lines of region, administrative authority, economic interest and philosophy; it pits farm owner against field worker, farm bureaucrat against health bureaucrat, rural legislator against urban legislator, scientist against scientist.

The members of the pesticide establishment are the people who use pesticides (growers, foresters, home exterminators), the people who make and supply them (chemical companies, farm service and supply companies), related business interests (aircraft applicators, manufacturers of farm machinery), a number of farm organizations, a bloc of legislators from farm districts, the DFA (always responsive to the needs of its client group), the farm publications (heavily supported by pesticide advertising) and a large segment of the academic community of agricultural scientists. Many would add to the list officers of rural banks, who often require pesticide use as a condition of loans, operating on the assumption that it is a necessity for profitable farming.

The antipesticide coalition consists of environmentalists, consumer groups, some labor organizations (chemical plant workers, farmworkers), some urban legislators, some bureaucrats, the federally sponsored

California Rural Legal Assistance (CRLA), a few renegade farmers, people interested in integrated pest management (the most credible alternative to current pesticide-use practices) and a segment of the academic community. The most vociferous of the antipesticide scientists was Robert van den Bosch, who died last year after a long career of making himself unpopular with advocates of pesticide use. Van den Bosch, a professor of entomology at UC Berkeley, believed that the farmers were being taken in on a grand scale by the pesticide manufacturers, hustled into adopting practices that were not only ecologically dangerous but likely in the end to produce more crop damage than they prevent.

How strong are these two opposing coalitions? At the moment the weight appears to be decisively on the side of the propesticide forces. The farm bloc in the legislature is not a majority in either house, but it is a solid and cohesive group that has been able, year after year, to beat back legislative attempts to set up stronger worker-protection programs, take worker-safety regulation out of the DFA, or outlaw the practice of licensing pesticide advisors who work for chemical companies.

The most promising road out of this wilderness is the approach called integrated pest management (IPM), which is a combination of techniques, including close monitoring of pest populations, crop rotation, biological controls and selective use of pesticides.

The University of California—stung by criticisms that it has been too much oriented toward a heavily mechanized and chemical-dependent agriculture, and not sufficiently concerned with the interests of farmworkers and consumers—is now proposing a major new statewide program of IPM research that would involve massive computerized data collection of all the information needed for sophisticated pest management.

Improvements in IPM capabilities should lessen the dependence of farmers on agricultural chemicals, and make it easier for them to see their interests as in harmony with those of workers and consumers.

This is a hopeful prospect, but more than 300 million pounds of lethal chemicals will be used this year in California, hundreds of people will become ill from working with them, and millions of consumers will take still more poisons into their bodies. As long as such dismal statistics continue to measure the reality of how we get our food, there will be a need for vigorous political action.

• A frequent contributor on agricultural topics was E. Phillip LeVeen, the director of Public Interest Economics West and an incisive critic of farm and water policy. LeVeen emphasizes the fact that modern mechanized farms depend as much on energy-hungry technology as they do on fertile soil—and as the price of energy rises, so must the price of everything grown. We are "growing food from money."

E. PHILLIP LEVEEN
and WALTER TRUETT ANDERSON   1980

Growing Food from Money: An Interview

PHILLIP LEVEEN: I came to the conclusion that our agricultural policies are basically inflationary—and, what's worse, that there are forces currently at work that are likely to drive food prices up sharply in the future.

WALT ANDERSON: *How did this come about?*

PL: The 1970s really saw the opening up of the world economy to United States farmers. Prior to that we gave food away, we didn't sell large amounts of it overseas. Our exports have tripled or quadrupled in the last 10 years. That was a deliberate policy of the United States. The idea was to give farmers foreign markets so they wouldn't need the government to buy their surpluses, then we wouldn't have to give them price supports and they'd be happy. The additional logic is that we need these exports because they generate the money we need to buy oil.

WA: *It sounds very sensible.*

PL: At first this strategy of exporting large amounts of food was successful; farm incomes went way up. Then, in 1975 and 1976, the export boom leveled off, ceased to grow. At that time farm costs were rising but farm prices weren't, so by 1977 the farmers were right back where they started—their incomes had fallen and they were being squeezed again. This led to a whole new set of agricultural policies in 1977 by which the United States was still trying to make it possible for farmers to conquer new markets. We have foreign trade offices all over the world to push American commodities. We subsidize their sale through credit, especially to Eastern European countries.

WA: *And U.S. agriculture was increasing its output during this period.*

PL: It was, but it's pretty definite now, if you look at the data, that U.S. agricultural productivity has begun to slow down.

WA: *Why is this occurring?*

PL: The rapid increase in our yields per acre in the 1950s and 1960s was related to what we might call the biological and technical revolution—high-yield varieties of seeds, plus the development of fertilizer technology that allowed fertilizer prices to decline throughout the 1950s and 1960s. Also, the revolution in chemical pesticides allowed yields to be increased. One other important factor was the continued increase of irrigation in the West. Irrigated land is very productive.

But now the increased yields may be ending. Farmers have adopted these technologies, to the extent they can be adopted, and have reaped whatever gains can be reaped, so we have a kind of saturation. Now, whether we have a good year or not basically depends on the weather, especially in the Midwest; it's not a question of whether the farmers are using enough fertilizer or the right seeds—they do, that's all there is to it. And the universities are simply not producing as many new major-breakthrough ideas.

Since the 1973 price increase in oil, the basic costs of those kinds of technologies have risen very, very rapidly because they're based on fossil fuels. So in addition to the fact that we are reaching natural limits in technology, the technology itself is becoming increasingly expensive. Our whole agricultural technology is fossil-fuel oriented. Most people think that just means diesel fuel in the tractor, but fossil fuels figure in every aspect of our technology: fertilizers, chemicals, energy to pump water, energy embodied in the equipment of farming, whether in the truck or the tractor or the processing machinery or the shed.

WA: *So, directly or indirectly, food prices are linked to fuel prices.*

PL: What we did was design an agricultural technology premised on the idea that labor was expensive and energy was cheap. Our research facilities have not been able to make the switch to thinking about what kinds of technologies we should develop in an energy-scarce world, as opposed to an energy-cheap world.

WA: *Are they making much effort to do that now? I know there's pressure on the university to move into some new kinds of agricultural research.*

PL: There is also counterpressure. When the university people started to develop integrated pest management they found themselves meeting a lot of resistance from the chemical companies. Similarly in irrigation; farmers have been very reluctant to see much work done on conservation of water in agriculture. As far as they're concerned, the answer to their problems is to build more projects and bring in more water—that's the solution farmers have always sought.

One of the things we're learning is that, in addition to energy being scarce, water is scarce. We've developed water resources over the West essentially as well as we can without huge and very, very costly projects—so at this point, if we're going to create more cropland or western cities are going to grow, it's going to become necessary to have much greater conservation. And since agriculture uses roughly 85 percent of all the water, it has to be conserved in agriculture.

WA: *What are likely to be the consequences, for agriculture, of rising fuel costs?*

PL: It's probably going to mean that we're going to have to relearn what we knew many years ago, which is that you don't grow all your vegetables in California and ship them all over the world by expensive transportation means. In the old days, vegetables were grown around cities where they were consumed, and the transportation part of the process was a relatively brief trip from the countryside to the city. In California and Florida now, we produce most of the nation's vegetables. It's not because vegetables won't grow in other areas—New Jersey was a great agricultural area: "The Garden State." It's because the big marketers of the vegetables decided they didn't want a summer system and a winter system. They wanted one year-round system and so they concentrated their activities in areas where the vegetables were easily grown, and they adopted the widespread transportation and distribution systems that were, in effect, based on cheap energy.

That's all changing. Last year alone the cost of taking a truckload of vegetables from the West Coast to the East Coast doubled, from $2,000 to $4,000, and that was before the most recent runup of gas prices; I don't know what it is now. So I'm saying that, at least in the summertime, people are going to start growing their vegetables in the East and they're not going to depend on California. Maybe you're even going to see the dairies reappear around the cities instead of being miles away so that you need a huge trucking system to get the milk to the consumer.

WA: *Despite all the policies that are trying to support close-in agriculture, it keeps disappearing.*

PL: What I'm worried about is, we know those effects are coming, we know high energy costs are going to have fantastic implications for almost all aspects of our life, and we still make decisions as though that wasn't the case. And the problem is, the decisions are frequently irreversible.

WA: *Are there other hidden costs?*

PL: I suspect so. Let's look again at what happened in the 1970s. In 1973 and 1974, when we took the controls off agriculture, everyone thought farmers would start producing a lot more. In fact, they didn't. We found that when they tried to expand on marginal land, to increase production to meet the international demand that was so high in the early 1970s, they were really unable to. It appears that the capacity of the system to produce large quantities of food is more limited than anyone realized. And at the same time they were trying to expand on marginal land, they began to create additional environmental problems, perhaps the most important of which was erosion.

We city dwellers don't know much about it, but erosion is a very, very difficult problem for the midwestern farmer, particularly when he's farming on hillsides. I suspect erosion in California is not quite so important, but I do think there is a similar problem here that we don't talk about, which is salinity buildup from our irrigation systems. The salinity problem is much bigger than anyone realizes, and it's going to come back to us in the next 10 to 20 years in terms of much higher costs of draining the land. For example, the southern San Joaquin Valley has to be drained. If it isn't drained, it's expected that upwards of a million acres will be forced out of production.

WA: *So a system has to be built?*

PL: That drain system is going to cost as much to build and operate as did the original irrigation systems that bring water to the valley. This is the sort of hidden, long-run cost we've been living with—it's been building up but we haven't been paying it. And we are going to pay it.

WA: *Inflation?*

PL: Yes. Going back to the original discussion about agricultural policy, if we continue to insist that the United States feed the world, we're going to have to continue to intensify production. Farm costs are going to have to rise, and I'm sure that will mean higher food costs. What it will mean in the long run is that the effort to feed the world is going to be very, very destructive to American consumers. What we should be doing, instead of spending more money to intensify U.S. production, is concentrating on countries where production is at a much lower level. Food production could be increased there without putting additional strain on our own system.

337

17 *The Impossible City Revisited*

• During the years of Bill Bronson's editorship, *Cry California* had made rather a specialty of Los Angeles stories. Along with reports on current Southern California issues, its pages held some impressive dreams and schemes concerning the metropolis: ideas for super-parks, super-transit, super-developments and redevelopments. Planners wrote zestily of new governments, new ways of living, billion-dollar expenditures. It was a heroic view of things.

Ten years later the scenery had changed. On the one hand, nobody seemed very interested any more in proposing fundamental transformations of Los Angeles or any other city—or, if they were, the would-be transformers were not writing for *Cry California*. In a decade of shocks and shortages, most thinkers seemed content to work on ways of muddling through.

But if the dreams of planning had faded, the reality had rather improved. For the first time, governments in Los Angeles County were facing up to issues of sprawl, pollution, and auto-dependency, and policies were slowly, creakily shifting. There was a major federal park project under way in the Santa Monica Mountains (though suffering badly from inadequate funding). Southern California had a regional transportation plan of sorts—and so on.

More modest visions, more encouraging real efforts; to some extent, the "is" and the "might be" were converging. But at how high a level? In this late piece, Walt Anderson surveyed the new Los Angeles scene.

WALTER TRUETT ANDERSON   1978

Super City at the Interchange

Los Angeles is the prodigal city, a gigantic consumer of such resources as energy, water and land. What are its chances for survival in the age of limits?

As we look at this subject, let us understand that we are dealing with a statewide issue, at the very least. The future of Los Angeles is not of interest solely to people who live there now or who may live there sometime. Home rule is a fine principle, but the truth of the matter is that modern American cities depend for their existence on massive support systems and are in no way self-contained or self-sufficient. When New York City came to the brink of financial collapse, the problem was immediately recognized as a national one. And in Los Angeles, where you drive to work on petroleum from Saudi Arabia and run your car through a carwash that is connected to the Owens Valley watershed, few things are as local as they may appear.

I also want to make it clear that we are not sitting down for a few hands of the Los-Angeles-is-just-awful game commonly played by easterners, Northern Californians and, sometimes, even Los Angeles natives. Personally, I would take Los Angeles—sprawl and all—over most American cities. I can well understand why people would choose to live there, and I expect that lots of people are going to want to live there in the future. It is worth our concern.

That said, let us proceed to the difficult subject of the future of the supercity, its painful and so far not-too-effective effort to grab the reins and move itself along a different line of development. Start with the item that is so close to the center of the Los Angeles lifestyle and the Los Angeles problem: the car.

Los Angeles was the first city to emerge as a major metropolis after the price of the automobile came within reach of the average American. Actually, the area was moving toward a pattern of dispersed urbanization even before the advent of the mass-produced automobile. Although it seems hard to believe now, Los Angeles at around the turn of the century had one of the country's best mass-transit systems, with fast, clean, cheap and far-ranging electrically powered streetcars—an early stimulus to scattered and leapfrog patterns of settlement.

The era of the streetcar came and went, and by now is largely forgotten. Now it appears the era of petroleum may also be finite, may hit its limits in the next decade. To warnings about this, the general response has been rather like that of a pack of lemmings who break into a gallop as they get nearer the edge of the cliff—perhaps hoping the cliff will turn out not to be there, or maybe that somebody will build a bridge across it before they arrive. Petroleum consumption continues to increase. In Los Angeles, the single-occupant car continues to be the dominant mode of transportation. One of the hottest political potatoes of recent years was the diamond-lane flap, when the California Department of Transportation tried to force carpooling. (Ironically, the only city in California with a stronger addiction to solitary commuting is Sacramento, hometown of the heavy thinkers who tried to make Los Angeles mend its ways.)

It is not too hard to see where this is leading. Congestion is serious on most of the freeways already, and it will get worse.

CalTrans, working with local governments and the United States Department of Transportation, has a four-point program to prevent this projection from becoming a reality. It consists of:

— Greater use of buses on the freeways.

— A 15-mile rail rapid-transit line.

— Downtown people-movers—an overhead rail system to get bus commuters to their workplaces and to move tourists and shoppers about the central business district.

— A "systems management" package of such devices as carpools, ramp-metering and diamond lanes for handling the flow of freeway traffic and increasing the vehicle occupancy. (CalTrans estimates that a very small change in vehicle occupancy—increasing the average to 1.4 persons per car from the present 1.2—would solve the congestion problem.)

The four-point program seems promising, until you take a look at the points.

— The bus-on-freeway program is limited by several things. One is congestion: it doesn't pay to run more buses on congested freeways, because people won't ride them (this may not sound entirely rational, but it's true) and consequently they don't reduce congestion. Another is money: it costs a lot to add new freeway lanes or even (as has been proposed) build new freeways especially for buses. Funds may become available for some projects, but a major busway system is definitely some years away.

— The rail transit line is similarly bound by time and money problems that are of course compounded by inflation: the longer it takes to get it started (and it is still in the concept stage), the more it costs.

— The downtown people-mover is a localized operation that basically serves as a "feeder" to the bus-on-freeway system and does not—by itself—have much effect on freeway traffic. It is about five years away.

— The "system management" approach is limited by the willingness of the system to be managed. After the diamond-lane controversy, CalTrans adopted a policy of no reduction of existing freeway lanes. Diamond lanes will have to be new lanes added (time and money again) rather than existing lanes converted for bus or carpool use.

It is quite possible the problem will find its own solution at the end of the petroleum era. A period of gasoline shortages coupled with rapidly rising prices could do what CalTrans couldn't: get people to change their commuting habits. This is a very likely scenario, but hardly one to cheer for. It would be a time of severe hardship for many people.

The Politics of Sprawl

The Los Angeles transportation system developed as it did because large amounts of energy were available at low prices. The land-use patterns developed because of the transportation, and because large amounts of *land* were available at low prices. This too is changing.

The Southern California Association of Governments (SCAG) has outlined several possible scenarios of future land development. One of them is "concentrated" distribution of growth in which there is more infilling of urban areas and recycling of existing housing. Another is the familiar "dispersed" pattern in which development proceeds as it did in past decades—spreading out over the farmlands and deserts, putting new suburbias wherever the open space for them can be found.

Which way will it go? Probably a bit of both, although the "most likely" forecasts and the official growth policies tend in the direction of higher density. This depends partly on public policy, and partly on economics and lifestyles.

The custom of early marriage and sizable families that supported the growth of suburbia is changing and the change is reflected in the population forecasts that underlie planning decisions. Later marriage, later childbearing and fewer children affect the kind of housing people want; at present there is faster-growing demand for apartments.

341

Yet the developers, local officials and planners seem extremely reluctant to let go of their old low-density ways, as long as there are open spaces and unbuilt-over hillsides left in the basin and higher-income families willing to buy houses built on them.

People in the Los Angeles basin have rarely shown much interest in planning issues that affect the entire region; there have been many squabbles between developers and controlled-growth groups over specific local projects, but little public debate on the major issues. There is, however, one active alliance of citizen groups—calling itself the Coalition for Los Angeles County Planning in the Public Interest—that *has* taken on the whole subject and has been making life miserable for the official planning establishment for several years. The coalition was organized for the specific purpose of challenging the official Los Angeles County blueprint for the future, the General Plan of 1973, which it called a "blueprint for urban sprawl."

The challenge was a smashing success. In June 1973, Judge David A. Thomas threw out the plan, finding the environmental impact report supporting it to be totally inadequate—especially on the issue of why the county had more than doubled the amount of land it was making available for current and future development at a time when the population was declining. The plan was found to have been developed "largely to conform to preexisting zoning and to individual requests of property owners for particular treatment of specific parcels" instead of on the basis of environmental information, comprehensive goals and policies, population-growth projections and sound evaluation of alternatives.

The planners went back to work and a new Los Angeles County General Plan has now reached the public-hearing stage. The coalition has scrutinized the county's new version of where it is going and finds it improved over 1973, but still not improved enough.

Sherman Griselle, the coalition's chairman and a professor of Urban planning at California State Polytechnic University, Pomona, thinks the lust for sprawl still burns in the hearts of county planners. Griselle agrees with the goals expressed in the new general plan, but says, "There's a lot of difference between glittering policies and the hard follow-through implementation. Los Angeles County traditionally has not been willing to follow up grand plans with tough regulatory controls—and that's what it's going to take."

That shift—the emergence of a new generation of planners who are as dedicated to urban renewal as their predecessors were to urban sprawl—is the change the coalition is struggling to bring about.

342

Planners, of course, are supposed to be nonpolitical. But the current struggle for their hearts and minds is one of the most important political controversies in Los Angeles—however little it may interest the average citizen—and its outcome will have a great impact on the area's future.

Is the People Boom Ending?

For as long as we've been hearing about it, Los Angeles has been growing—sometimes faster than any other part of the country. Consider that the population of Los Angeles County was about 3,500 in 1850, 170,000 in 1900 and over 4 million by 1950 when it was just hitting its stride. The flow of new residents into the basin seemed as limitless as the gasoline they would use to drive about and the land that could be built over to house them and the water they could use to fill their swimming pools and irrigate their lawns. Then the growth began to slow, and in the early 1970s the *Los Angeles Times* presented its readers with the surprising news that more people were leaving the county than were coming in—the population was dropping by the thousands. In 1974, population began to inch upward again—*very* slowly.

Yet most planners do not appear willing to accept the possibility that the people boom has come to an end; planning documents—even those that consider several alternative projections—gravitate toward scenarios of another million people in Los Angeles County by the end of the century. Most projections run considerably higher than that. The baseline projection in the new version of the Los Angeles County General Plan shows a 700,000 increase by the year 2000.

Griselle says: "There is no trend or any other indication that the population of Los Angeles County will have increased by 700,000 people by the year 2000." He expects that for some time to come—over the next seven years or so—population in the county will remain about where it is. This is a mighty important variable: A stable population would make it easier to change transportation systems before the freeways become seriously clogged, give Los Angeles a better chance of getting away from its leading position on the air-pollution charts, slow urban sprawl, and help hold down water consumption.

One of the most striking features of recent population trends in the Los Angeles area—and one of the things that makes it inadvisable to rely too confidently on *anybody's* projections into the future—is the change in ethnic makeup. In 1950, Los Angeles County's population was 86.3 percent Anglo with a small black minority and an even smaller Spanish-surname minority. The Spanish-surname segment is increasing rapidly, and by 1980—according to a recent study—Anglos will have slipped to 49.4 percent of the county's total (in the city of Los Angeles, 44.4 percent). Most projections show the Spanish-surname population continuing to grow faster than the Anglo and black populations.

This has already had unpredicted impacts on the city's growth and development. A large segment of downtown Los Angeles is no longer the Anglo business district it once was—but neither is it the decayed core it seemed on the way to becoming. It is a thriving Latin shopping center. In so many American cities, downtowns have died as shoppers shifted their business to the new suburban centers where they could park their cars. But downtown Los Angeles is very much alive, and a large part of its business comes from people who get there in public transportation. Bus service is heavily used between the downtown area and the Spanish-surname residential districts to the east of it.

Conservative Water Conservation

No other city on earth has achieved such remarkable feats of importing vast quantities of water from great distances. The sources of Los Angeles' water supply extend to a sizable part of the western United States, including the mountains that drain into the Colorado and the watersheds on both sides of the Sierra Nevada.

The Los Angeles basin water supply comes from four sources:

— The "in-house" water that reaches the basin from rainfall and from the inflow of local rivers, and is held in underground aquifers.

— The first of the city's great outreaches, the Los Angeles Aqueduct, that brings water from the Owens Valley on the eastern slopes of the Sierra Nevada.

— The Colorado River, whose waters—diverted by various dams and aqueducts—supply Southern California cities and agricultural areas such as the Imperial Valley.

— The California Water Project, which directs water southward from the reservoirs on the Sacramento River through the canals of the Central Valley and then up over the Tehachapi Mountains.

The local water tables and the Los Angeles River are totally inadequate—would support about 20 percent of the present population.

The Owens Valley supplies most of the demand for the city of Los Angeles, but not for other cities in the basin. In the case of a prolonged drought, Los Angeles would, like adjoining cities, become more dependent on the other sources—the Colorado River and the State Water Project.

Water from the Colorado and the SWP is pumped to Los Angeles over mountain ranges. Consequently, water supplies in the basin are connected to energy supplies. As energy grows more expensive, so will water. Some people predict that the cost of water in the Los Angeles basin will double; others say it will increase tenfold. Such high water costs could deal a death blow to the remaining agriculture in the area and will also create still further incentives for more dense urbanization. The outlying and hillside areas, where heavy watering is a shield against fire, will become much more expensive to live in.

The possible brightener for this generally gloomy picture would be an increased reliance on reclaimed wastewater for agriculture, park and freeway landscaping, fire protection and other purposes. So far this alternative has been used only to a very limited extent in the Los Angeles area (or in most other urbanized parts of California).

Increasing water costs—if nothing else—will gradually make Los Angeles a much more frugal water-user than it has been in the past.

These are important changes. It seems most unlikely that the graph lines on energy, land, population and water will continue to zoom merrily upward as they have for so many decades. (I have not said much about a fifth commodity—air—because it is not a variable; the limits of supply were exceeded years ago and nobody has ever figured out a way to bring in more of it. The transportation and land-use trends should help reduce air pollution, however.)

Los Angeles is well into a new transition, groping uncertainly and sometimes reluctantly for new ways to develop. We can see some of the bare outlines of the way things will probably change: fewer solitary drivers, more compact urban development, a more stable (and much less predominantly Anglo) population, a more frugal use of water, and somewhat cleaner air. But the projections do not tell us about the *quality* of the changes. A ride to work on public transportation could be a pleasant experience or a nerve-shattering disaster. Living in a more densely populated area could be congenial and satisfying, or merely crowded. Such differences will depend largely on how well the people and the decision-makers of the Los Angeles area understand the nature of the forces that are now shaping urban change, and how creatively they deal with them. If it can manage this transition well, greater Los Angeles may turn out to be the city of the future after all.

345

18 *The Urban Strategy and the Tax Revolt*

• Late in the 1970s, two new pressures came to bear to alter the pattern of California's growth. One was applied from the governor's office down, the other from the electorate up. Though antithetical in rhetoric and intent—though the supporters of one were largely the opponents of the other—they combined in unexpected ways to put a premium on the kind of compact, city-centered growth that planners had been talking about for years.

The first of these forces was Governor Jerry Brown's Urban Strategy. The second was Howard Jarvis's Proposition 13. By a hair, the Urban Strategy arrived on the scene first.

After the fiasco of the "State Planning Program Goals and Policy Report," the legislature decided to try state planning again. In 1970, it abolished the State Office of Planning and set up in its place an Office of Planning and Research in the governor's office. Like its predecessor, the new office was supposed to produce a wide-ranging report on the state's environmental goals and policies, to be updated every several years. The first such effort was published in 1974. Like the 1969 state planning document, this one was long on data and short on recommended action; nobody paid much attention to it; but it *did* become administration policy. It was a stubby trunk on which more productive branches might later be grafted.

On his way to becoming governor in 1974, Jerry Brown made land-use planning one of his major campaign themes. At the time he had little regard for the Office of Planning and Research. But Bill Press, head of the lobby called the Planning and Conservation League, suggested to Brown that OPR could be a very effective body indeed—if it had the governor's full backing.

Once in office, Brown changed his rhetoric and began to mock the very notion of planning. "Planning," he is supposed to have said, "is something people do in government when they don't have anything worthwhile to do." His actions, though, gave the lie to his words. He gathered around him capable people who *did* believe in the uses of planning. One of them was Bill Press, who in 1976 became the head of the bureau whose possibilities he had pointed out—the Office of Planning and Research.

Press and his people set out to produce a set of "partial updates" to the original Environmental Goals and Policy Report. Though only one of these was ever completed, that one was already more of a step in the direction of effective state planning than all previous efforts combined. It was called "An Urban Strategy for California." Brown made it a selling point in his campaign for the 1980 presidential nomination, and for one brief moment it figured as a national example in the field.

Cry California tracked the progress of the Urban Strategy with care. Alfred Heller made this buoyant early assessment:

ALFRED HELLER   1978

California's New Grand Strategy

Californians can be hopeful, even joyful, about the state's new "Urban Strategy" unveiled by Governor Brown just five days before the vernal equinox.

California's new what?

You won't be likely to know much about "An Urban Strategy for California," to be sure, if your source of information has been the local papers. You'll know more if you have been reading the *Washington Post* or the *Christian Science Monitor,* or watching the PBS MacNeil-Lehrer Report. The eastern press, it seems, accepts the strategy as a serious policy document. I think they're right, though their distance may lend enchantment to the view.

The heart of the Urban Strategy is this passage:

New urban development in California should be located according to the following priorities:

First priority: Renew and maintain existing urban areas, both cities and suburbs.

Second priority: Develop vacant and underutilized land within existing urban and suburban areas and presently served by streets,

347

water, sewer and other public services. Open space, historic buildings, recreational opportunities and the distinct identities of neighborhoods should be preserved.

Third priority: When urban development is necessary outside existing urban and suburban areas, use land that is immediately adjacent. Noncontiguous development would be appropriate when needed to accommodate planned open space, greenbelts, agricultural preservation or new-town community development.

These priorities may seem quite reasonable, but reason has not always been a big factor in state policy making. For example, the state's loss of rich agricultural land to urban development, in the millions of acres, has gone on more or less unabated since V-J Day. This has surely been the scandal of a generation—yet the government of this state has never faced up to its own full responsibility for it. State-funded freeways, water lines, canals and sewer systems, state purchases of materials, state planning standards for local governments, the organization (or disorganization) of the state's political subdivisions, state taxing policies, state aid and programs of all kinds—all have helped to create the slurbs, instead of putting a brake on their growth. Among the stated goals of the new urban strategy is "curbing wasteful urban sprawl and directing new development to existing cities and suburbs." And Item 20 of the strategy's 45 action proposals is:

Protection of Agricultural Lands. The Administration will support legislation which protects California's most productive crop and rangelands from premature or needless conversion to urban uses. Guided by State policies and subject to State review, cities and counties should take the lead in identifying lands to be preserved and assuring their protection. Property assessments for agricultural lands should be reduced and local governments reimbursed for lost tax revenues.

The specific aim of saving the state's prime agricultural lands has never before been expressed, much less adopted, by California. And a determination to renew existing urban areas, curb sprawl and save prime agricultural lands, all together, represents an important new commitment for our state.

The Urban Strategy is important as a policy document. It would be important, I maintain, even if there were no immediate move to carry out its provisions, because this is not a fuzzy restatement of a problem, as previous California planning reports have been. It is a set of actions and programs for resolving some of the most intractable problems connected with urban development in California, social and economic as well as environmental. And it is written in a simple and straightforward style, obviously intended to clarify instead of muddy. As a document of substance and suasion issued by high authority, it is bound to change the way we do things in the future, if not right away.

Clearly, the Urban Strategy is a political report produced in a political year. Brown expects the strategy to form the basis for a "political debate not only this year, but over a decade." He says the strategy is "not some government-imposed piece of paper" but a "flexible format for urban and suburban action" in the state. He believes the strategy is "in harmony" with what he describes as a "cultural, economic, environmental, and demographic thrust" toward urban revitalization instead of sprawl.

The strategy is divided into two sections: one presents the goals and priorities already referred to; and an "urban action program" presents various initiatives to "improve existing housing and encourage new development," to "improve urban social and economic conditions" and to "resolve inter-jurisdictional conflicts." There are in addition two subjects proposed for "further study": sharing property and sales taxes among the cities and counties in our metropolitan regions (an idea that has already been thoroughly studied in government and the academic world), and finding acceptable tax incentives to encourage economic development in the cities and suburbs.

Fourteen goals are stated; most of them seem unexceptionable, almost obvious. Yet where in a state policy document have they ever been gathered together before? Thus, the strategy aims to: protect the state's natural environment, particularly the land and air and water quality; improve the quality of public schools; revitalize the central cities and neighborhoods and eliminate urban blight; improve the efficiency of government and limit taxes to the lowest practical level. The strategy does not isolate issues concerning land use or environmental quality from closely related economic issues, and several of the goals emphasize economic and social concerns—employment, housing, transportation, health care.

Urban Action

The "urban action program" focuses state programs and administrative activity on improving the quality of life in existing urbanized areas. A few specific items from this important section. To help curb sprawl by

349

discouraging land speculation, the strategy proposes legislation for a capital gains tax on real estate held only for short-term purposes. The provision of new housing through rehabilitation as well as new construction receives strong emphasis. The strategy recommends: a $300-million appropriation for housing rehabilitation and construction; constitutional amendments that will allow tax exemptions for housing rehabilitation and permit tax forgiveness for industrial and commercial rehabilitation in appropriate locations; changes in building codes to make rehabilitation simpler; and the creation of a "housing task force" to help "satisfy the future housing needs" of the state.

In its emphasis on "environmentally sound" economic development the strategy also proposes:

— An immediate inventory of state-owned lands in urban areas, to find land that can be made available for low- and moderate-income housing or commercial or industrial development.

— Legislation to encourage public retirement systems to invest money in mortgages "that are consistent with the goals of the urban strategy."

— A state program of grants to be awarded to local governments that include energy-conservation elements in their general plans.

Several items direct state agencies to amend their policies (where they legally can do so) to correspond with the priorities of the strategy— agencies such as the Department of Water Resources, the Department of Health, and the Department of Transportation. (If the roads and sewers and water lines can be prevented from spreading into the fertile valleys, then so can a great many people.) It is proposed that in reviewing and approving federal grant applications, state agencies should give priority to projects that support the strategy. And there is a "California Urban Forestry Program"—tree-planting for the cities.

Proposals to "improve urban social and economic conditions" range from improving urban parks to prosecuting career criminals to improving community mental health. In this group, as in other parts of the strategy, past and new legislative recommendations of the administration are lumped together, along with proposed policy directives that do not require legislation. The end result is a long, somewhat disparate list—yet it does suggest in its entirety that programs and policies of the state can be grouped and integrated so that they work together to solve major problems. In this sense the strategy is the closest thing to a comprehensive plan yet produced in California. It contrasts strikingly with the traditional "single-purpose planning" of the past. Brown, of course, eschews the term "comprehensive" and even the term "plan." The urban strategy, he insists, is "not a plan but a process." So be it!

Regional Planning

Several of the proposed actions would illuminate, if not eliminate, the worst effects of the mishmash of local and regional governmental jurisdictions, taxing agencies and purposes within our metropolitan regions. Press calls these proposals "the most important part of the urban strategy." Legislation is proposed to direct the voluntary councils of government (COGs) of the state's largest metropolitan areas to "assess regionwide needs and available resources for housing, industrial sites, solid-waste disposal sites, open space, air and water quality, transportation systems, and other regional public facilities." The COGs are then supposed to identify "areas" where these needs should be met. General plans of cities and counties are then to show that each city and county is doing its part in meeting the regional needs identified by the COGs. Each COG will then "assess the cumulative effects" of all the local plans and report annually to the governor and the legislature on whether the regional needs are being met.

To help local governments make the various assessments of regional needs, the strategy proposes that $5 million a year from the general fund be allocated locally by OPR, and an additional $2 million for the COGs—not much, all told, for a big job.

Various special districts and agencies will be required to prepare "memoranda of understanding" with the COGs so that they too will help to implement regional needs. All of this amounts to a complex, essentially toothless regional planning procedure, far short of the multipurpose regional responsibility and authority needed, but it is probably better to have such a scheme than not to have it. It may turn out to be an important first step, and *any* step has been a long time in coming.

It seems to me that the very real contributions of the Urban Strategy may be overlooked by those who would like it to be something it is not—a comprehensive state conservation and development plan or a state land-use plan (whatever that might be). The strategy represents, in fact, yet another move in what has been over the past two decades a clear swing toward larger and more comprehensive efforts at planning in California. When the governor says we are going to concentrate on improving the quality of life in our existing urbanized areas and save the

351

best agricultural lands in the state, he is filling in two very large pieces in a picture that has, in large part, taken form since the early 1960s.

A sequel to the Urban Strategy, now under consideration by OPR, will deal with "proper management of nonurban land." It might make more sense to concentrate on two additional strategies that would complement the urban strategy: a state resource-use strategy and a state economic development strategy. Together with an updated version of the Urban Strategy, these could represent the state's first complete Environmental Goals and Policy Report—in effect a state conservation and development plan.

Making It Happen

At the conclusion of the Urban Strategy there is a chart summarizing what actions will be taken to implement it. Thus, for each of the 45 points of the strategy there will be either new legislation, a constitutional amendment proposed, an executive order, a change in the budget act, a new administrative regulation or policy, or a combination of such actions. There are 18 items requiring new legislation. Bills have been introduced for each one. Protection of agricultural land is already the subject of legislative action. Perhaps a well-timed push from the governor would move it along.

The bills having to do with regional planning and administration have been introduced by Assemblyman John Knox of Richmond, long a champion of improved regional government structure.

Of equal importance to the legislation is Executive Order B-41-78, issued by Governor Brown: "All state agencies, departments, commissions, boards, and offices shall, within the limits of law, conform their policies, actions and programs to the California Urban Strategy." This order has been followed up by OPR in meetings with each of the important action agencies of the state to discuss how it will be carried out. Changes have already taken place. For instance, the state Public Works Board has drafted a policy providing that new state buildings will be built in existing urban areas near public transit. OPR is working with the Department of General Services to find ways of aligning state purchasing policy with the priorities of the Urban Strategy.

The city of Oakland is to be a leading example of the Urban Strategy at work. There will be housing rehabilitation, job training and job creation for young people, experimentation in energy conservation, building of state and community facilities. This effort will need an

352

infusion of federal money and perhaps also long-hoped-for private commercial development. A five-member state team led by OPR is now working in Oakland Mayor Lionel Wilson's office to help coordinate the various programs.

Thus a push for the Urban Strategy is on, and my general impression is that Brown is firmly committed to it and won't waver from it. What if a later administration were to introduce policies contrary to the Urban Strategy? As I see it, many if not all of the strategy's features are long overdue and will have popular acceptance. To the extent that the Brown administration succeeds in making them law or bureaucratic habit, they will remain as state policy no matter who may become governor in the future.

- Somewhat earlier—before the Urban Strategy had received the governor's blessing—Samuel Wood had surveyed its key provisions with a cooler, if still approving, tone. His main complaints: the regional planning provisions were weak, and the piecemeal nature of the program—"incrementalism"— made it liable to fail.

SAMUEL E. WOOD   1977

The Urban Strategy:
Bold but Flawed

The regional-planning arrangement is one of the main weaknesses of the Urban Strategy. The existing Councils of Governments (COGs), which the strategy would make the keystone of its regional planning, have already shown themselves to be failures at regional problem-solving, lacking either the funding or the power to carry out such responsibilities.

The report makes much of the proposal to have the COGs identify regional needs and allocate them to local authorities, as if this procedure would solve local imbalance. It will not; most local plans, as every planning professional knows, already contain enough commercial and industrial zoning to satisfy an entire region. If this verbal legerdemain is designed to escape the truth of the need for real comprehensive regional

PETALUMA, CALIFORNIA

planning for conservation and development, then the effort is wasted and the reader confused.

Also, financing is necessary for regional planning. In the report, financing of the program is to be provided to COGs by federal money with matching state funds totaling up to $2 million a year; locals would be reimbursed up to $1 million a year by the state for their cost in meeting the program's responsibilities. These are piddling amounts.

The Urban Strategy seeks to divide planning responsibility. The day-to-day management of urban affairs remains basically with the cities, counties and special districts, while the state "retains the responsibility to establish overall goals that give direction to the actions of local government." There is nothing particularly new in this hierarchy, but there is also no answer to the question of how a major state effort is going to succeed if all the local governments and special districts don't happen to be in full agreement with its goals. "Cooperative regional planning" is a useful concept, except when the participants fail to cooperate. The Urban Strategy proposal makes no provision for the COGs to prepare regional plans in face of local intransigence, or to turn down local plans that fail to "relate to" regional needs and state policy.

The other weakness of the report is its self-confessed incrementalism. The Urban Strategy is being published now, and the other elements of the overall Environmental Goals and Policy Report are somewhere down the line.

There are good bureaucratic and political reasons for taking the incremental road, choosing to bite off a piece of the problem at a time. But somewhere at the state level there should be a holistic picture of where we are and where we are going, a clear vision of how the pieces fit together—and if this is not going to come from the agency that is specifically authorized by law to produce long-range and comprehensive planning, then where is it going to come from?

The action programs connected with each recommendation will have to be fought for item by item at the local, state and federal levels. There are any number of places where the whole strategy may collapse. With incrementalism, the barriers are multiplied by the number of increments.

Certainly the governor can—if he adopts the Urban Strategy wholeheartedly—get most of it into operation. It is equally certain that he cannot assemble all of it—line up the full complex of local, state and federal bureaucracies, legislative and judicial bodies, interest groups and private organizations—in a united march in the same direction.

The most important question is whether the Urban Strategy itself moves in the right direction, toward what needs to be done. The answer is yes.

- How effective was the Urban Strategy?

By some measures, not at all. Of the many implementing actions the legislature was asked to take, very few made it into law. Nothing was ever done about the regional planning mechanism; about changing the tax structure to discourage speculation; or about protecting agricultural land. If the success of the Urban Strategy had depended solely on the legislature, it would have to be judged a failure.

However, there were two ways in which the strategy made a real, and immediate, difference. The first was that it did change the actions, and to some extent the attitudes, of the powerful state bureaucracies. On March 18, 1978, Brown signed an executive order requiring all state agencies to "conform their policy, actions, and programs to the California Urban Strategy." By and large, they did; and because state actions themselves have a lot of influence on the course of development, this was not by any means just a change-on-paper.

355

— In Ventura County, the state had planned to extend water and sewer mains to an outlying Health Department facility. The city of Camarillo alerted OPR to the fact that this tie-in would encourage growth in an area meant for agriculture, and the project was scrapped.

— It was noticed that the Cal-Vet home-loan program had an army of functionaries at an office in suburban Walnut Creek and only a token office in Oakland—an accurate reflection of the way in which such programs have encouraged growth on the fringe. The staff was shifted, and the enlarged Oakland office was told to get moving on loans to rehabilitate older housing.

— In accordance with the strategy and San Jose's request, the Department of Transportation planned the 101 freeway south of that city without interchanges in an area San Jose desired to keep open. (Unfortunately for the success story, San Jose was soon to change its mind.)

— The Department of Transportation began to take more seriously the need to find replacement housing for people who lose their homes to freeways; it also began to repair and put in service the hundreds of houses it actually owns in the rights-of-way of unbuilt freeways.

The second manner in which the Urban Strategy made a difference? It was, for want of a better word, psychological. For the first time the state had put its weight behind the much-admired, little-practiced notion of compact, city-centered growth. This was, if not a turning point, another in a series of shoves tending to discourage the familiar sprawling style of development.

And now, barely two months after Brown's executive order to the bureaucrats, there came a much stronger and yet more ambiguous message: the passage, in June 1978, of Proposition 13. Overnight, the revenues that local governments derived from the property tax were cut by 57 percent. What this portended, for the Urban Strategy and for every other element of California life, was slow to emerge.

As a means of reducing the tax burden, Proposition 13 was a blunt instrument. It went into effect instantly, with no phasing-in period to allow governments to adjust. Its costs and benefits were brutally uneven. Communities with large tax bases or high

356

tax rates were relatively little affected; cities that were already pinching pennies found themselves in immediate trouble. The proposition cut taxes on business property as well as those on residential property, and in time the business share would decline further (because properties are reassessed only on sale, and business properties change hands less often). Then there was the provision that a two-thirds vote of local electorates was required to raise taxes—thus allowing a minority to veto taxes and programs the majority might desire.

Most Californians agreed, in the abstract, that such provisions were unfair; but this did not change the way they voted. "The arguments that Proposition 13 took a 'meat ax' approach were of no avail," Walt Anderson noted in a *Cry California* analysis. "The voters wanted a meat ax."

The passage of 13 had an immediate and rather shocking effect that nobody had talked about much in the campaign: it made local governments dependent on the state for funding. The result was a huge pilgrimage to Sacramento. The state had a swelling surplus in 1978—that was one reason people hadn't listened to the anti-13 scare stories—and it was immediately passed out to cities and counties to make up much of what they were losing in the first year. But the state money arrived with strings attached. The Fall 1978 issue of *Cry California* explored the new realities.

RICHARD A. GRANT   1978

City Hall Has Moved to Sacramento!

A startling form of statewide planning is here. With it has come a whole new set of game rules.

The first rule is: Don't bother going to city hall any more, go to Sacramento.

By voting in Proposition 13, the electorate has voted out local government. One has only to recall the hassles that accompanied the allocation of this year's state bail-out money to realize where the action is now. There has been a real shift of power.

The next rule: Make sure there's a surplus of state funds.

The legislature will be subjected to the pushes and pulls of powerful interest groups vying for their share of the largesse, and many beneficial programs will suffer for lack of political clout, but local governments will manage to carry out what are perceived to be essential services at pre-Proposition 13 levels, thanks to the surplus.

The final rule: Keep the inflation rate high to generate a hefty state surplus.

Abiding by this rule will insure bail-out funds and postpone indefinitely all those dire preelection forecasts of governmental chaos and disruption.

But it's a short-lived game and one that bodes ill for California's hallowed home-rule concepts. The Proposition 13 time bomb ticks on and the explosion will come when there is no more surplus. Tax-cutting binges aside, the challenge is to prepare for that day.

• Sherman Griselle, professor of Urban Planning at California State Polytechnic University, Pomona, elaborated the theme. To hold onto its authority, he wrote, local government must become more efficient. And he offered a hope that many shared for a few months in 1978: that the shock of Proposition 13 would lead the state to insist on, and local governments to welcome, an improvement in regional planning on the lines of the one proposed in the Urban Strategy—or better.

SHERMAN W. GRISELLE   1978

Requiem for Home Rule

With one pull of the Proposition 13 trigger, California voters have critically wounded home rule. The initiative will transfer to the state decisions formerly made by local governments (cities, counties, school districts, special districts) and local governments must acquiesce to state controls or risk having the plug pulled on their life-support systems.

The strings attached to the $4 billion in emergency funds authorized by Senator Albert Rodda's SB 154, the "bail-out bill," prohibit local governments from sharing in state surplus dollars if they give employees salary increases higher than those given state employees. Percentage cuts in local services are also regulated, as are the levels of service for special fire districts, and police and fire protection must be given first priority for state surplus money.

As the legislature debates second-year funding, it is a safe bet that Sacramento will attach many conditions tying local governments tightly to state and regional requirements, with home rule declining rapidly as the state prescribes local programs and service levels. This means that the traditional "bottom up" approach in local decision-making will quickly give way to "top down" directives from the state.

Local governments, as a matter of self-preservation, are obliged to provide the legislature with workable solutions to the problems they face. Some have retreated into a siege posture, determined to fight on for home rule and the status quo until rigor mortis sets in. Others have begun to discover available alternatives and to discuss a number of innovative ideas that fall into three major categories: instituting new user fees, contracting with private business to supply public services, or taking advantage of volunteer help to provide services.

This pay-your-own-way movement is becoming a key ingredient in growth-management systems. Local governments are withholding zoning, subdivision or building approval for developments that don't intend to pay their way through property taxes and service fees. This means that future growth will be allowed only if it is financially self-sufficient and requires no hidden subsidies from taxpayers over the years. Six years ago, Petaluma introduced by city ordinance a more cautious approach to development, and Proposition 13 now makes it an imperative.

The self-sufficiency arrangement requires local government departments and agencies to develop independent financial bases divorced from property taxes. Police and fire departments together consume upward of one-half the budgets of many cities. It has been proposed that these services be funded, partially or completely, through a Public Safety Policy (PSP) that would be subscribed to by the community's property owners. The PSP would be provided to the owners by local governments (singly or in cooperation with other jurisdictions) who would provide police and fire protection and insurance against fire loss, paid for by the PSP.

Proposals to use private firms to deliver services currently performed by public employees are gaining popularity. Entire cities could be managed by municipal management firms offering a package of police, fire, recreation, planning, public works and other services on a

359

contractual basis. Clusters of cities could go together in a single contract to obtain unified services over a large area from private-sector contractors. Another cost-cutting alternative local jurisdictions have just begun to tap is the large potential for volunteers that exists in all communities.

Planners throughout California should be involved in recommending solutions. Unfortunately, a number of shortsighted local politicians are cutting planning budgets drastically. Planners must rise to the challenge and openly champion proposals for change.

The philosophy expressed by the catchy phrase "home rule" entails costs conveniently overlooked by its advocates. California's multitude of local government units generate excessive expense to its taxpayers.

The ultimate correction is broad consolidation of existing units and transfer of those functions that can be performed on a regional basis. Only the legislature can bring about such reform. It is time for the legislature to stop ignoring the potential of region-wide governments and to oversee their emergence as a beneficial blending of local and state interests.

California's existing councils of government (COGs) are established under the Joint Exercise of Powers Act and are straightjacketed by the cities and counties from which they are created. Even if no further regional reforms come about, the control of COGs by locally appointed officials is ruinous and the legislature must immediately *require* COG membership and financial support on the part of local governments.

It is to be hoped that the long-term effect of Proposition 13 will be a major restructuring of government in California. It is time for local governments to take their home-rule elixir off the market and to promote the salubrious product of regional cooperation. Locals must face up to the fact that they are going to lose long-held "bottoms up" decision-making powers. If they want to avoid "top down" state controls, it would be well to get behind "midway" controls placed in the hands of representative regional organizations. Metropolitan areas in California must follow the example of the Twin Cities in Minnesota, Dade County in Florida, and the Portland, Oregon, area by creating popularly elected regional governments.

Short of centralized control at the state level, regional organizations are the only ones that can deal with such tough, areawide needs as low- and moderate-income housing; control of urban sprawl and inner-city decay; equal educational opportunities; public transportation; clean water and air; and open space preservation. These are all issues that local and state politicians avoid like the plague and should be more than happy to consign to a regional body.

The legislature also must align Local Agency Formation Commissions (LAFCOs) with the newly created regional entities to effectively coordinate policies and programs. In pursuit of this, LAFCOs must break away from traditional thinking and prescribe such innovations as municipal adoption of school districts to combine and coordinate the formerly separate functions of education, recreation and cultural services in a single city department capable of operating economies. LAFCOs would perform the surgery and grafting needed to restructure local governments into efficient units supportive of regional plans.

Financial ills at the local level will worsen as the effects of Proposition 13 are felt over many years, and reliance on the home-rule remedy will fade as it proves to be quackery incapable of curing its patient. Responsibility will fall squarely upon the state to prescribe the strong medicine needed to overcome years of accumulated government deficiencies. Only then will the voters be assured of getting the biggest bang for their Proposition 13 bucks.

- This belief—that the Proposition 13 shock might well lead to stronger regional government—was widespread. Some thought that the existing councils of government might gain in stature; others expected these bodies to be scrapped and replaced. Sam Wood spun out this scenario in the same *Cry California* issue, writing: "Councils of governments, with the loss of their major financial support, will fade away. In their place the state will create fiscally viable regional governments with wide powers for regional planning and development, and with responsibility for overseeing local conformity to state policy and the regional plan."

But the hope that Proposition 13 would lead to a period of reform was not borne out. Rather, 13 was interpreted as a sign that the public was fed up with government—any government—and that the last thing it would stand for was any reshuffling that appeared, however incorrectly, to be creating more of it. The legislature, in the wake of the tax revolt, became very cautious about tinkering with government, and completely closed to experiments demanding money.

At the local level, planning departments withered; many

communities simply abandoned any attempt to get a fix on any future more than a few years away. Ambitious local programs like the open-space acquisitions of the early 1970s lost momentum or stopped cold.

Proposition 13 seems to have rendered still more intense the competition among growing cities to attract tax base and avoid expenditures. More than ever we see the struggle for new industry and commerce, an even greater proliferation of redundant "regional shopping centers," an even greater tendency to zone for industry while hoping the next town down the line will find housing for the workers thus attracted.

If these were the only effects, Proposition 13 would have to be judged a disaster, the complete undoing of any progress possible under the Urban Strategy.

But these negative effects were offset, at least in part, by another result lightly touched on by Griselle: the new local skepticism about sprawling forms of growth. To build extensive new neighborhoods on the fringe, where expensive basic utilities have yet to be installed, is very unattractive for a city in the post-13 world. For this reason, Proposition 13, warts and all, may be the most effective antisprawl device California has invented yet.

The Urban Strategy, meanwhile, was still in place. It soon ceased to be "news," even in Sacramento; there was even an impression that it had gone away. It had not. As the following update pieces from *Cry California* show, the strategy was quietly, almost invisibly, at work.

BILL PRESS   1979

The Strategy after 13

To those who say Proposition 13 meant the death of the Urban Strategy, I caution you to look again. The strategy has not only survived, it is more important and more relevant than ever before. Proposition 13 forces decision makers, particularly at the local level, to carefully weigh and consider the costs of new development. In the community assistance division at OPR we see city after city and county after county now giving development priority to existing urban areas.

A recent example is the city of Anaheim. It received a proposal to build 900 dwelling units on undeveloped land in an outlying area. The fiscal impact study showed a net loss to the city of $5.9 million in the first five years of the project, with revenues of $3.7 million in taxes and fees and with expenditures of $9.6 million for extending and maintaining services. From the sixth to the tenth year, revenues to the city would amount to $7.5 million while expenditures would total $10.7 million, for a $3.2-million deficit. Thus Anaheim's total deficit after ten years of the 900-unit project would be $9.1 million.

This is the kind of economics cities are bound to consider today. This is the kind of project to which cities are more and more often saying "No!" In future years, as the state surplus shrinks and bail-out funds are no longer available, the crunch at the local level will be even more severe and even tighter management will be required.

We made some significant achievements this year with the Urban Strategy. 20 bills were actually introduced in the legislature. Seven of them passed and were signed by the governor.

On the administrative side, the survey of vacant state lands has been completed. About 30 communities have shown interest in purchasing state parcels. Consistent with the goals of the strategy, these parcels are being made available for low- and moderate-income housing in existing urban areas.

Another OPR administrative action requires the Energy Commission to grant funds to local agencies for land-use planning that encourages conservation. Grants totaling $1 million were made last year under this program, and $750,000 more will be allocated in 1979–80.

Another accomplishment of the Urban Strategy is that now, for the first time, state public-works facilities—sewer plants, freeways, water

363

supply systems, public buildings—will be built according to population projections adopted by councils of government (COGs) and approved by OPR. Population estimates will no longer be made in the back rooms of Sacramento, they will be shaped by cities, counties and COGs—with full public hearings—and approved by state policy makers at OPR.

A new policy of the Public Works Board, adopted in conformity with the Urban Strategy, provides that new state projects will be approved only in existing urban and serviced areas. The housing task force, appointed by the governor in March 1977, has been very active and will soon present its own legislative program to make sure that California meets its housing needs and does so in localities suitable for new growth.

Most important, we are beginning to see the broad policy concepts of the Urban Strategy creep into the daily vernacular, into the thinking, into the plans and programs and budgets of state agencies. We now find, as we review these plans and budgets, that more and more of them are couched in the language of the Urban Strategy. That's the real battle—the real evidence that we are winning the minds and the hearts of people.

E R I C   B R A Z I L   1 9 7 9

The Urban Strategy, Round II

Round two of California's Urban Strategy has begun, with the administration taking the wraps off a bundle of proposals to put new zip in the policy Governor Edmund G. Brown, Jr., hailed as "a document that sets a direction for the rest of this century."

Recently a package of 53 recommendations (the first installment of Urban Strategy II) thunked onto Brown's desk. This document lacks the glossy appeal and pioneering elan of the original Urban Strategy, which was a policy map to show the state out of the wilderness of haphazard development. But taken together they are a fairly convincing testament to the administration's will to push ahead with the revitalization of California's cities—given the surly, pennypinching mood of the electorate and its representatives.

This year OPR has 10 specific legislative proposals in the works; most of them are new. One carryover from last year is a bill requiring cities and counties to amend their general plans to make them consistent with the Urban Strategy: The plans would have to show their intent to renew and maintain existing developed areas, develop vacant and underused land currently receiving city services, and practice contiguous development. Last year this was one of the few bills the administration pushed to a vote in the face of a probable adverse outcome, and it was killed on the Assembly floor, with the real-estate lobby doing a clog dance on the corpse.

The administration has budgeted $149 million for Urban Strategy programs this year:

— $100 million to increase homeownership and rental opportunities for low- and moderate-income persons under a program still being shaped in the legislature.

— $25 million for a job-training program for the unemployed and underskilled, to be administered by the state Employment Development Department and the departments of industrial relations at California's community colleges.

— $10 million for urban parks.

— $9 million for the California Department of Transportation to replace the housing it demolishes.

— $5 million to establish a child-protection hotline, statewide.

Urban Strategy II proposals also include: tax investment credits to foster inner-city business and industrial development; reducing the collateral required of banks receiving deposits of state funds for other institutions that make loans in older cities and suburbs; and requiring state agencies to replace, one-for-one, all low-income housing demolished because of state construction.

Also part of the package is legislation that will authorize cities and counties to impose standby fees on vacant, serviced land in built-up areas and will broaden the authority of local governments to levy assessments to finance new capital facilities.

Proposition 13 took away millions the administration wanted to make the strategy go, but OPR Bill Press emphasizes its positive side.

"Proposition 13 quickened the acceptance of the Urban Strategy more than anything we could have done. We have seen city after city and county after county, in fact, either adopt the policies of the Urban Strategy or use those policies in making their decisions. Proposition 13 may prove the most effective slow-growth initiative ever, and the person who may get all the credit for slowing down growth in California won't be Alfie Heller or Bill Press, it'll be Howard Jarvis. Irony of ironies."

- A year later, Brazil again surveyed the scene. At this point, Press had left the administration, and Sacramento generally supposed that "he took the strategy with him."

ERIC BRAZIL   1980

The Invisible Strategy

While it's true that no one talks much about the Urban Strategy anymore around the capital, the reason is more likely that it has sunk so deeply into the consciousness of state agencies, and percolated so fully into city and county planning departments, that repeated verbalization isn't necessary.

"Certainly more and more people are talking about infilling and contiguous development," says Deni Greene, new director of OPR. "One builder has even proposed standby charges on open land. When we mentioned that a while back, people just yelled and screamed."

Greene calls the $100-million affordable housing program approved last year "a cornerstone of the Urban Strategy." She also cites the Century Freeway project—a multi-agency effort involving the relocation and construction of some 4,000 houses, plus job development in a blighted area of central Los Angeles—as a major example of the Urban Strategy in action.

It is true, however, that many of the key points in the original document have wound up on the cutting-room floor, defeated by the legislature or abandoned by the governor's office. The whole notion of beefing up regional planning capabilities and equipping councils of government with enforcement fangs, for instance, has been laid aside.

- There was nothing in the least *neat* about the way the Urban Strategy and the tax revolt were interacting as shapers of California growth, but a change of direction does seem to have occurred.

  The effects did not end with the election of George Deukmejian in 1982. Though Governor Deukmejian had and has no use for Brown's policies in general—and though the Urban Strategy as such is long abandoned—the concepts it incorporated have not lost their commonsensical force.

In 1983 the *real* budget crunch—the one the opponents of Proposition 13 had tried unsuccessfully to get the voters to fear—arrived. The state's lavish budget surpluses, parceled out year after year to local governments, were gone, replaced by an equally lavish deficit. Meanwhile, the Reagan administration in Washington was cutting nonmilitary expenditures, including programs for local government. All over California, the effects of Proposition 13—the good, the bad, the mixed—became unmistakable. Planning to guide growth was (in many jurisdictions) out; but so was the old habit of subsidizing growth, and that is a profound, implicit change.

In its very last issue, Spring 1983, *Cry California* (by now renamed *California Tomorrow*) focused on the budget battle then going on in Sacramento. Venturing into an area that the organization had not before made its own, Volume 18, Number 2, had a controversial theme: that major tax reforms and—yes—major tax increases were now essential.

MARY ELLEN LEARY   1983

The Politics of
Tax Reform in California

The central message in Proposition 13, which some have forgotten, some distorted and some never perceived, was the public's demand for tax equity. Fairness in apportioning the costs of government was what the 1978 revolt was all about. Homeowners saw that their property was disproportionately overburdened as tax assessment skyrocketed—property taxes had become California's heaviest and most painful levy. In 1977–78 they totaled $10.3 billion, more than the combined yield that year from both state sales taxes ($5 billion) and personal income taxes ($4.6 billion). Homeowners clamored for relief.

When the lawmakers failed to provide it, voters took matters into their own hands and cut property taxes by more than half. Such direct citizen action sent shock waves across all the other states. Inside California, the tremors are still rattling the dishes. The striving for equity in California's tax structure goes on. Proposition 13's work is unfinished.

What that initiative did, along with subsequent reductions in income taxes through indexing and the abolition of the business-inventory tax, was wipe out, from July 1, 1978, to the present, over $60 billion worth of taxes, state and local, personal and business. That money stayed in people's pockets. One comment from Sacramento: "No other state and no country in the 20th century ever cut taxes so dramatically or so swiftly." The marvel has been that the great machine of California's economy kept pouring out enough revenues to cushion that loss the past four years. That is, until this year.

The deficit has focused, with laser-like intensity, a dazzle of controversial opinions about state financing in California. Suddenly the whole of California politics centers upon the adequacy of revenues for state support, for local government and, most important, for schools. Ideas about tax reform, about equity in allocation of tax burdens, about where responsibility lies for providing services, and about the need for specific services have all come bubbling up.

Sacramento doesn't look for a popular revolt against Proposition 13. No one (well, almost no one) speaks of boosting property taxes. What many ponder is whether voter opinion in California is shifting away from the cynical hostility toward government, the post-Watergate and post-Vietnam distrust of government, that was a factor in the Proposition 13 vote. More than that, is the public mind regaining confidence that government is a proper instrument for carrying out some tasks? Are voters moving toward a willingness to back government adequately at those tasks? That is what political circles chew over.

But more than the intensity of interest or volume of rhetoric, what is new this year in Sacramento is the way various public interests, social concerns, labor, parent groups, consumers, and churches have clustered into a network of coalitions. Organizations that usually center on their own unique interests are now arguing ways the state could raise a billion here or a half-billion there. Their own stakes may be far down the line as the money gets distributed but the central question of bolstering tax resources to keep state government as a whole going enlists the interest of groups close to the grass roots.

Notable among these interests, Leary says, are environmentalists, whose favorite programs Deukmejian sought to cut, and local governments, sick of depending on uncertain and tardy driblets of state aid.

Equally ready for conflict are those who speak for local government: cities, counties, school districts and the host of other districts that until now have made do with the "bail-out" to supplement their halved local support. Now, with no surplus to dip into, local governments are in confusion or even collapse. Los Angeles County has had to borrow $100 million from the state; some small cities are near bankruptcy and so are many school districts. Funding is critical. But equally critical is the question of legal relationships between state and "home rule" government. This reaches deeper than mere tax equity—this touches Californians' concept of how they should govern themselves. A state that since 1910 has boasted unique, nonpartisan, independent, and highly professional public service at the local level now erodes that standard almost by chance. Concentrating in the state legislature decisions on how much money local governments will get has had a profoundly unsettling effect at the local level. Cities, counties and school districts cannot plan ahead, cannot budget until after state funding is settled, cannot structure their personnel plans, cannot foresee long-range pay levels. Now they are demanding some reliable and fixed portion of state money. Even if one concedes that prior to 1978 local government had overexpanded its undertakings and its cost, the attrition now seems an excess in the opposite direction.

> Leary explores a number of the possibilities for getting more revenue. Among the items: amendment of Proposition 13 to reinstate higher property taxes for business holdings; other new or restored taxes on business; a tax on the extraction of oil; the closing of various tax loopholes and "tax expenditures" (special credits and exemptions); and "sin taxes" on hard and soft liquor and on cigarettes. But progress for would-be tax-increasers is not easy.

These clusters of varied interests confront a legislature whose Democratic majority is somewhat sympathetic, whose Republican minority is an effective bar and whose overall opinion is that they don't yet know whether the voters' tax-revolt fever has subsided. Besides, legislatures are lethargic. Getting votes to support change is much harder than outsiders realize, especially since new taxes require a two-thirds vote in each house.

Assemblyman Tom Hannigan (D-Fairfield) has said: "Our stock declines in the public eye when we are unwilling to deal with substantive issues. In the budget discussions of the last years we have avoided major problems and they have gotten progressively worse. I think the people

369

elected us to make decisions. I don't take lightly the idea of new taxes. But it is irresponsible simply to close your mind against them when the operation of the state is imperiled."

- And Weyman Lundquist, not long retired from the post after five years of hard work as president of California Tomorrow, made no bones about it.

WEYMAN I. LUNDQUIST   1983

Increase Taxes!

Tax reduction has gone too far. The time has come to raise the taxes we need to spend for public purposes that positively shape everyone's future.

Voters are beginning to indicate again that governments legitimately can raise monies for good works. In California, for example, according to the *Cal-Tax News,* "Voters around the state on November 2 passed 61 percent of local ballot revenue-generating measures requiring a simple majority and passed 24 percent of those needing two-thirds majority."

Very few would question the need for greater efficiency and effectiveness in our government's performance. It was a recognition of that latter need that led to the spirit of tax cutting. But tax cuts have not proved to be the correct instrument for improving government performance, and the public is learning that. Awareness is growing, too, of the urgent need to maintain the physical infrastructure and to support public services, especially education.

In a business, the necessity for investment is unquestioned, yet we question the necessity for investing in government's productive function. Perhaps because the goods and services government produces are now such an integral part of our environment, we take them for granted. Yet our society depends utterly on the continuing presence of roads and bridges, a reasonably educated populace, public health measures, and a certain level of public security: Without taxes, none of these benefits would be freely available to the whole of society.

The idea of spending public money on such things, and even on the cultural riches of art, drama, music, and dance, is not new; it became a fact of life during the New Deal. Indeed, we continue to enjoy today the tangible and intangible assets created during that era, which far exceed in value the modest deficit spending they then cost.

Unfortunately, politicians have been unwilling lately to lead the way in raising the tax revenues necessary to maintain and improve such public goods as schools; health care; libraries; roads and highways; support for the young, the elderly, and the unemployable; arts programs; and even police and fire protection. Deferring investment in such reasonable public purposes today will cost us dearly tomorrow.

It is becoming increasingly clear that numerous government functions cannot or will not be performed by the private sector, for lack either of wherewithal or incentive. In addition to the aforementioned public works and support services, the regulations apparently needed to maintain a decent environment also must be funded by taxes. Citizens have clearly demonstrated their support for all of these values.

The time has come, then, for us to recognize that these things must be paid for—now, and in the future—and to direct our political leadership to tax and plan accordingly.

- Stephanie Mills, editor of the last issues of *California Tomorrow,* analyzed the governor's 1984 budget proposal and found it disastrous for environmental quality—and in other ways: "Immediate and widespread personal survival issues are raised by Governor Deukmejian's proposed cuts in spending on welfare." But she cautioned against a too-enthusiastic return to belief in the virtue of big (and rich) government.

371

STEPHANIE MILLS   1983

Maintaining Compassion,
but Not the Status Quo

Acknowledging today's need for increased taxation doesn't imply that having a well-heeled state is desirable or that we hope to increase the state's role in our futures: We've all read *1984*. We need to simplify and devolve back to particular places, as much as possible, the power and responsibility to care for this piece of the Earth and its people. We must evaluate what the state is genuinely good at, continue to support that, and reclaim the rest. Some such reevaluation is called for by scarcity. Will it be democratic and gradual or oligarchic and abrupt?

At some point we need to deliberate on what money can and cannot buy.

We are not proposing a "let them eat ideas" program. Action is called for. But we had best start thinking about, or better yet planning toward, running California on a much higher ratio of community self-reliance to government spending, with less consumption overall, especially by the affluent. A leaner mix of government and resources in our lives implies change. Which leads us around to a paradox.

We've got to raise taxes to save the Earth and take care of people, yet we've got to reduce our dependency on taxes and the large institutions that supply and disburse them.

We look for grassroots involvement in the design of a transitional strategy. "Only a systems analysis of our situation will get us through this," says futurist Robert Theobald. "We've got to look at all the implications of what we're doing." It's like laboring to repair the roof of an edifice while devising the plans for erecting something different on the same site. What we are talking about is unprecedented in history—a long, peaceful revolution in which responsibilities are reclaimed, as well as rights.

V *California 2000*

19 *The California 2000 Project*

• Late in the 1970s, the California Tomorrow Board of Directors began to develop an idea for a new major undertaking on the scale of *The California Tomorrow Plan:* not a repeat performance, but a second, similarly ground-breaking effort.

The project was originally labeled "The California Tomorrow Plan, 1982." But in a time when the turn of the century was coming plainly into view—when agencies and groups across the country were using it as a horizon, a limit within which certain things should be done (or averted)—California Tomorrow chose to join in the millennial theme. The undertaking became the *California 2000 Project.* Slogan: "To Turn the Century."

Simply to restate and update the original plan was not in question. Since 1972, the issues had changed to some degree; public attitudes had changed a great deal. Environmental consciousness remained high, but a new skepticism about the effectiveness of government was also abroad. Regional and statewide planning were definitely not in vogue. What was needed, the directors thought, was new study of California's future, made from the ground up, with no prejudgment as to the conclusions. (Some believed that the results would necessarily bear quite a resemblence to *The California Tomorrow Plan,* after all; some didn't.)

One thing the directors wanted, this time, was to go to school to the public early in the game, before a document existed. They also felt a need for a more thorough and statistical, less impressionistic, picture of the kind of future toward which present trends supposedly compel us.

The course was set at a meeting at Nevada City in the spring of 1978. The general head of the project would be Charles Warren, the chairman, until a few months earlier, of President Carter's Council on Environmental Quality. Work would consist of three elements. First, a series of regional meetings would be held to determine what the public was most concerned about—"to discover," Warren wrote, "how people perceive the problems they face, what goals they want to achieve, what measures seem likely to succeed, and what sort of effort they are willing to support." Second, a staff of researchers at the University of California (Davis) would put together information about current trends and future possibilities. Finally, all these results and data would be studied and boiled down to produce a set of recommendations for the future.

All of this conferencing, collating, and analysis would cost a great deal more than the less formal and more personal effort that had gone into *The California Tomorrow Plan*. President Weyman Lundquist and Executive Secretary Richard Grant put their fundraising skills into operation, with remarkable success. During the four-year period when its energies were focused on the California 2000 Project, California Tomorrow enjoyed a relatively opulent operating budget approaching $200,000 a year. Key donors included the Atlantic Richfield Foundation, the Heller Charitable and Educational Fund, the Michael J. Connell Foundation, the San Francisco Foundation, the T.A.T. Communications Company, and the William and Flora Hewlett Foundation (a longtime California Tomorrow supporter).

The early emphasis was on the regional meetings, six of them. The first group gathered in Sacramento in May 1980; the last in San Francisco a year and a half later. Intervening sessions were held at Eureka, Riverside, San Diego, and Los Angeles. In each case, a local steering committee set the agenda and suggested speakers and panel members. The organizers bent over backward to avoid "packing" the panels with environmental types. Some objections to the final casts of characters came both from environmentalists and from business leaders—proof, Richard Grant remarked, "that something is being done right."

Perhaps the liveliest and most controversial of these confabulations was the one held in Eureka, the capital of the North Coast timber region, in the autumn of 1980. A portion of the conference summary follows.

JOHN HART   1980

The North Coast Speaks Out

It wasn't your typical conference crowd, those like-minded, looka-like people all set to applaud. This audience was diverse and largely skeptical: timber company executives and architects, farmers and for-esters, students, fishermen and Native Americans. One fellow wore a protest sign: *"2000,"* it said, *"is planned socialism."*

Northcoast 2000—the second in California Tomorrow's series of regional meetings, groping for a vision of a future California. In this case it was something of an achievement that the conference was held at all. Much more than the earlier meeting in Sacramento, it brought together people of contrasting attitudes and interests—people not much accustomed to talking together. It is good to report that, at the end of it, no party felt it had been taken for a ride.

"To be honest with you," said Humboldt County Supervisor Danny Walsh afterward, "I didn't know what to expect." Walsh's board de-clined to endorse the conference, though both Supervisor Walsh and his colleague Eric Hedlund spoke before it. There was worry that North-coast 2000 would be a stacked deck: a place for environmentalists and bureaucrats to lecture a captive audience, another attempt to impose on the North Coast standards and priorities designed for it by outsiders.

This has been happening a lot to North Coast counties. It's been happening to areas throughout the nation that are rich in resources and poor in population—Alaska, the Rocky Mountain states, Utah, Nevada. The nation is calling on these hinterlands for oil, water, coal, timber and recreation. Simultaneously, the nation is setting rules that control the way the resources are managed, and setting aside some lands as absolute preserves. This rule-making and preserving are aimed at protecting the environment and the long-term economic future, but to local people it doesn't look that way. To them it looks like unnecessary, heavy-handed intervention.

The North Coast is in some ways typical. It has seen the creation and then the expansion of Redwood National Park, which the timber indus-try and local public opinion opposed; the imposition of stricter controls on private logging; controls on coastline development through the Coastal Commission; and a number of other government actions widely perceived as attacks on local autonomy. In other states, similar issues

377

have given rise to the "Sagebrush Rebellion." In the North Coast region you might speak of a "Redwood Rebellion." There is talk, mostly symbolic, of secession. One common bumper sticker on Eureka streets reads *Alta Libre—Free the North*.

One thing the north would like to be free of is a long-standing local recession. For all its natural wealth, the region has been economically depressed for years. Timber harvest has been dropping since 1959; the fishing fleet has grown, but is bringing home less; tourism is growing rapidly, but not fast enough to take up the slack. Unemployment is chronic, and it is high.

It is not surprising, then, that the 2000 conference focused almost entirely on the state of the natural resources of the North Coast and of the industries that depend on them. There were, in essence, two positions. Some held that the natural resources of the region have been badly managed, and that this must first of all be corrected by government regulation, if necessary. "The unemployment picture in the year 2000 could be much worse if the resource base is depleted," warned biologist Gary Rankel.

Other speakers denied there has been a problem. "The land," insisted Supervisor Walsh, "is essentially well cared for." No one quite argued that government regulation is the single cause of the North Coast's economic difficulties, but many felt that regulations hamper every attempt the region's people make to improve their situation.

That so fundamental a disagreement could be resolved in a single day was not to be expected. But the courteous statement of positions to an attentive, varied audience had value of its own. There were, moreover, some important if undramatized points of agreement; and some new ideas were offered that cut across the seeming gulf between the pro- and the anti-regulators.

Charles Warren opened the morning session with a briefing on the *Global 2000 Report* issued by the President's Council on Environmental Quality—a grim projection of a world moving faster and faster into a crisis of dwindling resources. Since the effects of that projected crisis would strike first in the Third World, the relevance of *Global 2000* to Northcoast 2000 was not at first clear. ("Maybe," one conference participant offered, "we should move the 2000 Project to Bangladesh.")

The link was somewhat clarified by Raymond Dasmann, professor of Environmental Studies at the University of California, Santa Cruz, in his lunchtime keynote address. In several ways, Dasmann suggested, the North Coast of California resembles a Third World nation economi-

cally subject to a foreign power. Like an economic colony, the area provides raw resources for other areas: water for central and southern California, protein in the form of fish for many western states, timber for the nation. Yet the profits from these exports tend to flow out of the region of origin, too. Again, most of the North Coast land is controlled by absentee owners—not just the federal government, with its extensive national forests, but also the large timber-owning corporations head-quartered elsewhere in the United States.

How can the North Coast break these "colonial ties"? Dasmann offered a three-point program:

— *Local profit from local resources.* Dasmann pointed out that environmentalist advocates of parks and wilderness are by no means the only outsiders with whom the North Coast has to deal. "How much timber wealth stays in the region?" he demanded. "How do we keep it here?" And he raised the possibility of a regional organization analogous to OPEC—an OTEC (Organization of Timber-Exporting Counties) or an OWEC (Organization of Water-Exporting Counties).

— *Regional self-reliance.* Wherever possible, the North Coast should work to supply the needs of its own people. This could be done most easily in the energy field, with abundant supplies of wind and water for power, along with plenty of "biomass" (such as logging waste) that could be either burned or fermented into fuel.

— *Sustained yield.* "By the year 2000," Dasmann said, "every major economic activity must be ecologically sustainable." He seemed here to align himself with those who feel the timber industry and others are not now on this sustained-yield basis.

Dasmann's formula—with its combination of ecological dictates and sympathy for local feelings of powerlessness—seemed to puzzle the conference; at least it drew little direct response. More challenges were directed at Charles Warren. "Can anybody rank preservation higher than such needs as food and water?" one listener demanded. "It is our purpose," Warren replied, "to avoid having to make that decision. With rational thought and community participation, the choice can be avoided."

The morning section of the conference was planned to focus on natural resource problems, and it did. The afternoon session, programmed to deal with human problems, dealt largely with the same issues discussed in the morning. In the North Coast region, perhaps more than anywhere, any distinction between land and livelihood is artificial.

> The account goes on to sketch the debate on the topics of major concern: the future of the forests and of the ocean and river fish populations; the fate of the rivers themselves; the problems of the region's limited but valuable farmlands and grazing lands.

Out of the assorted viewpoints at the Northcoast 2000 Conference there did emerge some notable points of agreement.

It was generally agreed that the North Coast economy will continue to depend largely on natural resources; on timber, fish, soil, water. Other kinds of industry, it was agreed, should be encouraged, but the land-based enterprises would continue to dominate.

It was agreed that the North Coast resources must be managed on a basis of sustained, long-term yield. Some felt this sustained-yield state had already been reached, while others saw it as a difficult future goal.

It was agreed that government regulations affecting the resource-dependent industries should be clearer, simpler and more rational. It was not-so-generally agreed that they should be weaker.

It was agreed that outright, negative regulation—the ubiquitous government "thou shalt not"—is one of the clumsiest and least-desirable tools. Where other forms of guidance are possible, the conference seemed to feel, they should be preferred. Incentives are better than penalties.

"What is planning?" Supervisor Hedlund asked the meeting. Too often, he remarked, it is nothing but enforcement of regulations and the granting of permits. It should be based instead, he said, on a definition of common goals.

The North Coast community has not settled on common goals. But, if the experience of the Northcoast 2000 Conference is any guide, it has a good chance of developing some. "I was happy to see a balance," remarked Supervisor Walsh. Supervisor Hedlund agreed. The diversity of represented interests, he said, "is a significant accomplishment, and it shouldn't stop today."

• Here is a portion of Raymond Dasmann's keynote address:

RAYMOND DASMANN   1980

Ending the War against the Planet

There is one goal for the year 2000 that we must regard as essential. By that time every major economic activity we are engaged in must be ecologically sustainable, or well on the way to becoming so. There is no other option if we wish to continue to inhabit this planet. We're running out of time.

It is difficult to look at the state of the world today and find much to be cheerful about. Obviously we live with a continued threat of war, a big war, the final war.

Not everyone seems to realize there is another vicious world war already under way—the war against the planet. It is an ecological war, and the weapons being used are more powerful every day. This war is being won, rapidly. The antiplanetary forces have all the big victories. By the end of the century they will be well on their way toward exterminating the tropical humid forests on earth, with their tens or hundreds of thousands of species. Outstanding victories against the planet Earth are being gained along the edges of the world's deserts. We are told that in some places the antiplanetary forces are advancing the desert edge, creating lifeless land at a speed of 16 kilometers a year. According to the United Nations, the battle against agricultural land is also going strong; by the year 2000, one third of what now remains will have been destroyed.

Meanwhile new recruits flock to the antiplanet armies—around 80 million people are added to the world's population each year. When this war is finally won, the consequences will be as severe and irreversible as though we had fought a nuclear war with the Soviets. It is strange how invisible the war is to politicians, even when it is described in the government's own *Global 2000 Report to the President.*

All of this may seem peripheral to the subject of Northcoast 2000, but it is the setting against which you must plan your program. It is the reason I say time is running out. It is the reason why it is foolish to pretend that things will go on pretty much along the lines they have in the past. They won't. There must be new directions, and they must be

381

sustainable. For this region they must take into account the necessity to achieve a maximum degree of self-reliance.

By self-reliance I am not suggesting the region become totally self-sufficient. Self-sufficiency in a full economic sense is probably both an unrealistic and an undesirable goal, since it involves sacrificing the natural advantages of the region in favor of emphasizing activities that are best performed by other regions. At worst, it means going back to what would be for most people involuntary simplicity—doing without too much. Self-reliance, as I see it, involves development of the capacity to supply the basic needs of people—food, energy, water, clothing, shelter—but more particularly taking control of and understanding the processes by which those needs are met.

What you must achieve is the *development* of this region. You have a choice between two ways of looking at the concept of development. The old way, followed during the idiot years of the 1950s and early 1960s, was supposed to benefit the developing countries but, in fact, it did not. It was successful, however, in its primary objective—the rich got richer. The new concept of the 1980s has been stated by K. Dadzie in the September 1980 *Scientific American:*

Development is the unfolding of people's individual and social imaginations in defining goals and inventing ways to approach them. Development is the continuing process of the liberation of peoples and societies. There is development when they are able to assert their autonomy and, in self-reliance, to carry out activities of interest to them. To develop is to be or to become. Not only to have.

The same definition can be applied to the concept of ecodevelopment—ecologically sustainable development. Ecodevelopment is based on three premises:

— It must meet the basic needs of people, and in particular the poorest people, before attending to the wants of the well-to-do.

— It must encourage self-reliance and a degree of self-sufficiency in essentials, based on the knowledge, traditions and skills of the people concerned.

— It must be based on a symbiosis between people and nature, to maintain the diversity of the natural world and to provide for diversity in the social world. Through this it can help to guarantee the sustainability of all essential activities.

I would suggest that these premises also be your guides toward reaching your goals of California 2000 and Northcoast 2000.

• After the last of the meetings, Richard Grant summed up the lessons of this valuable exploration of the public mood and expert opinion of the early 1980s.

RICHARD A. GRANT   1981

Taking Stock

There were threads linking the issues discussed at the six meetings up and down the state, but each also had its distinct theme.

As Sacramento looked 20 years ahead, a good part of the state's growth was seen to be taking place inland. Industry is expected to move in, agricultural land to be converted to other uses, and an already sensitive air basin to come under further assault.

In Eureka, the chief problem for the North Coast was perceived as sparse population and not enough industrial growth as the economy, now based mainly on fisheries and forestry, declines because of habitat destruction and the depletion of resources.

In Riverside and San Bernardino, people were concerned about air quality and waste management, problems compounded by the housing pressures that grow as neighboring Orange and Los Angeles counties fail to meet their own housing needs.

San Diego saw immigration and the economic and social adjustments to be made by a joint San Diego–Tijuana metropolis as its chief concerns.

The critical challenges for Los Angeles will be the likelihood of more expensive energy and poorer air quality as it deals with the need for a skilled labor force and an affordable urban lifestyle.

High on the agenda in the San Francisco Bay Area were the need for affordable housing, the loss of farmland to urban sprawl, and the effect of toxic wastes on the waters of the bay.

Taking the six regional conferences together, a composite of the problem areas discussed would have to include energy, water, air quality, land use (both urban and agricultural), housing, economic development and jobs.

Energy. Utility company executives, regulatory agents and public-interest representatives were agreed: that cost has replaced demand as the key planning factor in power production; that projections of the demand for power are down considerably, to a manageable annual increase, half the amount predicted as recently as 1974; that because of high interest charges on long-term financing, new central-station power plants are too expensive, and geothermal, hydroelectric, fuel-cell and cogeneration systems will be more rapidly developed; and that by the year 2000, fossil fuels will still take up about two thirds of the state's energy budget, with the largest share going to transportation.

Water. Here there was no such meeting of minds. Based on what came out at the meetings, the debate falls roughly in two camps. On one hand are those who maintain that satisfying water demand is the primary criterion for any water policy, and that if demand is not met there will be critical shortages, growth will halt and economic decline will be inevitable. This group tends to support expansion of existing delivery systems as the best way to meet future needs.

In the opposing view, California has ample water supply systems in place and problems of supply, distribution and allocation are not physical but legal and political. This group argues that water should be priced more realistically statewide; that because water is limited, market forces should play a much greater role in determining how it is allocated and used. Instead of building more delivery systems, existing water compacts could be revised to make regions of the state more nearly self-sufficient in handling their needs.

Air quality. There emerged general agreement that air quality will suffer in all the state's urban areas as the year 2000 approaches, given projected increases in population, economic growth, automobiles and vehicle trips. There was unanimity on all sides that the public wants clean air, that the effects of air pollution on human health must be taken into account, that industrial polluters should be required to retrofit their plants with the best controls available and, finally, that without a significant technological breakthrough, the automobile will continue to be the main source of air pollution.

When strategies for improving air quality were discussed, opinion was divided. Citizen groups working for clean air see mass transit and management of growth by government as solutions, while those in industry want regulatory reforms to speed up permit procedures and encourage new designs for plants and equipment that will generate less pollution.

Toxic wastes. Next to air pollution, this was the issue of environmental quality most frequently raised. The feeling was that the generation of poisonous residues should be controlled as much as possible at the source, rather than trying to permanently monitor their safe containment in scattered disposal sites.

Land use. Citizens, planners and developers all predicted more-compact cities. This will translate into higher densities, rehabilitation of existing structures (one speaker forecast that today's parking garages are tomorrow's offices and apartments), redevelopment of blighted zones and infilling of vacant areas. An important component in making these urban-core areas livable will be to locate workplaces, residential areas and social and cultural gathering places close to mass-transit corridors.

At San Diego, a commercial developer opined: "By the year 2000 we'll be living the genuinely urban life in vertically integrated surroundings . . . and we'll find it just as much to be desired as the rose-covered cottage was just after World War II."

The question of how much metropolitan areas can or should be allowed to grow was raised in both Los Angeles and San Francisco. Mayor Bradley saw 4.1 million as a realistic population projection for Los Angeles, but noted that the city, currently with some 3 million people, is zoned for 10 million. In the San Francisco Bay Area, cities in Santa Clara County have zoned themselves for 250,000 new jobs but only 80,000 more dwellings. The only frank plea for more population came at the Northcoast 2000 Conference in Eureka.

It was widely conceded that mass-transportation systems will have to play an important role if densely populated urban-core areas are to be livable and workable.

Agricultural lands were discussed at nearly every conference. From Eureka to Riverside, the fact that urban sprawl continues to take over flat, rich-soiled farmland was a matter for concern. The importance of these lands was acknowledged both for food production and as open space when adjacent to metropolitan areas. "They are the irreplaceable

basis of economic prosperity and they determine the quality of life. If we destroy them there is no substitute," said a speaker at Riverside.

In this vein, growth-control ordinances came under fire, as the result is often to push urban development into outlying unincorporated areas, displacing agriculture in the process.

Housing. Some viewed the price of homes as the most controversial and intractable problem in California, the binding constraint on all the population projections and rosy economic forecasts being offered.

California already has the most costly housing in the nation. Because workers cannot afford to live in Orange County, pressure falls on such places as Riverside and San Bernardino counties to fill the need. When workers must commute, the result is more pollution and congestion and more energy used. In the end, high housing costs drive wages up and lead businesses to seek more favorable locations.

Several speakers saw the cultural tradition of the single-family house as a dinosaur doomed to extinction in the coming struggle between the need for housing and the need to grow food.

Employment. One prerequisite for a prosperous California 2000, with its high-technology, service-oriented industries, is a highly skilled labor force. Unskilled jobs will be available, but well-paying blue-collar jobs are expected to decline. The impact will be felt most by minorities and immigrants. The concern expressed here was twofold: without a skilled labor pool the state's high-technology future will have trouble materializing; and as the number of unskilled workers grows, one danger is the further separation of society along economic lines, leaving an underclass permanently trapped by disadvantages, chiefly inferior education.

Planning for disaster. The most frequently mentioned worry in this area was not fire, flood or earthquake—though all are seen as threatening and inevitable—but devastation from nuclear war.

Tying together some of the threads that connect the six regional meetings, an idea begins to take shape of what the major questions will be for California moving toward a new millennium.

— As the number of urban dwellers continues to increase, to what extent can California's air, land and water be expected to support her population?

386

— To what extent will urban California decide it must preserve its natural resource and food bases in rural California?

— Architects, planners and builders all foresee more densely populated, vertically integrated urban centers as the key to viable and resource-efficient metropolitan areas. Will housing and land costs continue to push development into outlying regions at the expense of agricultural lands and natural areas?

— Will California be able to develop the highly skilled work force needed to make its high-technology economy work?

If California Tomorrow were to have a theme song, it could perhaps borrow from the words of the old spiritual, *Dem Bones:* "The ankle bone connected to the leg bone, the leg bone connected to the knee bone . . ."

The problems confronting California are connected and interconnected, and then connected again. In the end, a healthy environment and a healthy economy depend on one another. The challenge is to search out the connections and interconnections, to understand and interpret them correctly, and then to decide what to do.

- "And then to decide what to do"—or what to recommend be done: this was inevitably the toughest part of the California 2000 Project. Back when *The California Tomorrow Plan* was being put together, it was Alfred Heller who decided, when the experts disagreed, just what to advocate. But the 2000 Project had a collective leadership, and that leadership was by no means of one mind about just what it should recommend. Some members of the advisory group, for instance, favored strong government planning and regulation; others now had doubts about it. Some saw hope in new laws, others in individual actions and changing attitudes. Some saw the population issue as paramount, others did not. By the time the final work began, the balance of opinion had shifted away from belief either in the reliability of projections or in the efficacy of government-imposed solutions. In effect, the basic philosophy of the California 2000 Project had changed.

  The task of synthesizing viewpoints, and culling the great mass of information gathered under Charles Warren's direction, fell chiefly to author Richard Reinhardt, a familiar *Cry California* contributor. After passing through the hands of several editors, the book-length final report appeared in

September 1983. Its title and theme: *California 2000—The Next Frontier*.

California 2000—The Next Frontier was not quite what had been advertised. It did not incorporate, in any very obvious way, the findings of the regional conferences, or the masses of information provided by the U.C. Davis staff. Instead, the statement was what, under the circumstances, it had to be: an intriguing, well-written exploratory tour, a think piece, asking as many questions as it offered answers. It faithfully reflected the struggle of a number of deeply concerned and knowledgeable people to work out, not so much a path into the future, as a set of working ideas with which the future may be approached.

There follow five passages from *The Next Frontier:* its introduction (originally entitled "The Trouble With the Future"); its discussion of projected population growth and change; its viewpoints on energy planning and environmental health; and finally the conclusion, "Opening the Next Frontier."

RICHARD REINHARDT   1982

From *California 2000: The Next Frontier*

Whatever became of the future?" a friend asked the other day. "We used to love to talk about it."

Back when the future was in fashion, not so many years ago, novelists and architects and comic-strip cartoonists used to let their imaginations soar away on rocket voyages to Plexiglas planets, and the rest of us rode along with them, enjoying what we assumed was an advance peek at the wonders time and technology would unfold.

Lately, notwithstanding the success of space films, the future has lost its charm. Science fiction thrives, of course. But real scientists (along with most politicians, economists, and historians) disclaim the power of prognostication. Even the breed of social scientists known as futurists generally say they do not *predict;* they merely describe alternatives.

At the same time, however, most people carry around with them personal visions of the future—unspoken, sometimes unspeakable perceptions of things to come.

Two visions, totally divergent, dominate the thinking of Americans nowadays. One is a vision of a world threatened with chaos. Overpopulation, depletion of resources, destruction of fertile soils, and toxic pollution of the environment are pushing humanity rapidly toward catastrophe—famine, plague, and the possibility of thermonuclear war. The opposing vision is that human ingenuity, efficiency-seeking economic systems, and new applications of technology will lift the world of the future to unprecedented heights of material abundance. As for the explosive growth of world population that appalls some demographers, it is all to the good and will cause economic expansion, because more people generate more production.

Different as they are, the two visions have something in common. Both conjure up images of a world beyond control, rushing headlong into a strange twilight that could be the dawn of a new era—or the sunset of civilization. One vision suggests resignation, the other optimism, but neither really suggests that we can *act* to create the future we would like. It is no wonder so many people have lost their curiosity about what is to come, or manage to believe the best and the worst at once, carrying both visions as they would an umbrella and a bottle of suntan lotion on the way to a football game.

> Pages omitted here explore some of the hazards of prophecy, and the many complex factors that combine to make things turn out the way they do—instead of the way we expect them to.

Very well, then. Let's admit that certainties are few: really, *change* is the only certainty. Let's admit that, down the road, we will be facing whole new problems, yet unknown. Let's admit that we cannot concoct a panacea, design a universal program, to make the future what we would like it to be.

Having admitted these realities, however, we can go on to the next step. For we do have some knowledge, and we do have some power. Individuals and their attitudes and actions obviously do have an effect on the future. And though the future as a whole is unpredictable, many aspects of tomorrow can be foreseen as the direct consequences of today, just as certain aspects of today are consequences of yesterday. We can see, for example, that past policies of keeping fuel costs low and spending immense sums on highway construction virtually assured our present dependence on the private automobile as our primary means of transportation. The same thing could be said of current policies: that, for instance, a policy of providing cheap water almost guarantees a future in which water will be used copiously and wastefully. It is only common sense to try to make out where we are going, and to try to alter our course when this seems necessary or desirable. This process is what we mean by "planning," and it is something that must go on continuously in any society interested in self-preservation and progress.

It must be admitted that "planning" has lately acquired a rather bad name. Fairly or unfairly, the word has become associated in many people's minds with vast, empty, sterile malls, decorated with meaningless statuary and expensive wastecans; with traffic routes rammed through beloved landscapes and comfortable old neighborhoods; with obnoxious regulations imposed by Those-Who-Have on Those-Who-Have-Not—in short, with schemes applied from above to enforce the tastes, social theories or economic interests of one set of people on another.

This negative image has been darkened by the repeated failure of planning, in the 1950s and 1960s, to live up to its promises. In this period, we saw grandiose designs to remove slums, remodel neighborhoods and restore dying business districts. The results, at best, were mixed. At the same time, state and local governments tried to improve their general planning work. Though some of their efforts have benefitted California, they have typically been hampered by disjointedness, a lack of sound information, and an ultimate lack of the authority to carry out what they plan.

But whatever past failures and abuses have occurred in the name of planning, the need to plan, to guide the decisions that will shape the future, remains. Indeed, the activity of planning is unavoidable. We do it well or badly, blindly or intelligently, but we do it. And a properly designed planning process can give people more control, not less, over the things that affect their lives.

What constitutes good planning? Not making an inflexible design for the future; not building a petty government tyranny; but achieving a process for agreeing on common goals and effecting them. It is a system by which day-to-day decisions on the use of land and other resources can be measured against the long-range needs of a community.

It is not always easy, of course, to define what makes up the "community" and to decide how its members will express their goals. Is the community a local neighborhood improvement association? A chamber of commerce? A supervisorial district? The state? Or perhaps the whole human race? The answer may lie in choosing the correct level at which to attack each problem. Just as a decision on the location of an airport cannot very well be left to a single neighborhood, so a decision on the preservation of a unique wilderness area or a specialized ecosystem will have effects beyond the jurisdiction of a county board of supervisors, and it should be made accordingly.

Policy, of course, does not arise in a vacuum. It must be motivated by certain overriding concerns. An important aspect of the California 2000 Project has been to identify what those prime concerns are now—and what they are likely to become.

Goals of Necessity

California Tomorrow has attempted to define basic goals for our state as we approach the year 2000. We call them the imperatives:

— To husband the irreplaceable land.
— To allocate water wisely.
— To conserve energy.
— To restore environmental quality and promote health.
— To protect human dignity and freedom.

These goals may sound obvious—even simple. But "simple" is not "easy." California is far from approaching any one of them. In some cases we have been going in exactly the opposite directions.

These goals cannot be achieved by technical solutions or political innovations alone. In order to bring about the positive changes the goals imply, we, as individuals, will have to alter our habits and attitudes profoundly.

One widely shared attitude in notable need of change is that technology is, in itself, good or evil—that it can destroy us, as pessimists hold, or solve our problems for us overnight, as some optimists still seem to believe. (Applied technology generates problems along with solutions. The real and net effect of any innovation depends on us.)

In order to shape a livable California, there is one attitude that we must adopt. We must accept responsibility for the future, uncertainties and all, understanding that we create the future in myriad daily decisions. We can work on the problems and possibilities of California's next frontier with cautious optimism, by correcting our course into the unknowable through broad participation and mustering the best information we can. We must discover the current direction of change, understand the forces that drive it, and select among alternative courses: We must *plan* for a better future.

The Pressure of Population

Who will be living in California in the year 2000? Will they be a new breed? Sharper? Duller? Younger? Older? Lighter? Darker? Speakers of a babble of exotic tongues? Or, give or take a few hundred thousand births and deaths, essentially the same old us?

Demographers in various state agencies, projecting birth rates, immigration rates, and other data forward two decades (a dangerously long time for statistics to keep their shape), give this picture of California 2000:

— Population growth will continue in all parts of the state except a few of the older urban areas. Most of the future growth will result (as usual, in California) from immigration, stimulated by the ambiguous prospect of employment. The birth rate in California, like that of the rest of the United States, recently has been slightly below what demographers coldbloodedly call "the replacement level."

— The greatest *absolute* growth will be in Southern California, where half the population will be concentrated in one eighth of the area of the state.

— The greatest *percentage* growth (hence the heaviest strain on housing, schools and public services) will be in the central coastal area, the Sierra Foothills, the counties north of San Francisco Bay, and the Central Valley.

— Older age-groups will dominate the population, with the greatest increase occurring in the segment aged 45 to 64 as the post-World War II "baby boom" becomes a middle-age boom.

— The proportion of Hispanic persons could reach one third of the state's total population.

— Ethnic minorities will constitute a majority of the population, consisting largely of people to whom English is a second language or who do not speak English at all.

— There will be a tendency for city people to move voluntarily to rural or semirural areas of the state.

— The average household will be smaller.

— If all these state projections stay on course, California's population will increase overall by about one third, from less than 24 million to more than 31 million.

The report considers, and discounts, the efficiency of growth control at the local level and the possibility of population control by the state.

For the state as a whole, it is probably more practical to direct the location of population growth than to limit it. No one really knows what is an "ideal population" for California. We don't really know how many more people can live here without causing a serious decline in the quality of life. The lesson for California in its postwar population boom was that enormous change in patterns of settlement, industry, and culture can come about startlingly fast. The question for California 2000 is can we learn how to direct such rapid demographic change into patterns we desire?

For the time being, it is not the *number* of people here, but our way of life and the patterns of consumption that support it that will determine the comfort and well-being of Californians to the year 2000 and beyond.

The energy section begins with an amusing (and distressing) recital of the past record of energy "experts"—the constant visions and revisions, promises and threats, the continual near-reverses of policy course. "Small wonder," it concludes, "that many Americans entered the decade of the 1980s disillusioned, frustrated, and confused. We felt we had been scolded, lied to, manipulated, overcharged and inconvenienced—and all to the end that we would pay more and use less. . . . But the real 'crisis,' the long-range depletion of energy resources, remains unsolved."

The document next turns to the latest prognostications of the California Energy Commission, and finds them unappealing: "The 'current trend' projection describes a California in which dependence on fossil fuels continues; dependence on imported oil increases; and the pollutants of petroleum combustion are a growing cost and a health hazard."

Another Energy Road

While preparing the current trend projection, however, the Energy Commission also developed an alternative projection. It shows that California could meet the energy needs of its growing population and economy in the year 2000 with an energy supply only slightly larger than today's: 7,661 trillion British Thermal Units, as compared to the 7,408 BTUs we logged in 1979. Per capita use, in this projection, actually drops by 22 percent. How can this conserving future be achieved?

Complex as it is, the energy problem has only three possible solutions, three strategies by which energy supply and demand can be brought into balance. The first is to increase the supply of available energy by developing or inventing new, renewable sources; the second is to stabilize supply and demand by modestly increasing the supply and modestly decreasing the demand; and the third is to reduce permanently—and dramatically—the demand for energy by structural changes in the ways we live, work, and build. Every proposal for "solving" the energy problem, whether it be political, economic, or scientific, is only a variation on these three ideas. It is possible to pursue more than one of them at the same time, and California in recent years has been toying with all three.

Consider how each strategy might affect the construction of a building. A policy of dealing with energy by increasing the supply might suggest, for example, the installation of a windmill on or near the building to generate electric power. A policy of modest energy

394

conservation might prompt the construction of solar panels to heat the water supply and the installation of a thermostat to control temperatures inside the structure. A policy of energy-use *reduction*, however, would mean locating and designing the building to minimize *forever* its energy requirements for heating, cooling, lighting, maintenance, and access.

A more complicated example is the problem of solid-waste disposal, an activity that consumes huge amounts of energy. An energy-increasing approach to waste disposal would be to burn or volatilize waste materials to generate power. An energy-conserving approach would be to compost organic waste for use as a soil nutrient and to sort out materials—glass, etc.—for reuse. The energy-reductive approach would be to limit the generation of waste by manufacturing longer-lasting vehicles, tires, appliances; by selling foods and beverages in returnable, reusable containers (or in bulk); and by packaging other products in natural, biodegradable containers rather than in plastics that deteriorate slowly if at all.

Our recent success in conserving energy has convinced many Californians that we can solve our long-range energy problem by the relatively painless middle course—that is, by finding some new sources of supply, by driving smaller or fuel-efficient cars, by insulating our houses, by not heating our swimming pools and by substituting 60-watt for 100-watt bulbs.

The trouble is, energy conservation of this sort only delays the inevitable day when energy demand has doubled and the supply is dwindling out of sight. Only a permanent reduction in our structural dependence on energy can alter this grim prospect.

For individuals, a genuine reduction in energy dependence will mean less travel to and from work, more residential clustering near places of employment; less transportation of goods and people, more communication by telephone, television, or computer links; less consumption of energy-intensive products such as processed and packaged foods, more reliance on bulk products, home and community gardens, reusable containers; less long-distance vacationing, more close-to-home recreation.

For communities, real reduction in energy dependence will mean smaller, denser, more self-contained neighborhoods that require less transportation and offer diversions, services, and protection. For agriculture, real reduction will mean less reliance on fertilizers and pesticides derived from petrochemicals, more reliance on manures, composting, mulches, cover crops; less large-scale, mechanized,

395

centralized farming and animal husbandry, more small-scale, dispersed farming to bring crops closer to consumers; less processing of food products, more marketing of fresh and unprocessed foods; less energy-consuming packaging, more bulk sales.

For industry, real reduction will mean less planned obsolescence, more manufacture of durable, easily repaired goods; less wasteful manufacturing processes, less production of energy-consuming gizmos and nonbiodegradable materials; capture and reuse of heat and of materials that are now wasted; dispersal of manufacturing to produce goods close to market; emphasis on craftsmanship rather than quantity; development of sophisticated new information technologies.

Despite the inevitable depletion of fossil fuels, and the confusion of our past energy policies, Californians have reason for hope. There are possible goals within each of the three strategies for balancing energy supply and demand. Human inventiveness is daily bringing forth technological advances to help us along the path to a sustainable society.

Pollution, Health, and Hurry

In California, particularly, it is impossible to think about the future without considering the possibility of "running out" of fresh air. In such regions as the Los Angeles basin, the Central Valley, and the southern lobe of San Francisco Bay, where geographic and atmospheric barriers trap the air in great inverted bowls, there already are what might be called periodic shortages of clean air. Can these areas endure the exhaust fumes exhaled by a still greater population, more numerous cars and trucks, and continuing industrial development? Can there be health without clean air? Is clean air worth its cost? Is *anything* worth the cost of poisoned air?

If air pollution were merely a nuisance—an unesthetic, eye-stinging, foul-smelling cloud over the business district on certain autumn days—it might not deserve much attention. Unfortunately, there is evidence that air pollution has lasting consequences. It is an increasingly severe hazard to the health of humans and their agriculture, and to Earth's forests and watersheds.

Moreover, air pollution typifies a whole class of environmental hazards that are either new, or increasingly lethal. These factors appear to be displacing disease-causing organisms as the greatest threats to human health.

Measured by the standards of the world, and of the past, California

is a relatively healthy place. The number of deaths due to infectious diseases has fallen dramatically, as it has throughout the United States, since the beginning of this century.

At the same time, however, the rate of chronic diseases has risen sharply. Four of the five leading causes of death in California (heart disease, cancer, stroke, and cirrhosis of the liver) are attributable, in some respect, to the way of life or the environment of the victim; and the other leading cause of death—accidents—clearly is related to our system of high-speed highway transportation. Our technological society is creating new killers to replace the killers it has conquered. The World Health Organization has estimated that as many as eight of ten cancers are precipitated by environmental factors: carcinogens in the atmosphere, workplace, and the food supply, as well as by overall stress.

In California, injurious substances are becoming pervasive. Our industries, agriculture, and vehicles throw off about 5 million metric tons of hazardous wastes a year—corrosives, explosives, flammables, poisons—and only about a tenth of these waste materials are destroyed or disposed of without adverse effect on the environment. Several years ago the National Institute of Occupational Safety and Health estimated that some 26,500 toxic chemicals were in common use in the United States, of which 2,100 were suspected of causing cancer, 40 could cause mutation, and 400 could generate monstrosities in the reproduction of living creatures. Of the toxic chemicals, 2,200 were pesticides. The number and volume of synthetic organic chemicals grows in magnitude every year.

Air pollution, though probably not the most dangerous part of this "hazardous waste stream," is the most visible and ubiquitous manifestation of it. Approximately 85 percent of Californians live in areas where bad air is a constant or at least an occasional threat. Not only lung cancer, emphysema, asthma and other respiratory diseases, but also heart disease and diseases of the nervous system, are believed to be caused or exacerbated by exposure to polluted air.

Of the many reasons (economic, esthetic, spiritual) for minimizing pollution, none makes more immediate sense than preventing illness. However, many Californians don't understand the connection between maintaining environmental standards and maintaining public health.

Environmental hazards, unlike acute illnesses, are slow to reveal their effects, and the origins of environmentally related illnesses are extremely difficult to pinpoint. So it seems almost necessary to overlook the gradual deterioration of one's health, to accept as "normal" the poisonous influences of impure air, degraded water, adulterated foods, nervous tension. Many people, understandably, resent being warned of dangers in the things they customarily eat, drink, breathe, or do. Add to this a reluctance to accept the increased cost of living and the inconveniences that might result from strengthening environmental standards, and the result is a spreading, fatalistic acceptance of conditions that can and should be corrected.

Looking ahead toward several decades of growth in California, one can anticipate an increasing output of toxic wastes, much of which will wind up in the air we breathe. Yet, at the time of this report, there are strong political pressures to weaken or even abandon the clean air standards established by the state and federal governments. "Nonattainment," a bureaucratic term for failure, is in effect becoming an acceptable goal. Clearly, if life in California is to remain endurable for the next two decades and beyond, the standards for maintaining air quality and other environmental values should not be lowered but raised.

> In the matter of air pollution, the report reminds us, there is (in California) one primary culprit: the private automobile. But involved with that is a more fundamental demon: our lust for rapid, frantic, often meaningless travel, unequalled in the world.

Almost without exception, the seers in business and government believe something is going to happen—*must* happen—to change California's present dependence on large, gasoline-powered private automobiles. In the year 2000, when 22 million Californians have become more than 30 million, they will hardly be able to use automobiles, gasoline, and freeways the way they use them now. Yet short-range predictions assume that the car, the freeway, and the gasoline station will be with us indefinitely, only in some slightly modified form that will achieve efficiency and economy.

The commitment to automotive transportation perpetuates itself and intertwines with land, water, and energy consumption. For instance, our

way of using land contributes to our need to transport people to and fro each day in ever-increasing numbers. Through zoning, we restrict certain large areas to residential use. Other areas are to be used exclusively for offices, or industry, or retail shops, or entertainment, or agriculture. While this practice has certain evident virtues, it also necessitates the daily shuttling of innumerable people between their homes and their places of work. Single-use zoning, as it is now applied in most of California, forces all of us to *depend* on transportation, no matter how costly it becomes.

The corner drug store, the nearby market, the branch library, even the neighborhood school owe their decline, in part, to the success of automobile transportation. Transportation triumphs even over reason. The homemaker drives to market for a single purchase; the salesperson reports to headquarters for a 10-minute meeting before going into the field; two dozen committee members gather to transact an hour or two of business that could have been handled by letter or telephone.

399

Freeing the Movement of Information

As we wheel busily toward the 21st century, our dependence on automobile transportation—on transportation in general—will become more costly every year.

We should be considering coherent alternatives to travel, to shipment, to storage—that is, the shaping of a culture in the 2000s and afterward that moves people and goods only when it is necessary to do so, that encourages the movement of information rather than the movement of people, and that discourages aimless personal mobility as a form of exultation.

Such alternatives exist. We can bring jobs and people closer together, locate processing plants closer to raw materials, decentralize retailing and service businesses. We can develop more sophisticated people-moving systems: high-speed trains, fleets of electric minicars in central cities, moving sidewalks, jitneys. In transporting goods, Californians will perhaps rely increasingly on pipelines, beltlines, and multimodal vehicles.

These are undertakings that require huge investments of capital and entail relatively high risks. But what better direction could economic enterprise follow, in a resource-hungry world, than toward new ventures that rely on capital and skills rather than on energy and natural resources?

Californians should constantly be searching for ways to substitute communication for transportation. As a hotbed of high technology, California is ideally situated to demonstrate that integrated computers and other sophisticated communication devices can, in many cases, transfer information more reliably, quickly, and efficiently than humans riding or flying can.

Although it is unlikely that we will shake off our dependence on the automobile during the next 20 years, we could begin to settle our bodies and let our intelligence travel faster, through accelerated communication. Progress, in this instance, consists in speeding up some things and slowing down others.

Opening the Next Frontier

The new frontier that awaits us in the coming decades will differ radically from the American frontier of the 18th and 19th centuries. It will not offer free homesteads, fur pelts, or lamp oil oozing from the rocks. Like the old frontier, however, it will impose demands and put its mark on its inhabitants. As the pioneers of the last frontier were compelled to adapt or discard many customs and ideas they had brought with them from the "Old Country," so will the pioneers of the next frontier be forced to find new attitudes and institutions. As the earlier frontier had its distinctive characteristics—emptiness, abundance, isolation—so will the next frontier have its own peculiarities: depletion, acceleration, interdependence, change.

Depletion already is upon us, and has been evident for many years. We see it in shortages of cheap, developable land; of capital for public improvements; of electric power and transportation fuels; of housing, open space, prime agricultural land, timber, additional water resources, and specialized ecological systems such as wetlands, wilderness, and primal deserts. Depletion is evident, too, in the deterioration of environmental quality resulting from the presence of countless waste products of modern life. Depletion lurks in the side effects of drugs, dyes, pesticides, and preservatives. It is shockingly manifested in the extinction of whole species of plant and animal life.

Acceleration is characteristic of almost every aspect of contemporary life. It took millennia for people and grazing animals to denude the Middle East of its luxuriant forests; nowadays, a forest habitat can be destroyed, more or less permanently, in a few weeks. In one full century, between 1850 and 1950, the per capita consumption of energy in the United States roughly doubled. In slightly more than 30 years since 1950, consumption doubled again. During the first hundred thousand years of human existence, the extermination of other species of life was negligible; now, human enterprises, appetites, and whims destroy species at the rate of one per day. Scientists who study extinction estimate that the rate will increase to one per hour by the year 2000.

Interdependence is a phenomenon that is visible in the food chains and life cycles of plants and animals. It also is characteristic of many modern institutions. A zoning law that excludes development from one area, for example, may cause development pressure in another place. A highway that carries suburban commuters to the city may also bring congestion, air pollution, and rising land prices to the country. A pipeline to an arid valley may create additional demand for water by encouraging cultivation and development on desert land. A system of taxation that treats profits on the sale of undeveloped land as "capital gains" may discourage economic enterprise by drawing capital away from productive investments into land speculation. Actions taken in one subsystem have inevitable, if unpredictable, consequences in others.

401

Change is the aspect of the future that causes the greatest apprehension and resistance. Much of our political activity nowadays consists of trying to prevent change. Seldom do we make the effort to anticipate, accommodate or channel change. Yet change is an absolute certainty; and, in the nature of the next frontier, it will occur at an accelerating rate. Although the outcome of change is largely unpredictable, this fact does not mean we have no influence upon it. Nor do we have any excuse for failing to develop clear images of what the future *might* be. Allowing for change and attempting to deal with it, that is what we mean by "planning." Planning for change, acceleration, depletion, interdependence—this will be the key to survival on the next frontier.

The underlying problem for the future, however, is not in our institutions—our monetary system, our governments, our schools, our churches, our families—but in our attitudes toward the Earth and our place in its sphere. And, to change our attitudes, we will have to arrive at a new perception of California and of the life it could offer.

In many ways, California has been the ultimate frontier of the Old World—the place, above all others, where the dream of America seemed possible, the place where there appeared to be limitless soil, air, space, fuel—limitless opportunity. This vision of material abundance, combined with our characteristic American urge to share paradise with as many immigrants as could be enticed across the prairie and over the Sierra, created the prototypical Californian—a boomer and a spender, whose measure of success was growth: more products, bigger projects, higher towers, larger cities. Success on the next frontier will be measured by a different set of standards: resourcefulness, imagination, thrift. Many vestiges of the old mentality will have to be put aside.

To succeed on the next frontier, the people of California will have to learn to live, as much as possible, as part of the natural environment—not as its conquerors, manipulators, and exploiters, but as its loving and careful caretakers. We will have to accept new standards of material well-being, new definitions of comfort, convenience, and achievement. Our aspiration has been to make good by making California grow. Now, it must be to recognize the limitations of the resources that support life on Earth; to strive for a more equitable distribution of resources among all people; to dedicate our communities to realizing the full potential of every human being; and to create institutions that will protect and nurture the Earth.

Two decades ago, in an essay on the destiny of California, George

B. Leonard wrote: "The best place in the world for facing the problems of the future is California, where the future is happening every day."

California is a bellwether, for better or worse. As surely as the world is the sum of its parts, a change of attitude in the neighborhood called California could contribute to a new ethical climate throughout the world. The future—unpredictable, obscure, and perilous—*does* depend on us.

Editor's Afterword

- California Tomorrow began as a hybrid, a compound of two social movements that ordinarily don't mix. One was the environmental cause. "That gave us our base," Alfred Heller notes. The other movement, more cerebral, more technical, was what might be called the "good government" tradition. Since the turn-of-the-century Progressives, a certain number of people in each generation have insisted on the importance of keeping government tuned up, so to speak, to meet the changes and challenges of the century. The League of Women Voters has been a tenacious supporter of such ideas. California Tomorrow, with its doctrines of state planning, metropolitan government, and multipurpose policy-making, fits right in.

When California Tomorrow began publishing, the environmental side of its message was, in itself, news. (Its grim view of a misplanned future was headline material—and what other conservation group of the day was paying as much attention to urban issues?) As the rest of the environmental movement gradually broadened its focus, this distinctiveness became less marked. What remained unique about California Tomorrow was the linkage of concern for the environment with the other side of its case, the stubborn conviction that the workings of government do matter.

Not that California Tomorrow ever ignored policy in favor of pursuing an abstract efficiency. Good policy was always its first and last demand. But its founders had the stubborn conviction that good policy can be carried out only if the institutions of government can be made more capable, more responsive, and more understandable.

This belief finds easy acceptance among certain groups of people: most planners, many academics, many habitual observers of government. It has rarely captured the interest of the general public. California Tomorrow tried hard to arouse that interest; to some extent, first with *California Going, Going . . .* and later with *The California Tomorrow Plan,* it succeeded.

During the later part of the 1970s, however, public belief in—even interest in—the usefulness of government was on the decline. Whether or not one thing resulted from the other, it is interesting that California Tomorrow suspended its work at a point when the antigovernment

405

feeling seemed to have reached an extreme. At that point, the audience for planning appeared to be limited to the long-converted.

Government—so we might paraphrase today's prevailing attitude—is just something we have to put up with. Who cares how they organize the desks? All you can really do is find something you care about (as local and specific as possible) and work on that. Save the local scrap of open space, steer the affordable-housing project through the hurdles, build the energy-efficient windmill. And other voices: "What we do in our daily, individual lives may matter most of all."

Critics point out the natural cussedness of human institutions and the limits of reform: that a change that looks good on paper may yield no real improvement in action; that a fine-sounding policy may never be carried out; that, indeed, a fine-sounding policy carried out this year may prove to be next year's disaster. They also observe that an efficient government setup is liable to fall, sooner or later, into the "wrong" hands. What is the point of gathering the scattered offices that manage federally owned land together into one department (as reformers have long proposed) if that department is to be headed by a James Watt? What is the advantage of having a State Planning Council if its members are appointed by a governor who believes in development at any cost?

David Brower of Friends of the Earth is just one strong voice that has frankly counseled against the pursuit of "better" government—he equates the seeming chaos of some present arrangements with the diversity so often found in healthy ecosystems.

Such views have their attractiveness. They provide a needed corrective against the tendency to count too much on government, to overlook the ways that plans go wrong, to assume too readily that—once we make the right promises, pass the right laws, get the lines of authority right—good results will follow of themselves. It ain't necessarily so.

Nevertheless and after all: government is not something that we can dispense with. It has and will have many jobs to do. It is in nobody's long-term interest that they be done badly. And if reform by itself does not guarantee success, the lack of it can sometimes be a guarantee of failure. Sometimes the existing structures are so clumsy, so hard for the citizen to influence, so convoluted that they simply cannot move . . . or cannot move in any new direction.

We have a tendency to equate in our minds efficiency and authoritarianism. California Tomorrow, on the other hand, always insisted on government that was both democratic and effective—effective because democratic, democratic because effective. This is no doubt a difficult goal. But one thing is very clear: there is no magic about inefficiency. It does nothing to increase the citizen's control of government. Rather, it hampers it. Inefficiency can be a form of tyranny.

Good tools may not make the carpenter, but it is easier to be a carpenter if your tools are suited to the job—and don't break in your hands.

—Take the National Wilderness Preservation System, the form of national zoning by which certain wild areas are kept inviolate. Does any wilderness advocate seriously believe that the cause of wilderness protection would be as far along as it is today if this particular reform, this changing of the rules, had not occurred in 1964?

—Take the Bay Conservation and Development Commission. As I write this, Governor Deukmejian has just appointed to that commission some new members: people more in favor of bayshore development than their predecessors were. Conservationists are objecting. But this is the point—they know, at least, exactly where to direct their complaints and how to make them effective. Because there is a Bay Commission, a body with the power to plan and the power to decide, people know where to apply pressure. For this reason, I am fairly sure that, in the end, little damage will be done. Structure does matter.

—Today the Bay Area organization called People for Open Space is trying to put together a campaign to set aside vast stretches of open land around the area's present cities as a permanent metropolitan greenbelt. Because there is no competent regional body to consider the merits of such a plan or to carry it out, the POS campaign must be put together out of a multitude of local campaigns, one in every jurisdiction in which a piece of the proposed greenbelt lies. It is a magnificent effort made doubly difficult by a gap in the government setup: structure again.

Any government, needless to say, is going to make its share of mistakes. Any government will have its bureaucratic tangles, its inertias. Any government, if let, will tend to overtax and overspend. Any government has to be watched.

But this is in itself a reason for reform, because one of the most distressing things about the present system is how difficult it is to watch. It takes a broadly informed citizen to know where the important decisions are being made and a tireless citizen to have any hope of influencing them. Often, as in the greenbelt case, power is so diffused that the voter is disenfranchised. "Home rule" means that, with your authority as a constituent, you can influence one board of supervisors, one city council; but you have no standing with the board or council next door, no matter how much its actions may concern you. (Your future is also in the hands of a number of special single-purpose districts. Do you know what these are—and who is supposedly your representative on each of them?)

Since the publication of *California, Going, Going . . .*, many of the fears of that period have been partially allayed. Things are certainly not as bad as, 20 years ago, it appeared they were going to be. Population growth, for one thing, has slackened, allowing us more time to find the answers to many questions; and some disturbing trends of the past have tapered off. Ten years ago, utitlity companies were still forecasting the need to build nuclear power plants every few miles up and down a thousand miles of coastline!

But if the fears of an earlier time have not, by and large, been realized, neither have the hopes. The balance of forces today seems to be nudging us, not toward a nightmare, but into a depressingly modest—a mediocre—future.

(Some parkland, but not really enough. Some transit systems, but not very efficient ones. Some "affordable housing," but not all that affordable—and not all that good to live in. A seemingly permanent poverty problem, somewhat moderated but never successfully confronted.)

We even have to wonder whether we have actually gotten off the bleak road sketched in *California, Going, Going . . .* and again in the California One scenario of *The California Tomorrow Plan.* Have we really changed course that much, or are we merely traveling the same old course a bit more slowly? In some respects it seems the latter is so. Our cities are oozing out across the landscape not quite so rapidly as before, but they are still on the spread—indeed, recent developments have lower densities, on the average, than those of a few years back. Our energy appetite is rising more slowly than before—but it is rising. Vigorous control measures have knocked air pollution levels back a decade or two—but, experts suggest, they are due to increase again as the numbers of cars and miles driven continue to climb. And so on.

Our tools of government have improved somewhat since the early 1960s. If they had not, we would be in much worse shape than we are. But if we are to avoid fighting a long, slow, losing battle to hang on to the quality of life in California, we will have to do better than that.

We have not gained control. We have only gained a little time.

For a few years on either side of 1970—a moment, historically—

change in government and law seemed not only possible but almost easy. Reformers and reform ideas seemed to be everywhere; the brew was boiling. Before more than a part of the promise of that time was fulfilled, the energy faded, and left us with the present inertia. As problems continue to mount, however, another period of opportunity, another fertile moment, is likely to present itself.

If in fact that day is coming, it is important that we organize our thinking about the sorts of changes it is worthwhile to pursue.

Whether California Tomorrow was exactly right in its prescriptions for reform is naturally a matter for debate. Certainly change in the real world is unlikely to come in the neat packages that Alfred Heller and Sam Wood envisioned at first. But to my mind, at least, there is no question about the rightness of their two or three basic themes: that some form of unified regional government is necessary in the metropolitan areas; that the state must equip itself to adopt, and carry out, a general scheme for the conservation and development of California; that single-purpose plans in government must be brought into line with the goals of such a general vision.

During the next decades, whatever the surprises they bring to California, we are going to be looking again to the adequacy of our government tools. It is then, I think, that California Tomorrow, that old toolshop, will be most appropriately valued.

The Contributors

John W. Abbott, public relations expert and journalist, lent his skills to many organizations and causes. Involved with California Tomorrow almost from its beginning, he served as executive secretary and editor for nearly five years before his death in 1976.

Gerald D. Adams is a feature writer for the *San Francisco Examiner;* he specializes in urban affairs and environmental topics.

Walter Truett Anderson is a political scientist and writer. Among his numerous books is *Rethinking Liberalism,* a collection of essays.

Nicholas Arguimbau is a San Francisco attorney, now in private practice, who specializes in constitutional and environmental law. It was Arguimbau who first suggested forcing a referendum on the proposed Peripheral Canal.

Gil Bailey, a veteran reporter, was Washington, D. C. correspondent for the Ridder newspapers during the 1970s; he is now on the *Seattle Post-Intelligencer.*

George Barrios is the pseudonym of Los Angeles writer Walter Houk, who lives on the north slope of the Santa Monica Mountains.

Karl Belser, planning director for Santa Clara County from 1950 to 1967, was a pioneering figure in county-level planning.

Harold A. Berliner, formerly district attorney of Nevada County, now an attorney in private practice, works especially "to protect the environment and to cure fraud." He was a director of California Tomorrow for 23 years.

Daniel J. Blackburn is a political writer and columnist, and a frequent contributor to the *California Journal.*

Eric Brazil is Los Angeles Bureau Chief for *USA Today.*

William Bronson, the first editor of *Cry California,* was also the author of many articles and several books including *How to Kill a Golden State.* He died in 1976.

Willie L. Brown, Jr., is a San Francisco attorney and represents the 17th District in the State Assembly, of which he was elected speaker in 1980.

Sterling Bunnell is a psychiatrist who has been active in conservation education.

Lou Cannon is White House correspondent for the *Washington Post* and a biographer of Ronald Reagan.

Marion Clawson is Senior Fellow Emeritus of Resources for the Future, Inc., and former head of the U.S. Bureau of Land Management.

Stan Cloud, a journalist, is now Executive Editor of the *Los Angeles Herald-Examiner*.

Thomas H. Crawford is a San Francisco attorney; he was country director for the Peace Corps in the eastern Caribbean from 1979 to 1982.

Raymond F. Dasmann is Professor of Environmental Studies at the University of California, Santa Cruz. Among his writings is the book *The Destruction of California*.

James Deacon is Professor of Biological Sciences at the University of Nevada, Las Vegas.

Elizabeth Dickson is currently Director of the Policy Analysis Division of the New York City Office for Economic Development.

Harrison C. Dunning is Professor of Law at the University of California, Davis. He was staff director of the Governor's Commission to Review California Water Rights Law in 1977–78.

Garrett Eckbo is a private architectural consultant and Professor Emeritus at the University of California, Berkeley.

Douglas Foster is now Senior Editor at the Center for Investigative Reporting in San Francisco.

Curt Gentry, noted California writer, is the author of numerous books including *The Last Days of the Late, Great State of California* and *Helter Skelter: The True Story of the Manson Murders*.

Adriana Gianturco was director of the California Department of Transportation under Governor Jerry Brown. She now writes on public policy issues for several California newspapers and magazines.

Charles R. Goldman is Professor of Limnology in the Division of Environmental Studies at the University of California, Davis, and director of the Tahoe Research Group at the Institute of Ecology there.

Richard A. Grant was executive secretary of California Tomorrow from 1975 to 1982. He is currently working with several charitable trusts in Southern California.

Professor Sherman W. Griselle was founding chair of the Department of Urban and Regional Planning at California State Polytechnic University, Pomona; he is a former president of the California Chapter, American Planning Association.

John Hart is a San Francisco writer specializing in environmental and literary subjects. His writings include *Walking Softly in the Wilderness: The Sierra Club Guide to Backpacking*.

Alfred Heller, founder of California Tomorrow, now edits the magazine *World's Fair*.

Van Herbert was the pen name of a prominent San Francisco psychiatrist.

Richard D. Hedman is Principal Planner for Urban Design in the San Francisco City Planning Department.

Ira Michael Heyman is the Chancellor of the University of California at Berkeley.

Joseph C. Houghteling has served on the California Highway Commission, the California Park Commission, and the San Francisco Bay Conservation and Development Commission—as well as on the Board of Directors of California Tomorrow.

Barbara Ward Jackson, now deceased, was a distinguished British economist and authority on Third World development, as well as on urban affairs.

Dr. Robert E. Jenkins of Arlington, Virginia, is director of the science department and national vice president of The Nature Conservancy.

Steven M. Johnson is staff artist on the *Sacramento Bee* and author of *What The World Needs Now,* a book of cartoons portraying whimsical inventions.

Harold Keen, now deceased, was a prominent San Diego journalist best known for his daily show "People in the News" on KFMB-TV.

Mary Ellen Leary writes for the *Economist,* the *Nation,* the *California Journal,* and the Pacific News Service.

Daryl Lembke, for 21 years a reporter on the *Los Angeles Times,* is now Press Secretary to State Senator David A. Roberti.

E. Phillip LeVeen is the West Coast Director of Public Interest Economics, a research and educational foundation located in Washington, D.C. and Berkeley, California.

Martin Litton, a conservationist, writer, and champion of difficult causes, was senior editor at *Sunset;* is now proprietor of Grand Canyon Dories.

Weyman I. Lundquist, a San Francisco attorney, was for five years President of California Tomorrow; he is an activist, in and out of the courtroom, on behalf of environmental and other causes.

Ray March has contributed to *Time,* the *New York Times, New West,* and many other publications. His book *Alabama Bound: 45 Years inside a Prison System* was a 1978 nominee for a National Book Award.

Stephanie Mills is a freelance editor and writer on environmental subjects; she has edited *California Tomorrow, CoEvolution Quarterly,* and *Not Man Apart;* and is currently Director of Development at World College West near San Francisco.

413

Victor Palmieri is a businessman and former Ambassador at Large and U.S. Coordinator for Refugee Affairs.

Bill Press was director of the State Office of Planning and Research under Jerry Brown and, earlier, director of the Planning and Conservation League; he is now a political commentator on KABC-TV, Los Angeles.

Richard Reinhardt, a San Franciscan, is the author of numerous books and articles.

Hal Rubin spent many years as a technical editor "turning jargon into English"; he now lives in Sacramento and is a nationally-published freelance writer specializing in environmental topics.

Pat Washburn Rubin, a freelance writer, specializes in state politics and horticultural subjects. Pat and Hal are married.

John Seginski is a freelance garden and natural history writer.

Robert C. Simmons, for many years a reporter with KNXT-TV, Los Angeles, is now at KING-TV, Seattle.

The Stanford Biology Study Group, a loosely-organized working group of graduate students and professors, was formed in 1970 to evaluate available information about the ecological impacts of the Vietnam War.

Frank M. Stead, formerly with the California Department of Public Health, is a consultant in environmental management who lives in Piedmont, California.

Allan Temko is architecture critic for the *San Francisco Chronicle.*

Jay Thorwaldson was a reporter with the *Peninsula Times-Tribune* for fifteen years; he is currently Director of Community Relations with the Palo Alto Medical Foundation.

Mark von Wodtke is Professor of Landscape Architecture at California State Polytechnic University, Pomona.

T. H. Watkins, a widely-published writer on environmental affairs, is former editor of *American Heritage* and present editor of *Wilderness,* the magazine of The Wilderness Society.

Caspar W. Weinberger's public career has included major cabinet posts in both California and federal governments.

Steven Witt is director of the California Agricultural Lands Project, a nonprofit information clearinghouse that conducts information on agricultural topics, and author of *Genetic Engineering of Plants.*

Samuel E. Wood has spent much of his life working for local, state, and federal governments in various planning capacities; he was co-founder and first executive director of California Tomorrow; and is now a planning consultant in Sacramento.

414

A Short Bibliography
of California Tomorrow

*This list includes writings produced
by or published by California Tomorrow,
with the addition of several especially
pertinent "outside" sources.*

Abbott, John W., and John Hart, "Democracy in the Space Age: Regional Government under a California State Plan," California Tomorrow, San Francisco, California, 1973.

Abbott, John W., editor, "Private Property and the Public Interest: Summary of Proceedings of a California Tomorrow Legal Seminar on the Use and Regulation of Land," California Tomorrow, San Francisco, 1974.

Cry California (later *California Tomorrow*), periodical, published four times a year from 1965 to 1983. Volume 1, Number 1 was published in Winter 1965–66; Volume 17, Number 2, Spring 1982, was the first issue to be called *California Tomorrow;* the final issue, Volume 18, Number 2, appeared in Spring 1983.

Gantner, Anthony F., editor, "Resource Allocation and Comprehensive Planning: Summary of a California Tomorrow Seminar on the Use of Land Resources," California Tomorrow, San Francisco, 1975.

Heller, Alfred, "California Tomorrow: A Voice for State and Regional Planning," an oral history conducted in 1981 by Malca Chall, in *Statewide and Regional Land-Use Planning in California, 1950–1980 Project,* Volume I, Regional Oral History Office, The Bancroft Library, University of California, Berkeley, 1983.

Heller, Alfred, editor, *The California Tomorrow Plan,* William Kaufmann, Inc., Los Altos, California, 1972 (also published in *Cry California,* Summer, 1972).

Heller, Alfred, editor, "The California Tomorrow Plan: A First Sketch," California Tomorrow, San Francisco, 1971.

Olmsted, Roger, "A Long Look Ahead: Are you Making a Better Plan?," *Sierra Club Bulletin,* December, 1972.

Reinhardt, Richard, principal author, "California 2000: The Next Frontier," California Tomorrow, San Francisco, 1982 (the Summer 1982 issue of *California Tomorrow* magazine).

415

Stanford Biology Study Group, "The Destruction of Indochina: A Legacy of Our Presence," California Tomorrow, San Francisco, 1970.

Wood, Samuel E., "Administration, Research, and Analysis in Behalf of Environmental Quality," an oral history conducted 1981 by Malca Chall, in *Statewide and Regional Land-Use Planning in California, 1950–1980 Project,* Volume I, Regional Oral History Office, the Bancroft Library, University of California, Berkeley, 1983.

Wood, Samuel E., and Alfred Heller, "California Going, Going . . .," California Tomorrow, Sacramento, California, 1962.

Wood, Samuel E., and Alfred Heller, "The Phantom Cities of California," California Tomorrow, San Francisco, 1963.

Wood, Samuel E., and Daryl Lembke, "The Federal Threats to the California Landscape," California Tomorrow, San Francisco, 1967 (also published in *Cry California,* Spring 1967).

Availability: Many libraries have files of *Cry California*. All of the above listed publications, and an abundance of additional original materials can be found at the California Historical Society Library, 2099 Pacific Avenue, San Francisco, 94109. Many will be found at the new office of California Tomorrow at Fort Mason in San Francisco, Building B, Room 305; the mailing address is Box 421201, San Francisco, 94142–1201. The Heller and Wood oral histories are available at the Bancroft Library at the University of California, Berkeley; at the California Historical Society; and at the libraries of several campuses of the University of California and the California State University System.

The People of California Tomorrow 1961–1983

Founders

 Alfred Heller
 Samuel E. Wood

Presidents

 Alfred Heller 1961–1974
 William M. Roth 1975–1976
 Weyman I. Lundquist 1977–1982
 Ronald L. Olson 1982–1983

Board of Directors

The four founding directors of California Tomorrow were Harold A. Berliner, Alfred Heller, William M. Roth, and (until her death in 1964) Catherine Bauer Wurster, the eminent authority on public housing. In 1972 the board was expanded. The following people served for varying periods on the larger board:

 E. Jane Arnault 1980–1983
 Standish Backus, Jr. 1972–1976
 Harold A. Berliner 1972–1983
 Mignon Bowen 1982–1983
 Lewis H. Butler 1976–1977
 Diane P. Cooley 1974–1976
 Ira De Voyd Hall 1972–1974
 Howard H. Hays 1975–1976
 Alfred Heller 1972–1975
 Clarence E. Heller 1972–1983
 Flora L. Hewlett 1971–1977
 Joseph C. Houghteling 1977–1983
 Robert C. Kirkwood 1972–1980
 Weyman I. Lundquist 1976–1983
 William R. Marken 1982–1983
 A. Hamilton Marston 1977–1983
 Proctor Mellquist 1978–1983

Versia M. Metcalf 1975–1980
Ronald L. Olson 1977–1983
Nathaniel A. Owings 1972
Harvey S. Perloff 1972–1980
William M. Roth 1972–1976
Edward A. Smuckler 1980–1983
Martin Stone 1972–1973
F. Jerome Tone 1982–1983
Esteban E. Torres 1972–1974
Carol L. Valentine 1977–1983
William L. C. Wheaton 1972–1976
Alfred S. Wilkins 1977–1978
Richard A. Wilson 1976–1983

The Advisory Board

The California Tomorrow Advisory Board was a complement to the Board of Directors. Many people moved from the advisory group to the policy-making body or in the opposite direction. Listed below are those advisors who did not at some time serve as directors:

Harvey O. Banks
L. M. K. Boelter
Tom Bradley
Willie L. Brown, Jr.
Eugene Burdick
George A. Dudley
Simon Eisner
Marc Goldstein
Allen Griffin
Ellen Stern Harris
Robert E. Kelly
Marty Kent
T. J. Kent, Jr.
Russel V. Lee
Francis C. Lindsay
Rex Lotery
Neil Morgan
William Newsom
Victor H. Palmieri
Roy Sorenson
Dwight Steele
Wallace Stegner
Caspar W. Weinberger
Charles A. Wellman

Executive Officers

Samuel E. Wood 1961–1968
John W. Abbott 1971–1975
Richard A. Grant 1976–1982
  (Director, Southern California office, 1972–1975)
Isabel Wade 1982–1983

Staff

Jean Fortna, Office Manager, 1970–1982
Fran Chiappetta, Membership Secretary, 1971–1973
William L. Kahrl, Administration, 1971

Cry California

Editors: William Bronson 1965–1971
John W. Abbott 1972–1975
Richard A. Grant 1976–1982
Walt Anderson (Annual Review issues)
  1976–1981
Stephanie Mills 1982–1983

Cheryl Brandt, Assistant to the Editor, 1967–1982
John Beyer, Art Director, 1971–1982
Alfred Marty, Art Director, 1967–1971
Anne Jenkins, Editorial Assistant, 1965–1967
Judy Tuttle, Editorial Assistant, 1965–1967

California Tomorrow joined forces with several other organizations along the way. The *California Center on Environment* merged with California Tomorrow in 1969; its headquarters became the Southern California office, and its director, Richard Grant, became Executive Secretary of the larger organization. The *Planning and Conservation Foundation* combined with California Tomorrow in 1975, contributing its President, Richard Wilson, and others to the Board of Directors. A third organization, the *California Environmental Intern Program,* was affiliated with California Tomorrow from 1976 until 1980. This career-development service works to match people trained or training in environmental and planning fields with short-term projects in private and government agencies (object: to open doors for permanent employment). On the program's staff, during its association with California Tomorrow, were Charlotte Symons, Robert P. Lawrence, Sheila O'Rourke, and George J. Geer.

Index

420